How to make money while you sleep!

How to
make
money
while you sleep!

A 7-STEP PLAN FOR STARTING YOUR OWN PROFITABLE ONLINE BUSINESS

Brett McFall

Wrightbooks

First published 2008 by Wrightbooks
an imprint of John Wiley & Sons Australia, Ltd
42 McDougall Street, Milton Qld 4064

Office also in Melbourne

Typeset in Palatino Linotype 11/14pt

© Brett McFall 2008

The moral rights of the author have been asserted

National Library of Australia Cataloguing-in-Publication data:

Author:	McFall, Brett.
Title:	How to make money while you sleep : a 7-step plan for starting your own profitable online business / author, Brett McFall.
Publisher:	Richmond, Vic. : John Wiley & Sons, 2008.
ISBN:	9780731407293 (pbk.)
Notes:	Includes index.
Subjects:	Electronic commerce. Web sites. New business enterprises--Computer networks. Success in business.
Dewey Number:	658.84

Cover design by Mike te Wierik
Author photo © Melbourne Headshot Company

Printed in Australia by McPherson's Printing Group

10 9 8 7 6 5 4 3 2 1

Disclaimer
The material in this publication is of the nature of general comment only, and does not represent professional advice. It is not intended to provide specific guidance for particular circumstances and it should not be relied on as the basis for any decision to take action or not take action on any matter which it covers. Readers should obtain professional advice where appropriate, before making any such decision. To the maximum extent permitted by law, the author and publisher disclaim all responsibility and liability to any person, arising directly or indirectly from any person taking or not taking action based upon the information in this publication.

Contents

What people say about *How to Make Money While You Sleep!*

How to Make Money While You Sleep! is so informative — it showed me step by step how to put together an online business. Brett's BURPIES copywriting formula blew me away.

Henry Gosling, retiree with no previous internet experience, Queensland

I've set up two websites, with another three to come, and in the past five weeks I've made over $4000 through my online businesses. There are two reasons for my new-found success — Brett's seminar and *How to Make Money While You Sleep!*

Grant Neilsen, 54, retired small-business owner with no previous internet experience, Queensland

Starting an internet business is so daunting a task that I put it off for years. Thankfully, Brett makes getting started quick, easy and so much fun. This book has really helped to give me a competitive edge in the online-business market.

Trish Madison, 44, accountant with no previous internet experience, New Zealand

I knew there was a lot of money to be made online, but felt lost as how to go about it. Full of simple and practical advice, *How to Make Money While You Sleep!* has made me much more confident about achieving success.

Carol Brown, 59, pensioner with no previous internet experience, New South Wales

This is a fantastic book. Brett exposes the tricks of the trade, provides plenty of time-saving techniques and explains internet marketing in an easy-to-understand, step-by-step process.

Eva Lopez, 36, printer and internet novice, New South Wales

Online marketing was so confusing until I read *How to Make Money While You Sleep!* It's filled with unique marketing ideas that anyone can easily put into effect. If you're serious about earning money on the internet, this book will get you there fast.

Laurel Stevenson, 65, retiree with no previous internet experience, New Zealand

How to Make Money While You Sleep! has saved us money, not to mention valuable time. This book is now our internet business bible. Thanks, Brett!

Heather Smith, 50, and Dr Len van Ingen, 63, Queensland

I've just started in the internet-marketing game and this book has been a great resource. Brett provides useful information, step-by-step instructions and lots of insider tips that are fast-tracking my internet-marketing business.

Mara Dower, 37, stay-at-home parent with no previous internet experience, Victoria

Thanks Brett, you really know how to mentor your marketers! I get so much out of your approaches and strategies. It's wonderful that you share so much so clearly and simply. I'm now ready to get my online business underway.

Serena Scarlett, 47, New South Wales

Packed with useful tips, formulas and ideas, this book provides everything you need to develop an automated internet business that delivers cash to your bank account while you sleep.

Susan Burgess, 62, no previous internet experience, New South Wales

I felt so motivated after finishing *How to Make Money While You Sleep!* that I read it again and have started the processes Brett outlines. I'm really looking forward to the day I can throw in my day job and make an income from the internet.

Sylvia Marino, 49, stay-at-home parent with no previous internet experience, New South Wales

I've completed a lot of internet courses and have come out feeling really overwhelmed by all the information. Written simply, *How to Make Money While You Sleep!* has everything you need to create a successful internet business.

Suzanne Evans, 54, no previous internet experience, New South Wales

Congratulations, Brett. You've made what I thought was complex simple, and I'm now working on my first product!

Daryl Patterson, 66, retired manager, Tasmania

Foreword

This book provides hope for budding entrepreneurs. It explains how you can use the most significant communication medium — the internet — to create a successful, sustainable business that you can run from home part time. Whatever your current occupation, you can use the concepts in this book to provide a side income until your business becomes self-sustaining — with a view, of course, to having the incredible lifestyle that an online business can offer.

Who wouldn't want to be able to run their business from a yacht in Spain, a country farm in France or a sunny beach in Australia? Brett really does 'walk his talk', living this internet-marketing lifestyle.

In my company, I aim to be innovative. I know that for something to work effectively it has to be simple. That's what I like about *How to Make Money While You Sleep!* It breaks new ground by making the process for setting up a business online extremely easy for beginners to follow.

Like Brett, I also used the internet to realise my dreams. I went from being in gangs, dealing drugs and declaring bankruptcy, to training people around the world in using the internet to create a full-time income. Brett started my international speaking career and together we have 'spread the message' to people in the United States, United Kingdom, Australia, Singapore, India, Indonesia, Malaysia, China, Japan and the United Arab Emirates.

Starting a business can be scary — mostly because of the costs that are involved. But on the internet, those restrictions are almost gone. You can start an online business, create your own product and market it to the masses for less than the average weekly wage. And after reading this book, chances are you'll feel like you're working too hard!

What you read here could provide you with an income, a passion and a purpose that I, too, discovered long ago. I encourage you to grab the opportunity with both hands because it could indeed be the ride of your life.

Best wishes

Stephen Pierce
Business Optimisation Strategist
<www.dtalpha.com>

About the author

Best known for teaching people how to make money on the internet quickly and easily, Brett McFall is an international speaker, copywriter and internet marketer. His websites turn over in excess of $500 000 a year practically on autopilot, allowing him to take a holiday somewhere in the world every eight weeks and live the life of his dreams.

A failed English student from the western suburbs of Sydney, today Brett is regarded by many as Australia's best direct-response copywriter. He's written over 10 000 advertisements, sales letters and marketing campaigns for 153 different industries.

In 2002 he began his first internet business selling his books, CDs and DVDs that taught business owners how to write advertisements for themselves. Two years later he co-created a four-day seminar — the World Internet Summit — where he and selected experts could teach others how to make money online. Today it is a multi-million-dollar company and the biggest internet business event in the world, teaching thousands of people in Australia, the United States, the United Kingdom, Singapore, Malaysia, Japan, China, Hong Kong, Thailand, Indonesia, India and Dubai.

Brett has shared the stage with marketing consultant Jay Abraham and motivational speaker Jim Rohn, as well as the best internet marketers in the world. He has been featured on ABC Radio and *National Nine News*.

For more information about Brett and to register for the *How to Make Money While You Sleep!* seminar, visit <www.brettmcfall.com>.

Introduction

It was July 1997. I was 26 years old and working as a copywriter for an advertising agency in Penrith, in Sydney's west. And I was bored. After only two years there, I simply wasn't learning anything new.

I loved my job, but there seemed to be very little future staying where I was. (Have you ever felt like this? You don't know where your life is going, what you're going to do or how you're going to do something about it.)

I didn't know what I wanted to do with my career, let alone how to chase it. No-one was beating my door down headhunting me; a pay rise wasn't coming any time soon; and I didn't fancy looking for another job closer to Sydney. I lived at least an hour and 15 minutes away from the city by car — on a good day. In heavy traffic it could take nearly two hours, which wasn't an appealing thought.

There were no opportunities in the advertising industry close to where I lived, so my future was stuck between 'Should I move to the city?' and 'Should I just stay in my present job and hope for the best?'

I thought about these two options for several months until one lunchbreak when I found myself in a newsagency looking for something to take my mind off things. As I looked over the myriad magazines on the rack, one caught my attention. It was a magazine about business opportunities.

I bought it and sat eating my lunch, reading every page and discovering one opportunity after another. They all sounded great.

I'd always wanted my own business. I'd bought how-to books and watched countless television programs about entrepreneurs. Owning a business really fascinated me. The trouble was I didn't have any experience and I didn't have any models to follow.

In short, I was scared to take that step. In the past I'd made every excuse under the sun like 'I'm not good enough' or 'I'm not ready', and the biggest of all, 'I'd hate to fail'. But this magazine was helping me get over these self-limiting beliefs. Even better, I could call and leave my details with many of the companies featured in the magazine, and they would send me more information about the opportunities they offered.

I was so excited. I called about five or six of the companies and couldn't wait for the packages to arrive. Doing this changed my life. Instead of feeling sorry for myself working in a job that wasn't good for me, I took control. And as a result, I discovered something quite interesting.

One of the packages I'd sent for revealed that I could run my own business from home, without staff, and still make upwards of $100 000 a year. For a guy on around $30 000 a year, that was big news. I couldn't even imagine what it would be like to earn $100 000 in a year.

The problem was that I couldn't afford that particular business opportunity. Any business opportunity has a purchase or investment cost, and that one was $10 000 — way out of my reach.

So I ordered one of the more affordable products from the company's business products catalogue instead. It was a manual on how to create advertising that worked, and it included a bonus audio tape. It cost me $67, which, at the time, felt like a lot of money for a manual and a tape, but I suspected that if I could just see what was inside the product, I might be able to create a similar product of my own and sell it in the same way. After all, that's what I would have been doing if I could have afforded the business opportunity — selling the manual and the audio tape — so why not create my own product? I had solid knowledge of writing advertisements. I didn't mind doing the work to create my own manual — it sounded like fun — and I'd saved myself $10 000, which I didn't have anyway.

A few days later I received the manual and the audio tape in the mail, and at that moment my future was sealed. I couldn't believe it — I already knew the information in the manual. In fact, I knew it even better than the person teaching it. Not only that, but the manual and the tape had been published by the author himself. The manual was a ringbinder with photocopied paper. And the audio tape had a homemade label.

The presentation wasn't very impressive, but the content certainly was. And really, isn't the information the most important thing?

It was then that the possibility of a new future dawned on me. If I could create my own product just like this one — with my own information — then why couldn't I sell it, too? Even better, I didn't have to leave my job — I could do it while I worked.

This to me was one of those 'aha!' moments in life — the moment when you know for certain that this is what you should do. The thought that I could actually publish my own product was so exciting and so liberating. I could instantly see my future. And then another thought came to me, 'What is the worst thing that could happen?' Not much, right? I couldn't really lose, could I?

I knew that even if I came up short and sold only a few copies of my self-published manual, I would still be better off than where I was right then. I might be behind a hundred dollars or so, but I'd have gained some experience and would own a product that I could keep improving until I got it right.

So, was my first product a success? I'll tell you shortly, but first here's how all this applies to you.

Use the internet to make money

The same opportunity that existed for me back then still exists for you today. In fact, not only does it exist, but it's bigger and better than it was when I started. Why is that?

Because since then an important piece of technology has come along and swept the world off its feet — the internet.

Never before has there been such freedom, such opportunity and such possibility to build wealth, and it's because of the internet.

Let me paint a picture for you of what your life could be like if you not only read every word in this book, but actually applied them, too.

Imagine if, while working at your current job or business, you were bringing in an extra $500 a week. And you were earning it without doing much extra work. Money that came in consistently and basically equated to a $26 000-a-year pay rise.

What would you do with this kind of money? Pay off some of your mortgage? Go on a holiday? Get your credit card balance back to zero?

I'm a big believer in being clear about your dreams, so for a moment let's just suppose that it is one year from today. In your mind I want you to travel to the future:

- You have a little internet business that sells products 24 hours a day to customers around the world. The products you sell are information products created by you, not someone else. They're unique and your customers love them. In fact, happy customers often write to you asking when your next product is coming out.

- Your products sell so well that you are able to leave your job and concentrate on your internet business. Your employer was shocked when you resigned. In fact, you swear that you saw a little bit of jealousy in the eyes of your manager as you left the office for the last time.

- A typical morning for you starts with rolling out of bed at a time that suits you. No longer are you a slave to the alarm clock. There's no traffic to worry about, either. You don't have to work in an office or a factory any longer; your internet business allows you the freedom to operate from anywhere you want.

- You enjoy your breakfasts more now because you don't have to rush them. You even have time to flick through the morning newspaper as you relax in your pyjamas.

- You like to flick through the paper for the latest holiday ideas, too. For the first time in your life, not only can you choose the holiday you want, you can actually make as much money while you're on holiday as when you're at home and working on your internet business.

- When you're ready, you stroll over to the computer and check your email. This is the part you've grown to love the most. Why? Because often most of the messages are notifications that you've received payments — $100 here, $200 there. Even better is the thought that while you're earning that money, you're normally fast asleep in your bed. Funny how you sleep much more soundly these days, too!

- Speaking of money, when someone orders a product from your website, their credit card is automatically debited and the cash is placed straight into your account. It doesn't matter what time it is, your business functions 24 hours a day. It's so nice to check your account balance every day and see deposits of hundreds of dollars, sometimes even thousands of dollars.

⬿ Your family notices the differences, too. They say you're a lot more relaxed than you used to be. Quality time with your family used to be hard to fit in, but now you have the freedom to revolve your business around your family commitments. You're so glad that you can actually be at school to see your kids perform in a play or play sport. This is the stuff that never seemed possible in your previous life. And your family loves it.

⬿ That new car you just brought home looks fantastic, and the feeling you had when you chose it still lingers. The part you like most is that your internet business pays the lease on that car. That's right, week in, week out, you don't have any worries about meeting the payments, because your business brings in the money practically on autopilot.

⬿ You're getting used to this new lifestyle of making money while you sleep. In the past you had hoped that one day you would have enough spare cash to help your favourite charity in some way. Today, the cash from one of your businesses funds the charity. Actually, it's the best solution because the charity can benefit long term from it. Instead of a one-off donation, it receives regular donations from you. And the more your products sell, the more donations the charity gets. What's more, you were able to do the work once, so you could 'set it and forget it'.

⬿ Your ideas didn't stop there. You decided to buy an investment home and create another internet business to pay off the mortgage. Even if you can't find tenants, you still don't worry. The business covers the mortgage easily. You never imagined it could be like this. These days, when you want something, you know that it's really just another internet business away.

🖎 Not only that, but you've grown to love doing something else too. Your family loves your sense of playfulness these days, particularly as you've begun to surprise them with outrageous gifts, like that day you hired a limousine to pick everyone up from home to go shopping for the day.

Okay, come back to today. Now, how does that feel?

Wouldn't it be great if, in a year from now, you were living this kind of lifestyle? Would that make reading this book worthwhile? Wouldn't this be a great goal to achieve? Some of the things I mentioned in that time-travel exercise may not be your cup of tea. That's okay. Simply paint in your own dream. I'm not here to tell you what to do — just how to get there.

What I'm going to teach you in this book is possible, very possible. In fact, my own life now mirrors what I just had you imagine, but it wasn't always like this. I've been able to do this only because I learned how to use the internet to make money.

You could be doing many things right now other than reading this book. The fact that you are reading it tells me that you want something different from your life. You're not satisfied with what you're achieving, with what you've got or with where you're going.

I want you to know that the level of freedom an internet business can give you is extraordinary. Hopefully your mind is beginning to tick over with ideas already. What I'm going to cover in these pages goes away from the 'norm' and may at times sound outlandish, so if you want to get a lot out of the time you're going to spend here, then open your mind.

Try not to judge what I'm presenting until you look into it further, or, better still, try it out. It's no help to you at all if you think, 'Huh, that'll never work' or 'Who does this guy think he is?' Thoughts like that will automatically block out what I'm trying to teach you.

If you see something that's new to you and that sounds almost impossible, rather than saying to yourself 'This guy's crazy', I'd like you to say something that a friend of mine taught me: 'Hmm … isn't that interesting!'

Throughout this book you'll come across sections that I call 'light bulb moments'. When you read these, in particular, it will be beneficial for you to say, 'Hmm … isn't that interesting!' This way you won't block out the ideas and concepts I give you before you've had time to evaluate them. And this is very important to your learning. Simply applying this rule alone will open your mind to so much more information. Not just throughout this book either, but in life too. If you just use these four words, 'Hmm … isn't that interesting!' more often, you'll find life so much more engaging, rewarding and satisfying.

Making things easier for you

The internet has plenty of websites available that can help you to 'make money while you sleep'. Throughout the book, I suggest many different websites for you to visit.

Another way I'm going to make this journey easier for you is this: I'm not going to tell you 'everything'.

Too much information can paralyse your progress. It really doesn't take much for your brain to feel overloaded, and when that happens, you stop moving forward. You need breathing space. You need time to accept new information.

So this book is not a comprehensive resource about marketing on the internet. It's about understanding the basics so that you can take action immediately. You can learn all the fancy stuff (such as search-engine optimisation, viral marketing and AdSense) later on, but it won't make sense to you if you don't understand the basics first.

I've seen so many people become absolutely overwhelmed and desperate to take action, but unable to even decide which direction to take. That won't happen here if you just follow my simple system.

You may be wondering what I mean when I refer to 'making money while you sleep'. It's quite simple, actually.

This book will teach you how to set up your own internet business. Even if you're a complete beginner, it's quite simple to do once you have the right information, which I share with you in this book.

The great thing about an internet business is that it operates 24 hours a day. Customers can visit your website and order your product, no matter what time it is. You don't need to be there to process their credit cards — it's not like a regular shop, where you have to open between 9 am and 5 pm.

You don't even have to package the product for your customers. In many instances, they can download it to their own computer immediately. An information product like an e-book (electronic book) is an electronic file, nothing else. Sure, you're selling something — a book that your customers can read just like a regular book, except on their computer screen — but it's intangible, so effectively, you're selling 'nothing'.

This all means that you can be working, exercising, holidaying and, yes, even sleeping, while your business operates.

ॐ ॐ ॐ

Now, back to my first information product.

I knew absolutely nothing about creating my own product. I'd never written any of my advertising knowledge down, let alone tried to write a course based on it, so here's what I did.

I basically knew that I wanted to create a manual that helped business owners increase the response to their advertising. After all, that was my expertise — I worked with businesspeople every day writing advertisements for them.

It made sense to me that my first product should contain some of my experience showing business owners how to quickly and easily increase the amount of money they make from advertising.

Because writing a manual like that would take a long time, I came up with the idea of creating a monthly newsletter called the *Brett McFall Advertising Letter*. It was an eight-page newsletter that I produced once a month. (It's always a good idea to 'chunk' things down into smaller parts, and that's what I did with this project.) But, of course, I had no subscribers.

My next step, then, was to advertise in the same business opportunity magazine where I first began my adventure. I wrote a half-page advertisement that offered 12 issues for $127.

When the first fax came through with an order for the newsletter, I couldn't stop staring at it! Someone was actually paying me for something I hadn't even created yet. Someone I didn't know. Yet, they had read my ad, liked the sound of it and had given me permission to charge their credit card for $127. Boy, was I excited! But then I realised … I now had to actually write the newsletter.

Taking the first step is always the hardest. I procrastinated for a few more nights, then finally sat down and wrote my first newsletter. I was so happy with myself — I must have read it at least five times.

I printed the eight A4 pages, took them to a photocopying shop and had them turned into two double-sided A3 sheets of paper stapled together to make a simple newsletter. I was in print!

From there, my business grew. Every month I produced that newsletter, and I really loved doing it, too. The whole process fascinated me. After 12 months, I had just 18 subscribers. But that was still $2286 dollars I had earned from my idea, and nothing could take away the excitement of that. Remember, though — I had a plan! The next step was to take those 12 newsletters and turn them into 'chapters'. By doing that, I had a manual.

Here's the really good part. The manual I created from those newsletters became *Inside Secrets of Advertising* — a big manual that you can still buy from my website.

Over the next two years that manual became a huge success, making me over $400 000! And it's helped business owners in many countries around the world. The amount of positive feedback I received was amazing. Not only that, but the more manuals I sold, the more people wanted me to write for them personally, allowing me to leave my job in 2002 and start my own business. The dream had finally come to fruition.

Today, there are much quicker ways to create your own information products. With the internet, you can sell your products around the world in a heartbeat — and you can do it all from home. In fact, chances are you don't realise how much opportunity is out there waiting for you, how much money is being spent online, how many people are crying out for products that you can create and how you can identify them before you even create the product.

This is your awakening. If you're ready to find out how you can make money while you sleep, then it's time to get started.

Part I

Welcome to the new world

The first part of success lies in 'believing it can be done'. With so much confusion about how the internet can be used as a business medium you need to know what sort of business you should set up, what you should sell and how it's possible. In this part, I take a look at each of these elements, and more.

Chapter 1

Why the internet is the best way to make money while you sleep

If you wanted to start your own conventional business on any high street near you, what sort of costs do you think you might be up for?

Let's say you wanted to open a clothes shop. To begin with you'd probably need to lease premises. Standard rent is between $1000 and $2000 per week. So before you do anything, you'd have an average of $75 000 a year to cover in lease payments. Then you'd need to:

- ✐ order stock to fill the shelves (you'd need to pay for the shelves too, and maybe even a small refurbishment)
- ✐ hire one or two employees

- take out insurance to cover your business, stock, fit-out, yourself, your staff and customers

- perhaps install some security to protect your stock and your premises

- pay for utilities

- spend time in the store — six days a week is not uncommon — as you wait for customers to come in

- provide for other, unexpected, expenses along the way.

This is before you've earned a single cent or even spent money on advertising. Is it any wonder that it's so hard to start your own business and make enough money to live on too?

I've worked in 153 different industries, and you would be alarmed at the number of small-business owners who are scraping by week in, week out. The owners would be better off if they just had a job in their chosen industry — a predictable income without the stress of trying to run a business.

My aim is to make you aware of a new business medium. Something that puts the rules back in your favour. Something that gives you half a chance of success. And, yes, it lets you make money while you sleep.

Seven reasons an internet-based business makes such good sense

It's time now to get to the bottom of what an internet business is all about and take a look at the advantages of setting one up.

1   No premises to rent

You don't have to pay for a lease because you don't have a business that operates out of a shop or an office. If you can keep your costs low right from the start, you will have a much higher chance of success simply because you're neither being weighed down by a big debt before you get going nor feeling the pressure of having that debt.

Instead of a shopfront, you'll have a website. Many people choose to design their own website on their laptop or desktop computer. (I explain a much easier way to do it though, in chapter 7.) Either type of computer is fine, but you should consider how much portability you want. These days you can get a perfectly adequate PC with everything you need for under $2000.

If you buy a laptop computer and expect to travel or commute with it a lot, consider getting a pull-along bag. It's much better for both your body (because laptops can feel quite heavy the longer you hold them) and your computer.

The next thing you'll need is an internet connection. If you can afford it, get a broadband internet connection. It's much faster than dial-up, and while it's not critical to have this speed, broadband will certainly make your online life much easier.

Hosting

In the online world there *is* an equivalent to the lease, and it's called hosting. Let's say that you create your website and store it on your computer. In order for anyone in the world to be able to see that website, you have to upload (move) it to a much bigger computer that is 'hooked in' to the internet. This is called a server. (I'll discuss creating and putting your website online in chapter 7.) An internet server is switched on 24 hours a day so that people across the world can look at and interact with what is stored on it.

When you store your website on a server, it's called hosting. The server hosts your website for the rest of the world to see. You're charged a fee for this, making hosting very similar to leasing premises in the real world. But the good news is it's very cheap. You can find hosting for as little as $10 a month. Can you imagine if leasing premises was this cheap in the real world?

2 No staff to pay

Staff can be a great asset to your business, and you'll probably want to hire some if your business gets really big. But they are also a great responsibility, and when you're starting out, your goal is to keep costs to a minimum so that you can build enough profit to survive.

One of the great things about having a business on the internet is that you can do almost everything yourself. You don't have to — sometimes you'll actually want people to do some of the work for you — but at least you have a choice.

If you've ever employed staff before, then you may also agree that managing staff is a job within itself. Again, the internet allows you to bypass this for as long as you need.

For instance, a salesperson is one of the most valuable staff members you can ever have. Without sales, you don't have a business. On the internet, you can have a 24-hour salesperson working for you. This salesperson requires no pay, no superannuation, no holidays and no sick pay. In chapter 6, I'll tell you all about this, but for the moment you just need to understand that the words on your website are your salesperson. Your website merely needs to say the same things that an actual salesperson would say to your prospective customers to make them want to buy your product.

The great part is that, once you've got these words in place, you don't have to keep saying them or rewriting them. They work day in, day out. You do the work once, but benefit over and over again.

3   Your business can be automated

This is the part I love most. When I first learned about automating my business, I couldn't believe the implications. It was so exciting. This is what it means for you:

- Your website can be advertised 24 hours a day for very little cost.

- People from all around the world can join your email list (a critical tool discussed further in chapter 9) and receive emails, lessons and tips from you for as long as you want, automatically. This enables you to build a relationship with them that helps them to trust you and want to become your customer.

- You can send an email to everyone on your list at once (a broadcast), and you can even set the time and day it is sent. You don't have to physically send the email to every person on your list — software does it for you automatically. Can you imagine making an offer to 1000 people at once? If just five people out of those 1000 buy your product at, say, $100, that's $500 for simply sending an email.

- ✍ Money can be processed and put into your bank account automatically.

- ✍ A thankyou message can be sent to customers a split second after they buy your product.

And the best part? This all happens while you sleep, holiday or watch television! Never before have you had such freedom and leverage. It means that a one-person business can function with the efficiency of a big business.

4 Beginners can do it

As I've said, I teach internet marketing all over the world. Most of the people I teach are absolute beginners. Very few can type their name on a computer let alone do it with any great speed. Yet many of these people can have a thriving internet business — and you can, too.

You don't need to know everything about business or how the internet works to succeed — all you need is to understand the following concept: *be the general of the army, not a soldier in the trenches*.

Let me explain what this means. If you are a soldier, you will be doing a lot of hard, physical work. One day you might be on guard duty; another on reconnaissance; and another on patrol. Or you could be digging trenches, cleaning firearms or practising drills. The general doesn't do these things. The general just moves all the pieces around like in a chess game. From one location the general can control an entire army.

With that idea in mind, when it comes to your internet business, you want to be the general of the army, not a soldier in the trenches. The internet gives you the freedom to *not* be the one running around designing your websites, creating your product, writing your sales copy (the words that sell your product), promoting your site, processing the money, delivering the product and so on. You *can* choose to do this (and many do), but the good news is you have the freedom to choose *not* to.

This freedom comes from working smartly by:

- using template software to design your website
- utilising other people or tools to create your product
- using software to write the copy for your website
- splitting your sales profits with partners who will promote your site to the people and companies listed in their databases, at no up-front charge
- making your product downloadable so your customers can access it when they want and at any hour of the day.

Get the idea? By doing things cleverly from the start, a beginner can master the internet. What you need are the ideas and the knowledge. As long as you take responsibility for these, there are other people, tools and software that can do the bulk of the work for you.

Maybe you're already in business. Maybe you're an employee. Maybe you're out of work, a parent wanting to get back into the workforce, a retiree, a university student or just a kid with a dream. Regardless, the internet can be your key to freedom. An online business doesn't need to replace your current job or role (not yet anyway); you can simply use it to generate extra income while you work, study or play.

I've been using the internet as my sole source of income since 2002. Prior to that I never would have thought it was possible to use the internet to make enough money to live off. Perhaps you feel that way, too. If so, then you need to break through these limiting thoughts, just like I did. The world has changed, and it's not too late for you to change with it. You just need to *want* something more.

For the moment, that desire is all you need. The internet is *not* overcrowded with ideas. The internet is *not* just for 'nerds' and 'geeks' — it's for anyone who wants to build wealth.

Forget about the limitations you may perceive. The only person stopping you from doing something profitable on the internet is you. You can learn how to do this, no matter how long it takes. And there are plenty of tools available to help you.

Just make a big promise to yourself (say this to yourself right now): *I won't give up until I reach my goal.*

Having the will to get there, the desire to do something different from everyone else and the strength not to give up until you achieve your goal are the qualities of the great entrepreneurs of the world.

I'm not a technical person. I don't really understand how computers operate. Like me, you may not know the difference between RAM and ROM, but the thing is you don't need to. The great news is only the business medium has changed, the principles of business remain the same.

What I did was focus on the things that make money, rather than try to learn everything about the internet. So don't worry too much about your computer, the software, which search engine you like the most or which operating system your computer uses. The combination of these items is like the engine of your car. You don't need to know how every part of your car's engine works for you to be able to drive.

If you want to build wealth using the internet, then *sell stuff that people want to buy*. That's how simple it is. It's very important to remember this. And just for the record, if you want to build a lot of wealth, then *sell the systems that help others sell stuff that people want to buy* (but that's a lesson for another day).

5 Create as many businesses as you want

Is time important to you? What do you want to spend your time on? And who do you want to spend that time with? Is time perhaps one of the core reasons for reading this book in the first place? So that you can earn more money and therefore have more freedom to do what you want?

If you had that clothes shop I mentioned earlier, a lot of your time would probably be spent in the shop — perhaps 50 to 60 hours a week. If you decided that you needed to have two or three shops to make more money, you would be looking at even less free time.

So, your end goal is still not being achieved. Very few business owners, unless they're extremely disciplined and quite visionary, have that freedom from their businesses.

However, with the right internet-based business running practically on autopilot you can have that freedom from your business. Even if you decide to have two internet-based businesses, or three, or four, or 10, it's not going to mean huge chunks of your time are taken away. You could have one website producing $1000 a month over here and another producing $1000 a month over there. And because you've set them up smartly, all you have to do is monitor them. You'll be working *on* them, not working *in* them. This may seem daunting, but you *can* do it.

Light bulb moment

In 2005, I created a copywriting software program that helps people write the words for their website so that their product sells. I don't know a thing about programming, yet I created this software using a program called Make Your Own Software (<www.makeyourownsoftware.com>).

My copywriting software sells for US$97 (approximately AU$113). It took me about three weeks to create it, and I haven't done anything else to it since. I sell at least two copies nearly every day (at US$194 per day, that's around US$5820 a month). Imagine if this was your product—and if you sold 50 of these a month—you'd have made almost US$5000 with only one website! Is it easier to make money this way than at your current job or business? What if you had two, three or five sites making $5000 a month? That's pretty exciting.

6 Work when you want

Are you a morning person or an evening person?

If you're a morning person, wouldn't it be great to get all your work done early and then have the freedom to do whatever you want in the afternoon? Or if you're more of an evening person, wouldn't it be great to sleep in until midday and then start your work? So when your brain is really pumping at night you have the freedom to work like crazy, when it's right for you.

If you're a parent, wouldn't it be handy to be able to work around your kids' hours? No longer would you have to race to get to work after dropping the kids off at school or worry about leaving work to pick them up on time.

Most regular jobs and businesses just don't give you this freedom. The internet, however, does. There's no 'nine to five' online.

When I was an employee, I used to daydream about having the freedom to go to the movies whenever I wanted. A lofty goal, I know! But when you're an employee or stuck in a regular business, that's not something you can do. To me, at that time, going to the movies at 2 pm on a weekday represented a greater life — a life of freedom and choice.

This is the life I'm very lucky to lead right now. And it's a life you can have, too. You may have different reasons and different goals, but one thing you need in order to be able to do them is the *freedom*. And would you believe that now that I have the freedom, I hardly ever go to the movies during the day!

7 Work where you want

When I truly realised that my internet business enabled me to work wherever I wanted, it had a huge impact. In fact, it can take a long while to accept. Our lives are so dominated by our work that when that restriction is taken away, it can be hard to adjust.

Chances are that you are living where you are because it's close, or at least relatively close, to your work. There may be other reasons for your location — for example, schooling or family — but work is a big influence on where you choose to live, wouldn't you agree?

What happens then when suddenly your work is on your laptop computer? Wherever your computer is, that's your business. What does that mean if you are living where you are because of proximity to your job? It means that you no longer have to. That's right; you can actually work where you want!

As long I have my laptop with me and an internet connection, I'm in business. And so, after a few months of contemplating this, I decided I wanted to live elsewhere.

For 30 years or so, I'd quite happily lived in the western suburbs of Sydney. But then it dawned on me that I had the freedom to move where I wanted so I decided to move to a place that I'd thought about for a long time. As I write this, I'm living near the sea, on the Gold Coast in Queensland, simply because I can!

Who knows? I may move somewhere else in the future. Perhaps to a snowy alpine forest in Canada, a sun-drenched island in the Caribbean, or to London, Paris or Rio de Janeiro! This sort of freedom is almost unheard of for most people.

If you like the summer months, how great would it be if you had a home in the opposite hemisphere, so that when it's winter in your neck of the woods you can take off and enjoy summer? You could constantly live in warm weather if you wanted to.

If you like skiing, why be limited by the seasons? Simply grab your laptop and go to where it's winter. Your customers don't suffer — they won't even know where you are.

The internet gives you a global business. And suddenly, when you have a choice, it can actually be a hard thing to even consider where you might want to live. So for now I just want you to say, *'Hmm … isn't that interesting!'*

Remember the start-up costs for a conventional business that I mentioned at the beginning of the chapter? Let's take a look at how the internet business model stacks up against the regular small-business model. In my internet business, I have hardly any of these costs.

- I don't pay for a lease because I don't have a business that operates in a shop or office (I just have a laptop computer).

- I don't need to order lots of stock to fill my shelves because I can either produce the physical products on demand (that is, only when orders come in) or have products that are downloadable (that is, they can be downloaded hundreds of times a day, with no production process or additional work required).

- The only insurance I need is the one that covers me personally. (There are no premises to insure, and my house insurance covers my computer.)

- I don't have to hire security to protect my stock because I don't have any. Any physical products I sell are produced on demand in a warehouse, which also ships them to my customers when required.

- I don't have any staff. (Software can automate up to 80 per cent of my business so that it operates as if it *did* have staff working in it. For example, it does things like sending thankyou emails to customers.)

- No staff means I don't have to provide holiday pay, holiday loading, sick leave, superannuation or workers' compensation insurance.

- I don't have huge electricity bills. (I'm not running a store that needs lighting and heating.)

 ✍ I don't have to be in the shop over a weekend, during public holidays or late at night. My website is my shop and it works 24 hours a day whether I'm awake or asleep, giving me the freedom to use my time the way I want.

Is this sounding like a slightly better business model than the conventional one? For the cost savings alone, it's pretty inviting. But the lifestyle is by far the best.

Any day of the week, I can go for a drive, go surfing, take in a movie, watch television, chat on the phone or fly somewhere any time — and my business still runs. To me, the freedom is the greatest part of all. If you don't feel like working, you don't have to.

Now, you're probably thinking, 'Can I really do this?' In the next chapter I explain why I think you can.

Summary

 ✍ A regular business can put a lot of pressure on you right from the beginning because of the costs and effort associated with getting started. And we've all heard how hard it is for small-business owners to actually succeed. An internet business, however, removes most of those restrictions.

 ✍ The seven reasons the internet is the best way to make money while you sleep are:

1 *no premises to rent*. You can run your business using a laptop computer and an internet connection.

2 *no staff to pay*. You can do most of the work yourself and ultimately, your website itself becomes a 'staff' member.

3   *your business can be automated.* Using tools, partners and software, you can automate a lot of the normal business tasks.

4   *beginners can do it.* By being the general of the army, not a soldier in the trenches, you won't get bogged down with technicalities and tasks.

5   *create as many businesses as you want.* Unlike a regular business, creating more internet businesses won't have a massive drain on your time.

6   *work when you want.* You can make your business work around you, giving you the freedom to sleep in or get up early.

7   *work where you want.* Yes, it's true. Once you have an internet business, you don't need to be close to your customers — they can be anywhere in the world, and so can you.

Chapter 2

The keys to your internet success

Perhaps you're wondering if you really can do what I'm suggesting. If you've never done something like this before, it makes sense to wonder if it's truly possible for you to succeed.

Indeed, it is possible. However, there's one very important thing that could stop you from succeeding before you've even switched on your computer, and it has nothing to do with the internet, your ability, your skills, your environment or your education. What it has everything to do with is your mindset.

In other words, it's your ability to talk yourself out of doing something; to allow irrational fears to creep into your decision-making process; and to focus on what could go *wrong* rather than what could go *right*.

One day you're feeling focused, confident and excited, and the next you're feeling directionless, unsure and in doubt about whether you can actually pull off what you've planned. Frustrating, isn't it?

The trick to getting through this, however, is to not let these things rule your life. These stoppages are caused by your fears. Fear of making mistakes. Fear of attempting something and failing. But if you don't attempt it, then you've failed already. If you don't actually try to do something, then you certainly can't succeed at it.

While your fears can protect you from harm and help you to make well-balanced decisions, they can also halt your progress. It all depends on how much you let them influence you. It's okay to listen to your fears, but don't let them drown out your hopes. Your hopes deserve the same level of respect that you give your fears. Why should the negatives have a louder voice than the positives?

What if everything I tell you in this book actually works? What if you could leave your job or current business and work from home, or wherever it is that *you* want to work from? What if you could pay off your home because of the extra money you bring in? What would your life be like if you did succeed?

Either way, whether or not you succeed, you're in control. You're in control of your mind, not the other way around. Your mind simply helps you make decisions. You decide what result you get.

You are completely in charge because you can determine what to focus on. You can choose to focus on what could go wrong … or what could go right, and either can happen. You simply choose which one rules your life.

There are six keys to success with an internet business, and most are related to having the right mindset. The success keys are:

1   you don't need to know everything to succeed

2   the internet is the cheapest place to fail

3   outsource much of your work

4   target niche markets

5   give people what they want

6   let software do most of the work for you.

I'll take a look at each of these in turn.

1 You don't need to know everything to succeed

Feeling like you need to know everything is what you're worried about, isn't it? You're concerned about all the things you may need to know to get started, such as:

- How will I design a website?

- How will I process money from my overseas customers?

- How do I create a product?

- How much do I charge?

However, when we can't answer these questions, we stop taking action until we can gather enough information to move forward.

As I've mentioned, I don't know how the internet comes together. I don't really understand how all the cables work to send me the information I want. And I can't understand how video and audio is transmitted through tiny little wires. It amazes and confuses me, but it hasn't stopped me earning my living from the internet. And it doesn't have to stop you either. I just want you to focus on the principles of business. What's most important is that you start somewhere.

The internet is simply the medium through which you will do business. All you're doing is selling something. That's it. You need to sell something to create cash flow, and then make sure that you bring in more money than you spend — just like a regular business.

2 The internet is the cheapest place to fail

The internet is a very low-cost place to start and run a business, which means it's not going to hurt so badly if things don't go right. You're not going to have to mortgage your house to pay for an internet business or take out a huge loan to get started.

You can make mistakes on the internet and still survive. In fact, I've made hundreds! But guess what? Because I made a lot of mistakes, I found out what worked very quickly. The mistakes actually helped me to succeed.

So there's my success secret — *win by making mistakes*. The more mistakes I make, the more I win. I can tell you that it's not just a success secret of mine but of nearly every successful person I know.

As long as you learn from your mistakes, you will succeed. This is because on the internet a product that doesn't sell won't bankrupt you. By selling information products such as e-books, audio files, video files, CDs, DVDs and software, you can manage your costs very easily.

For instance, if your product is an e-book, there's no inventory. It's just a digital file that your customers download to their computer. It's the same as a book in a bookstore, except your customers read it on their screen or print out the pages. If you sell one a day or 100 a day, there's no difference. Every customer downloads the same file.

If you sell a CD product, you can often produce just 50 to 100 copies — not thousands. There are companies that do short-run productions. This ability to print on demand means that you won't be under pressure to sell thousands of copies of your product just to break-even.

I use a 'fulfilment house' in Queensland, which ships all my tangible products (CDs, DVDs and manuals) for me. I send the warehouse an email each time a customer orders a product from me, and it takes care of the rest. It even lets me know when stock is getting low, so I can advise how many more sets to produce. It's fantastic. For a product that retails for around AU$2000, the actual cost to me of having a fulfilment house take care of it is approximately AU$150.

When you're starting out, however, you don't need to use a warehouse. When I began my business I did everything myself — buying folders from an office supply store, having the pages photocopied, wrapping the product in bubble wrap and posting it. I loved doing this, because it meant I was 'in business'.

The point is the internet is a cheap place to do business. It costs almost nothing to send an email to tell people about your offer. It can cost as little as $10 a month to have your shop (that is, your website) on the internet for all to see. When you do get sales, the banks' merchant fees for processing them are very low — for example, 2 per cent of the sale price, sometimes even lower.

This all means that even if you experience a worst-case scenario and for whatever reason your product doesn't sell, your costs are manageable and you can survive to try again another day. When a regular business doesn't work, however, it can cost you a fortune in expenses that you may never recover (which is probably another reason the internet is becoming so popular).

3 Outsource much of your work

It's your choice how you run your internet business, but there are people and tools that can help you do most of the work. You just need to decide what you want to do and then see who or what can help you do it. The great news is that most of the people and tools that can help you on your journey are much less expensive than the costs associated with setting up a regular business.

For instance, if you want to have a fancy-looking website, you can hire a designer to create one for you through a company called Logoworks from just US$1500 (approximately AU$1700). Visit <www.logoworks.com> to check it out. This is a very good rate to have someone design a professional-looking website for you.

As an aside, you may have noticed that I reference US companies as resources. The reason for this is that, at the time of writing, they are more advanced than most Australian internet companies — but, of course, this will change over time.

'Are there cheaper suppliers out there?' I hear you ask. There sure are. Elance (<www.elance.com>), for example, is another great place to find website designers. You can pay a designer as little as US$500 (approximately AU$570) to design your website. In fact, Elance does more than this. It's a place where writers and designers go to find work. They will actually bid to write your sales messages for you, design your website, write your e-book, translate your information into another language and much more. It's a great service, and it means that you don't have to hire full-time staff if you don't want to. You can just hire people as you need them.

Another option is to hire a local student to do it, but because this is your business, just make sure the student knows what he or she is doing.

By outsourcing, you're being the general of the army, not a soldier in the trenches. You can focus on the tasks you want to do instead of getting bogged down with every single task.

Light bulb moment

Wouldn't it be great if you could create a new product every month or year? You simply generate the idea and have other people execute it for you. Once you know the steps (which I'm showing you in this book), you can just repeat them over and over and then monitor that they are being done correctly. You don't have to get closely involved if you don't want to, and you can do this while working at a job, going to school or running a household.

4 Target niche markets

What is a niche market? Put simply, it's a group of people who have an interest in a particular hobby, sport, profession or trend. Because their interest is so specific, we can tailor a product to suit only them.

For instance, 'people interested in cricket' is a very large market, depending on the country in which you live. However, a niche market for cricket might be 'indoor cricket'. Another niche market is 'women's cricket'. In fact, 'women's indoor cricket' would be another niche market.

The more specific you get, the more defined the niche market is. For example, 'New South Wales women's indoor cricket' would be an even smaller group, because I've used the state boundary to isolate the group. You could choose any criteria such as age, location, gender or income.

How defining a niche market will help you succeed

The big players (large companies) out there tend to chase volume money — that is, the 'mass market'. Smaller markets don't have that same appeal because they simply don't offer the same high profits.

When you run your own internet business, however, you can still make a decent profit by targeting smaller markets. Plus, there's less competition, so marketing to them is easier and less costly. Why compete with the big players if you don't have to?

Another reason I recommend you search for a niche market is that you'll have a much higher chance of success because you'll be finding out what people want first. For example, if you were hungry and felt like eating an ice cream, and I was looking to make some money, it would make sense if I asked you what you wanted to eat before I tried to sell you something. Otherwise, I might try to sell you a hamburger, Chinese food or a soft drink. But that's not what you want. So if I find that out beforehand, all I have to do is offer you an ice cream and my chances are much higher that I'll get a sale.

Simple logic like this can really make a huge difference to your success in business, which leads me to the next success key.

5 Give people what they want

Give people what they want — this is a super-powerful marketing secret.

If you find out what your niche market wants to know, solve or buy (I explain how to do this in chapter 3), you can give it to them on a platter. Why try to reinvent the wheel when people will happily give you their money if you just give them what they want?

So many people come to me with great product ideas, but they are actually working too hard. You don't need to create a brand-new hamburger — you just need a starving market. If your niche market is telling you what it wants to eat, then to make money just find the food it wants and sell it to the group! That's it. It doesn't take a revolutionary idea to create a thriving business, just a willingness to give a certain group of people what they want.

In 2004 I created a $40 000-a-year business from scratch by following this principle. Have you heard of scrapbooking? It involves taking your photos and memories and turning them into something amazing. Usually it's done by adding ribbons, cards and different bits of art to bring out the emotion of a special occasion. It's about making photo albums into unique mementos. But it's about so much more than that, too.

Scrapbooking a niche market that I tapped into and made over $40 000 from in the first year. In fact, I still sell the product I created for this market — it's an e-book called *Scrapbooking Profits* (<www.scrapbookingprofits.com>). I simply set up a web page (I'll show you to create your own web page in chapter 7) that said this:

> **Dear Friend,**
>
> Thank you for reaching my new website. I'm writing an e-book on how to make money from scrapbooking and I need your advice.
>
> **Could you please tell me: What is your most pressing question about making money with scrapbooking?**
>
> Your feedback is valuable to me. And as a gift for leaving your most pressing question, I'll happily send you a copy of the e-book ($27.77) when it's finished.

Below this I created a form where respondents could leave their name, email and their question.

For four days I took some paid advertising on the search engine Google, which cost me around US$50 in total. These are called 'Google Ads' (for a step-by-step tutorial visit <www.adwords.google.com>), and they send people to the advertised site. The result was that 30 people left me their question about making money from scrapbooking.

So what was I doing? I was finding out what the market wanted.

Now, if just two or three people had left a response, that would tell me something, too. It would tell me that if very few people were prepared to even leave a question, then there wouldn't be much chance of them spending money when I wanted to sell them the e-book. At that stage, I would have stopped that project and looked for something else after having spent very little time, money or effort.

Having flexibility like this is incredible. By 'testing and measuring' the response to your product idea, you can reduce your failure rate, thereby improving your success rate. The bottom line is you can test the waters every step of the way — your market will tell you whether to keep going or to change strategies. This is very smart indeed, and I suggest you adopt this method of testing, too.

As it turned out for me, I had a great response. I took those 30 questions and hired a writer through Elance. Many people bid to do the job, which basically involved them researching and finding the answers to the 30 questions my prospects had left. From the 12 writers who put in a bid, I ended up selecting a writer who had an interest in scrapbooking. She charged me US$800 (approximately AU$910).

Fourteen days later, the writer sent me the finished work. She'd created the whole e-book and written around 80 pages. I paid her and then began to sell the e-book on my website. It was as simple as that.

I paid for some more advertising on Google (around US$20 a day — approximately AU$23) to bring people to the site, and almost overnight I began selling, on average, three copies a day at US$27.77. Every day I made a profit of US$63.31 ($83.31 in sales, minus $20 advertising costs), and my initial investment was recovered in as little as 15 days.

That $63.31 a day added up to $23 108.15 (approximately AU$26 330) for the year — profit, not sales. I then found ways to increase sales (which I will explain in chapter 10). As a result, I sold four e-books a day, quickly taking the yearly sales to around US$40 000 (approximately AU$45 560), of which over US$33 000 (approximately AU$37 600) was profit. Not bad, huh?

I still sell *Scrapbooking Profits*. Would you believe that I don't even think about it? I don't even pay for advertising. And apart from reading over what the writer created in the first place, I haven't done any more work on it.

All I did was find out if people in that niche market would like to know how to turn their scrapbooking hobby into a business. I asked them what they wanted to know and then gave them the answers based on the most popular questions. It doesn't get much simpler than that. Without actually creating it, I provided a quality product that gave my market exactly what it wanted.

You may be wondering how I sold this e-book when I have no track record or background in scrapbooking. The answer is quite simple. I didn't have to establish *my* credibility; I just had to prove that the e-book was credible.

To achieve this, I did two things. Firstly, on my website I told the visitors exactly how I created the e-book — that I took the most common questions about making money from scrapbooking and answered them. Secondly, I emailed the 30 people who gave me the questions in the first place. I gave them a free copy of the e-book and asked them for their thoughts about it. These are called testimonials. With their permission, I put these testimonials on my web page. This gave credibility to both the e-book and me, and I haven't looked back since.

Light bulb moment

You could be involved in a niche market right now. Do you play a sport? Do you have any hobbies? Is there something in particular you love to do on the weekend? Do you read a certain magazine more than any other? Do you spend a lot of time researching information on something you love? What is your greatest interest? By thinking about these questions, you may stumble upon an untapped market for which you could create a product.

---

6 Let software do most of the work for you

In most regular businesses, you need staff to help run things and do things such as send information to customers, process orders, manage your customer list so that each person gets what was ordered, tally the weekly sales and pay your salespeople their commissions.

The good news is that for an internet business, software programs exist that can do all of this for you and more. I use software from WorldInternetOffice.com and this takes care of around 80 per cent of my business for me. It's priced from US$29 (approximately AU$33) a month. Visit <www.worldinternetoffice.com>.

WorldInternetOffice.com enables you to work less and still run a thriving business. Your orders can be fulfilled, payments received and emails sent with very little input required from you. This software also makes sure you are completely 'spam' compliant and allows customers to opt out of (unsubscribe from) your automated email messages at any time. In short, you can relax as it takes care of almost everything for you.

For example, if visitors choose to leave their name and email address to receive more information about my product, over a number of days they will receive messages from me telling them more about the product.

This happens automatically. Before the website goes 'live', I write the messages that I want them to read, and then use WorldInternetOffice.com to send the emails for me at specific times. It doesn't matter if 1000 people sign up for these emails, it takes no extra effort from me. I don't have to write 1000 sets of messages; I simply write them once and the software sends them out to each person automatically.

Software such as WorldInternetOffice.com allows you to use your time wisely. The work that it can automate for you is the equivalent of having three or four staff on your payroll. And when you're a small business, like you will be when you start out, it's a great asset that can speed your success along.

Now that you know what the keys to internet success are, it's time to move on to the next chapter and take a look at how to succeed at making money selling 'nothing'.

Summary

✎ There is only one thing that will stop you from being successful — your *mindset*. Don't let your fears control your life. To succeed, you need to realise that you are in control of your mind and of what you tell yourself. And your thoughts become actions, good or bad.

  The six keys to your internet success are:

1 *you don't need to know everything to succeed.* You don't need to know how the internet works to run a successful internet business.

2 *the internet is the cheapest place to fail.* Failing is a great thing on the internet. You can try new ideas out and then shut them down in a matter of days if you don't like them or they don't work, without it costing you a fortune.

3 *outsource much of your work.* There are plenty of people out there who can write copy for you and design your websites. Most are low cost and you can hire them as you need them.

4 *target niche markets.* Focus on those smaller, tight-knit, easy-to-identify groups that have a passion for something. This way there'll be less competition, and they will be easy to please.

5 *give people what they want.* Find out what your market wants before you spend too much time or money on your product or business. Test ideas and measure the response to them. This way you'll have a much greater chance of success.

6 *let software do most of the work for you.* The right software can run up to 80 per cent of your business for you, including sending emails, processing orders and sending thankyou letters.

Chapter 3

Why sell information?

As you now know, I sell information. I sell it both physically (manuals, CDs and DVDs) and digitally (e-books, software, audio files and video files).

The physical products I sell are stored in a fulfilment house, which is designed solely for shipping products like mine anywhere in the world. I'm charged for the production and the shipping, which means I don't pay to lease or staff the premises. It's a very economical service — it costs approximately 7 per cent of the sale price.

The digital products are delivered automatically to customers online. There is no physical component to these products.

I like information products because they:

- *are unique*. I am the only person customers can buy them from; they are not available in bookshops or libraries.

- *are high profit*. Because the products are unique, I can charge the price they deserve to be sold at, instead of having to discount them in order to survive.

- *are quick and easy to create*. Using the technique I outline in chapter 5, it can take as little as one hour to create a product that sells for between US$20 and US$50 per unit. And you don't need much expertise.

- *are low-cost to produce*. Digital files downloaded to a customer's computer have a one-time production cost (remember, it's one file that is downloaded thousands of times). Ringbinders (to hold a manual), CDs and DVDs are all cheap too — costing less than a few dollars each. Another important point is that I never have more than 25 of each product in stock, so I don't have to produce big print runs. If I do get a rush of sales, it only takes a day or two for the fulfilment house to produce more.

- *have a long shelf life*. The information can be updated quickly and at no cost, so the overall product can remain viable for many years. Compare this with selling a physical product like fitness equipment. The fitness trend my change, and suddenly, you're left with a shop full of equipment that no-one wants. A person buying an information product in five years' time should receive as much value from it as someone buying it now. In the introduction I told you about the first manual I created, *Inside Secrets of Advertising*; with periodic updating, I expect it to keep selling for at least the next 10 years.

Light bulb moment

'Information products' are the best products to sell over the internet. Items like manuals, CDs, DVDs and software are easy to create, produce and store, and they are profitable to sell. Customers can also download some products, such as e-books, straight to their computers, so no delivery is needed.

A CD that costs around AU$5 to produce and send to your customer can often sell for around AU$47. Any businessperson would consider this a decent profit. A whole series of CDs can sell for AU$497, sometimes more, depending on the content, yet your costs can be less than AU$50. (If you're wondering why I use '7' a lot in my prices, it's because I've tested a lot of different numbers to end a price with, and '7' is the most successful! Amazing, but true.)

If you're wondering how much to sell your product for, the general rule I use is '× 10' — that is, whatever your hard costs are, multiply them by 10 to find your selling price. Profits need to be this high to keep you excited, to put some money into your bank account and to allow you to expand the business (that is, to sell more products) so that you can keep providing the services your customers want.

So many small businesses struggle or, worse still, fail because they're not making enough money. If they don't survive, everyone loses out — the business owner, the supplier and the customer. With an information product, however, everyone wins. You make a decent profit, and as long as you produce quality information, your customer gets great value for money.

Because I sell information, I essentially sell 'nothing'. My products are generally just words, sounds or images. Now, you can sell almost anything you want over the internet, but if you truly want to experience the lifestyle that an internet business can provide, I strongly encourage you to sell information products.

Five ways you can create an information-product business

By now you're probably thinking, 'That's all well and good, but how do I get started? How do I decide what information product to sell?' Well, in this chapter I explain how you can figure all this out. Consider the following five questions to help you tap into your knowledge and experience, and perhaps find a great product idea:

1   What skills do you have?

2   What skills or knowledge does someone close to you have?

3   Can you solve a problem?

4   Can you help sell someone else's product?

5   Can someone else create a product for you?

I'll take a look at each of these questions in turn.

1   What skills do you have?

Think about this — what knowledge and skills do you have?

For example, I'm an expert at writing advertising. I've been doing it since 1989, and after that much time, I've become very good, which is why my first information products were about writing advertising.

Have you been doing something for at least 10 years? It could be a career, sport or hobby — maybe even watching television. (Who knows? Perhaps your expert knowledge of TV shows could be turned into an information product!) Are you a good cook? Are you great at being on time? Are you someone who deals well with stress?

Do you have knowledge that could benefit someone else? Something you do, if it was taught to someone else, could help that person do it more quickly or efficiently. Do people ever ask you to explain to them how you do what you do?

These are all skills that you may be able to use to create great information products. It's time to get started by putting some things on paper. Don't worry about how the ideas will work just yet, just get some down first.

List five skills, ideas or areas of knowledge, expertise or experience you have:

_____

_____

_____

_____

_____

_____

_____

_____

How did you go? If you haven't written anything, then please go back and do it now. It's important that you participate in this exercise if you want results. Thinking about your answers isn't enough; you need to engage your brain and actually write them down. It's a powerful way to learn and to think.

Now that you've thought about what skills you have, I'm going to change the question slightly.

2 What skills or knowledge does someone close to you have?

The great news is that you don't have to be the sole source of inspiration. You may know someone who has greater knowledge of a topic or a better skill than you.

Do you have a friend who does something interesting for a living? A family member who others rely on for certain skills or knowledge? Does someone you know run a business already? Is that person a professional in some capacity?

Now, think outside your circle of friends and family. Are there people you look up to, but who you don't know personally (that is, experts, leaders or entrepreneurs)? It's okay if you don't have a relationship with them yet. All it takes is an idea from you, and then who knows what could happen?

Have you thought of anyone yet? Even if you had some great ideas in response to question one, don't ignore this one. Your goal is to have plenty of ideas to choose from — the strongest will stand out later on.

List five people (you may know them or know of them) and their valuable skills:

_____

_____

_____

_____

_____

_____

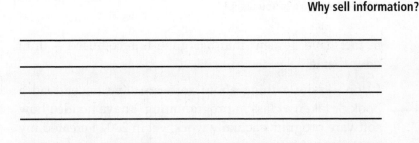

Once you've completed this exercise, you may be surprised at some of the potential ideas and areas of expertise that are available to you. We all have people around us who can help. You're truly never alone.

Another way to tap into your brain for an information product is found in the next question.

3 Can you solve a problem?

Are you a problem-solver? For instance, are you the type of person who can see what's wrong with a situation and come up with solutions to fix it? If so, that's great news. You should write these problem-and-solution ideas down every time they happen.

If you're not this type of person, don't worry, you can be. Here's what I mean.

Do you ever get annoyed with things that don't work properly? Do you ever ask yourself, '*Why* did that happen?' Do you ever get so frustrated with the way coworkers or friends do a certain task that you say, 'Don't worry, I'll do it!'?

If you said 'yes' to any or all of those questions, you could be staring an information product right in the face. You see, if you can solve a problem or simply have a better understanding of something than other people, you may in fact have a talent that has gone unrecognised — until now, that is.

I don't know a thing about software. I've never read a book or taken a class in programming. I have no idea how software programs actually work, yet in 2004 I created my own piece of software!

How? I simply thought of a problem and a way to solve it. All I needed was the idea, not the know-how. Then I came across some software that solved my problem.

This software is called, of all things, Make Your Own Software (<www.makeyourownsoftware.com>). At the time of writing, it sells for US$197 (approximately AU$220) and enables you to create your own software. (It's especially useful for beginners.) You simply download it to your computer, and you can begin using it straightaway. I found it really easy to use and chances are you will too.

I knew that many people find it hard to write their own advertising. To me it's easy because I've been trained, but for a beginner, it's difficult to get it right. That was the 'problem'. So I thought, 'Well, what if I could create some software that did most of the work for them?'

That was it. That was all I needed to create the product. I used Make Your Own Software and after about three weeks of finetuning it was done and available to purchase online. It really was that quick. The software I created is called BURPIES (see figure 3.1). Visit <www.burpiesbybrett.com> to check it out.

BURPIES helps people to write their sales message in as little as 30 minutes (something that could normally take you a day or two on your own). I sell it for US$97 (approximately AU$110). I haven't done any more work on this product since I created it, but it continues to sell. I've sold over 2000 copies so far (and made over AU$220 000), and could have been selling a lot more if I'd focused on it.

Figure 3.1: my BURPIES software

What tends to happen is that once a project starts selling well, you move on to the next project simply because it's exciting to do something new. Had I spent more time on this project, I could have sold at least 5000 copies of it by now. I would have done so by initiating joint ventures with people who have large databases. I could have run advertisements for it in the mainstream media and on other websites. And I could still do all that and so much more.

Instead, I have used just one method of marketing simply because it suits me. I have affiliates who sell BURPIES for me (these are people who promote the product for me and are paid a commission from every sale they make — this is covered in detail in chapter 10), so the marketing takes care of itself. From the beginning, I wanted to 'set it and forget it', and today I still make money from it while I sleep.

Never underestimate your product-creating power. You, too, could put together your own software. You just need to find a problem to solve. In fact, have a think about that right now.

List five everyday problems or frustrations you have:

_____

_____

_____

_____

_____

_____

_____

_____

_____

_____

List the best solutions you can think of to solve those problems or frustrations:

_____

_____

_____

_____

_____

_____

_____

_____

_____

_____

At this stage I just want you to get these potential product ideas down on paper. You never know what might come of these once I show you how to create the products.

Let's move on to the next question.

4 Can you help sell someone else's product?

My goal is to help you get started making money from using the internet. Until now I've focused on showing you how to create the product based on your own research. But let's say that you want to get involved in an internet business straightaway, just so that you can get your feet wet. What then?

That's what this question is all about — making money by helping others sell their already-existing product. This way you don't have to do any of the groundwork or, in fact, much work at all — you just do the promoting. And in the meantime, you can work on your own project.

Now, what if there was a place you could go where a lot of top-selling information products were available for you to sell on commission? At this place, you could simply choose one of thousands of products to sell that each came with its own website and sales message and that didn't involve you having to accept cash — it's all done for you. What if you didn't even have to register a domain (website) name, do any product research or even make sure your customer received the product?

Well, the great news is there is such as place — ClickBank (<www.clickbank.com>), see figure 3.2 (overleaf).

This site is amazing. It gives you access to over 10 000 digital information products (that is, downloadable products) — ranging from health and fitness to home and family, and from fun and entertainment to sports and recreation. There are e-books, audio products, video products and more ready for you to sell.

Figure 3.2: ClickBank's home page

Reproduced with the permission of ClickBank.

If you're asking, 'What's the catch?', well, there isn't one. ClickBank is simply a marketplace where you can sell other people's products on commission — in fact, up to 75 per cent commission. This means that if a product sells for $100, you keep $75!

Nearly all the work is done for you — the website has been set up, the sales letter has been written, and credit card processing and delivery of the product has been organised. All you have to do is send people to the product's site. You don't even have to host the website. You can simply visit ClickBank, join up for free and look around its marketplace for a product that you would like to promote.

When you select a product you'd like to sell, you'll be given an exclusive web link (a line of numbers and letters called code). This is your code to place as a link on your website or in emails. When someone clicks on that link (for example,

<http://nettips07.hotcopy.hop.clickbank.net>), they will be taken to the web page of your chosen product. If those people buy the product after doing this, then ClickBank automatically knows that they bought the product using your link and sets money aside to pay you a commission.

It really is as easy as that, and it's completely safe and reliable.

The website you are advertising has been set up by an information marketer like yourself. That person has done all the hard work — researching a market, creating a product, designing a website, writing the sales message and then allowing ClickBank to process the money and help affiliates (like you) to sell the product on a commission.

It's a great way to get started. In fact, I know people who make their sole income from ClickBank. I still use it myself. I sell a few different types of products from its catalogue. Figure 3.3 shows the total sales I made over three months from one of those products.

Figure 3.3: total sales made over three months using ClickBank

2007-03-14	02:43	TBKVH69B		MSTR	Sale	1	$88.72
2007-03-07	13:19	GNS9NJ8B		MSTR	Sale	1	$87.45
2007-03-02	17:07	LMXH408B		PYPL	Sale	1	$88.72
2007-02-26	15:00	DFD02L7B		PYPL	Sale	1	$43.72
2007-02-22	18:22	99JHQ47B		MSTR	Sale	1	$88.72
2007-02-21	09:18	N377907B		AMEX	Sale	1	$87.45
2007-02-19	21:03	Z4L7HV6B		PYPL	Sale	1	$88.72
2007-02-18	15:53	DSBLLQ6B		MSTR	Sale	1	$43.72

all 44 results.   Total: $3,330.58

Reproduced with the permission of ClickBank.

If you look at the bottom of this screen shot, you'll see US$3330.58 in sales over the three months — and just to be clear, I don't do any work for this money. Every month or so, ClickBank sends me a cheque for the money I've made.

I make this money by emailing customers who have bought something else from me. For instance, people who buy my *Scrapbooking Profits* e-book may also be interested in digital photography (they may want to learn how to take digital photos to put in their scrapbook).

A few weeks after they buy my scrapbooking product, my database software (WorldInternetOffice.com) automatically sends them an email about a product that teaches beginners about digital photography.

That's all the work that I do. My link from ClickBank for the digital photography e-book is in the email, and every now and then someone clicks on that link, visits the website and buys the product. I get paid 50 per cent of the purchase price.

If you're wondering why this service exists, it's pretty simple, actually. Just think, if you had your own downloadable information product, would you mind if other people helped you to sell it? And would you mind if for every dollar they helped you make, you gave them 50 cents? Or maybe even 75 cents? So it's a win for the person without a product to sell and a win for the product owner.

Ultimately, you will need to create your own information-product business to survive long term, but I thoroughly recommend this system. Think of it as a form of diversification — investment managers and financial planners will tell you not to put all your eggs in one basket, and that's what I'm saying too.

5 Can someone else create your product for you?

Now, I don't know how lazy you are, but if the previous method was still too much work for you, then this is the way to go.

It is possible and viable to get someone else to create your product for you, so you don't have to do any of the 'hard' work. If you remember, that's what I did with my e-book, *Scrapbooking Profits* — I had a ghostwriter write the book for me.

You can do the same. As I've explained, you can go to Elance and hire someone to create your product, website and sales copy, all while you lie on the beach or travel the world.

This is where some of the ideas you wrote down earlier in the chapter could come in handy. If you know something about the topics you listed, all you may have to do is outline what your e-book should cover. You can then hire a writer to create the content according to your instructions.

You may have someone bid to do the project for, say, US$1500. But someone else may bid to do it for US$300. You can read a profile of each of the writers who bid and feedback about them from past clients to help you make a decision. At these prices, having someone else create your product for you is great value, especially if it means you can get on with other things, like your job (you can be at work getting paid, while someone else does the research and writing of your book). You will outlay more cash up-front as the general of the army, but as I'm sure you're beginning to realise, the benefits can far outweigh the cost.

Now that your brain is beginning to turn over ideas, it's time to take a look at my seven steps to creating a profitable online business.

Summary

✐ The best product to sell is *information*, because:

- ▣ it's easy to be unique

- ▣ profits can be high

- ▣ it's quick and easy to create

- ▣ production costs are minimal

- ▣ it has a long shelf life.

✐ There are five ways to start creating an information product business. Just ask yourself:

1 What skills do I have?

2 What skills does someone close to you have?

3 Can I solve a problem?

4 Can I help sell someone else's product?

5 Can someone else create the product for me?

Part II

The seven steps to creating a profitable online business

I've been teaching internet marketing since 2003 when I was first asked to speak at a seminar in Atlanta, Georgia, in the US. Since then, I've noticed two issues in most people's approach to learning about starting an internet business and applying that knowledge.

The first issue is information overload. Online business is a relatively new field of wealth creation. Because it is so foreign compared with other, more tangible methods of building wealth — like real estate or share investment — most people want to absorb as much information as possible before they start. However, the sheer volume of information that is available is astounding.

This leads to the second issue I've observed, which is that people become so overwhelmed by information that they end up immobilised. They want to take action towards their dreams, but find that they don't know which way to turn. They have too many options, so they end up doing nothing at all — this is often referred to as 'analysis paralysis'.

These two issues are why I believe that too much information can be bad for you. To help you avoid information overload, I have compiled a list of seven critical things you need to know to set up a business on the internet. If you can master these steps first, you will have a greater chance of success.

As you progress, you will discover the other amazing benefits that the internet business world has to offer, such as different tools, helpful software, cutting-edge marketing techniques, search-engine optimisation tricks and payment processors. For now, though, let's focus on the seven steps that will put you on the path towards making money while you sleep.

1   Find a hot niche market.

2   Create a product that gives your market what it wants.

3   Create a powerful and compelling sales message.

4   Design a simple website that converts prospects into buyers.

5   Bring traffic to your website.

6   Use email to turn even more people into customers.

7   Recruit an army of people to sell your product for you.

Chapter 4

Step 1: find a hot niche market

Unfortunately, there's no way to guarantee that your product will be a winner. However, there *is* a way to maximise your long-term chances of success, and as I've hinted already, it has a lot to do with researching what your market wants before you create the product.

What you need to search for is something that prompts an emotional reaction within the market — a problem that people would pay to have solved. So it has to be a frustrating matter or concern, not just a minor issue. The group of people that search for a solution to this issue is called a niche. If they're really passionate about that solution, then they're called a 'hot' niche.

If you follow this rule, you will have a much higher chance of creating a successful product, because the decisions you make will be based on good information rather than guess-work. You'll simply be giving your customers what they're telling you they want.

And the great news is that the internet makes doing your research easier than it's ever been. If all businesses could research the way you're going to, there would be fewer business failures.

Here are some great tips for researching your hot niche market before you do any serious work:

ᵆ Become an internet keyword spy.

ᵆ Listen to your market.

ᵆ Tune into the latest buzz.

I'll take a look at each of these in turn.

Become an internet keyword spy

To locate the group of people you're going to sell to, you'll need to identify the best keywords for your product. A 'keyword' is like an internet version of a word you might look for in the index of a book. When customers look for information on the internet, they type in the word (or words) most relevant to their topic. One tool to help you identify appropriate and useful keywords for your niche market is Wordtracker (<www.wordtracker.com>), see figure 4.1.

Wordtracker will enable you to see how many people are searching for a particular word or phrase on the internet, which can help you decide if your idea is a good one or not. This service has a subscription fee of US$329 (approximately AU$365) per year, and it's absolutely worth it. Fortunately, there's also a free trial version of this software. Just visit the website for details.

Figure 4.1: Wordtracker's home page

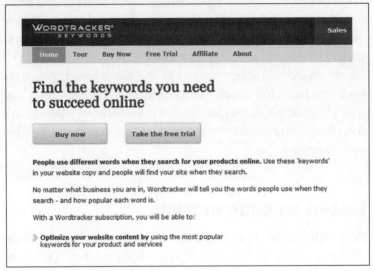

Reproduced with the permission of Wordtracker.

This kind of research helps you eliminate weaker ideas from the very start. You may have a great product idea, but what if no-one is actually looking for it online? After all, if there aren't many people searching for your product, then it's going to be much harder to sell. If, however, you found out that up to 40 000 people were searching for information related to your product idea every month, then that might give you cause to keep pursuing that idea.

What you're looking for are keywords that a lot of people are looking for but for which there is little competition — in other words, *high* interest, *low* competition. High interest means 20 000 to 40 000 people a month searching for information on a particular topic. Low competition means only one or two other internet businesses are providing that market with the information they want. If you find this combination, then you're off to a great start.

The Wordtracker software also enables you to compare your keywords against potential competitors' keywords, so you can see how many competitors you have before you begin. You may find that you have no competition and plenty of potential customers looking for your solution (if so, you'll be in the box seat). On the other hand, you may find you have too much competition. In this case, you can quickly change strategies and try something else. That's the great thing about the internet; it lets you be as flexible as you need to be.

Listen to your market

Research your hot niche market by visiting online discussion groups before you begin your journey. There are thousands of discussion groups (also known as forums) on the internet for all different subjects, and people wishing to discuss their favourite topics or issues contribute to and read them.

For budding internet entrepreneurs, discussion groups are valuable places to visit as they provide insights into the minds of your potential customers. Here you can discover what people are talking about, what their passions are, what their problems are and what their questions are.

Two places to find discussion groups are Yahoo! Groups (<http://groups.yahoo.com>) and Google Groups (<http://groups.google.com>). These groups are truly the 'secret weapons' of internet marketing. When you base your decisions on real research, your results are much more predictable.

What if, having visited a couple of discussion groups, you noticed that a certain question or two kept popping up? For example, say that within a discussion group on baseball, the question 'What is the best grip for holding a baseball bat?' appeared multiple times. It would make sense to develop a product, such as an e-book, called *The 5 Best Batting Grips for Hitting Home Runs!*

By listening to the questions your market is asking, you have the inside edge on their problems and what they want to know. Your customers will love your work simply because you found out what was on their minds *before* you created your product.

You can spend many hours doing this kind of research, and it's generally worth every minute. However, while research is critical, you don't want to get stuck evaluating and contemplating until you end up taking no action. Indeed, while the internet makes researching easy, it's important to use your internet research tools (such as search engines and forums) efficiently. You can research forever, but the money only starts coming in when you take action towards selling a product to your market.

This 'disease of perfectionism' is a common problem; the best way to avoid it is to set a time limit on your research. I recommend setting aside seven hours. Whether you complete your research in one day or spread it out over several days, seven hours equates to a fair day's work and is all you should need to research and evaluate the feasibility of your idea.

Tune into the latest buzz

'Ezines' are another great way to tune into your market. Ezines are online magazines that feature articles, reviews, advice and general information about certain topics. The great thing is that they are usually targeted towards a specific market.

Through ezines you can find out what products and services your market really likes and why. You'll discover the latest trends, and you'll probably even hear about the things your market doesn't like.

To find an ezine simply type into a search engine (such as Google or Yahoo!) '(your topic) ezines' — for example, 'car ezines' or 'African violet ezines'. If no ezines appear, then this could be a good indicator that your market isn't very big or very interested in finding out more information — a handy discovery at this stage.

If you do find a relevant ezine (or ezines), spend some time reading it. Usually you can sign up for the ezine's newsletter, which notifies you whenever any new information is posted. Generally, ezines are free.

Other good sources of current information are blogs. A blog (short for web log) is an online diary or journal where people post their thoughts, questions and discoveries. Blogs are free to view and anyone can leave their comments, which means they get a very high participation rate. If you see the same questions posted repeatedly, then there could be many thousands of other people out there with exactly the same question.

To find blogs related to your market simply type into a search engine '(your topic) blogs' — for example, 'poodle blogs' or 'indoor cricket blogs'.

Another great way to benefit from a blog is by joining the discussion. The best way to do this is to actually give something of yourself rather than just asking a question. Leave a comment first about a certain topic and then ask what others think about the same issue. This way you're contributing as a whole and not just using the service for your own gain. These 'communities' exist because visitors share and become involved. If you respect this, then you'll find blogs to be a great resource.

Ask about people's frustrations, dislikes and problems. Find out what needs are not yet being addressed. You may come across some gems of information that you hadn't yet thought of. Of course, the best problem is something that can be solved with the right information.

Once you've found a potential market or two, check out the competition. Let's say that 'knitters' is your potential niche market. You've found out how many people are searching for knitting-related topics every month, you've found relevant discussion groups, ezines and blogs, and overall you feel you've identified a need in that market.

The next step is to use a search engine to find sites that are related in some way to knitting. You may need to narrow the search by typing in the need you've found in the market — for example, 'knitting baby clothes'.

When the results of this search appear, look for the advertising on the right-hand side of the page — it may be from someone else who's already created a product for that market. Click on the ad to find out what that website is offering and perhaps even buy the product. This can sometimes be the greatest research of all because you can see what is already being produced for this market.

Once you know what the competition is producing, you can find a way to make your product different or better. That's why having some competition can be good — it gives you something to measure your product against. Chances are your future customers will not only buy your product but that of your competition, too.

So, what is your niche market?

Write down what your niche market is and the problem you are going to solve for it (for example, 'My niche market is knitters who can't find enough patterns for baby clothes, so I'm going to tell them the best places to find these patterns and how to create their own'):

_____

_____

_____

_____

_____

_____

_____

_____

It's important that you can identify your niche market precisely. If I was to ask you who it is, you should be able to tell me in 15 seconds. If you can't do this, then you don't know your niche market well enough, which means you need to spend a little more time researching. Once you can identify it in that time, then you've completed the first step.

Summary

✍ Research your product and market before you move ahead by using Wordtracker, visiting discussion groups and blogs, and researching ezines.

✍ The two best search engines to use when you research are Google (<www.google.com>) and Yahoo! (<www.yahoo.com>).

✍ Sometimes the most valuable thing you can do to research your hot niche market is to buy your competitors' products — find out what they are *not* offering and make that your selling point.

Chapter 5

Step 2: create a product that gives your market what it wants

Now that you've done your research you're probably starting to focus on what form your product should take. My goal is to make it as easy as possible for you to create your first product, so in this chapter I'm going to cover how to fast-track putting something together that your niche market needs.

Interview experts from your niche

Interviewing is your saviour when it comes to creating information products quickly, especially if you've never written a word in your life. By interviewing an expert in your chosen area, you can actually create a product that is full of good, solid information and that people will enjoy using and would have no hesitation buying.

Remember, people use the internet to find information. It makes sense, then, that if you create a product that provides information that people want, you're going to find people who are prepared to pay for it. I've made many products using interviews — products like CDs, manuals, online videos and online audio of me interviewing an expert in a chosen area. People love this type of product.

The best part is that it takes only around one hour of your time to interview an expert. That's right; a one-hour interview is all you need to create an information product.

Now, you might be wondering, 'Why would an expert let me interview him or her? And how much will it cost?' In fact, you'll find that most experts will let you interview them without any strings attached. Quite often, all you have to do is ask.

Experts aren't considered 'experts' unless they teach people what they know. If they don't get their 'genius' out there, then no-one will know they're experts, so the interview is free publicity for them. All they have to do is answer your questions for an hour and their work is done. By selling this interview, you're promoting them without any charge, but you're still going to get paid for giving them free publicity.

Another reason interviews are relatively easy to get has to do with something slightly more basic and human. Most people are flattered to have the opportunity to present their point of view. It makes them feel valued. And don't we all like to be valued?

I'm not necessarily talking about interviewing experts you see on television, hear on the radio or read about in magazines. Experts can be the heads of associations, successful local entrepreneurs or leading people in your community. They are people who are an authority in a particular area. It's a win–win opportunity — the expert ends up with free publicity and you end up with a saleable product.

What if someone offered to write a book about you and your business? The book would be released across the nation and available in every bookstore. Would you want to be part of it? You'd be crazy not to! Think about it — you have to advertise yourself somehow, otherwise no-one is going to know about you or your business. But advertising is usually very expensive and takes a fair bit of work to do effectively.

While you won't be offering the opportunity to be on the shelves of every bookstore in the country (yet!), you will be promoting these experts who are not household names at this stage. You're going to help them reach their goal.

For most experts, any promotion is good promotion. Once you truly understand what a great opportunity you are offering them, you will feel much more confident in approaching them.

Should you pay an expert for the interview?

In most cases, you shouldn't need to pay interviewees. I've never paid for an interview. You don't even need to offer to split any profits from the sale of the product.

Any expert should value the opportunity of having a quality promotional vehicle out there, especially a free one. This is a quality promotional tool — not a 30-second radio advertisement or small newspaper article. You're recording an interview that showcases the expert's knowledge and skills. Customers who listen to this advice are likely to be highly motivated to buy the expert's products or pay him or her to consult.

If it all goes according to plan, you both should benefit financially from the process. If experts are presented with the opportunity in the right way, nine times out of 10 they will agree to be involved.

To help you out I've included a script you can use when approaching experts for an interview, see figure 5.1. By using it word for word, you should find it very easy to get experts to agree to an interview.

Figure 5.1: getting-an-interview script

'Hi Mr/Mrs/Ms/Miss/Dr Expert,

I was wondering if you would be interested in letting me promote you/your expertise/your business. If so, there's no charge.

What I would like to do is interview you and turn the recording into an e-book, CD, DVD and/or audio tape. This way I can showcase your expertise by asking you questions that you can answer with ease.

Then, at the end of the recording, you will have the opportunity to promote your company/website.

I'll do all the promotion for the interview. All you have to do is allow me to interview you for one hour.

Would this sort of promotional tool interest you?'

If you follow this script, you're in business! It really is this simple.

If the expert wants to know more about how you're going to promote the interview, tell him or her everything — that you're going to turn the interview into a product that sells over the internet; that you will take all the risk; that you will pay for it out of your own pocket; and that you will produce, edit, market and deliver it. This makes it a very risk- and hassle-free proposition for them. You can do this in writing or verbally. The bottom line is don't offer to pay for the interview. You're starting a business from scratch so you need make sure you keep your costs low.

There are many people out there who would happily be interviewed for free, so if someone does demand payment, find another expert to interview. You're offering a win–win opportunity only for those who see it for what it really is.

You can also let the expert have the rights to the interview, which means that you will each own it. The expert can do what he or she likes with the interview, but most likely he or she won't do anything with it. You know how to market it (by reading this book), so you will likely be the only one selling the interview as a product. I don't always offer the rights of the interview to the expert, but if it helps get the deal, then it's fine.

Is a written agreement with the expert necessary?

You're creating a great promotional device for both you and the interviewee, so there should be very little reason to get bogged down in legalities. However, occasionally I do have an agreement depending on how well I know the expert and how well I know he or she understands the process. When I do, it's usually a simple written document stating that both parties:

- own the rights to the interview

- agree that the product will be promoted to the public

- will act in good faith and carry out their responsibilities to the best of their abilities

- agree not to defame either party at any stage.

I'm not a lawyer or legal professional, and these are my recommendations only. For anything that is legally binding, you should always seek legal advice.

When I don't have a written agreement, I sometimes just have the expert agree verbally to the above terms at the start of the recording. This is, of course, deleted from the final recording, but kept on file privately.

Tips for a great interview

Here are my top tips for interviewing experts:

- *The interview needs to be relaxed and conversational.*
  A great way to do this is to have a list of questions prepared beforehand and to allow the expert to see them a few days prior to the interview. This way the expert can think about what he or she is going to say.

- *Ask your question and then keep quiet.* It's important to let the interview flow by allowing the expert to do his or her thing. That means letting the expert answer without you interrupting too much or, even worse, adding 'ums' and 'ahs'. When I ask attendees of my seminars to practise by interviewing fellow participants, one of their biggest challenges is keeping themselves from saying 'Yeah', 'Mmm' and 'Uh-huh' during the interview. It may sound like a small thing, but it can make a huge difference to listeners. So remember to keep quiet while your expert is answering.

✐ *Get the first interview out of the way.* In truth, your first interview will probably be quite average, and it's important for you to accept that this will be the case. The good news is that every interview you do after that one will be much better. Remember not to let your 'perfectionist' gene stop you from taking action, though. Practise by interviewing a friend or family member first because nothing can take the place of actually *doing* an interview. You learn so much — things that you won't discover by just reading this book. So make a start — it gets much easier after the first one.

✐ *Ask 'open' questions.* Your goal is to make it easy for an expert to give good, information-packed answers. Don't ask 'closed' questions which will result in 'Yes' or 'No' answers. Ask questions such as:

▣ 'What is so good about XYZ topic?' (Not, 'Is XYZ topic good?')

▣ 'What are the top three things people should know about XYZ topic?'

▣ 'What are some of the common problems people experience?'

▣ 'Can you talk about some real examples of XYZ topic?'

While I think it's a great idea to create your own questions to ask your chosen expert, I'm going to give you a head start. In figure 5.2 (overleaf), you will find the questions

I use when interviewing experts. I call it my 'Interview Maximiser' as it strengthens the quality of your interview by zoning in on what your customers will want to know.

The great thing about my Interview Maximiser is that it can be used for an expert in any field. They are excellent questions to ask for getting quality information, but they are also very general. I've left space for you to add in the field of expertise appropriate to your interview, meaning my Interview Maximiser can become your new best friend. (If you'd like to print out a copy of the Interview Maximiser for your own use, you can do so from <www.brettmcfall. com/maximiser>.)

Figure 5.2: Interview Maximiser

1   What is so good about _____?

2   Can you give us a little bit of background about how you got involved in _____ and what led you to become such an expert?

3   What are the top three things that someone should know in order to be successful in _____?

4   What is the best way to get started?

5   How long does it take to become proficient at

    _____?

6   Will your methods or advice work in any area and for anyone?

7   How much experience does a person need to

    _____?

8   Can you provide some real-life examples of other people who have followed your advice?

9   If you had one secret to give about _____,
     what would it be?

10   What are some of the common problems that people
     experience in _____?

11   Some people might think that it all sounds too good to be
     true. Is there a catch?

12   What sorts of things can someone do to stay on top?

13   Where can people find more information about

     _____?

14   How can people contact you?

Here's how you would use one of the questions in my
Interview Maximiser. Let's take the third question: 'What
are the top three things that someone should know in order
to be successful in _____?'

All you need to do is insert the subject or focus of your
interview at the end of the question. If the interview is
with a rugby league expert, then your question would
read: 'What are the top three things that someone should
know in order to be successful in playing rugby league?'
If you decided to focus on a certain area of the sport, your
question would be even more precise: 'What are the top
three things that someone should know in order to tackle
an opposition player?'

See how you just adapt the question to suit your interview?
Basically, the questions are written for you; all you have to
do is insert your chosen topic.

I've used this template for five years, and it can turn
what would normally be a good interview into a great
one. This means you can relax and just let the interview

flow. An interview usually lasts for an hour when you use these questions.

Remember, if you've noticed any common questions popping up during your research in step 1, you can add these to your interview questions, too.

Light bulb moment

If you're not comfortable with interviewing an expert yourself, that doesn't mean you can't create the product. Simply find someone else to interview the expert for you. If you have a friend who might be a good interviewer, then ask him or her to do it. Another option is to hire a professional from a talent management agency.

Just remember that you *don't* have to be a professional interviewer to create a product this way. What's important is the content of the interview, not necessarily your interview style.

Here's another tip: find out if there's a community radio station near you. The people who work there are often trained in interviewing and are at the station to gain experience before moving on to commercial radio. Why not see if someone there would like to do the interview for you as a way to get even more experience?

You may be an expert in a certain area yourself. In fact, your first interviewee could be staring at you in the mirror. If this is the case, then you have two options — interview yourself or have someone interview you.

If you have someone else interview you, then it's simply a reversal of roles. If you want to interview yourself, however, then all you have to do is turn the questions into statements. For example, the question 'What is so good about XYZ hobby?' would become 'You know, many people ask me "What is so good about XYZ hobby?" and my answer usually goes like this ...' It's as simple as that.

How to record a telephone interview

Most of my interviews are conducted over the telephone. It's the easiest option, really. The expert doesn't need to be in the same room as you, so you can revolve the interview around his or her schedule or location. Indeed, it means you can even record an interview with experts who live overseas over the phone. It also means you can be relaxed at home and dressed in your pyjamas if you want — no-one will ever know!

There are many different, technical ways to record a telephone conversation, but they usually require a little bit of know-how. The alternative, and the easiest way by far, is to avoid purchasing any special phone recording equipment. All you have to do is visit No Cost Conference (<www.nocostconference.com>), a free teleconferencing service operating out of the US. At the time of writing, it's actually much cheaper to use US-based teleconference services than Australian ones.

No Cost Conference provides you with instant, unlimited, automated and free conferencing calls, and is available 24/7 with no scheduling required. You simply sign up at no charge, and you will be given a phone number to call, a conference identification number and a moderator number. These are the numbers you use to access your service.

You can also record the call via the website, and there are simple instructions for doing this. Once the call is over, you can download the recorded call to your computer as a 'WAV' file. Using software that I discuss in the next section, you then open the 'WAV' file and convert it to an 'MP3' file.

How to record a face-to-face interview

Fortunately, you don't need much equipment to record a face-to-face interview, and the equipment you do require is not expensive.

To record an audio interview, you can use your own computer and a program that I'll tell you about shortly. You can record interviews straight to your hard drive as long as your computer or laptop has a microphone input.

The microphones you use are important, so it's not a good idea to buy the cheapest ones you can find. Your customers will want a good-quality recording that's easy to listen to, but this doesn't mean that you need to spend thousands of dollars (yes, prices really do go that high for microphones). You should be able to buy a pair of headset microphones from your local electronics store. They look like a regular set of light headphones, except they have a boom microphone attached. These cost around $60 to $70 each.

You'll need to ask someone at the electronics store for a jack that will enable you to connect the two headset microphones to your computer. Different computers have different options, so make sure that the supplier understands the requirements of your computer. If you have a laptop, this should not be an issue as you can take it to the store with you.

You then connect the two microphones to your computer so that you can record both yourself and your expert as the interview occurs.

An alternative to using the two-microphone set-up is to get an MP3 recorder. An MP3 recorder is a portable digital device that records audio; as it's a digital recorder, there are no tapes or discs. Make sure you have an MP3 *recorder*, not just an MP3 *player*; not all MP3 players have this functionality. You'll need one that records good sound quality (ask your local dealer for advice).

MP3 recorders can be found at electronics stores and most department stores. You'll have to pay around $200, which isn't bad for a piece of equipment that will help you create a very profitable product.

MP3 recorders are great little tools as you can often record up to nine hours of audio on them. That's almost nine interviews. Of course, don't forget to buy spare batteries — the last thing you want during an interview is to run out of power!

Once the interview is recorded, you simply transfer the audio file from the device to your computer. It's simple to do and the device will come with instructions on exactly how to do this.

The MP3 file is actually what you'll be selling to your customers. You don't really need to understand what an MP3 file is, but, in short, it's the preferred format for transferring audio because it doesn't take up too much room on a computer's hard drive.

What to do once the interview is on your computer

During the interview, what if you coughed or sneezed, there were long pauses or there were things mentioned that you didn't want in the final recording? Well, fortunately they can be fixed easily using a fantastic — and free — software program called 'Audacity'. You can download a copy from <http://audacity.sourceforge.net>.

This software is about to become your new best friend. Not only will it help you edit the recording, but it can actually do the recording for you, too. (Generally, recording straight to your computer will produce a high-quality result.)

Here's how to record your interview directly to your computer:

1   Connect the two headset microphones to your computer (following the advice of your local electronics store expert).

2   Launch the Audacity program on your computer.

3   Press the record button.

That's it!

The operation buttons within the Audacity program are shown in figure 5.3. They function just like a regular audio recording device with 'stop', 'play', 'record' and 'pause' buttons.

Figure 5.3: the Audacity control panel

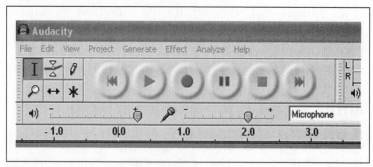

'Audacity' is a trademark of Dominic Mazzoni.

Once the software is recording, you'll see it representing your voice graphically as shown in figure 5.4.

Figure 5.4: the recording signal of your voice

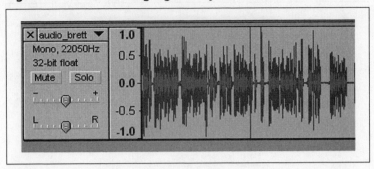

'Audacity' is a trademark of Dominic Mazzoni.

The vertical lines on the right half of figure 5.4 show the recording signal of your voice. When you're talking, the lines go up and down. When it's not picking up any noise, you'll see a flat horizontal line.

When you've finished your interview, simply click on the 'stop' button. You can then listen to the recording straightaway and delete the parts that you don't want. (Audacity provides simple instructions for doing this.) Basically, you just highlight any sections you don't want and click on the 'delete' button.

When you're happy with your recording, convert the file to an MP3 file. The software does this for you when you choose the 'Export As MP3' option in the 'File' drop-down menu, shown in figure 5.5 (overleaf).

This is all you need to do to record, edit and save your interview to your computer.

In summary, you can either record your interview to an MP3 recorder and transfer it to your computer, record it straight to your computer using the Audacity software, or record and download your interview via teleconferencing.

Figure 5.5: converting your recording to an MP3 file

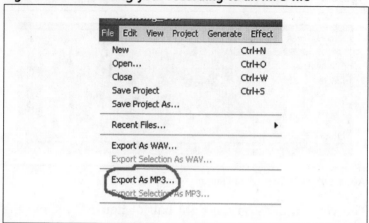

'Audacity' is a trademark of Dominic Mazzoni.

How much should you sell the interview for?

You'll generally be interviewing people who have not been interviewed before, which helps make your product unique. This means that you can sell it at a price that allows you to make a decent profit.

I recommend selling one-hour interviews for between $30 and $97, depending on how unique the content is. To make sure your customers get value for money, you can have the interview transcribed.

Transcription simply means having the audio recording typed out into what's called a 'report'. The report is exactly the same content, just a different delivery method. This is useful because some people like to listen while others prefer to read. By offering both, your customers can choose which way they want to learn, and without much extra effort, you effectively have two products — one audio and one written.

There are plenty of transcription services available on the internet, and it's worthwhile doing a search to find one that's right for you. CastingWords (<http://castingwords.com>) is one such transcription service, and it charges from US$0.75 per minute of recording. It provides a very quick turnaround service, usually sending the transcription back within a few days.

The best way to approach the sales process is to sell the audio interview and then include the transcribed report as a bonus. I used this method when I first started selling interviews and my customers loved it.

The first product I created was an interview with a mail-order expert who was making over $30 000 a month selling products via the mail. I knew there would be a lot of people who would like to know how he did it, and indeed there were. I earned over $28 000 a year for three years just from this interview. The audio quality wasn't very good, but the information was gold.

Then I did it again, this time with a real estate expert. This product became a $24 000 per year income earner.

I sold both of these interviews for $97 each. They were great interviews so my customers were very happy. My interviewees were happy, too, because it promoted them. And me? Well, I'd achieved my goal of selling information products.

How to turn your $30 product into a $300 product

Selling a product for between $30 and $100 will make you a decent profit. But there is a way to increase your return to around $300, or even $500. By following what I've already taught you, you're almost there.

All you have to do to create a higher priced product is conduct more interviews. So, instead of selling one product at up to $100, sell a package of three, four or five interviews for up to $500. All you need to do is interview more experts in that chosen field.

For example, if you were to interview an expert on property investing, you'd probably find that he or she had a certain area of expertise within that niche. Ideally, what you want to find are other interviewees who have expertise in a different area of property investing. This way your customers will get a much more rounded education. In this case, your product might look something like this:

- *Interview 1* — John Smith reveals how to buy investment homes at 30 per cent below retail value — even if you're a beginner.

- *Interview 2* — Kim Tran tells you the best regions to find property bargains.

- *Interview 3* — David Delosa explains how he's purchased 221 homes in the past three years using a financing technique that less than one in 100 investors know.

- *Interview 4* — Margaret Thompson reveals 10 secrets for buying real estate with less than $2000 to invest.

Can you see how this would be a very desirable product for someone interested in property investing?

The great part is that you can still ask each expert the same questions from Interview Maximiser. Each of their topics is slightly different, so each answer will be different, which means your listeners will never actually know that you're asking the same questions. Of course, you can change the questions as much as you want or need, but remember, these questions do get the sorts of responses that your listeners want.

The more interviews you include in your package, the more you can charge. Don't forget to include transcriptions of the interviews as bonuses.

Tips for creating your information product

The most important thing when creating your information product is to keep the quality high. Your product will live or die by the quality of the answers your experts give. If they just provide meaningless, vague answers to your questions, you are letting your customers down and they will not be happy. While you don't have to create a hard-hitting interview that you might see on a serious current affairs show, you do have a duty to work hard on the listener's behalf.

Don't let an expert glide through the interview. It's your job to get answers — real answers. You're on the side of your listeners, and that sometimes means that you need to make your expert work harder than he or she may have thought. Here's what I mean:

- *Get the details.* If your expert is not giving specific details, your listeners will not be happy. Don't be afraid to ask for further explanations or specific examples.

- *Don't let the expert ramble.* It's your role to respectfully interrupt if your expert doesn't answer the question quickly enough or stay on the topic.

✎ *Use 'Which means?' as much as possible in the interview.*
These two words force your expert to explain his
or her answers so that listeners will have the most
complete information possible. If your expert gives
an answer like, 'The main thing to remember about
investing in property is to be frugal', this is too
general to be useful. To fix the situation, simply ask,
'Which means?' and then let the expert answer. By
asking this question, your expert will naturally have
to get into more detail and will soon understand
what you expect.

Setting up a customer database

When you're looking for experts to interview, one of your
criteria should be that they already have their own database
of customers. Many experts already do and there is a way
to turn their customers into yours at no cost.

Light bulb moment

Apart from a great product, one of the most important things
for you to have in your business is a database of customers. This
is because on the internet you can make money just by sending
an email to your customers and offering a product related to
something they are interested in.

These days I can spend 15 minutes writing an email about a
product I'm offering, send it out to my database and generate
thousands of dollars in sales within 24 hours—something I
couldn't do before I had my own database. So make growing your
customer database a priority from the start. And offering one of
your interviews for free is a great way to do this.

Let's say you've interviewed five experts and each has their own customer database of 5000 people. Now, if you've decided to offer each of your experts the rights to the interview, then it means you have a copy and they have a copy. So while each expert owns the rights to his or her interview, only you own the rights to all five interviews.

If all of the interviews are on the same topic, you can approach each of the experts and ask them if they would like to give their interview, plus two more of their choice, to their customers as a gift. And a pretty substantial one too — potentially $300 worth.

If the experts want to add value to customer relationships, then this gift is perfect. The product is based around the topic their customers are interested in, and it features the expert too.

Simply ask the experts to promote the product to their customer databases and direct customers to the appropriate page on your website to download the interview package for free. The only condition is that the customers must give you their name and email address to access the three interviews. It's their choice — they can either pay $297 or get the package for free by providing their details.

What you are doing is giving the products to these people in exchange for their details. Yes, you lose the $297, but remember, these three interviews cost nothing to deliver — they are simply MP3 files that customers download to their computer.

What you are gaining is far more valuable. Let's say all five experts promote your special offer to their databases of 5000 each. If 2000 people from each database accept the offer and give you their name and email address in exchange for the interviews, that's a total of 10 000 people on your database, almost instantly.

The result is that now these people are *your* customers. In a few weeks you can email them an offer for one of the remaining two interviews or another relevant product. If you have 10 000 people on your database and you offer them an interview for, say, $27, it's highly likely that at least 200 (2 per cent) of them will buy it. That's $5400 (200 x $27) in your pocket just for sending one email. If 300 people were to buy just one of your interviews, then you would make $8100.

Is this strategy beginning to make sense? You're making money without doing much marketing. I have more marketing strategies for you in later chapters, but this one is about as easy as it gets.

Hopefully by now you're beginning to get excited about selling information over the internet. If you're also wondering, 'Well, once I've got my product, how do I sell it to my customers?', that question will be answered in the next chapter when I explain how to create a powerful and compelling sales message.

Summary

- ✍ By interviewing experts, you can quickly create your own original $30 product in as little as one hour.

- ✍ Use the getting-an-interview script to help convince potential interviewees to take part in the interview.

- ✍ Use the Interview Maximiser questions to get the best information from your experts.

- ✍ You don't have to do the interviews yourself; you can have other people do them for you.

- ✍ All you need to interview someone is your own computer or an MP3 recorder.

  ✐   You can use free software (such as Audacity; visit
<http://audacity.sourceforge.net>) to record and/or
edit your interview.

  ✐   To record an interview over the telephone, use a
teleconferencing service such as No Cost Conference
(<www.nocostconference.com>).

  ✐   You can easily turn your $30 product into a $300
product by adding more interviews.

  ✐   Keep the quality of your interviews high so that
your customers love your products — it's your
responsibility to dig for answers when interviewing
your expert.

Chapter 6

Step 3: create a powerful and compelling sales message

Now that you know your niche market and you've created a product that gives the market what it wants, it's time to learn how to describe your product in a way that will make people want to buy it. This is the skill of copywriting, and it is the most powerful marketing skill you will ever learn. Copywriting is simply selling in writing. The word 'copy' means 'text' or 'words'. The words you use to sell your product will be responsible for making your dream lifestyle a reality.

The words on your web page will be the only contact you have with your prospective customers. These words are you. They are your offer. They are everything when it comes to your business. Therefore, they need to be inviting, credible, helpful, succinct and clear.

In this chapter, I reveal my step-by-step writing system for captivating your prospects' attention, gaining their trust and interest, and then leading them to make their purchase.

> **Light bulb moment**
>
> Knowing how to write an effective sales message is a skill that anyone can use to create an income. A talented copywriter can always get work; it's worth learning this skill and encouraging your family and friends to do the same. Apart from selling products on the internet, you may one day want to get paid to copywrite for others.

My formula for an effective sales letter

After writing over 10 000 advertisements and letters, I discovered a way to write sales messages that, more often than not, made a lot of money for both my clients and me. Indeed, sometimes as much as hundreds of thousands of dollars in just a few days, even though previously many of my clients had struggled to break-even. This meant that the there was a difference in the way I used words.

I was also getting emails and phone calls from people asking me the same question: 'How can I write my own advertising that makes money?' What they were really asking was, 'How can I write like you *without* spending 10 years learning?' After all, that's how long I'd spent becoming an expert at it. I realised that if I created a simple system that people could follow, they would be able to write their sales messages in a way similar to me and achieve almost identical results.

I sat down one afternoon and looked at many of the advertisements, sales letters and websites I had created. Within an hour, I had identified a writing pattern that previously I hadn't noticed, and I knew instantly that I could help any beginner create their own sales messages, as long as they followed the steps.

Before I explain my formula for a great sales message, let me ask, have you ever written a letter to someone before? Some of the most effective sales messages I've ever written have *not* been advertisements — they've been *letters*.

Yes, the humble sales letter is by far the most powerful form of persuasion I've ever used, and it's the best way to sell a product from your website. Most retail sites prefer not to use letters to sell their products, but they're losing a lot of money by not testing out what I'm about to teach you.

It's a classic mistake — business owners assume they know what their market wants, but they're just basing this assumption on what they think looks good, or they're copying their competitors. Of course photos and flashy graphics look better than a sales letter. However, what I've found again and again is that a sales letter gets the best results every time.

Unless you are a huge company that is already widely known, you will need to have a sales letter on your website in order to convince potential customers of the value of your offer. Retailers like Woolworths and Coles don't need sales letters for their food products because they sell commodities. Their customers buy them week in, week out and in general their products are fairly low priced.

Websites that feature a catalogue of products don't usually need the long type of sales letters I'm talking about either. Though they still need to use well-written sales messages, catalogues usually feature shorter ones for each product.

All you're doing with your website sales letter is helping your potential customers make an informed decision. They need information if they are going to spend money online because they can't feel the product or pick it up. You need to help them understand what the product is about and why they should buy it. If you don't, you'll be losing sales.

If you're going to sell a number of products, then I recommend that you have a separate sales letter for each (and even separate websites). This way, you can tailor your website's sales message directly to your customers' needs and wants.

Now, when I went through a lot of the marketing material I had written, I discovered that there were seven main parts to the advertisements that I wrote. Many marketing books and experts recommend using the AIDA formula: attention, interest, desire, action. This represents the steps you need to take purchasers through in order to lead them to a sale. The AIDA formula is a great start, but it doesn't go far enough. Human emotions are much more complicated than this formula indicates, so I developed my own formula to address these. I call it my BURPIES formula:

- big promise
- use imagination
- rarity
- points
- irresistible offer

✍ evidence

✍ sign off.

I'm going to take you through each component to show you how to make people want to buy your product.

B is for *big promise*

There are three methods for making your 'big promise' — using a headline, audio and video. Together they have a massive impact.

Capture attention with headlines

The first thing you need to do on your website is grab your visitor's attention. To do this, you'll want to make a big promise. Something that makes people want to read on. The may not necessarily want to buy your product yet, but they will want to find out more about it.

The best way to do this is usually with a headline. It's the first thing visitors see. Did you know that 80 per cent of people read *only* the headline?[†] This means that if you don't have a headline on your website, 80 per cent of the people who arrive there may leave straightaway. In that split second, they simply want to know why they should stay on your page. A headline is great way to do this.

I love headlines that make you curious. The 'curiosity headline' has worked exceptionally well for my clients and me. In fact, it's one of my biggest secrets for getting results. Yet, strangely, few people ever try this tactic.

[†] David Ogilvy, *Ogilvy on Advertising*, Random House, 1998.

A great curiosity headline comprises two things — benefit and curiosity. When something interests you and then makes you think, 'Hmm, how could that be?', this is when you have a captivating curiosity headline. Here are a few of my most successful headlines:

REVEALED!
The sneaky little secret banks use to turn their foreign exchange mistakes into YOUR FAULT! *(What you'll discover here could be the most important news you read all day.)*

The embarrassingly simple secrets of an expelled high-school rebel, who consistently makes $27 000 on EVERY house he buys in just 2 short years … and the best part? You can see how he does it for FREE!

The astonishing secrets of a western Sydney nerd … *who failed his high school English exam* … yet NOW writes ads that bring in thousands of dollars in sales EVERY TIME!

See what I mean? These headlines contain a benefit for readers and they also raise your curiosity.

It's also important to test headlines against each other. Figure 6.1 shows the headline I use on the website selling my e-book, *Scrapbooking Profits*. It was the winner out of six different headlines that I tested. It gets more sales than any other headline I've tried.

Changing a few words in your headline can make a huge difference to your results. Some words increase sales while others decrease sales. Even the order of the words can affect sales.

This headline paints a clear picture of why scrapbook enthusiasts should buy my product. It makes the reader curious to find out more, which is the sole reason for having a headline. Your headline needs to do the same.

Figure 6.1: the headline on my *Scrapbooking Profits* website

> # Congratulations ...
> ## 30 days from now you could have your own thriving Scrapbooking business ... you can work your own hours from home ... <u>wake</u> when you want ... revolve it around family commitments - and take control of your financial destiny once and for all doing something you LOVE!
>
>
> From: Brett McFall, 9.18am
>
> Hi ,
>
> If you are interested in making money from your favourite hobby, scrapbooking ... then this is going to be the most exciting message you ever read.

Light bulb moment

In chapter 2, I talked about creating a research web page that allows visitors to leave their biggest question on the topic related to your proposed product. An added bonus of doing this is that you can create headlines based on the most popular questions asked!

> **Light bulb moment** *(cont'd)*
>
> For example, let's say the most common question was: 'What is the quickest way for a beginner to make money online?' Your headline would read something like this: 'How To Quickly And Easily Make Money On The Internet ... Even If You're A Beginner!' It's tailored to what your market wants to know.

The bottom line is you need to make a *big* promise to your prospective customers — even if it's just the promise of something more interesting further down the page. Here are some thought starters:

🖋 What is the biggest benefit your product produces?

🖋 What is the biggest problem your product solves?

🖋 What *specifically* does your product offer?

Now it's your turn to have a go at creating a headline. (By taking part in exercises like this, you'll remember twice as much of the information.)

Based on what you've learned so far, write a potential headline for your product:

_____

_____

_____

_____

What do you think of your headline? The most important thing right now is that you had a go. Just getting your brain into the right frame of mind for writing headlines is quite an achievement — and it can be fun, too.

Use the power of audio

Audio is very popular on websites these days undoubtedly because it is one of the least expensive ways to grab attention. All you need to do is repeat the headline in the audio and a few of the major points contained in the sales message. I've created a software package that enables you to put playable buttons on your website. It's called Audio Wiz and can be found at <www.brettmcfallaudio.com>, see figure 6.2.

Figure 6.2: my Audio Wiz software

You can record a message for your visitors to make them even more interested in what you are offering. You simply record your message on your computer using the headset microphone and Audacity software mentioned in chapter 5, and then use Audio Wiz to turn it into buttons you can place on your web page. Figure 6.3 (overleaf) shows how I've used the audio buttons on my *Scrapbooking Profits* web page.

Figure 6.3: the audio buttons on my *Scrapbooking Profits* web page

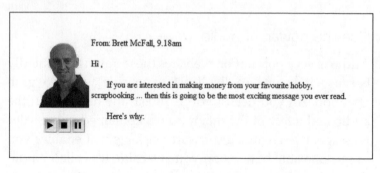

Surprise your visitor with video

Video is another real attention getter. You record your video using a digital camera or webcam and then upload it to your website.

The very popular video-sharing website YouTube (<www. youtube.com>) allows you to upload raw video files to its website, and then place that video (using YouTube's special encoding process) on your website. It's just about the easiest way to add video to your site, and it costs nothing. There are easy-to-follow instructions on YouTube to help you upload your video and then put it on your web page.

Figure 6.4 shows how I use video on one of my websites. Visitors simply click on the play button in the centre of the screen to watch the video.

In this particular video, I talk for around six minutes (without any make-up!) and in that time I basically follow my BURPIES formula. So it's a sales letter on video.

Now let's take a look at the next part of the formula.

Figure 6.4: video on my Lightbulb Experience website

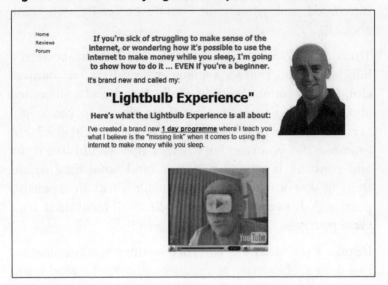

U is for *use imagination*

The next section of your sales letter should engage your visitors by having them use their imagination in relation to your product. You must get them to see, hear and feel what it is they truly want … or don't want. This is important because if you've done everything I've shown you up to this point, then your product answers a need in your market. That need is what you want people to remember when they reach your website.

I've discovered something interesting about how we behave when it comes to the buying process, but to understand it fully you need to think about the way you feel after you purchase something. When you buy something that you really like, your brain experiences a mini overload of emotion. The excitement takes over, and you do things like imagining the ways you're going to enjoy what you've purchased and what your friends or family will think about it.

Think back to when you bought your last car, booked a holiday, or purchased a piece of jewellery, an item of clothing, or something you really loved and got excited about. Did you wonder what those closest to you might say about your purchase and how they might feel? For example, did you wonder whether they would like it too and consider it a good purchase, and what they would think of you now that you have it? Or if was an expensive purchase, did you think to yourself, 'Will I still think it's a great purchase three weeks from now?'

If you ask yourself these sorts of questions, you're not alone. I've done this exercise at seminars all over the world, and most people do think about their purchases this way. It's not always because we need the approval of others. In our minds, we simply go through the process of wondering about the consequences of our actions. For example, we imagine what it's going to be like to drive that brand-new car, the smell of the leather and how great it will feel showing it to your friends or family for the first time. All these thoughts make us feel excited about the purchase.

So, if we know this is how most people will react *after* they've purchased something important to them, then why not ask them to experience this feeling *before* they make the purchase? This is why I started writing sales messages that 'use imagination' straight after the headline.

Sometimes I ask readers to imagine what they want to experience. Other times, depending on the product, I ask them to imagine what they want to avoid. Either way, I give them a reason to be interested in what's on offer.

Everything we buy is a solution for something — an aspirin is a headache solution; a DVD is an entertainment solution; a packet of chips is a hunger solution; an e-book is an information solution. You need your visitors to imagine what it would be like to have your solution already working for them. Get them thinking about what life would be like if they had your solution right this very second.

Figure 6.5 is an example of how I use imagination from my *Scrapbooking Profits* website. Notice how every sentence leads readers to experience what it would be like to own my own product.

Figure 6.5: using imagination on my *Scrapbooking Profits* website

Imagine being able to set your own hours

Would that be nice? Doing what you love - scrapbooking ... and doing it when it suits your lifestyle. And can you imagine how great you'll feel if you were getting PAID to do it?

Wouldn't it be great to work from home? Not having to battle the peak hour traffic or sit on dirty public transport? How would it make you feel to be your own boss ... and for people to be proud to be have you 'scrapbook' for them?

Just a few weeks from now you could be earning between $50 and $100 an hour doing what you love.

Did you hear that? *$50-$100 an hour!* Some professional business people don't make anywhere near that per hour.

And imagine being able to start your scrapbooking business while you're working at your current job? You can definitely do that. *Imagine being in control of how much money you make.* Some scrapbookers can easily make over $5,000 a month *(that's $60,000 a year)*. Not bad just for working from home, huh?

Now that you've seen an example, write down some sentences that will make your readers imagine what their life will be like once they own your product. (You can use sentences similar to the ones in figure 6.5 as idea starters.)

Write down two sentences to inspire your readers to imagine their lives *after* they own your product:

_____

_____

_____

_____

R is for *rarity*

Do you own any antiques or rare paintings? Do you know anyone else who owns either of these things? Do you own something that you treasure? Something that may be old and worn, but to you it's irreplaceable.

Why do you like this item so much? When we treasure something, we know exactly why. It may be a piece of jewellery that your late grandmother gave you or perhaps something from your childhood such as a trophy or an award.

Now, think about an antique chair that someone would pay over $1000 for. The chair was worth much less when it was made, but because there are so few of this type of chair now, its value is much higher.

Remember, when there are many of a particular item, its value is low. However, when there are few of that item available, its value increases.

We love things that are rare and unique. It's a universal human trait. That's why antiques sell for much higher prices today than when they were first created — their rarity makes them more valuable.

How does this apply to you and your product? Well, if you know that people value rare things, then you have to find a way to make your product rare. If you can do this, then not only will you sell more of your product, but you'll be able to sell it at a higher price than you would ordinarily.

As long as you understand how the uniqueness of a product affects its value, you will be able to use this as a marketing tool for your own product.

What is your unique selling proposition?

Why is your product unique? What about it is so special?

If you cannot answer this question with a clear, concise answer, you are going to struggle to make sales. Without even knowing what you're going to sell, I can safely make that prediction.

In training seminars, I often spend an entire session working through how people find their product's unique selling proposition (USP). It's an old advertising term and it's one of the most powerful marketing concepts. I'm going to give you the key to finding your USP — write it down and memorise it. It's something that is responsible for helping me build a great deal of wealth, and it can help you do the same.

You need to be able to answer the following question with a clear and specific response: 'Why should I do business with you over anyone else?'

When I invite people on stage at seminars so I can help them find their USP, they usually don't answer the question. They think they are answering it, but they're not. I usually listen to around five minutes of general answers — answers that people have been conditioned to say or that they think mean something to their customers. But they're not honestly answering the question. However, I don't let them get away with it because it's so important to get right. I keep asking and asking until the audience agrees that the people on stage are actually providing a unique reason for others to do business with them.

It can be a hard and confronting process for the people on stage, but when they finally 'get it', their eyes light up and they feel 10 feet tall. And so they should because they've finally uncovered their unique reason for being in business, which means they can finally be competitive.

The interesting thing is that the USP is always there — it's just hidden. I haven't had a business owner on stage yet that hasn't uncovered his or her USP. It gets buried under layers and layers of bland statements and generalities that cost business owners everywhere hundreds of thousands of dollars.

I once had a man on stage who pleaded with me that there was nothing unique about the gym that he owned. He just didn't have an answer to 'Why should I do business with you over anyone else?' What he was really telling me was that he didn't know how to look for it. He couldn't see what was unique about his business. He'd accepted that his gym was like every other gym that was struggling to survive.

Ten minutes into the exercise, the audience was beginning to agree with the gym owner. So I took the pressure off him for a moment and started talking to the audience about what I was doing and how it works. Suddenly, after the focus was taken off the owner, his brain began to stop resisting. He interrupted me with, 'Brett, I actually think I've got it! I own the only gym in my town!'

The audience went into raptures and could not believe the man was sitting on such a unique selling proposition. The stress on the man's face was replaced by utter joy.

Even if you think your product may not be unique, it is. Here are some questions about your product to get your brain thinking:

- Is your product the only one that looks at your subject in a certain way?

- Is your product the first of its kind?

- Is your product better than any others? If so, how?

- Does your product answer questions that others don't? If so, which questions?

- Is your product easier to understand than others?

- Is your product more comprehensive? Or is it shorter and more succinct?

- Did you interview experts that haven't been interviewed before?

- Did the experts reveal new secrets?

- Do you have more after-sales service than other products of this type? If so, what?

Figure 6.6 (overleaf) shows how I described the rarity of my *Scrapbooking Profits* product. I simply told the truth about how I collected the information inside the book, and this made it unique.

Investing time and effort into this part of your letter is really valuable. Your USP will often compel your prospects to make the purchase. Even though you'll give them so many other reasons to buy your product, when they tell others about it, this is the one thing they will refer to.

Figure 6.6: how I made my *Scrapbooking Profits* e-book different from the rest

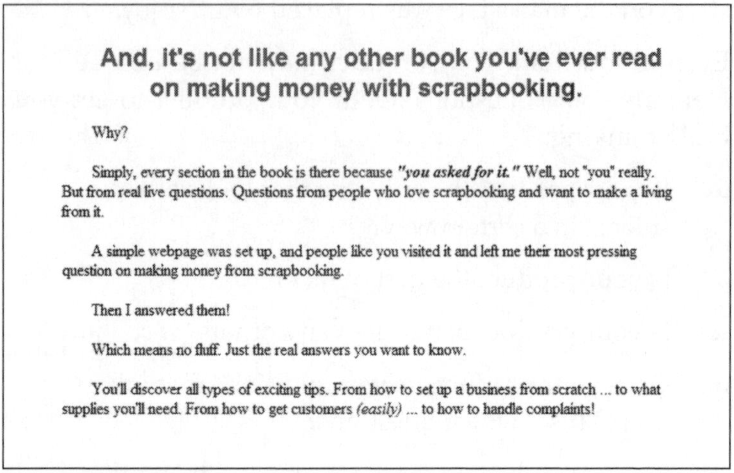

And, it's not like any other book you've ever read on making money with scrapbooking.

Why?

Simply, every section in the book is there because *"you asked for it."* Well, not "you" really. But from real live questions. Questions from people who love scrapbooking and want to make a living from it.

A simple webpage was set up, and people like you visited it and left me their most pressing question on making money from scrapbooking.

Then I answered them!

Which means no fluff. Just the real answers you want to know.

You'll discover all types of exciting tips. From how to set up a business from scratch ... to what supplies you'll need. From how to get customers *(easily)* ... to how to handle complaints!

Now it's your turn to come up with a unique selling proposition. Why should someone buy your product over any other? Write down the answer here and be specific:

_____

_____

_____

_____

Once you've completed this exercise, it's time for the next section of your letter.

P is for *points*

Here is where you get the chance to tell your reader about all the great things they are going to discover when they buy your product. The best way to tell readers about the great things your product contains is by writing the information in point, or bullet, form. It's important that you hold your reader's interest, and the most effective way to do this is to focus of the product's *features and benefits*.

Most people miss this completely when writing their sales letter or web copy, and then wonder why so few people respond to their marketing efforts. The main problem is that people confuse what they *think* people want to know with what readers *actually* want to know.

Interesting and effective sales copy does not focus on the features on your product such as what it is (an e-book, audio download or CD), what the product consists of (pages, chapters or two CDs), or what it does (explains scrapbooking, for example). Copy that sells focuses on how the reader will benefit from these features. Remember:

- a feature is a component of your product
- a benefit is what the feature does to solve a problem for the customer.

Without describing the benefits, your copy sounds flat and boring — people will simply leave your website and you'll lose a sale. The following are some examples of features and benefits:

- If you buy a car, one of its features may be air bags. The benefit of the air bags is that they protect you from being hurt in an accident.
- If you buy a home, one of its features may be ducted air conditioning. The benefit of the air conditioning is that it keeps the house cool during warm weather.

Here's a great little tip for highlighting the benefits of any feature — after any feature write 'which means'. For example, if your e-book *Handy Fishing Tips* tells readers about eight different types of fishing rods, all you have to do is add 'which means' after this to describe the benefit to readers. It may read something like this: 'When you read *Handy Fishing Tips,* you'll discover the eight different types of fishing rods you can buy, which means you'll know which one suits your age, experience and height'. By adding 'which means' straight after writing a feature, it makes your copy more interesting and effective. An alternative to 'which means' is 'so that you' — use both.

Additionally, by describing the benefits of your product you are creating a higher perceived value, which means your readers will start to regard the information as special and something they really want to own. You won't have to wonder if people will read everything that you've written if you've hammered home the benefits throughout your letter.

Remember, you're trying to solve your customers' problems, and the only way they can know whether you can do this is if you tell them how your information will help them. This is how big sales are made from any website. You need to do a better job than your competitors of describing how your product will help the reader.

At the same time as you describe your product's features and benefits, you also need to arouse readers' curiosity. This is about telling readers how you can help them, but not telling them everything. The 'everything' is saved for inside your product itself. For example, if, during an interview with an expert on handy fishing tips, he or she revealed an exact method for catching fish while others are going home empty-handed, this is very powerful.

If you were to reveal this tip in the sales letter, then there would be very little reason to buy your product. So while you want to let your readers know that this tip exists, you don't want to give away the punchline. Here is how I would handle this in the sales letter:

> You'll discover a little-known casting technique for catching fish even when it seems they aren't biting — which means when your friends are going home empty-handed, you'll be guaranteed to have one fish in your bag at the very least (*this simple secret is revealed on page 43*).

Wouldn't every budding angler want to know what this fishing technique is? This is what makes people desperate to get your product — the power of curiosity. In this example, I've even included the page that the secret is featured on, so readers know that they can find it easily when they buy the product.

Take a look at figure 6.7 (overleaf) — it's a screen shot of some of the bullet points I wrote to describe what's inside my *Scrapbooking Profits* e-book. Notice how the points are about the benefits to the customer and how they also make you curious.

I is for *irresistible offer*

We all love a bargain. No matter how high the price that we pay — even if it's millions of dollars — we still love to feel that we've achieved a good deal. So you must work hard at your offer. You must create offers that make people want to take action right away. Give until it hurts!

I prove this in my seminars where I sell a regular bottle of water (that you'd pay around $2 for) for $100 right there and then. How do I do this? First, I ask for a volunteer from the audience who has $100 cash on them. I then tell this person that I would like him or her to pay me $100 for the bottle of water. Naturally, the volunteer refuses to pay that much for it.

Figure 6.7: bullet points describing the benefits of my e-book

- Another amazing place WHERE you can get your hands on scrapbook layouts ... project videos ... new methods ... helpful tips and ideas for your scrapbook

- The single biggest complaint customers have about Scrapbook Artists *(once you know this, you'll be able to create an ultra successful business while your competitors remain oblivious)*

- **How to market your business so well that your customers are desperate to do business with you ... literally waiting in line for "only you"**

- How to do more of the kind of work that YOU love most ... and get paid top dollar for it

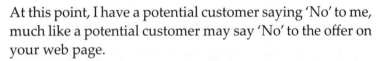

- No customers to sell to yet? Here's a secret almost nobody *(except the few successful Scrapbook Artists making good money)* know about building a huge list of customers at lightning-quick speed – even if you've never sold a thing in your life

- Are there any copyright laws when you sell a Scrapbook spread? This is what you MUST know to sail past any legal hassles with ease

At this point, I have a potential customer saying 'No' to me, much like a potential customer may say 'No' to the offer on your web page.

In this example, it's quite obvious why someone would say no to paying me $100 for a bottle of water — the same bottle of water could be bought for $2 outside the venue. Next I say that the bottle of water comes with some bonuses. At this stage the volunteer's attitude changes to, 'Oh, okay … so what bonuses are you talking about?' This is just what you want your readers to do.

I outline the bonuses, the first of which may be my *Lazy Way to Advertising Riches* manual, selling for AU$119 on

<www.brettmcfall.com>. At this point, the volunteer on stage with me looks a little more interested but not quite ready to part with $100.

The second bonus that comes with the bottle of water could be my Inside Secrets of Advertising course, retailing for AU$397 on <www.brettmcfall.com>. Sometimes I even show the website on the big screen to prove I'm telling the truth about how much it sells for.

By now the volunteer usually starts to show some signs of weakening, like fidgeting and generally giving the impression that he or she is considering handing over the $100. But sometimes I stop him or her, explaining that the bottle of water comes with one final bonus, which may be my Ad Pack program, which sells for US$2497. It trains you in how to become a copywriter, how to increase your sales overnight, and much more. It includes DVDs, CDs and manuals.

In a matter of seconds, the volunteer usually slams that $100 into my hand and says, 'I'll take it'. I'll generally play with him or her a little and say something like, 'What? You now want my bottle of water for $100? But just a moment ago you said "No" to it! What you are trying to pull here?' (Cue audience laughter ...)

But at this point the volunteer and the audience both know that something quite powerful has just happened. We've taken a prospect from a 'No' to a 'Yes' in a matter of minutes. How does this happen? The prospect becomes a committed customer the moment he or she understands that the item being bought holds much more value than the amount paid.

So, the volunteer on stage isn't really paying me $100 for the bottle of water. He or she is buying the bonuses. This is an incredible shift in understanding what marketing is all about. All along I've talked about your product and about telling your readers how good it is, but in fact, you can sell more of your product if you don't sell the product at all!

What if you could do the same on your website? If I can sell a bottle of regular water for $100, surely you can sell your unique information product for around $30. If you're wondering how you do this, it's really quite simple. All you have to do is use the power of bonuses to move the customer from a 'No' to a 'Yes'. Find some bonuses or create your own, and add them to your offer.

Let's say that instead of interviewing just one expert in your chosen niche, you actually interview five. You could simply turn one of those interviews into the product and use the other four as bonuses. Or, you could use all five as the product and then do another five interviews to add in as bonuses. You could keep on adding interviews until your offer becomes irresistible to refuse.

By now it should be obvious that you can make a lot of sales if you just get your marketing right. It's all about the offer. At the end of the day, your customers will always make a decision based on how much value they get. Your goal is to help them get so much value that they can't possibly lose.

When you sell downloadable products, it doesn't cost you any more to deliver 10 products than it does to deliver one. They are all just digital files that will be downloaded by your customer. That's how you can still provide hundreds of dollars worth of value for a meagre $30 and still make a profit.

Take my *Scrapbooking Profits* product, for example. I didn't just sell the e-book; I included a number of bonuses to entice customers. The first bonus was a 106-page e-book, *101 Scrapbooking Tips*, which is longer than the actual (90-page) e-book they're buying, see figure 6.8.

Figure 6.8: the first bonus with *Scrapbooking Profits*

FREE BONUS #1 - 101 Scrapbooking Tips

This *106-page* e-book is something every serious scrapbooker should have - you'll never be lost for ideas with this resource by your side. For instance, you'll discover:

- **What you need to start scrapbooking** *(and the best news is, you don't need much more than these few essential items ... and they won't cost you the earth!)*

- The <u>simple materials</u> you can get your hands on for next to nothing and without going to a supply store, but which make your scrapbook look simply sensational

- **Do you know what "weaving photographs" is?** Tip No.19 reveals what it is and how you can use it to create a 3 dimensional artist look in your layouts

- REVEALED! **<u>The simple way to create fake "wax seals" in your layouts</u>** *(incredibly effective and creates a beautiful finish, but use Tip No.26 and you won't have to get your hands anywhere near messy hot wax)*

- Ever wondered how to make a "pop-up window" - yes, just like the ones you see in children's books? No problem - **Tip No.60 tells you exactly how to do it ... and it's super-simple too**

Then I added more bonuses — 12 separate bonuses to help customers market their scrapbooking business — valued at $348. Not bad for a $27.77 purchase. For most prospects, this is an irresistible offer. These bonuses are shown in figure 6.9 (overleaf).

If you understand what I've just explained, then you stand to make a lot of money and have very profitable businesses on the internet. Make yours an irresistible offer and sales will happen automatically.

Figure 6.9: more bonuses that come with
Scrapbooking Profits

E is for *evidence*

By this stage, your readers should be very keen and quite excited about the thought of owning your product. At the same time, however, they're likely to be thinking that it sounds too good to be true. This is where most people lose the sale. It doesn't mean they don't want to believe you; they are simply being cautious.

You probably react the same way when you're buying a product, especially if it's online. It's not that you don't want the product; you're just afraid of being ripped off. We've all seen the shows on television or read stories in the paper about people losing money through scams — which is why the saying 'If it sounds too good to be true, it probably is' can be good advice.

But as a marketer of your own product, it's you who is being evaluated by your visitors. So at this stage of your website sales letter, you need to provide some information that proves to them that you're credible and trustworthy. There are three really good ways to do this:

- Prove your claims.
- Let others say how good the product is.
- Include a strong guarantee.

Let's take a look at each.

Prove your claims

Explain what makes your interviewee an expert in his or her field by talking about the interviewee's experience and achievements, including any media coverage, such as newspaper stories and magazine articles, he or she has received. For example, if your interview is with an expert in surfing, then you'll need to mention any awards he or she has won, include photos of him or her surfing and perhaps provide information about surfing classes he or she teaches.

On some of my own sites, where it's appropriate, I even show photos of my income just so my visitors can see that I actually make money on the internet. The bottom line is prove your claims!

Let others say how good the product is

Including comments from satisfied customers is by far one of the most powerful techniques to help you gain your visitors' trust. While it's fine to talk about how good you are or how good your product is, unfortunately it's never as believable as when someone else says it. People tend to trust what others say rather than what we say about our own products. These comments are called testimonials.

There's a simple formula I use when it comes to writing testimonials and it works better than any other. After reading thousands of testimonials during my career, I began to notice how some really grabbed me while others had very little impact. The ones that were most effective were made up of two parts — once I was lost; now I am found. That is, the first part of the testimonial talked about the past and about how hard life had been before discovering this product. The second part highlighted how great life was now because of the product. Once I was lost; now I am found. It's a simple formula, but it really does work.

You're probably wondering how you can use this formula when you're not the one writing the testimonial. What tends to happen is that your customers will want to write a testimonial for you, but most will feel unsure about how to write a good one. So they put it off and put it off, until it never gets done!

You need to help your customers out. Contact them personally to find out their thoughts, ask them if they would mind if you put that down on paper and then send the testimonial to them for approval. This makes it much easier for them as all the hard work has been done for them. It also means you can use my two-step formula when describing their thoughts.

A good testimonial always features the person's full name and suburb, as well as job title if it's related to the product or industry. Once you've written a draft of the testimonial, ask the customers to approve it or make any changes they see fit. Make sure they are 100 per cent happy with it. Finally, ask them to sign a copy of it and keep this in your records.

Keep and use any testimonial you get. They are an important part of helping your visitors to realise that your product is everything you say it is. Figure 6.10 shows two of the many testimonials customers have given me and that I use on <www.scrapbookingprofits.com>.

Figure 6.10: testimonials on my *Scrapbooking Profits* website

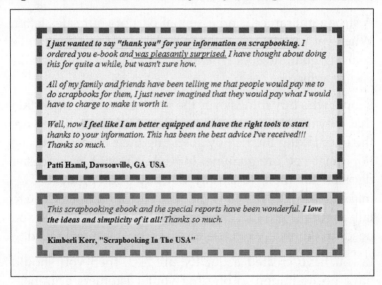

> *I just wanted to say "thank you" for your information on scrapbooking. I ordered you e-book and was pleasantly surprised. I have thought about doing this for quite a while, but wasn't sure how.*
>
> *All of my family and friends have been telling me that people would pay me to do scrapbooks for them, I just never imagined that they would pay what I would have to charge to make it worth it.*
>
> *Well, now I feel like I am better equipped and have the right tools to start thanks to your information. This has been the best advice I've received!!! Thanks so much.*
>
> **Patti Hamil, Dawsonville, GA USA**

> *This scrapbooking ebook and the special reports have been wonderful. I love the ideas and simplicity of it all! Thanks so much.*
>
> **Kimberli Kerr, "Scrapbooking In The USA"**

Light bulb moment

If this is your first product, how do you get testimonials unless someone buys your product? That's easy—let people have the product for free on the condition that they give you feedback about it.

....

: **Light bulb moment** *(cont'd)*

: If 20 people take you up on the offer, only about eight may actually
: follow through and give you a testimonial, which is a good start.
: Remember, it doesn't cost you anything to give these 20 people
: your downloadable product, but it does mean that within a
: week you'll have the testimonials you need to start charging for
: the product.

....

Include a strong guarantee

A strong guarantee is an essential part of your sales letter.
Whatever you do, you must include one. If you don't have
a strong guarantee, don't expect sales to reach the heights
you imagine.

People who buy things over the internet want to be certain
that they're getting value for money. At this point they are
the ones taking the risk by spending their money with the
hope that you are genuine. Indeed, it would be an easier
decision for them to simply not buy your product. This
makes sense really, as they can't see you or meet with you to
talk about the product. So you need to settle their fears. You
need to completely remove the risks, no questions asked.

If you have created a quality product, then you should
have no hesitation in offering your customers a money-
back guarantee. Remember, they are not customers until
they buy your product, and they won't buy it until they
feel secure. This will require a rock-solid guarantee that
states if the product isn't everything you've promised, they
can have their money back.

Your guarantee should be at least 30 days long. Sixty days is
better, and 90 days is fantastic. Ideally, a lifetime guarantee

makes your customers feel the most secure, and the more secure they feel the more likely they will keep it.

Figure 6.11 shows the guarantee I use for *Scrapbooking Profits* — feel free to model yours on this one if it suits your product. You'll notice that I reduce the risk even further by letting my customers know that they can keep the product, as a gift from me, even if they want a refund.

Figure 6.11: the guarantee I use for *Scrapbooking Profits*

> ### 100% RISK-FREE
> ### MONEY BACK GUARANTEE
>
> Hey, you're my customer. And if you're not happy, it looks bad on me. So if you're not happy with what you discover from *"How To Make Money Scrapbooking"* I don't expect ... or want ... to keep your money. Just simply whip off an email to me and I'll happily refund your money in full *(in fact, I'd be embarrassed to keep it).*
>
> **But... the book is yours to keep no matter what,
> as a "thank you" gift from me!**
>
> *Okay? So you really can't lose! The book's yours no matter what.*

Will people rip you off?

I've found, and all of the top marketers I've met over the past few years agree with me, that only around 2 per cent of people will take you up on the guarantee when they haven't even used the product. These buyers are different from those who do use your product and don't believe it delivered on your promises — that is, legitimate customers who take you up on your guarantee because they're not happy. There's no problem with this, and it's why the guarantee is there. Besides, if you have a quality product, then there will be very few of these customers.

What this really means, though, is that around 98 per cent of people will keep the product because they love it. Your goal is to focus on these people and just accept that there will be others that don't like the product as much. Don't get caught up worrying about the people who don't keep the product; it's part of doing business. Your business will still be profitable.

S is for *sign off*

After all this, your job is done, right?

Not on your life! This is where a lot of website sales letters drop the ball. You must tell your visitors to order now and then explain how to do so. This is easily done by reminding your visitors, in summary form, of all the great things they're going to receive by taking advantage of the offer now.

If you want a lot of sales, you can't leave it to your visitors' discretion to decide when the right time to buy is. If your visitors leave the decision to buy your product until later, chances are it will never happen. This would be a real shame because, having reached this part of your sales letter, your visitors want your product — otherwise they would have left the website by now.

So, at the end of your sales letter, take readers back to where it all began by reminding them of the original problem that made them read the web page in the first place. Remind them of the major benefits they are going to get, including the bonuses, and of the money-back guarantee. Then let them know that to receive all of these benefits they should order now so they can start enjoying them immediately. I also let my visitors know that the bonuses may not be there forever — another reason to buy now. (I often test different bonuses, too, to find out which ones motivate more visitors to buy.)

Finally, tell them step by step what they should do to take advantage of the deal they've been reading about. For example, 'Simply pick up the phone right now and call 00 0000 0000. Our friendly staff will take your details and send the product off to you today'. Or, 'Just click on the order link below to enter your credit card details through our secure network, and in a matter of minutes you can be enjoying *XYZ* e-book'.

Something else I like to do in the sales letter at the very last moment is to add in another bonus gift to really tip my visitors over the edge. So in summary, put a time limit on all the bonuses, remind the visitors of the biggest bonus and then add in a new bonus at the very end. This is shown in figure 6.12.

Figure 6.12: the final part of my *Scrapbooking Profits* sales letter

But ... I don't know how long I'll keep these bonuses up there. It's part of a marketing test I'm doing. They're worth a lot to me in my heart, and at any time I could take them down forever. So if you want them, get in quick.

<u>Click Here To Order Securely Through Click Bank</u>

Wishing you great success .

Warmly,
Brett McFall

P.S. Don't forget , you're getting **$348 worth of bonuses** for just a fraction of that price. Everything to get you started in making money with scrapbooking. So if that's what you want to do, this is the opportunity you've been waiting for. <u>Click Here To Order Securely Through Click Bank</u>

P.S. LAST MINUTE BONUS!! If you're a scrapbooker, then you love to sketch your designs out before you do it for real for your clients, right? So I'll include a *"Sketch Template"* which you can use to plan out your pages. *The page layout is done for you, all YOU have to do is add your genius!*

The postscript is a very important part of your letter. In fact, it's the second most-read item on your web page after the headline, so it's important to remind the reader what your deal is all about. However, one thing *you* should remember is *never mention the price!*

Many people will scroll to the end of your sales letter to see what's there, perhaps to find out who it's from or what the offer is. If you place the product's price here, then your customers may decide that they don't want your product for that price. But how can they possibly gauge whether it's good value or not? They don't know anything about it!

They may have originally been searching the internet for free information, but if you can prove that paying for yours is worthwhile, then they may just consider buying it. You don't want to let your customers make that decision without the right information. It's better to keep the price in the 'irresistible offer' section so that they can evaluate everything in its entirety.

Adding an order link

I recommend getting an order link through ClickBank (<www.clickbank.com>), which I discussed in chapter 3. By visiting this website, you can learn how to use this service to sell your product. ClickBank will accept the credit card payment on your behalf and then send you the money, charging a flat 7 per cent fee on every sale. It even handles refunds for you, too. It's a service that takes the hassle out of processing the orders yourself.

ClickBank will give you a link to put on your web page that takes customers to a site where they can securely enter their credit card details. It's a great system and one that I've used for many years.

Even if haven't ever considered yourself to be a writer and thought there was no way you could write a sales letter, hopefully my BURPIES formula has shown you that you can. I've used this formula for over 10 years now, and thousands of other people around the world have also used it. You don't need to be an expert; you just need to follow the formula.

Summary

✍ The best way to sell your product on a website is to write a sales letter — that is, a letter telling people why they should buy it.

✍ Copywriting is the skill of describing your product so that people want to buy it. It's an essential part of selling your product on the internet.

✍ My BURPIES formula takes you step by step through the process of writing an effective sales letter for your web page. BURPIES stands for:

- ▣ big promise — which is usually delivered through a headline

- ▣ use imagination — that is, paint a picture for your visitor about how their problem can be solved with your product

- ▣ rarity — that is, outline what makes your product different from any other

- ▣ points — that is, list the features and benefits of your product

- ▣ irresistible offer — that is, create an offer and value that is so inviting that visitors feel compelled to buy

- ▣ evidence — that is, prove what you say is true using tools such as testimonials and a strong guarantee

- ▣ sign off — that is, tell the visitor how to order and remind them of the main reasons why they must order right now.

Look at the sales letter I use at <www.scrapbookingprofits. com> to see how all these pieces fit together. By identifying the different parts, you can see how to use them to create your own sales letter.

Chapter 7

Step 4: design a simple website that converts prospects into buyers

This chapter is a relatively short one because I have a simple solution when it comes to designing your own website. To really learn about it, you just need to put the ideas in this chapter into practice.

What design program should you use?

When it comes to designing a website, the biggest hurdle for beginners is actually putting their website up on the internet. It sounds technical, it is technical and, ultimately, it can bog you down in tasks that don't make you any money.

In my experience, beginners who have used popular design software, including Microsoft FrontPage (no longer being produced) and Adobe Dreamweaver, tend to struggle. If they're really, really motivated they are able to create their own website, but not without some confusion and having to spend a lot of time doing so.

These are great programs backed by effective marketing. They do, however, require you to know things about the internet outside the software programs themselves, such as the different types of browsers that people use to view the internet, which can affect how your website appears.

Ultimately, this means that if you're a beginner using this software to design your website, it can take a long time and require a great deal of effort and patience.

This is why a lot of people end up hiring a website designer to create their sites for them. If you're a beginner on a limited budget, there are two issues here. Firstly, website designers are usually very expensive (sometimes charging between AU$5000 and $10 000 for a four- to five-page website). Secondly, most value design higher than sales, which means their main priority is to make your site 'look good'.

You may agree with this approach; after all, we all want our websites to be attractive. However, from an entrepreneur's point of view, your main priority is to generate cash flow. If you decide to update the design of your website later on, you can pay for a professional designer out of the profits from your business.

After you've started making good money, you can make your website look however you'd like (make sure you always test to see whether it increases sales or not), but don't invest thousands of dollars in design before you've made any money. You simply don't need to. There's a much easier way to go about this.

Website design with BigPixie

You no longer have to be a 'geek' to design your own website. In fact, I've been showing people for a couple of years how easily it can be done, and it never fails to amaze them. You can design your own website through BigPixie (<www.bigpixie.com>), see figure 7.1.

I searched for three years to find a system that would make website design easy, and now this is all you need.

Figure 7.1: BigPixie's home page

© Mezine.com, Inc.

BigPixie enables you to design a website and have it 'live' on the internet in around five minutes. Even if you're new to the internet and don't have any formal design skills, you can put together a professional-looking website. You don't need to know HTML code (the programming language for websites), you don't need any training and you don't need to wait for weeks for your site to be ready.

There are three steps to setting up a website:

1   Register a domain name (the name of your website).

2   Secure hosting space on a server.

3   Create your pages (and upload them if they're created on your computer and not on the server).

BigPixie can help you with the entire process. You can put together web pages with photos, newsletters, auto-responders (automatic, pre-written messages that are sent to your clients from you) and even a shopping cart (to hold the items your customers want to purchase). You can also register your domain name here (or transfer it from somewhere else if you already have one), as well as set up email addresses.

One of the great things about having your own domain name is that you can have multiple email addresses specifically for that domain name. For a larger organisation, say, Fred's Mowing, you might have <accounts@fredmow. com.au>, <bookings@fredmow.com.au> or <inquiries@ fredmow.com.au>. Different email addresses for different purposes allow you to identify the content of the email prior to opening it so that it can be 'sorted' as it arrives. Multiple email addresses probably won't be much help when you're starting out, but as your business grows, you'll find they come in very handy.

At BigPixie, domain name registration, hosting, website-building and email services are all done online, which means you don't have to buy or download any special software. You can make changes to your website from any computer, anywhere in the world as long as you have an internet connection. (This is very handy when you're travelling around the world enjoying your increased income!)

BigPixie is easy to use. You can sign up for a free 10-day trial and then choose from one of 1400 professionally designed website templates. Before you know it, you'll be looking at your own web page. A sample web page is shown in figure 7.2.

Figure 7.2: a sample web page created using BigPixie

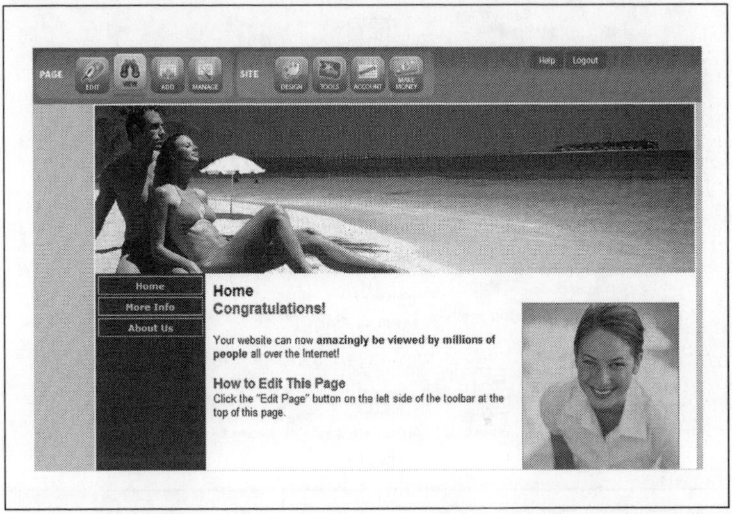

© Mezine.com, Inc.

As you can see in figure 7.2, I've started creating a web page by placing a beach scene as the header graphic (or picture). You build your site using the control panel at the top of the screen.

These tools make it very simple to create or change anything on your website, and they only appear on your screen when you've logged into your account. Visitors to your website won't see them.

I suggest you explore this system for yourself, only then will it really make sense just how simple it is to get started. After the free 10-day trial, it's AU$359.40 (per website) for a year (correct at the time of writing). This includes a domain name, hosting of your site, five email addresses, and use of all the design tools (see figure 7.3) and templates. There's also a 24-hour customer support team to answer your questions.

Figure 7.3: BigPixie's design tools menu

© Mezine.com, Inc.

BigPixie also enables you to:

- ✎ accept credit card payments securely (so your customers can do business with you at no risk)

- ✎ edit the words and photos on your website. You can upload your own photos and other graphics, too. The editor works just like any of the popular word processing programs on today's computers, see figure 7.4.

- add new pages to your site. You can add up to 500 different pages to your website such as a page for a feedback form, newsletter, contents list or photo album.

- change the whole look of your website by selecting a professional design from the library. Once you've selected a design, you can either keep it as is, or mix and match colours until you're happy. Page layout options are shown in figure 7.5 (overleaf).

- add photos to your website. BigPixie gives you access to over 2000 royalty-free, professional photographs, so you don't have to hire models or an expensive photographer. The photo gallery is shown in figure 7.6 (overleaf). You can also upload and use your own photos.

- make your information products downloadable.

Figure 7.4: Bigpixie's text editor

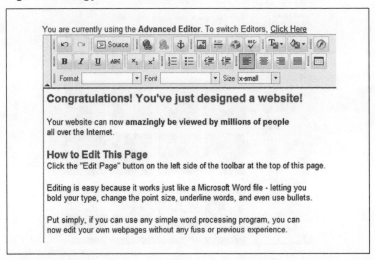

© Mezine.com, Inc.

Figure 7.5: page layout options

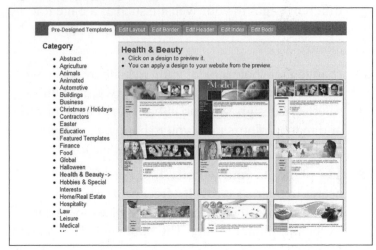

© Mezine.com, Inc.

Figure 7.6: BigPixie's photo gallery

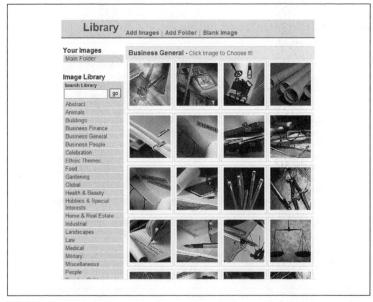

© Mezine.com, Inc.

If you're wondering whether my 'be the general of the army, not a soldier in the trenches' philosophy applies here — that is, whether you should have someone else use this system to design your web page — the answer is yes, assuming you're prepared to pay someone to do it. However, BigPixie is easy to use, so you can still be the general because the software will do most of the work for you.

The most important part of setting up your internet business is to get your product and your marketing working effectively. Your website is your shop. Once it's up and running, you can pretty much forget it, which gives you time to focus on marketing your product.

What sort of website should you design?

Would you like to know the secret to designing a money-making website? It's something that only successful information-product marketers know, and if you get it right, it can make all the websites you design in the future successful, too.

The secret is don't design your own website, or to be more precise, don't over design your website.

In chapter 6, I explained how to write a sales letter. This is essentially your 'salesperson', so it's actually all you need. People are often surprised when they find out that the website design that sells your product the most effectively just includes the words on the page. Black text on a white background is all you need. This is the style that I use, too.

You don't need a header graphic at the top of your website (many people like to have one because it makes them feel better about 'how it looks'). If you're going to use photographs on your website, only do so if they further your story or prove a point in your sales letter. Photos can make your website slower to load on your visitor's screen, so use them sparingly.

Other elements to avoid include flashy graphics, bold colours, backgrounds that sparkle and visual presentations that take a long time to load.

Other pages you may choose to include in your website are a frequently asked questions page, a testimonials page and, of course, an order page (so that your new customers may buy your product). Of course, these can all be put within the one sales letter page, which is what I recommend.

Marketing your website

Another feature of BigPixie is that it tells you how to market your website to your industry. You'll find a step-by-step plan when you click on the 'Make Money' button on the right-hand side of the control panel (see figure 7.2 on page 127).

The information provided here covers a range of topics, including how to get better search engine rankings, how to make money by selling space in your newsletter and how to do pay-per-click advertising.

The internet gives you so many options, usually too many. As I noted earlier, there are many other website design systems that you can use, and there are new ones coming online every day it seems — and you should look at these and make your own decision. But for the quickest and most effective solution, I recommend you try BigPixie. I searched for three years for a system this good, and when I found it, I bought the licence to it. You can make your own decision when you try it for yourself.

Once you have your product, your sales copy and your website, the next step is to go live. In the next chapter, I will explain how to bring traffic to your site.

Summary

- Anyone can build their own website using a user-friendly and affordable service called BigPixie (<www.bigpixie.com>).

- BigPixie will help you design your website, register your domain name (that is, the name of your website), accept money and start selling your product right away.

Chapter 8

Step 5: bring traffic to your website

You've done your research, created a product, written a letter that sells your product and designed a site that makes it easy to buy. The only thing you need now is for people to visit your website.

Visitors to your website are called 'traffic'. Expressions such as 'high traffic' and 'low traffic' refer to the amount of visitors you get. To get traffic, you have two choices — you can buy it, or you can get it for free. If you're like most people, you'd rather get it for free. However, 'free' traffic generally takes more work, so you'll want to weigh up what you've got more of — money or time.

Paying for traffic to your website

If you want results fast with only a small amount of work, then buying traffic is the best option. You can do this through 'pay-per-click' advertisements. These are available through the three major search engines — Google, Yahoo! and Windows Live Search.

You've probably seen this type of paid advertisement. They're generally on the right-hand side of the search engine results pages. They look like small, four-line classified ads that you might find in your local newspaper, except that you can click on these advertisements and be taken right to the advertiser's website.

Google is the world's number one search engine, and its advertising system, Google AdWords, is the one I recommend using. It's quite easy to learn and what I like about it most is that you can test up to nine different advertisements at once for no extra cost. Google will automatically rotate each of the nine advertisements and give you the results showing which one got the most 'clicks'. Basically, you're conducting market research to establish which of the advertisements is the most effective.

Figure 8.1 shows a sample of some advertisements I have run for my copywriting software.

In case you are wondering, the ad that received the highest number of clicks was the one with the headline that reads, 'Warning: Don't write a'.

If it's your first time using a pay-per-click service, I recommend checking out the step-by-step tutorial at <www.adwords.google.com>. But in short, here's how pay per click works. You tell Google the keywords you would like to advertise under. This means you can choose when your ad appears by telling Google to only show your advertisement when someone searches for a certain word or series of words.

Figure 8.1: pay-per-click advertisements for my copywriting software

Beats any letter you have
New software writes 80 per cent of your
sales letter—done in 30 minutes
www.burpiesbybrett.com

Sales letter in 30 mins
New copywriting software for e-books
makes it easier than any other.
www.burpiesbybrett.com

Sales letter not pulling?
New copywriting software for e-books
makes it easier than any other.
www.burpiesbybrett.com

Warning: Don't write a
sales letter again until you have
this new software—done in 30 mins
www.burpiesbybrett.com

Increase sales by 300 per cent
New software writes 80 per cent of your
sales letter—done in 30 minutes
www.burpiesbybrett.com

Silent salesman
New software writes 80 per cent of your
sales letter—done in 30 minutes
www.burpiesbybrett.com

Figure 8.1 *(cont'd)*: pay-per-click advertisements for
my copywriting software

Puts sell in your web page
New software writes 80 per cent of your
sales letter—done in 30 minutes
www.burpiesbybrett.com

Anything better?
New software writes 80 per cent of your
sales letter—done in 30 minutes
www.burpiesbybrett.com

Easiest in the world?
New software writes 80 per cent of your
sales letter—done in 30 minutes
www.burpiesbybrett.com

For instance, if you're selling an e-book about how to
improve your tennis swing, then you'll tell Google to
show your advertisement when someone does a search
using terms such as 'tennis swing', 'tennis swing tips'
and 'tennis tips'. In fact, you could have hundreds of
different combinations of related words. This is where all
that research at the start about what people are searching
for online comes in handy; the keywords you researched
become the keywords your advertisements appear under.

Following are some tips for writing effective pay-per-click
advertisements:

- *Always use the full nine-advertisement option.* If you
  use Google AdWords, make sure you take advantage
  of this option. It doesn't cost you more, and you
  only need to change the headline on each ad. It
  means you get to test your copy for as long as you

need, enabling you to identify and eliminate the poor-performing ads.

Think of your advertisement as one big headline. You don't have to sell your product in the advertisement. It just has to make people want to know more; your sales letter will sell your product for you. This advertisement has only one purpose — to get the click.

Keep the advertisement short and sharp. You only have a few words and a few lines to get your message across, so think about the nine main benefits you offer and turn each one into an advertisement.

Make a clear promise in your advertisement. As always, your prospective customers want to know what's in it for them, so sell them on what your product does. Sometimes the best promise to make is an irresistible offer like a free e-book, CD or DVD. This way you can turn prospects into customers after you've delivered good value to them.

Use the keywords you researched in your advertisement. If someone types 'karate secrets' into a search engine, it makes sense that he or she is more likely to click on your ad if you have 'karate secrets' in your first line.

How much does it cost?

You are charged for the number of people who click on your advertisements. For every 'click', you pay the search engine (hence the name, 'pay-per-click'). You do, however, get to choose how much you pay. You can offer to pay Google around 50 cents a click, but you can also offer to pay them more. It all depends on how 'high' you want your ad to appear on their search engine and how much competition you have for that keyword (remember, there may be a lot of other people wanting to advertise to the same market as you).

If there's a lot of competition for the same words, it's going to cost you more if you want a high ranking. While there are other factors that determine the placement of your ad, the people who offer Google the most money will go to the top of the list, which means their ad will appear ahead of the other entries.

Overall, pay-per-click advertising can be an incredibly fast and effective way to bring traffic to your site. Think of it as an investment, not a cost. If you've done your research effectively, created a great product that responds to your market's needs and written a compelling sales message for your website, then paying to send prospects to your website is a good investment.

If it costs you around $5 in advertising to get a $30 sale, this is a very good return on your investment. Even if it costs you $10, $15 or $20, you would still be making a profit — and this doesn't include other sales you'll make when you email your customers about other products that you have to offer. So I definitely recommend that you give this type of advertising a go.

How to get traffic for free

While more work is involved if you don't want to pay for traffic to your website, it isn't too difficult. Of course, if you don't want to do it yourself, you can always hire other people to do it for you at sites like Elance (<www.elance.com>).

People seeking to get traffic for free often want to know about search-engine optimisation (SEO) — until someone starts explaining it to them! In short, SEO is a way of making your website attractive to search engines so that they list your website towards the top of their results lists. If you're at the top of the search results lists, you'll get traffic for free. Unfortunately, SEO is also a very technical field and, as such, it's beyond the scope of this book. (Remember, this book is about making things *easy* for you!) If you use BigPixie to design your website, you will actually be able to 'optimise' it very easily by following the instructions provided in its help pages.

However, there are some simple things you can do — such as writing articles and using publicity — to bring free traffic to your website.

Write articles about your chosen field

To get free traffic to your website, you need to give your knowledge away, and the best ways to do this is by writing articles. It may seem like you're giving away too much information for nothing, but keep in mind that people primarily use the internet to search for information. You need to be the provider of that information.

In my case, when I was a copywriter, my business started overflowing with work when I began teaching people how to write copy themselves. It's amazing, but the more you teach others what you know, the more information they'll want from you and the more they'll pay you to teach them.

Write short 300- to 500-word articles that provide useful tips about your chosen field, and at the end of each article, include your website address. The idea is to give good-quality information so readers will be interested in visiting your website.

The next step is to publish your article on the internet. There are websites, such as Ezine Articles (<www.ezinearticles.com>), ArticleDashboard.com and GoArticles.com, that will do this for you for free. What's more, these websites allow newsletter publishers to use your articles for their own gain, but only if they use the entire article, even the part at the end that mentions your website. There are thousands of online newsletter publishers out there, and they all need good information to fill their newsletters. You can be a source of that information. All you have to do is provide good-quality content.

You could end up with thousands of people reading your article if a publisher promotes it to their customers. For example, if there's a newsletter on the topic you have chosen for your product it could be emailed to 30 000 people every week. Wouldn't it be great if you could get yourself in front of these people? Well, by writing an article, you can.

How to write a great article

If you're wondering how to write an article, the good news is that it's not all that different from writing your sales letter. Your article needs to include benefits for the reader and be based on their interests. Importantly, your article must give solid, practical information that people can use straightaway. If you visit Ezine Articles and type in my name, you'll find articles I've written that will help you and which you can model yours on.

Your article should not be a sales pitch for your product. It needs to be able to stand on its own as a piece of helpful information. This is the secret to writing articles. The goal is to deliver great information. If you do this properly, the reader will want to know more. Also, for your article to be published in the first place, it has to deliver. Publishers only stay in business if they produce quality publications; so they're always on the hunt for the best articles.

Use some of the information that's in your product as an article. This is a great way to advertise your product, because at the end you simply write, 'This article was taken from the new e-book *How to Make Cakes in 30 Seconds*. For more information, just CLICK HERE'.

Another option is to write new articles by taking 'chunks' of information from your product and turning them into a summarised list — for example, '5 simple tips for cooking the perfect cake every time' or '7 quick ways to cook delicious treats for the kids'. You're using information you've already gathered, but finding creative and different ways to promote your product with it.

At the end of your article include an 'about the author' section. Here you can talk a little about yourself and include your website address. For example:

> ABOUT THE AUTHOR: Brett McFall is Australia's most experienced direct response copywriter having written over 10 000 sales messages for 153 different industries. For instant access to free marketing reports, plus products and LIVE training, visit <www. brettmcfall.com>.

All it takes is for a few publishers to include your article in their newsletters and send it to their databases before hundreds, if not thousands, of people start visiting your website. Writing one article a week could provide you with all the traffic you need, and it won't cost you a cent.

Publicise your product

Many of the news stories you read in newspapers are there because someone sent a press release about it to the newspaper's editor. This is how much of our news becomes news. Quite often, journalists sift through the press releases that are faxed and emailed to them to find the stories that most suit their purposes.

Where do the press releases come from? From people just like you and me. If you can make your press release newsworthy, then you have a good chance of getting free publicity.

Publicity is the best kind of marketing because it's not advertising. While the public may be less inclined to trust you and your information when you have something financial to gain from selling your product, it's different when a media outlet does it on your behalf.

Would you like your new business to be featured on the news? In newspapers? In magazines? On trusted news websites? And not pay a single cent for it? Then you need to learn how to write a great press release. The secret to doing this is writing something that editors will consider to be newsworthy.

There are three ways to create a newsworthy press release:

1   *Do something good for others.* This is one of the easiest ways to help editors cover your story. It's true — the more you give, the more you receive, so see what you can do for charities. Don't just do it for the publicity. If you do something in the right spirit and give unconditionally, then the publicity will follow. This is the inside secret to getting publicity quickly for you or your product. My business partner and I once raised over $65 000 in three weeks for Red Nose Day (a charity set up to fund research into sudden infant death syndrome), and before we knew it television

crews from two stations were interviewing us for prime-time news. When we started running internet seminars, however, we couldn't get anyone to cover what we were doing. As soon as we started helping others, the publicity came easily. It's also the right thing to do.

2   *Make announcements that affect a lot of people.* That's what 'news' is. If you can do or create something that directly affects a lot of people, you'll find media outlets will be interested. Announcing a brand-new logo doesn't cut it. Things such as joint ventures with large organisations or unique product releases and ideas will interest many editors, particularly those who produce publications for your niche market.

3   *Have a strong and clear view on a news topic.* Editors love people who stand up for what they believe in. If you have something to say about a topic and you can back it up, then say it in a press release. Editors love opposing sides of a story. That's why it pays to keep a close watch on internet news sites that are related to your niche market, so you can make your opinion known whenever you feel it's warranted.

The bottom line is don't make your business the focus. You really do need to give of yourself first in some way, only then will editors allow you or invite you to talk about your product or business.

Let's take a look at an example of a good press release. Figure 8.2 (overleaf) shows one that I wrote for a seminar I was co-producing in Singapore, the World Internet MEGA Summit. This four-day seminar is a fantastic event, but that wasn't enough to get attention from editors. So I made an announcement before the event about how a previous attendee had made a lot of money using what we teach.

Figure 8.2: my press release for the World Internet MEGA Summit

MEDIA RELEASE — 21 MAY 2007

Busy mother of three makes $96 717 in five months selling 'nothing' (her secret revealed for the first time this weekend in Singapore)

Using just a laptop computer and an internet connection, Tracy Repchuk from Burbank, California came across an amazing money-making idea that looks set to make her around $250 000 this year.

This weekend over 3000 people will hear Tracy's remarkable story with the hope of copying her success. The four-day event in Singapore is the **World Internet MEGA Summit**.

At the summit Tracy will reveal exactly how she went from struggling mum to living the life of her dreams, travelling the world selling 'nothing'.

That 'nothing' is information. Even though she was new to marketing, Tracy simply started a blog in which she diarised her progress learning about how to make money on the internet, and online readers asked if they could pay her to teach them. Now she has clients paying her $5500 a time.

The event will be video-streamed over the internet to potentially tens of thousands of people watching online. It is the world's biggest internet business event and will feature internet business experts from the United States, China, Australia, New Zealand, Singapore and Thailand.

For more information or an interview with Tracy Repchuk or the creators of the event, contact Phoebe in Singapore on +65 00000000 or Brett McFall in Australia on +61 00000000.

Did you notice how the press release makes an intriguing announcement that's likely to appeal to a lot of people — in particular, stay-at-home parents who would like to be able to do the same as the one featured? It tells the story quickly and then provides contact details for more information. This press release led to coverage in a popular Singapore magazine.

Where do you send your press release?

A couple of good places to send your press release are PRWeb (<www.prweb.com>) and Medianet (<www.aapmedianet.com.au>).

PRWeb is an online press release service that will submit your release to hundreds of media outlets. It's free to join and sending releases is also free. There are also other options you can pay for if you require a more precise form of distribution. For example, it costs US$80 (approximately AU$91) to reach a specific branch of the media such as radio stations.

PRWeb also includes instructions about writing a good press release, and if you need more help, you can have the site write your releases for you.

✎ ✎ ✎

You now know about the most effective free and paid ways to bring traffic to your website. Using just one of these options could make a huge difference to your sales. Put all of them into practice, however, and you could be well on your way to having a profitable business.

Summary

✎ There are two ways to bring traffic to your
     website — you can pay for it or you can get it for free.

The method you choose will depend mostly on what you have more of — money or time.

🖎 If you want immediate results, then pay-per-click advertising through the three major search engines — Google, Yahoo! and Windows Live Search — is the best option.

🖎 To use pay-per-click advertisements effectively:

- ▣ always use the full nine-advertisement option if using Google AdWords

- ▣ think of your advertisement as one big headline

- ▣ keep the advertisement short and sharp

- ▣ make a clear promise in your advertisement

- ▣ use the keywords you researched in your advertisement.

🖎 To bring free traffic to your site, you need to learn about search-engine optimisation (SEO). However, SEO is quite technical, so you may want to focus initially on two other, easier methods of free traffic — writing articles and getting free publicity.

Chapter 9

Step 6: use email to turn more people into customers

I used to think that the internet-business model ended with what I discussed in chapter 8. Even though I'd been in marketing for a long time, I thought that if I just did my research, created a product, wrote a sales message, designed my site and sent traffic to it, I could then move on to my next project.

That was a big mistake. I knew that the right way to sell a product was by creating relationships and building trust with potential customers, but back in 2002 I didn't know how to do it online. I was used to having people join my mailing list, and then I would physically send them mail. As far as I knew, to do the same online meant sending each person an individual email, and that wasn't something I wanted to do.

However, I discovered that email programs could send an email to everyone in your contacts list, and initially this seemed like a good idea. Then I thought, 'What if I eventually have thousands of people in my database? What if I have many different types of prospects and customers?' For example, I could have:

✍ customers that hadn't bought the product yet and customers that had

✍ customers that wanted cheaper products and those that only wanted the more expensive ones

✍ customers that wanted me to send them information on one product but not another.

There was no way that a simple email program could handle all this. Fortunately, there was a better way. It's called list-management software, and it's going to become a very important part of your internet business.

Here's the great realisation I had as I started to sell my first product over the internet, a course I'd written called Lazy Way to Advertising Riches — most people didn't buy from my website the first time they saw it!

If 100 people visited my website, about three would buy my product. Indeed, from my experience and that of my peers, around 97 per cent of people will leave your website without making a purchase. This is still okay for you because, even if only three people buy your product, you will still have a profitable business. For instance, my product was selling for AU$119, so three sales a week meant AU$357. I had been earning only around $450 a week at my 38-hour-a-week job, so this was pretty good.

However, what about the majority of people who visit your site because they're interested in the information you have, but who don't buy your product? It may be that a few of those people just need more information from you to make their purchase decision. Perhaps it was simply the wrong time, or they were interrupted. This is where follow-up emails come in.

Email is almost free to send. The only cost you have is the service that enables you to email large numbers of people — that is, the list-management software. This costs around US$29.95 (approximately AU$34) a month, sometimes even less. Services like WorldInternetOffice. com are very affordable, and even BigPixie can help you with you this.

By using email as a marketing tool, you can contact your visitors (who are not yet buyers) and give them more reasons to consider becoming your customers. You can give them more information, supporting facts and proof that what you claim the product will do is true — basically, educate them about your product's true value. Of course, they can always unsubscribe. But those that don't are interested in your information or offer.

If you want to dramatically increase your sales, using follow-up email is a must. It enables you to find the right buying time for your customers. It may be two days, two weeks or even two months from now. Either way, you can be there to help them when they're ready. For me, it meant going from three sales for every 100 people who visited my site to as many as 18 sales in every 100 visitors. This is an amazing increase for not much extra effort.

Collect the email addresses of prospective customers

Before you can send those follow-up emails, you need to collect your visitors' email addresses. A great way to do this is to offer something on your website that makes visitors want to give you their details, such as a free report, newsletter or audio containing information they would want to know. This will help you to build credibility and help your prospective customers to trust your advice. Plus, you can provide the extra information at almost no cost (once they've signed up, at the click of a button you can contact them any time).

For instance, if you're selling an information product called 'How to Train Your Pekingese Dog', then offer a free report, such as 'Simple tips for walking your Pekingese' or 'The three things you must know before you toilet train your Pekingese', that would be of interest to people in this niche market. Another option is to offer one of your interviews with an expert Pekingese trainer for free. This would be a great way to show your prospective customers how valuable your interviews are.

Alternatively, you could offer a newsletter that contains weekly tips on the care and training of Pekingese. You could easily find these tips by going to Ezine Articles (<www.ezinearticles.com>). All you would need to do is type in 'Pekingese dog training tips' and then choose from one of the many different articles that reference Pekingese dogs. As long as you include the 'about the author' section at the end of the article, you could use any of these articles to send to your subscribers every week free of charge.

You could even take small sections from your information product and give them away — whatever it takes to get prospective customers to leave their details.

As you can see, there are plenty of options when it comes to enticing prospective customers. Even if they don't buy your product, it hasn't cost you anything to give away some great information that helps your readers. The main thing to remember is that the way to make more sales is to give away good information. That's what your market is looking for, so you must make sure that *you're* the one giving it to them, or at least in a better way than your competitors.

I covered the BURPIES sales letter formula in chapter 6. All you need now is more prospective customers seeing your sales letter in order for your sales to increase. Using email can get more people to take you seriously and visit your sales letter web page. Although initially they may have had a quick look and not really paid much attention, by having visitors register to receive good information, you can build trust with them. That way when they do read your sales material, they'll be much more likely to buy. This is so simple, yet so effective at increasing your sales.

Write a compelling subscription offer

Getting the highest possible number of people 'opting in' to your database (known as opt-ins) all comes down to the words you use. Take a look at figure 9.1 (overleaf) to see how I encourage people to join my *McFall Report* — a free newsletter I produce that gives people tips for increasing the response to their marketing. You can see that I haven't just asked visitors to leave their name and email address; instead, I've made what they will get quite clear so that they'll have greater motivation to subscribe.

To create a form like this on my website, all I do is write the copy that invites my visitors to sign up. I then use WorldInternetOffice.com to create the 'form'. The program gives me some code that I paste into the web page and this creates the 'Name' and 'Email' sections, and the 'Subscribe

Me NOW' button. Upon subscribing, customers begin to receive emails from me and some great information about advertising, copywriting and internet marketing.

Figure 9.1: the message I use to invite visitors to join my newsletter

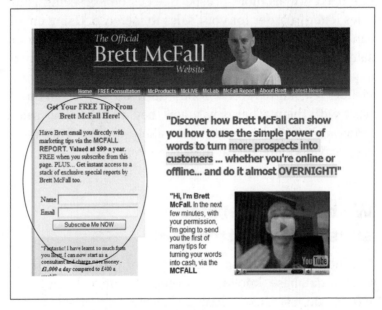

Let's take a look at another example. Figure 9.2 shows the form I used for the marketing seminar I co-created, the World Internet Summit (<www.worldinternetsummit. com>). This type of message is called a pop-in. It's not part of the web page itself; it floats onto the screen as a separate message while your prospective customer is viewing the page. A pop-in is usually in a box smaller than the main web page, and it can be closed easily by clicking on the 'Close' link. After submitting their details, subscribers are taken to another web page where they can access their free gift.

Figure 9.2: an opt-in message

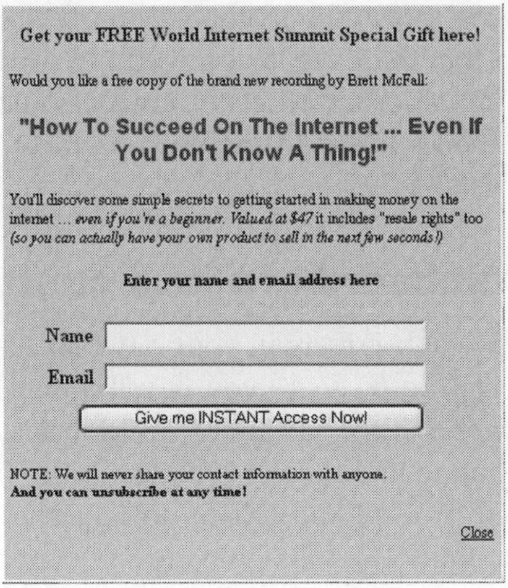

Get your FREE World Internet Summit Special Gift here!

Would you like a free copy of the brand new recording by Brett McFall:

"How To Succeed On The Internet ... Even If You Don't Know A Thing!"

You'll discover some simple secrets to getting started in making money on the internet ... *even if you're a beginner. Valued at $47* it includes "resale rights" too *(so you can actually have your own product to sell in the next few seconds!)*

Enter your name and email address here

Name

Email

Give me INSTANT Access Now!

NOTE: We will never share your contact information with anyone.
And you can unsubscribe at any time!

Close

This opt-in message offers a free recording by me, as well as the resale rights to the recording, so you can sell it or give it away to others (which means it's very good value). I do whatever I can to make it attractive for visitors to leave their details.

If you use WorldInternetOffice.com to create your opt-in form, as people sign up, their details are stored on a remote server. This means that they are stored within WorldInternetOffice.com's online system, so they are separate from your computer. You can download your customers' details at any time, and you won't lose these valuable contacts if your computer breaks down or is stolen.

Another advantage of using WorldInternetOffice.com is that if a subscriber wants to unsubscribe, it takes care of this too, without involving you. It's simple, reliable and easy.

What's most important is that your copy offers something of value. It's also a good idea to reassure your readers that their details are safe and will not be abused or sold. (Aside from the fact that there are laws governing privacy, no-one likes spam. It's important to let your readers know that you will not sell their address to any third parties.)

Turning subscribers into customers

Once you have subscribers in your database, how do you encourage them to buy? As you now know, you need to give away good information to build trust with your subscribers but, to make a sale, you need to go further. You actually must prompt subscribers to take the action you want them to take. The following are some guidelines you should adhere to:

❧ *Personalise the email by using your subscriber's name.* If you have your subscriber's name, you may as well use it. I've had almost a 200 per cent increase in response when personalising emails. Fortunately, software makes this easy to do. At the beginning of figure 9.3 (on page 158), you'll see 'Hi <$firstname$>' — this means that when the email is sent out by WorldInternetOffice.com the subscriber's name will be inserted automatically. And you can use the subscriber's name throughout the message. I also prefer to use 'Hi <$firstname$>' (that is, 'Hi Hahn' or 'Hi Julie') rather than 'Dear <$firstname$>' simply because it's more conversational and what I'd use if I was chatting to the subscriber in person. It's still respectful but less formal than 'Dear Mr Smith'.

❧ *Remind your subscribers why they joined your list.* It's possible that your subscribers also subscribe to other newsletters or reports. While it's obvious to you why they joined your list, some subscribers may actually have forgotten. So, in your emails, make sure you remind them about who you are and the benefits of your product.

Provide proof of satisfied customers. We all love to know that we're making the right decision, so seeing that others have purchased your product and are happy with it will make your subscribers feel more comfortable. I talked about using testimonials in you website sales letter in chapter 6. These are not just for your website; you can use them in your emails, too. It's okay that people may have seen them before; chances are they won't remember them.

Tell your subscribers to take action. If your product really delivers and your prospective customers really have an interest in the topic, then they're going to be very happy once they own your product. They should certainly be happier than they would be without it — after all, they were searching for this information in the first place, so it must mean something to them. You owe it to your subscribers to help them get what they want, so make sure you tell them that if they want a certain result, then all they have to do is take a certain action, which is to invest in your product.

Include three links to your website in the email. Your subscribers may decide at any moment that they want to visit your web page to order your product, so make sure that the emails you send contain three links to your website — one at the top, in the middle and at the end. This way they won't have to search for the link and potentially lose interest.

Figure 9.3 is an example of one of my follow-up emails that sticks to these guidelines. In fact, this product is purchased by up to seven people in every 100, and a large part of that is due to my follow-up emails.

Figure 9.3: one of my follow-up emails

http://www.burpiesbybrett.com/index2.html

Hi <$firstname$>,

Thank you for your interest in my new software program, BURPIES Copywriting Software.

Did you grab yourself a copy yet?

You do want sales letters to be made easy for you, don't you? You do want to save time?

And you do want the extra sales that a dynamic sales message can give you, right?

Well what are you waiting for?

After 17 years writing advertising both online and offline, I knew there was a way for novices to write their own copy. I looked at all the software programs on the market, and thought...

'Uh-uh, there has to be an easier way—people want to do as little thinking as possible.'

So I created my own software. And the good news? It's very easy to use.

Here's what one customer recently said:

'G'day Brett, Thanks a million for the great software—it really does work; you are very clever! After watching your bonus online video, I used it last night and, without any editing (just completely raw—straight to the page), I did it. Amazing really!'

Cheers from Peter L Miller

If you haven't done so already, grab it here:

http://www.burpiesbybrett.com/index2.html

And if you have any questions, just reply to this email and I'll be happy to answer them for you.

Warmly,

Brett McFall

http://www.burpiesbybrett.com/index2.html

Remember, when you write your follow-up emails, it's all about selling your product. This means that the same rules you followed when writing your sales letter also apply to the email. Your subject line in the email is your headline; you need to talk about the benefits; you need to show proof that what you say is true; and you need to get your readers to take action. After all, it's still a letter, but it's just in a different format.

Another tip when writing your emails is never use capital letters for the entire email. In the online world, this is interpreted as 'shouting'. While it's fine to use capital letters to highlight a word or two, keep them to a minimum.

How long should your follow-up emails be?

The length of your emails really depends on you. Overall, I've achieved the best results by writing to my subscribers in a sincere and succinct way. I aim to make the people receiving my email stop and take notice. This is done simply by respecting the readers — that is, not taking up too much of their time with an email that takes too long to the get to the point, or by sending an email that's too short and needs readers to click on the link to read the message. So it's a delicate balance.

Once you create your product, you'll begin to find your 'voice' and feel out what your readers need and want. Don't be too hard and fast with your rules on the length of emails you send; just be sincere and ensure every sentence has a purpose.

Tell subscribers about your other products

Ultimately, your aim is to turn prospects into customers and remember, those that do buy from you may still want other products along the same lines. Most customers who found your product useful will be open to getting more of the same, but if you don't tell them that you have other products, they may never know. In my experience, one-third of your customers will buy from you again if you just send them an offer. So if you don't ask via an email, you could be losing yourself a lot of profit. As always, the great thing about this email is that you can set it up so that it happens automatically.

Summary

- Most people — about 97 per cent — won't buy from your site the first time they visit.

- You should create an offer on your website that makes visitors want to give you their name and email address. This way, you can contact them again with follow-up emails at almost no cost, and increase your sales by having emails automatically sent to them informing them of your product.

✍ Your opt-in message needs to describe the benefits of the free offer so your visitors see the value of giving you their contact details.

✍ There are five guidelines to follow to ensure effective follow-up emails:

- Personalise the email by using your subscriber's name.

- Remind your subscribers why they joined your list.

- Provide proof of satisfied customers.

- Tell your subscribers to take action.

- Include three links to your website in the email.

✍ The follow-up email is still a letter and should therefore be as long or as short as it needs to be to motivate your subscribers into taking the action you're suggesting.

Chapter 10

Step 7: recruit an army of people to sell your product for you

In chapter 1, I suggested that your ultimate goal was to 'be the general of the army, not a soldier in the trenches'. Well, here is where it all comes to fruition.

By following what I'm going to explain in this chapter, you could have an army of people marketing your website for you. They'll promote your product, but you only pay them after they've made a sale. Even better, you can arrange it so that you don't have to be the one writing the cheques.

I'm talking about setting up an affiliate program. An affiliate is someone who will promote your website on the internet and take a commission. This means:

✍ no effort from you (the affiliate does all the marketing)

- ✍ no extra risk (you stay in control of your product and business)

- ✍ no up-front costs (you only pay them out of the sales they produce).

Figure 10.1 shows the business model I've been teaching up to this point, where you are solely responsible for the marketing of your internet business. Compare this with the affiliate business model shown in figure 10.2. This is the business model you want to evolve to, where other people — affiliates — are helping to market your internet business.

Figure 10.1: traditional business model

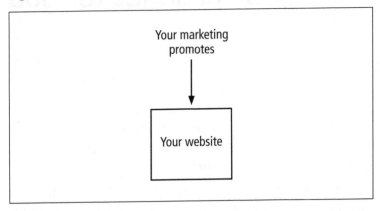

Today, I don't advertise my own products (so my advertising costs are zero) — my affiliates do that for me. It's great because it means I can move on to do other things while my affiliates promote my products. You can do the same, and as long as you make sure you have completed the previous six steps correctly, you'll do very well (and so will your affiliates).

Figure 10.2: affiliate business model

Wouldn't it be great if you could advertise in the mainstream media, such as on television and radio, and in newspapers, and only pay for it *after* you've made sales? Well, unfortunately this option is not available. However, it is on the internet, and that's what affiliate programs are all about.

Setting up an affiliate program

Setting up an affiliate program is relatively easy because software can look after almost every part of it for you. One great service for helping with affiliate programs is ClickBank (<www.clickbank.com>), which I first mentioned in chapter 3. The difference this time is that you're going to use ClickBank to help sell your own product rather than to find products to sell.

You register on ClickBank as a publisher at a cost of US$49.95 (approximately AU$56), and then simply follow the step-by-step process for listing your product for sale and setting up your account. ClickBank can accept all the payments from your customers on your behalf. Its fee is 7.5 per cent of your sale price, and the remaining 92.5 per cent is split between you and your affiliate at the rate you decide (paying affiliates is covered later in the chapter).

Instead of just you using the business system you've created to make your own sales, other people are going to use the system, too. Affiliates will send people to your website via links on their own websites or in their emails or e-newsletters. Every prospective customer who clicks through from an affiliate's link and buys your product will be making money for both you and your affiliate.

There is a common misconception that each affiliate requires a separate and exclusive website created for him or her to sell your product. For example, if you had 100 different affiliates, you'd have to create 100 different web pages so that the earnings of each could be accurately calculated. However, you don't actually need to do this.

ClickBank provides each of your affiliates with an exclusive affiliate link that they will include in their emails and on their websites. Each link leads to your website, but through some smart coding within that affiliate link, every prospect is 'tagged' as coming from a certain affiliate (this tagging is commonly referred to as 'cookies'). This way, when a sale is made, the right affiliate is attributed with the sale.

In addition, ClickBank's system tells you everything you need to know about the type of sale made, processes all the money for you, operates 24 hours a day and, here's the best part, not only does it tally the sales from each affiliate, it also writes the cheques to you and your affiliates. Moreover, you can check the calculations online at any time.

ClickBank isn't the only service you can use to manage your affiliates. WorldInternetOffice.com can also do this for you. It's more of a hands-on system, however. For instance, you will have to write the cheques every month to your affiliates, but WorldInternetOffice.com will provide you with a report so that you know how much to pay them. While it's more work for you, it does mean you'll have the cash immediately. Just enable it to accept cash using a service called PayPal (<www.paypal.com>) — full instructions are provided on the website. Overall WorldInternetOffice.com is a cheaper option; it just requires more effort from you.

I use WorldInternetOffice.com to manage my products that aren't electronic (ClickBank only looks after electronic products). WorldInternetOffice.com sends automatic emails to your affiliates letting them know they've made a sale, and it allows you to set other tiers of payment (for example, a two-tier system where the affiliates get paid for sales, and can also be paid if their customers become affiliates and start making sales too).

WorldInternetOffice.com does all the calculations for you and most of the paperwork, processes credit card payments, and allows affiliates to update their own information, check their own sales and more.

How much should you pay your affiliates?

I recommend paying your affiliates at least 50 per cent of the product's selling price as commission. (Seventy-five per cent is the maximum you can offer through ClickBank.) The reason for paying this much is so that as many people as possible will be motivated to promote your products. Remember, you only pay them when they make sales, so every sale is a bonus for them.

Do whatever you can to make it a winning deal for your affiliates. The more you can encourage other people to sell your product, the less work you will have to do. For instance, if you're selling 10 e-books a week at $27, your weekly sales are $270. But if you have 50 affiliates promoting your product for you and they each sell three copies of your e-book per week, your total weekly sales will be 160 sales (50 affiliates × 3 sales = 150 sales + 10 of your own sales = 160 sales a week) or $4320.

The service you use to manage your affiliates, such as ClickBank, will tell you that your affiliates have earned $2025 in commission (150 affiliate sales × $27 = $4050 × 50 per cent commission = $2025). This still leaves you with an income of $2295 for the week.

This isn't a bad return for very little work. What if you had 100, 200 or 500 affiliates selling for you? Once you have a product that sells and a system that others can also use to help sell your product, your business has the potential to grow at an amazing rate.

Recruiting affiliates

ClickBank will show you how to put your product up for sale in its 'marketplace', so that potential affiliates will be able to find your product and start signing up to sell it for you. However, I'm going to let you in on a secret about helping affiliates make more sales with just a little more effort on your part.

If you create marketing material for your affiliates and make it available on one of your websites, then it will be a much more appealing product for them to sell because they won't have to take time to put together this material themselves. This could mean the difference between 10 affiliates signing up and 100 signing up. Your goal is to make it as easy as possible for affiliates to make sales. At this stage no-one knows your product better than you, so you really are the best person for it. Besides, it doesn't cost much to pay someone else to do it under your guidance, does it, 'General'?

Simple marketing materials you can give affiliates include:

- email promotions
- banner advertisements
- product images
- articles.

I'll now explain each of these in detail.

Email promotions

Email promotions can be as long or short as you like, but it's a good idea to provide them in different lengths. This way your affiliates can choose which one suits their needs. The email should simply recommend the product. You can use just a headline, select some copy from your sales letter, use a testimonial, or include a fact or statistic that may interest your affiliates' readers. At the end of this copy your affiliates just includes their affiliate link, which takes their readers to your site.

Figure 10.3 (overleaf) shows some examples of email promotions that I make available to affiliates of my *Scrapbooking Profits* website. This sales copy can easily be copied and pasted into affiliates' newsletters, or even adapted to be used as pay-per-click advertisements.

Figure 10.3: email promotions for *Scrapbooking Profits*

Earn $50 to $100 An Hour
Scrapbooking is one of the fastest growing hobbies sweeping the world, and you can earn good money doing it for others. New book shows you how.
[INSERT YOUR AFFILIATE LINK HERE]

How To Make Up To $100 An Hour In Your Own Scrapbooking Business
[INSERT YOUR AFFILIATE LINK HERE]

New e-Book Reveals ...
How to work from home
doing scrapbooking for others.
[INSERT YOUR AFFILIATE LINK HERE]

Who Else Wants To Make Money Scrapbooking?
World's fastest growing hobby can now provide you a work-from-home income.
[INSERT YOUR AFFILIATE LINK HERE]

Figure 10.4 shows some email copy I give to affiliates of my copywriting software at <www.burpiesbybrett.com>.

Figure 10.4: email promotion for my copywriting software

CHALLENGE: Write down what you're currently earning from one of your websites right now.

YEARLY INCOME = _____

Okay, now, get a calculator and do the following:

Multiply that figure by 3.

Did you do it?

Good. Now let's say your yearly income from your website is $10 000 — just to be conservative, okay?

So if you multiply that by 3, you get $30 000, right?

Well how would you like to be able to ACTUALLY do that to your sales figures? Sound too good to be true?

That's what master copywriter Brett McFall does on a regular basis using his 'magic formula' for writing sales letters. Just one of the parts of his formula has increased sales by 300 per cent for both him and his clients time after time.

After 18 years of testing and measuring his craft, his formula now works like magic.

Would you like that power working for your web page? Now you can — with Brett's new software that automatically INSTALLS the 'magic formula' into your sales letter.

Just as if Brett had written your sales letter for you.

Check it out now at: [INSERT YOUR AFFILIATE LINK HERE]

By taking the time to do a little extra work for my affiliates, you can see how much easier it is for them to promote my product. I've found that the more work you do for your affiliates, the better your sales will be. Basically, they just want to promote your product. They don't want to have to come up with an advertisement for a product they don't necessarily know anything about.

Banner advertisements

Some affiliates will have websites that get a lot of traffic, so they may prefer to place an advertisement for your product on their home page. They simply 'attach' their affiliate link to the advertisement so that when someone clicks on it they are taken to your website.

Figure 10.5 is an example of a rotating banner advertisement I give to affiliates of the training seminar I co-created, the World Internet Summit. It's one advertisement, but the words scroll continuously so that the ad looks 'alive'.

Figure 10.5: a rotating banner advertisement

You can have advertisements like this designed at Rent A Coder (<www.rentacoder.com>) for less than US$20 (approximately AU$23). Just work out what you want the banner advertisement to say, and then let an expert create it for you. This is a great marketing tool to give to your affiliates.

Product images

As you now know, when you're selling a downloadable product, you're just selling an electronic file, which is rather boring. Of course, what's inside the electronic file can be quite exciting. So to help customers get the full picture, you can create a product image that represents your product the way a cover does for a book. This way, customers have an image in their mind of what the product is; it makes your electronic product more real and tangible. For your affiliates, it means they can use the image on their website to promote you.

Figure 10.6 shows some examples of product images that I've had designed for my affiliates. For around US$50 (approximately AU$57), you could have them designed for you, too, at Elance. There's also plenty of software that allows you to do this yourself. Simply search for 'e-book cover software' on Google, and you'll find a lot to choose from. Some software is even available for free.

Figure 10.6: product images I give to affiliates to help promote my products

Articles

If you think articles are a good way of promoting yourself for free (as discussed in chapter 8), then it makes sense that your affiliates would think so, too. However, unless they're serious promoters, they're probably not going to get articles written up just to promote your product (though if they did, they would definitely make more sales).

What you can do, then, is have articles written for them. By going through Elance, you could have a series of 10 articles created for around US$200 (approximately AU$230). Then your affiliates can simply insert them into their newsletters or websites.

A content-rich article is a powerful advertisement for any product. Just make sure you finish the article in such a way that all your affiliates need to do is insert their affiliate link at the end — for example, 'For more great tips like these, check out the new e-book *Growing Giant Pumpkins* at: [INSERT YOUR AFFILIATE LINK HERE]'.

Light bulb moment

A business opportunity you may not have considered is producing articles for people who have websites but who don't have the time or the desire to create marketing for their affiliates.

It may cost $200 to have 10 articles written, but there's nothing stopping you from on-selling them to various entrepreneurs in similar markets to give to their affiliates. After all, the articles just provide good information about a particular subject. If they're pretty general, they could be used to help sell various products in the same niche.

The people you sell them to could also insert their own additions to tailor the article to their product. If you were to sell just five sets of 10 articles for $200, that's $1000 in sales. Less the $200 they originally cost you, you've made a profit of $800.

How to have a constant supply of affiliates

This is the last step for recruiting an army of affiliates, and it's possibly the most important if you really want the lifestyle that an internet business can provide.

Put a link to join your affiliate program at the bottom of your website. This way, the more people you get to your site, the more people you'll have signing up as affiliates. Your visitors can choose to join as an affiliate even if they don't buy your product. (ClickBank has instructions for every part of this procedure.) An example of this from my *Scrapbooking Profits* website is shown in figure 10.7.

Figure 10.7: a link on my *Scrapbooking Profits* website to find out about becoming an affiliate

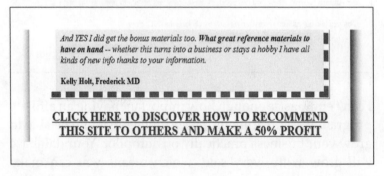

Figure 10.8 (overleaf) shows the page that visitors see after they click for more information about my affiliate program. I have a simple message that outlines my affiliate program and enables them to sign up.

Figure 10.8: information about becoming an affiliate

Scrapbookingprofits.com Affiliate Program

Scrapbookingprofits.com sells the Internet's top converting ebook on making money from Scrapbooking ..."How To Make Money With Scrapbooking".

Average conversion rates are **2.2%** *(these can, and will, vary)* and we pay a **50% commission on all sales through ClickBank**.

You can view our web site sales page by clicking here.

Here's How Our Affiliate Program Works

Our affiliate program is managed by ClickBank.

It pays a 50% commission for every sale your refer. The ebook currently sells for $27.77.

So for every visitor you bring to our site that buys the book, **you earn $13.88.**

ClickBank independently tracks all sales and issues commission checks.

Joining our affiliate program takes only a minute or two. After you join, you will be directed to our Affiliate Toolbox where you can access professionally written ads to promote the material.

You can join our affiliate program right now by clicking the link below:

Click Here To Join Our Affiliate Program

I can't emphasise enough how important having an affiliate program is. With affiliates promoting you, you'll be able to grow your business practically on autopilot. Your database will grow with every sale, which means you can make more sales later on from other products that you'll offer. And this is where it gets really exciting.

One day you'll be able to sit back and let your business tick over without your involvement. Of course, you may choose to stay involved and make it bigger and better — but wouldn't it be nice to have a choice?

You've reached the end of my seven steps to a profitable internet business. Now it's time for you to start taking some action, but before you do, I'm going to share some final secrets with you and provide additional proof that this process really works.

Summary

✍ If you want to be 'the general of the army, not a soldier in the trenches', then you need an affiliate program. The affiliates will sell your product for you and you only pay them after they've made a sale. It's a risk-free way to increase your sales.

✍ The affiliate-management service I recommend is ClickBank (<www.clickbank.com>). It takes care of almost everything for you, including paying your affiliates what they're owed.

✍ Pay your affiliates at least 50 per cent of the profits of each sale, perhaps even up to 75 per cent, so they are motivated to be your salespeople.

✍ To recruit a lot of affiliates create marketing materials for them so they can easily promote your product.

✍ You should create marketing tools for your affiliates, including:

- ▣ email promotions
- ▣ banner advertisements
- ▣ product images
- ▣ articles.

Part III

Real proof

When you learn about something new, it helps to know that other people have been in your shoes and triumphed. Therefore, the final part of this book includes two case studies that will hopefully inspire you to set up an online business, and unlike you, they didn't have a road map to follow.

It will also cover some of my most powerful strategies for reaching your goal. These are the beliefs and habits that helped me leave my job, offer incredible value to my customers and create the lifestyle of my dreams. I know they can do the same for you.

Chapter 11

The end of a book, the start of a new world

Congratulations! You've reached the end. This tells me that you are serious about using the internet as a business medium to change your life.

The seven steps to creating a profitable online business are incredibly powerful. They've made a lot of people a lot of money, including me. In fact, I estimate that I've used them to generate well over AU$5 million. Now that you've got the essential information, all you need is to get going. Here are some final tips:

✎ *Keep your ultimate goal in view at all times.* Having a dream is important. We all need things to focus on in our future; they're what pull us through when things get tough. So get excited about what you *really* want.

Imagine it. Think about it every day. And be specific. Write down exactly what you want your business to look like, how it runs, what it sells, how much money it makes and how much time you spend on it.

This is your goal. This is your driving force. This is what you'll hold up in perhaps one year from now and say, 'It's because I saw this, that I am experiencing it today'.

 Take one step at a time. Juggling a lot of things at once is not the best way to start your business. You need to focus. Overloading yourself with a million things to do will only slow your progress.

Pick one project and see it through. Dedicate yourself to mastering one website business. Once you can do this and you completely understand the process, then doing many things at once will become a real possibility.

 Where possible, aim to be 'the general of the army, not a soldier in the trenches'. For your first project, it will be beneficial for you to play a role in every part — but that's only so you can teach someone else to do these tasks for you later on. Utilising other people's talents and leveraging your own time by investing it in teaching others what to do will pay you back again and again.

Your main role should be to oversee everything so that you can keep your focus on the end goal. And if you can't do it on the first project, then promise yourself to do it on the second. You can't enjoy the fantastic lifestyle an internet business can give you if you're stuck in front of a computer screen all day, every day, can you?

⊘ *Spend at least 30 minutes a day on your internet business.* You need to train your brain that having an internet business is a priority. Even if it's time spent rereading this book, it's important that you set aside 30 minutes each day to work on you new internet business. Pretty soon you'll devote the time automatically because you'll love working on it. Running an internet business is something that draws you in the more you do it. And, yes, it does get easier.

⊘ *Keep learning.* What I've revealed in this book are only the basics of setting up an online business. There are many more ways to enhance everything I've covered and many more ways to make money online. Be disciplined in what you do, but also keep your mind open to other techniques. Look for new ways to get an edge and make things simpler. The more you learn, the more you'll find what works for you.

⊘ *Ignore the 'dream stealers'.* There are always going to be people who try to protect you — well-meaning family and friends who may try to discourage you from starting your business or who focus on the negatives. They're just trying to protect you from getting hurt. Well, you don't need protection. You're blazing new trails, and risk is part of the deal. However, you're choosing something that has few risks and is one of the cheapest places to make mistakes.

No matter what anyone else says, keep your focus. Only you have read this book, and now have the knowledge and skills to set up a successful online business. Judgement from anyone else isn't valid if they haven't learned what you've learned. The bottom line is don't let anyone steal your dream.

Case studies: how people just like you have created the lifestyle of their dreams

You've heard a lot from me throughout this book, about what I've tried, what works and how my journey has introduced me to a whole new world. Now it's time to find out how others have achieved their goals with their internet businesses.

Case study 1: Chris Elmore

In 2003, Chris Elmore (then aged 19) started his own information-product business in his parents' spare bedroom. By 2007, Chris's business, Elmore Music (<www.elmore-music.com>), was turning over $330 000 per year.

The turning point

Stuck in a dead-end job and making just $9 per hour, Chris believed that there had to be more to life. 'I was doing the same routine every day', he says. 'I was tired and I had a really nasty boss.' So he made the decision to set up an online business. The only problem was he didn't know what sort of business he wanted to establish — 'It took a long time to figure out the product and the strategy, but the idea was brewing.'

It wasn't until he received an email from a cousin that Chris realised what he could do. His cousin wanted to learn how to play guitar but couldn't afford to pay for lessons. While not an expert guitar player, it was something Chris loved doing. So, he decided to turn his passion into a business by putting together guitar lessons that not only his cousin could use, but anyone else could too, and sell them online.

Getting started

Working out what he was going to sell was the easy part. Putting the first product together involved a series of trial and error. The product began as a book and was mailed out to customers. However, requests for video and audio components led Chris to turn the book into an internet-based product. From there, Chris's business took off. These days, he 'can upgrade the course online, as opposed to printing another thousand copies. And there's no more hassle with sending physical products — the product is now digital'. Once logged in to the members' area, customers have access to 'instructions, songs, videos, sound and popular tracks from famous artists'. If users get stuck, they can email questions to a tutor.

Despite his enthusiasm, Chris had few computer skills, so setting up an online business was a challenge. Today, Chris has a team of four working for him, which allows him to do what he does best — 'creating a vision'. Chris advises that when starting out, 'It's really important that you begin doing things yourself. Eventually, though, you'll get to a certain point where you're just stuck, and you're too busy. So get people to help you out'.

Business development

After getting his website up and running, Chris turned his attention to developing the business. After the steep learning curve that was the first website, the other products were much easier to develop. His business is now comprised of five websites. The four new ones teach 'guitar songs, how to play popular songs, guitar theory and backing tracks, as well as with drum beats and the bass riffs'. According to Chris, this expansion is the result of giving customers a good-quality product. He adds, 'once you've got your customer, and your product is good, you can provide them with further products. And they'll just love it; they're actually looking for further products'.

For people seeking to set up an online business and those whose online business has become stagnant, Chris advises them to focus on increasing conversions rather than increasing traffic — that is, increasing the number of visitors who become customers. The best way to do that is to 'improve your sales copy, your product and your price'. The next step is to produce more high-quality products to sell to your existing customers.

Success mindset

For Chris, achieving success comes down to two things: passion and hunger. You have to really love what you're doing. This is crucial if you're in it for the long haul. In addition, you'll pick things up faster if you actually enjoy what you're doing.

> The first thing you need to do is sit down with a piece of paper and think about what it is that you love doing, or what things people come to you for advice on, or you've always wanted to do — just jot them down. From there you can research your market to find out what's needed. The next step is to develop your product.

Passion alone won't deliver success. You have to really want it. According to Chris:

> It's like the old saying, 'comfort always kills'. So it's a good idea to be around people who are a lot higher up than you are. Get upset; get angry with where you're at. Get frustrated and see bigger things that are out there that you haven't got. That's when you get hungry, and you'll progress from there.

You also need to have a vision, a clear idea of what you want your business to look like five to 10 years down the track. And think big! 'Know your numbers', Chris advises. That is, find out how many visitors your site gets, how many subscribers you have and the rate at which they're signing up. The next step is to work out a plan to grow the business. Network — talk to people who have been in business longer than you about different strategies and techniques to increase your market share.

Case study 2: Tracy Repchuk

Tracy Repchuk is a mother of three who wanted a slice of the internet pie. She wanted to be able to work from home and still look after her family. After attending the World Internet Summit in September 2006, she set up an online business (<www.tracyrepchuk.com>) and spent a few months thinking about what she was going to do. Within five months of getting serious, she had made over $96 000.

Getting started

In January 2007, Tracy set about building wealth using the internet. With no clear idea of her market or the type of product she wanted to sell but keen to get started, Tracy began writing a blog (an online diary). She knew from previous research into using the internet to create wealth that there was an overwhelming amount of information about this topic, so she decided to help others put all the pieces together. Her blog was titled, '31 Days to Internet Wealth'. 'I received such an unbelievable response through that blog that I just knew after the 31 days, I had to make a quantum leap from there', she says.

By including a form on her web page for subscribers, she was able begin accumulating contacts. Subscribers would receive a newsletter containing tips for and hints about successfully using the internet to make money, which Tracy had learned through her extensive research and time at internet seminars.

Amazingly, Tracy didn't have to pay to attract traffic to her website. Over the 31 days, people began contacting her, requesting one-on-one coaching. For Tracy, this was an unexpected bonus — people wanted to pay for something she was already providing for free. Tracy explains: 'The internet is an information medium. What I did was give away internet marketing information, and then people wanted to pay me to personally teach them how to do it'. What customers realised was that paying a few thousand dollars for personal coaching would reap rewards that would eclipse their initial outlay.

Business development

'Once I hit that 31-day mark and my blog was done, I had to decide what I was going to do next. And that's when I said, "I've got the content, I'm going to put this into a book".' The end result was a best-selling book, *31 Days to Millionaire Marketing Miracles* (available on Amazon.com). From there, Tracy's business took off and she was in high demand as both a speaker and coach. Commenting on her rapid success at the time she notes, 'In a one-week period, I made over $31 000 in coaching program earnings'. And things haven't slowed down.

Success mindset

Tracy puts her success down to two things — attending the World Internet Summit and having a mentor. It's also about putting in the hard yards. For budding entrepreneurs looking to follow in her footsteps, Tracy has this advice: 'Get your website up, get subscribers, network, enter into joint ventures and do this every single day'.

One last word

This book is about making money while you sleep. If you've followed the steps I've laid out for you, you should be well on your way to doing this. However, at the risk of taking the fun out of it, there's one more thing I need to mention — make sure you keep appropriate records of all your income and expenses and you pay attention to any taxation or legal requirements. If you're not sure what your tax or legal obligations may be, check with your accountant or tax adviser.

After all, you're in business now!

Appendix
Useful websites

Audacity
<http://audacity.sourceforge.net>

Audio Wiz software
<www.brettmcfallaudio.com>

BigPixie
<www.bigpixie.com>

BURPIES software
<www.burpiesbybrett.com>

Elance
<www.elance.com>

Ezine Articles
<www.ezinearticles.com>

Google AdWords
<www.adwords.google.com>

Google Groups
<www.groups.google.com>

How to Make Money While You Sleep! seminar
<www.moneywhileyousleep.com>

Logoworks
<www.logoworks.com>

Make Your Own Software
<www.makeyourownsoftware.com>

No Cost Conference
<www.nocostconference.com>

PayPal
<www.paypal.com>

PRWeb
<www.prweb.com>

Rent A Coder
<www.rentacoder.com>

Scrapbooking Profits
<www.scrapbookingprofits.com>

Lightbulb Experience seminar
<www.thelightbulbexperience.com>

Wordtracker
<www.wordtracker.com>

WorldInternetOffice.com
<www.worldinternetoffice.com>

Yahoo! Groups
<www.groups.yahoo.com>

YouTube
<www.youtube.com>

Index

Like some extra help?

Now that you've discovered my simple system for starting your own online business, you may be asking yourself, 'What now?'

I've created an opportunity to be trained *live* in these techniques so that you can build some momentum.

I want you to succeed. I want you to follow your plans through. I want you to keep your focus. In short, I want you to be making money while you sleep.

So this is your invitation to attend my *How to Make Money While You Sleep!* seminar.

Having someone else to work with will increase your chances of success, so both you and a friend can attend as my guests.

Normally, these two tickets sell for $497 each. However, by visiting **<www.brettmcfall.com/seminar>** the tickets are yours while seats are available, so be quick.

And if you have any questions about this book, you can send them to me via this website and I'll answer them at the seminar.

I look forward to showing you even more internet secrets and making it all easy to understand.

Till we meet!

Warmly,

Brett McFall

How to Make Money While You Sleep!
seminar voucher × 2 (valued at $994)

Congratulations on purchasing this book.

As a gift to you from Brett McFall this voucher entitles you and a friend to attend Brett's *live How to Make Money While You Sleep!* seminar, as his guest.

This seminar will provide further instruction on the strategies and steps in this book. It will cover how to start and profit from your own internet business, and include extra secrets that couldn't be put in this book due to space limitations.

STEP 1: to register you and a friend, visit **<www.brettmcfall.com/seminar>**.

STEP 2: you will be prompted to open the book to a certain page and find a particular word. This is to verify your right to these in-demand tickets valued at $497 each ($994 total).

After correct verification, you will be taken through the registration process for this event.

STEP 3: enjoy as you discover how to attend this *live* event!

Conditions

This offer is open to all purchasers of this book. Original proof of purchase is required. The offer is limited to the *How To Make Money While You Sleep!* event only, and your registration in the seminar is subject to availability of space and/ or changes to program schedule. This is a limited time offer and the seminar may cease at any time, although bonuses to the equivalent value will always be substituted on the above website. This voucher is valid for one event only and can only be used on one occasion. At the time of printing, the value of this gift is $994. While an administration fee will be taken upon registration, entry to the event is free with the use of this voucher. This voucher gains you entry to the event; it may not gain you access to all bonuses that full-paying attendees receive. Attendees are responsible for all other costs associated with getting to and attending the event; this voucher covers entry to the program only.

This is a promotional offer of the Author and all queries regarding this offer should be made via the Author's website <www.brettmcfall.com>. The Publisher takes no responsibility for the fulfillment of this offer.

DEVELOPING
POLICY RESEARCH

To the memory of my
GRANNY BOOTH
who died, in her 93rd year,
still full of life and
splendour and joy, on
13 January 1987

Developing
Policy Research

Tim Booth
Director, Joint Unit for Social Services Research,
University of Sheffield

Avebury

Aldershot · Brookfield USA · Hong Kong · Singapore · Sydney

Published by
Gower Publishing Company Limited
Gower House
Croft Road
Aldershot
Hants GU11 3HR
England

Gower Publishing Company
Old Post Road
Brookfield
Vermont 05036
USA

British Library Cataloguing in Publication Data

Booth, Tim, 1947–
    Social policy and government.
    1. Social policy —— Research
    I. Title
    361.6′1′072   HN18

Library of Congress Cataloging-in-Publication Data

Booth, Timothy A.
    Social policy research and government/Tim Booth.
      p.   cm.
    Bibliography: p.
    Includes index.
    1. Social policy——Research. 2. Social sciences——Research—
—Government policy. 3. Social policy——Research——United States. 4.
Social sciences——Research——Government policy——United States.
I. Title.
HN29.B64 1988   87–36543
361.6′1′072——dc 19   CIP

ISBN 0 566 05216 4

Printed and bound in Great Britain by
Biddles Limited, Guildford and King's Lynn

Contents

Preface

This book has been brewing for a long time. It started, I can see now, when I joined the fast-growing ranks of social services researchers appointed after the creation of unified social services departments by the 1971 Seebohm reorganization. Struggling to uphold academic standards of research (the only ones I knew) in an environment where they had no roots, I was soon trounced by a combination of bureaucratic politics and my own naïvety. The experience left its mark and set me thinking.

The ill-formed lessons I drew at the time to explain my failure as an in-house researcher have subsequently been refined over the course of a career that has kept constantly bringing me back to the same sort of problems. Over the years, almost without knowing it, many things have helped to shape my ideas but two in particular deserve a mention.

My continuing involvement with the Social Services Research Group (SSRG), reaching back to its inaugural meeting in 1972 when Sir Keith Joseph, of all people, told the assembled gathering of newly established researchers about the important role that awaited them, has given me a window on to the concerns, frustrations and achievements of people doing research for policy in an agency setting.

Equally, my colleagues – past and present – in the Joint Unit for Social Services Research (JUSSR) at Sheffield University have also helped to keep me in touch with the state of the art. JUSSR was set up in 1978 as a forum for collaboration between the university, local authorities and other statutory and voluntary agencies on research concerned with the organization, operation, management and planning of the social services. During the past ten years we have worked together on a large number of projects, big and small, and I have learned a lot from them in the process. Much more, I am sure, than they themselves realize and more, too, I suspect, than I myself might care to acknowledge. Probably unknowingly, they have contributed to the making of this book. Certainly, in the course of our work, we have often come up against the truth of Beatrice Webb's observation that in the rough and tumble of day-by-day public administration we cannot stand and wait for an authoritative social science: we have, here and now, to act or refrain from acting according to any clues that may be available (*My Apprenticeship*, Penguin Books, p. 257).

From the outset I had in mind that this book should serve three purposes. It is intended as a *textbook* on policy research, a *sourcebook* of examples of the use of social research in the making of policy and a series of *essays* on social planning. In line with this framework, the book is designed for dipping into as well as for reading from cover to cover. Each of the chapters has been written as a more or less free-standing piece in its own right but, taken together, they all explore an interrelated set of themes: namely, the failures of social planning, the role of research in policy-making and the relations between government and social science.

The thrust of the argument linking these themes and developed throughout the book was expressed by the Fulton Report on the civil service (1968) in the simple dictum that 'Research is . . . the indispensable basis of proper planning' (para. 173). More effective social planning depends on improved ways of monitoring social conditions, and better information about the state of society and about the working and impact of social policies. These will only come about when governments learn to make better use of the potential of the social sciences and when social scientists learn how to be of more use to policy-makers.

I have accumulated a large number of debts in preparing this book. While a brief acknowledgement here in no way writes them off, it is a small courtesy whose sentiments are sincere. My thanks are due to the Sheffield University Travel Fund and to the British Academy for financial help which enabled me to pay a short research visit to Washington, DC, in search of case material for inclusion in Part II. The Leverhulme Trust also awarded me a small personal grant towards my research expenses. I am very grateful to each of them for their interest in and support of this study.

While in the United States I met and made a lot of friends and abandoned a few preconceptions. Among the many people who made me welcome and willingly gave their time to answer my questions I should like to mention especially: William Gorham, of the Urban Institute; Henry Aaron, of the Brookings Institution; Harry Havens and Larry Thompson, of the US General Accounting Office; Robert Helms and Gerry Britten, of the Department of Health and Human Services; Carolyn Solomon, of the Evaluation Documentation Centre at HHS; and not least, Frances Goodman, of Davis House, for providing comfortable accommodation and a congenial retreat.

Closer to home, I have reason to be grateful to Jane Anthony, of

Gower, for the confidence she showed in the book when it was no more than a synopsis. My colleague David Phillips sportingly fielded my teaching while I was away on a term's study leave. Jill Sargent and Marg Jaram have nursed the manuscript through all its various stages with unwavering speed and efficiency; having them to rely on has eased my load immensely. Their mastery of the electronic office, its gadgetry and its language, is impressive although I still have not got used to being told to 'SROFF'. Goodness knows how I would have managed to whip my bibliography into shape without the expert help of Ken Simons.

Public Administration, Policy and Politics and *Research, Policy and Planning* readily gave their permission for me to use parts of articles which first appeared in these serials. Steve Bell of the *Guardian* has kindly allowed me to reprint the cartoon which appears on p. 78.

My sons, Matthew and Daniel, met my all too frequent flashes of temper when things were not going well with a tolerance and understanding that I did not deserve; I hope now to be able to make amends. Wendy Booth has read and commented on every chapter in draft. She has struggled gallantly to shorten the words, break up over-long sentences, cut the flow of adjectives and otherwise lighten the prose. If the result is still flawed, the fault is because I stopped my ears to her advice. More important still, however, she has also given me the stamina and the patience to see the job through. Thanks, Wend.

In the end, of course, there is no one but me to blame for the mistakes and, like most authors, I am left with the niggling feeling that somehow I haven't said quite what I meant. Enough of that, however, for the time has come to watch a spot of cricket!

TIM BOOTH
Sheffield University
June 1987

PART I
THEMES:
THE
UNDERDEVELOPMENT
OF SOCIAL PLANNING

1 The poverty of social planning

'Teach us O Lord . . . To train our minds to make no plan.' (Hymn and Prayer for Civil Servants, anon.)

Social planning is a term overloaded with meanings. In Britain it has been used most frequently to refer, narrowly, to the programming of resources and the co-ordination of policies and services. In this book it is used in a much wider sense to refer to the search for policies to meet the goals of social development (Ferge, 1979; Gans, 1972).

Social policy can best be seen as encompassing all policies which affect the distribution of resources and life-chances among individuals, groups and classes in society (Walker, 1981), including cash incomes, benefits in kind, capital assets, public services and status and power (Townsend, 1974). It may be explicit and deliberately formulated or implicit and accidental (Donnison, 1975a). It includes not only policies which are framed and implemented by central and local government, but also those of non-state institutions such as voluntary organizations, trade unions, private companies and firms.

From this point of view, the contribution of social policy to the production and distribution of welfare is measured by its impact on the structure of inequality in society. Inequality is one of the basic building-blocks of the social order. In changing or reinforcing the pattern of inequalities, social policy helps to shape the structure of society. In this sense, it may be conceived as 'the means whereby societies prevent, postpone, introduce and manage changes in structure' (Townsend, 1976). With this conception of social policy in mind, social planning will be defined as the deliberate selection and weighting of policies according to an explicit rationale with the aim of steering or guiding society along a particular path of social development.

Social planning in this sense calls for a strategic framework for the making of policy which explicitly links the choice of means with the pursuit of ends. As the Central Policy Review Staff (CPRS, 1975) has noted, such a framework for the making and execution of policies, and for the determination of coherent and consistent priorities, is lacking from government in Britain. Instead, 'policy is made by taking decisions about specific items. . .and then having a retrospective look to see what their combined effect turned out to be' (Social Services Committee, 1981). As a result, social planning is in the doldrums, badly thought of and badly done.

The reasons for this sorry state of affairs are diverse and complex, and form a good part of the theme of this book. The most fundamental among them is also the most straightforward: social planning is done badly, if at all, because it can't be done well. The force of this argument derives from the incrementalist critique of rationalist models of decision-making and the policy process.

Rationalism and the Incrementalist Critique
The rationalist model of policy-making is based on the simple premise that any rational action must have an aim or purpose and that an action is rational only to the extent that it pursues this aim consciously and consistently (Popper, 1957). If policy-making is to be construed as a rational attempt to manage our affairs and deal with problems, then it must involve the setting of objectives and the careful choice of means suited to the attainment of these goals. Otherwise it amounts to nothing more than hit-and-miss guesswork. Only when policy-makers have a clear idea – a blueprint – of what they are striving towards can they begin to consider the best ways and means for getting there and settle on a programme of practical action.

According to the rationalist model, policy-making comprises four steps or stages:

1 The definition of the goals or objectives that are to be pursued.
2 The ordering of priorities where it is not possible to pursue all these objectives at the same time or with the same vigour.
3 The review of different ways and means of achieving these objectives and of their probable consequences or outcomes.
4 The choice of that course of action which promises optimal success in realizing the agreed goals.

An important feature of the rationalist model is the link it establishes between policy-making and planning. They are seen to be part and parcel of the same process. In terms of the rationalist model, policy-making becomes planning: the two processes share the same methodology.

It is this implication, that policy-making and planning are really one and the same thing, which the incrementalist denies and which lies at the heart of the incrementalist critique of the rationalist model. For the incrementalist there is simply no way in which policy-makers can follow the rules of the rationalist method and do their job properly. A number of arguments underpin the incrementalist's case.

The first criticism voiced by the incrementalist is that, in the real world, it is almost impossible to secure agreement on ultimate goals or objectives because of conflicting values and interests. People do not agree on the ends that are worth pursuing, or on the priority that should be given to them; and there is no systematic and objective method for reconciling this plurality of viewpoints. The rationalist's injunction that the policy-maker must start by spelling out objectives will only serve to bring into the open and accentuate these conflicts. It will merely encourage fruitless squabbling and wrangling, and abort the possibility of practical action. If, the incrementalist retorts, we can only set about doing something once objectives have been agreed, then we shall never succeed in tackling the problems we face at all.

Instead of trying to articulate objectives, the incrementalist argues, policy-makers concentrate on the task of finding answers to problems. They seek to resolve or remedy known ills rather than try to work towards or bring about some desired future end, for the simple reason that pragmatic agreement on what should be done about a problem can usually be reached even when consensus on values or objectives is impossible. For the incrementalist, then, the ends which policies serve are governed by the choice of means rather than the other way around as the rationalist model suggests. Instead of striving to realize some vision or blueprint of a better tomorrow, the policy-maker concentrates on remedying the problems of today. This idea effectively severs the link between policy-making and planning forged by the rational model. It turns policy-making into a method of problem-solving with the focus strictly on the here and now.

It is at this point that another difference emerges between the incrementalist and the rationalist. In the rational model the choice of which policy to adopt is determined by analytical criteria. The policy-maker explores all the alternative ways of achieving a set objective and chooses the one which promises the most success on the basis of a comprehensive evaluation of their costs and benefits. The incrementalist challenges this model of decision-making, and the key role it assigns to research and analysis on three grounds.

First, because the policy-maker cannot rely on ends as a guide to means. As we so rarely agree on where we should be heading, we are rarely in a position to decide what is the best way of getting there. Consequently, policy-makers proceed by aiming to maximize agreement on ways of tackling specific problems. Instead of starting by defining objectives, they begin by clarifying what the problems are and then look for ways of tackling them which mobilize enough support to facilitate action. The test of a good policy for the incrementalist is that it forges agreement between people whose interests and values may differ substantially.

The incrementalist's second objection to the important place given to analysis in the rational model is that it is simply not up to the job; that the task of comparing policy options in terms of their effectiveness or efficiency is unworkable. We do not have all the information or the technical know-how necessary for this task. Our social statistics are inadequate; our knowledge of the workings of society is deficient; and our understanding of the effects and ramifications of social policies is too meagre – and the problems of measuring their impact or outcome raise unresolved, and perhaps insoluble, difficulties of a technical nature. Moreover, even if these obstacles could be overcome, the costs of acquiring such information are likely to outweigh any benefits which might accrue in the form of more efficient public policies. Finally, policy-makers cannot afford to wait for the results of analysis before making decisions. Analysis takes time, and the sort of exhaustive analysis entailed by the rational model would take a great deal of time. Policy-makers, on the other hand, are under constant pressure to make decisions quickly. Analysis simply would not be possible within the time-scale in which they have to operate.

For the incrementalist social problems are too complex to be well understood and too slippery to be mastered. The idea that analysis can provide the information on which to base action is seen as an illusion. Policy-makers have to adopt a strategy for problem-solving that enables them to cope under conditions of ignorance and uncertainty.

These points tie up with another important criticism which incrementalists make of the rational model. It overlooks the fact that even the most carefully planned actions or decisions often have unintended and unanticipated consequences: a contingency rooted in the unpredictability of human behaviour and the complex interdependencies on which societies are built. This criticism has a number of damaging implications.

It means that careful analysis and systematic evaluation is an inadequate basis for choosing among policy options because there is no sure way of finding out what their practical effects are likely to be other than by trial and experiment. Social policies are almost bound to produce some sort of second-order effects which were not foreseen, may very well be undesirable and might even prejudice or thwart the policy-maker's original objectives. If serious enough, they might upset or distort the analysis on which the choice of policy was grounded by introducing new and significant costs or benefits into the equation. They pose a serious dilemma for the rationalist.

Ignoring them may result in carefully laid plans being jeopardized. Responding to them entails either going back to the drawing-board or resorting to *ad hoc* improvisation, which is the very antithesis of the rationalist method. In this light, rationalism is seen to contain the seeds of its own failure.

All these problems are avoided, the incrementalist argues, if we recognize that policy-makers do not and cannot select means in the light of ends, or even distinguish between the two, but rather proceed by trial and error. For the incrementalist the method of trial and error is both a better description of how policy-makers in fact behave and a more realistic approach to the job of policy-making than the technique of systematic evaluation advocated by the rationalist. It faces up to the complexity of social problems, and acknowledges that in trying to tackle them, *caution* is a desirable virtue given our limited knowledge of their causes and character. Also it permits greater *flexibility* by encouraging a step-by-step approach to problems which allows for the possibility of mistakes. At this point, it can be seen that the incrementalist critique of the rationalist model in fact amounts to a fully fledged alternative view of the policy-making process.

Incrementalism and its Critics

The difference between the rationalist and the incrementalist is the same as the difference between a navigator and a pilot: one charts a course, while the other steers through troubled waters. Perhaps this is why the rationalist is often criticized for star-gazing and the incrementalist is accused of never looking beyond the near-horizon.

Certainly, unlike the rationalist, whose sights are set on some distant objective, the incrementalist focuses very much on the here and now. Incrementalism conceives policy-making as the business of doing something about today's problems rather than reaching out for some vision of a better tomorrow. Policies are evaluated in terms of the marginal benefits they offer in improving the status quo. The question is not how far this or that course of action gets us towards some clearly defined objective, but how far it is likely to bring about a change for the better in things as they are now.

The justification for this pragmatic approach rests on the belief that while agreement at the level of values is always difficult and often impossible, agreement at the level of policy on specific proposals for reform or change can generally be negotiated – if not always easily. Faced with a call to act, therefore, policy-makers seek out those measures which maximize agreement and mobilize the most support.

This test of consensus as the criterion of policy choice tends to favour gradual, small-scale, piecemeal change, for the simple reason that it is easier to get agreement for small adjustments and minor reforms, which bear on fewer people or threaten them less, than for major ones which impinge on more people or have more far-reaching consequences.

This little-by-little philosophy of progress is seen as having a number of strengths. It minimizes not only the political risks, but also the social costs of failure. Given our limited understanding of the workings of society, the complexity of social problems and the inevitability of unforeseen snags, mistakes are bound to be made. A gradual, step-by-step approach to policy-making means that what mistakes do occur are likely to be small and their repercussions manageable. Gradualism enables the policy-maker to monitor progress, to compare the results expected with the results achieved, to spot mistakes quickly and to correct them easily and to respond sensitively to political feedback about their impact so as to harness support and head off opposition. Within this model, then, policy evolves through a series of successive marginal adjustments.

From what has been said, it can be seen that incrementalism is incompatible with planning. It admits no strategy or guiding purpose; it is a way of coping with problems and no more, of 'muddling through' (Lindblom, 1959). As such, it meets a broadside of criticism from the advocates of the rational model. Four main charges are levelled against incrementalism.

The view that consensus marks the test of a good policy assumes a pluralist theory of society and of the state in which people are free to combine to pursue and protect their common interests; in which almost every interest has its own watchdog; in which all interest groups are equally adept at articulating and pressing their claims; and in which the government is open and sensitive to their pressures as well as even-handed and impartial in its stance. Just as free market theorists have argued that competition between self-interested individuals will produce an efficient distribution of resources, so the incrementalist assumes that free competition between group interests in the political arena will result in an agreement on policy based on a just distribution of benefits. Yet, say the critics, in the same way as there are imperfections in the economic market, so too there are imperfections in the political market. Some groups – like the poor, the old and the mentally handicapped – lack a powerful voice, while others mirror in political power the economic power they wield in the market-place. There are few reasons for believing that political competition will of itself produce an outcome that takes full account of minority interests or the general welfare of the community.

Moreover, it is claimed, the test of consensus provides succour to the forces of conservatism and inertia present in bureaucracy and society. It balks innovation and discourages risk-taking. The incrementalist's readiness to avoid conflict and to accept compromises for the sake of agreement too often means that decisions are reached which appease the powerful at the expense of the weak and the disenfranchised.

This leads to a third criticism: that policy-making by successive marginal adjustments could only be effective when all that was called for was fine-tuning of the system. It is incapable of bringing about the major shifts in resources and ideas needed to cope with the challenge of fundamental change. Incrementalism, its critics argue, presupposes that things are not too bad as they are given a few, minor adjustments here and there.

Finally, the argument runs, incrementalism, with its step-by-step approach, assumes that the problems facing policy-makers are unconnected with one another and may be tackled one-by-one. It eschews the kind of overarching analysis that would reveal the links between them and the larger social forces behind them. Such piecemeal reform, say the critics, is merely palliative. It fails to attack the root causes of social problems, but only mops up some of the mess. In short, it is not capable of initiating the major task of social reconstruction which many rationalist planners believe is required.

By way of an overview of the long-standing debate between rationalism and incrementalism rehearsed above, the differences between these two models of the policy-making process may be summarized as follows:

1   The rational model is oriented to the future, whereas incrementalism focuses on the here and now.
2   Rationalism equates policy-making with planning, whereas incrementalism sees it as problem-solving.
3   In the rational model ends dictate the choice of means, whereas for the incrementalist means are regarded as ends in themselves.
4   The rationalist strives to look at problems 'in the round', whereas the incrementalist tries to simplify them.
5   The rational model urges a strategic approach to policy, whereas incrementalism commends a piecemeal, step-by-step approach.
6   Rationalism emphasizes the role of analysis and evaluation in the formulation of policy, whereas incrementalism proceeds by trial and error.
7   In the rational model the comparative merits of different policies are assessed by analytical criteria, whereas incrementalism holds

that the acid test of a good policy is that it wins support and agreement.

Advice vs Analysis

The arguments of the incrementalist show up the failure of social planning in a stark and cheerless light. It is the inevitable consequence of the piecemeal nature of policy-making enforced by having to cope with problems which, for the most part, beggar our understanding. Moreover, it has to be said, these arguments are supported by the evidence from inside government itself about the workings of the policy process.

Few people within government have the inclination or incentive to look beyond the crisis of the moment or to 'penetrate behind the curtain of everyday decisions' (Heyworth Committee, 1965). As Lord Crowther-Hunt (1977) has observed, departmental planning in Whitehall is 'overwhelmingly dominated by, and almost entirely composed of, those who are heavily immersed in the problems of here and now'. As a result, according to the Fulton Report on the Civil Service (1968), 'In the press of daily business, long-term policy-planning and research tend to take second place'. As Fulton saw it, the future was being left to take care of itself, and forward thinking was being 'crowded out' by officials already 'over-burdened with more immediate demands arising from the parliamentary and public responsibilities of Ministers'.

To overcome this problem, Fulton proposed the setting up of departmental 'planning units' headed by a senior policy adviser. Freed from any involvement in day-to-day operations, they would assume responsibility for 'major long-term policy-planning'; their main task 'should be to identify and study the problems and needs of the future and the possible means to meet them'(ibid., para.173).

These units were never established. Perhaps because they threatened to give the minister an alternative source of advice not under the control of the Permanent Secretary. In any case, the outcome has been that research, which Fulton declared to be 'the indispensable basis for proper planning', has continued to play only a peripheral part in the process of departmental policy-making. As the Heyworth Committee (1965) had earlier foreseen, research and administration have continued to run on parallel lines and rarely meet.

This failure to integrate research and administration has helped to perpetuate the traditional Whitehall distinction between advice and analysis (Keeling, 1972). Advice draws on hunch, intuition and experience; analysis calls for investigation, objectivity and method. The preference for advice has preserved ways of thinking and decision-making which Wootton (1962) long ago chastized for paying too much attention to logic and too little to fact, a criticism echoed by Richard Crossman (1967) in a passage that might almost come from a script for *Yes, Minister*:

> [M]y quest has been not so much for the secret place where power is concealed as for the Committee whose decisions are taken in the light of available evidence. And all my life the vision has eluded me. Whenever I got myself elected to the Fellows Meeting at New College, to my Faculty Meeting, to the Oxford City Council, to Parliament, and, finally, to the Cabinet, the higher I climbed the more certain I was that on the next storey of the pyramid of power I would find a body of people making their decisions not on hunch and guesswork but on the basis of reliable information. Now I know that in Whitehall at least I was searching, not for a will o' the wisp, but for a pot of gold.

Nor is there any reason to suppose that things have changed much. Public administration still lacks a long-term perspective. Reviewing the failure to establish policy-planning units on the Fulton model in Whitehall, MacDonald and Fry (1980) conclude: 'In Britain the activities of government take place within an institutional matrix which, by imposing strictly short-term disciplines, lends an element of surprise or drama to virtually every single event within the public domain.'

More than any other postwar administration, the Heath government recognized these deficiencies in the machinery of decision-making at the centre. It lacked a framework for the strategic definition of objectives:

> For lack of such a clear definition of strategic purpose and under the pressures of the day to day problems immediately before them, governments are always at risk of losing sight of the need to consider the totality of their current policies in relation to their longer term objectives; and they may pay too little attention to the difficult, but critical, task of evaluating as objectively as possible the alternative policy options and priorities open to them. (Cmnd 4506)

The White Paper on the Reorganization of Central Government (1970) acknowledged that the essential basis of good government is better information. Ministers needed to 'have before them at the right time all the necessary information and the analysis to enable them to take decisions' (ibid., para. 15). It proposed the setting up of a central analytical capability (subsequently called the Central Policy Review Staff, CPRS), 'so that the government strategy could be continuously reviewed and regularly reported upon' (Heath and Barker, 1978). Its role, according to Douglas Hurd, Heath's Political Secretary, was 'to rub ministers' noses in the future'; the work of

the CPRS is examined in more detail in Chapter 8 of this book. It
survived for almost thirteen years before being abolished by Mrs
Thatcher in 1983. At the risk of some oversimplification, a review
of its history and its achievements, in relation to the purposes
outlined in Cmnd 4506, yields three main lessons (Williams, 1983):
first, neither ministers nor mandarins want policy analysis; secondly,
top civil servants have little understanding of policy analysis or of
how to use it; and thirdly, the enveloping secrecy of British
government and the obsessive departmentalism within Whitehall
have stunted the application and development of policy analysis,
especially on cross-departmental issues.

The pride of place given to advice over analysis, reflecting, as it
does, the respective roles and status of generalists and specialists in
the civil service, and the monopoly of advice enjoyed by top
mandarins, has inhibited the spread of more systematic and rigorous
techniques of policy evaluation. Williams (ibid.) concludes: 'The
lack of hard-edged policy analysis is a symptom of pre-modern
central government that has not faced up to the information and
analytic demands of running a complex welfare state.'

In the USA, too, federal policy-makers are not unknown for
shooting from the hip – acting first and thinking later. As one former
Secretary of Health, Education and Welfare, John Gardner, put it,
'We Americans have a great and honored tradition of stumbling
into the future.' This is a tradition which stretches back to the start
of the Union. Abraham Lincoln was certainly aware of it, and in an
address to the Illinois Republican State Convention delivered in
1858, he mapped out what he saw as a safer path: 'If we could first
know where we are, and whither we are tending, we could better
judge what to do, and how to do it.' This passage, then, neatly and
eloquently sums up the rationalist's case. It also shows that the
debate with those who doubt the wisdom of trying to steer a fixed
course in matters of public policy is by no means a new one, even
if it has come out mostly on the side of muddling through. Over a
century after Lincoln was speaking, for example, it was still possible
for a knowing insider within the giant federal bureaucracy to describe
the USA, in words echoing Williams' criticism of Britain, as 'an
undeveloped country' when it comes to planning for the efficient
allocation of national resources against competing needs (Mondale,
1967).

What distinguishes the USA in this respect is that, unlike Britain,
bold, imaginative and ambitious efforts have been made, over the
past twenty years, to harness the potential of the social sciences, to
integrate research into the making of policy, to improve the quantity
and quality of information about the state of society and to translate

this knowledge into action. Part II of this book reviews the most important of these initiatives and assesses their achievements and failings. Part III draws out the wider lessons of these case studies, charting the uneasy relationship between policy-makers and social scientists. For the moment, it is enough to note that these specific initiatives have been conceived and implemented in the context of a fundamental debate about the nature of the policy process, a debate which, among other things, focuses on the value of systematic analysis in the making of decisions.

An Artificial Debate

The fact that policy-making inside government generally shows itself to be a piecemeal process does not finally clinch the argument in favour of the incrementalist. It certainly suggests that incrementalism probably offers the more true to life account of how policy really is formulated but it does not vindicate the claim that this is also how policy should be formulated. Indeed, this book is partly an attack on the idea that the failure of social planning shows it to be a waste of time, which is another version of the idea that because things are done as they are, they could never be done any differently.

The crux of the matter is that the debate between rationalists and incrementalists is somewhat artificial, in the sense that for a good part of the time both sides are talking at cross-purposes (Smith and May, 1980). They look at the policy process from different angles. Incrementalism is best seen as providing a *descriptive* account of the policy-making process: an empirically grounded explanation of how decisions are reached. On the other hand, the rational model is best seen as offering a *normative* account of policy-making – of prescribing how decisions should ideally be made. Much of the argument generated by the debate between them arises because the advocates of each model insist on criticizing the other only on their own home ground. Thus incrementalists point out the inaccuracies of the rational model saying that is not the way things are done, while rationalists stress the shortcomings of muddling through saying that is not the way things should be done. The real issue is not who is right and who is wrong, but how far rationalist precepts add up to a workable formula for improving on established, incremental methods of policy-making.

The debate is artificial in another sense as well. The two sides are usually presented as opposing camps. In reality there is no precise, clear-cut line of demarcation between them. The battle hymn of the incrementalist may very well be 'Lead Kindly Light': 'I do not ask to see/The distant scene; one step enough for me.' But just how big that step might be, or how far-reaching its repercussions, is not spelled out (remember 'one small step for man, one giant leap for mankind'?).

The issue is, as Rule (1978) has pointed out, how piecemeal is piecemeal? The impracticality of trying to formulate anything resembling a total social strategy in which every existing policy and every new decision is related to every other is easily demonstrated. Any such attempt is destined to fail in the face of the fragmentation of powers, responsibilities and functions within government as will be shown in Chapter 2. But the alternative is not just disjointed incrementalism. There are degrees of co-ordination. For example, the Working Party on Collaboration between the NHS and Local Government (1973), set up to consider the relations between health and local authorities in anticipation of their reorganization in 1974, distinguished between co-ordination and collaboration. Co-ordination means working independently but in harmony; collaboration means working together. The Working Party stressed that the 'real objective is not to achieve the joint consideration of plans which have been prepared separately by the two sides and brought together at a late stage to see how well they match up', rather the aim 'is to secure genuinely collaborative methods of working throughout the process of planning'.

The point is that policy-makers are not really forced to choose between having an all-encompassing strategy on the one hand, or on the other allowing themselves to be carried along, like a cork on a current, by day-to-day pressures and the politics of drift and get-by. There is a middle-ground betweeen comprehensive planning and opportunism. The real challenge, as the CPRS (1975) acknowledged, is to improve the co-ordination of policies in line with a collective view on priorities.

Another key point of difference between the two sides is also blurred when theory is put to the test. Even if the policy-maker is not unlike a drunk staggering from one lamp-post to the next, as the incrementalist implies, he is more likely to find his way and keep his footing if the path ahead is clearly lit. Even a torch is better than no light at all. So it is with the use of research for policy. Research may not provide all the answers, some problems may defy precise measurement and comprehensive analysis may be impossible. But even incomplete information about the costs and consequences of policy decisions is better than wishful thinking as a basis for action. The real issue, then, is not, as it is often presented, about synoptic methods of policy-making vs sequential trial and error; it is about how to avoid repeating the sort of 'striking failures' in public policy and planning 'that seem in part attributable to the lack of adequate enquiry into social facts' (Rothschild, 1982).

Planning and Overload

Myrdal (1960) long ago argued that planning in the welfare state developed as a consequence of the growth of government and the increase in volume and complexity of state intervention. He observed: 'The regular sequence has been that intervention caused planning.' Planning became necessary as a means of co-ordination in order to preserve some measure of coherence in the administration of government policies. From this perspective planning, viewed as the attempt 'to co-ordinate public policies more rationally in order to reach more fully and rapidly the desirable ends for future development which are determined by the political process', is a response to the dangers of overload inherent within 'big government'.

The thesis of governmental overload began to achieve widespread currency in the mid-1970s. Several threads were woven into the argument. Partly it expressed the fear that modern governments, charged with managing the economy, might become ungovernable in the face of the failure of Keynesian economics (Douglas, 1976). Partly, too, it was seen as the culmination of internal contradictions in liberal representative democracy which result in an excessive burden being placed on the 'sharing out' function of government (Brittan, 1975). Marxist commentators located the problem in the capitalist productive system (Coates, 1976) which pushes the state into steadily increasing its activities and expenditure, in order to maintain the profitability of monopoly capital and to support the surplus population, until eventually it is pitched into fiscal crisis (O'Connor, 1973). And other political scientists saw governments becoming overloaded as spending commitments grew faster than the economy resulting in policy failures and a loss of effectiveness that threatened their legitimacy and authority (Rose and Peters, 1978; Rose, 1980).

King (1975) has provided a summary of the problem of overload that pulls together many of these threads. He argues that the reach of government now exceeds its grasp. Governments today are held responsible for far more than ever they were before and the range of problems with which they are expected to deal is still increasing. At the same time, their capacity to exercise these responsibilities has declined because of a shortage of resources exacerbated by a falling rate of economic growth and the loss of the fiscal dividend; because the growing scale of government has multiplied its dependence on strategically placed and powerful groups in the wider society; because these groups have become less compliant; and because of a lack of understanding of the problems. The consequences for government of a world at once more complex, more demanding and more intractable have been that policies more often fail, which is the symptom of overload in a nutshell. We have more government and less effectiveness.

A case example of the problem of overload can be found in the critique of the welfare state that has developed in the ranks of both liberal and conservative opinion since the early 1970s. Broadly speaking, the welfare state has been indicted on three grounds (Heclo, 1977):

1 *Cost* – the welfare state has fuelled excessive public expectations of government by extending the rights and claims of citizenship. The resulting pressure has pushed up social expenditure at a faster rate than the economy can sustain or taxpayers are willing to bear.

2 *Ineffectiveness* – the welfare state has failed to deliver on most of its promises. At best, social policies and programmes have failed to get money and services to those who need them most. At worst, government has been unable to fundamentally change social conditions for the better or to reduce inequality and deprivation.

3 *Over-regulation* – the pursuit of uniform national standards or norms of provision in the name of equity and fairness has led to the centralization of decision-making, the imposition of professional definitions of need, the growth of bureaucracy and the loss of democratic participation in the administration of services.

In sum, the redistributive aims of the welfare state have resulted in the gradual centralization of power and decision-making in massive bureaucracies whose paternalistic bias, added to problems of red tape and accountability, has contributed to over-regulation and ineffectiveness (Klein, 1977).

What can be done about the administrative overload on government posed by the welfare state? The solutions tend to fall into one or other of two broad categories: limit government's reach or improve its grasp. The differences between them are similar to those between supply and demand-side economics. Government's reach could be reduced by lowering public expectations (demands) of the welfare state. Essentially this means asserting political authority to redefine the balance of responsibilities between the state and the individual. In practical terms this might involve, among other things, cutting back statutory services, lowering the safety net, promoting the private market and stressing the virtues of self-help, mutual aid and informal support. On the other hand, government's grasp could be strengthened by improving the working of the administrative machine: overload is only a problem relative to the capacity to handle it (Crozier, 1975). In practical terms this could mean greater decentralization of decision-making. It certainly calls for better planning: planning as a means of improving co-ordination in the face of the growing complexity of Big Government; and planning to provide the social information on which effective government in an increasingly complex society depends.

If King, Crozier and others are right in arguing that the danger of overload is partly a consequence of the growing organizational complexity of government brought about by the drift towards an ever more highly organized and complex society, then somehow we must learn how to cope with this trend. Merely pruning the functions of government is no answer. There is no escape through the backdoor of history to earlier, simpler times. Governments have to live in the present and face up to the future like anyone else; they must organize their resources to meet their commitments.

The problem of co-ordinating activities to meet these commitments is greater within government than in the private sector because the number and variety of public outputs is larger, because there is no easy yardstick like profitability to measure performance and because there is no common denominator, such as money, for comparing the outputs of programmes and making trade-offs between them. Other types of information and analysis are required: *social monitoring* to provide information for policy-makers about trends and changes in society, about the relative social needs of different groups, about the impact of social policies and their distributional effects and about the effectiveness of programmes; and *social reporting* to provide information for Parliament and the wider public about the impact of government policies on the social state of the nation, so that they can better judge its performance. This book explores what is involved in trying to avert what some have seen as the dangers of overload, or what is here called the failure of social planning, through better methods of social monitoring and social reporting.

A Case Study of Social Services Planning
A case study might help to clarify the themes and issues introduced in this chapter and point the way for later discussion.

Central government has made three attempts since the early 1960s to introduce a national planning system for local authority personal social services. There were the Health and Welfare Plans of 1962–5. These were followed by the 1972 ten-year planning exercise. Finally, in 1977 a system of three-year planning was introduced, known as LAPS (Local Authority Planning Statements). Each of these initiatives was inspired by problems faced by the central department (Department of Health and Social Security):

(a) the problem of *co-ordination*, or how to ensure the co-ordinated development of the health and social services in the face of their administrative segregation;
(b) the problem of *control*, or how to ensure some uniformity in standards of provision between local authorities when they enjoy almost complete autonomy in the administration of local services;
(c) the problem of *implementation*, or how to get local authorities to do things they are reluctant to do such as, for example, shift resources from institutional into community care;
(d) the problem of *defending* the DHSS budget and the social services against the predatory instincts of the Treasury; without knowing what is happening in the country, the DHSS is ill-placed to hold its corner in the annual round of Rate Support Grant (RSG) negotiations and the public expenditure (PESC) review.

The recourse to the idea of a national planning system has been part of a prolonged attempt to find a managerial solution to these problems of government.

So far, however, none of these attempts has met with any lasting success. Shortly after the election of the Conservative government in 1979, the DHSS informed the local authority associations that it had decided not to ask local authorities to complete planning statements for the period 1979–80 to 1981–2, the third round in the annual LAPS cycle. Why, after all the efforts to set up a national planning system, extending over a period of almost twenty years, was the decision made to abandon LAPS just at the point when it appeared to have been established successfully? Why was LAPS allowed to lapse?

The answer is by no means clear-cut. Indeed, two competing explanations of events may be discerned, each of which puts a somewhat different gloss on the matter. Let us call one of them the cynical option, and the other the softer option.

The Cynical Option
The fact cannot be concealed that the change of government in 1979 was a major blow to LAPS and marked a fundamental shift in government's stance towards social services planning.

None the less, it would be wrong to argue that it was simply the change of government that undermined LAPS. After all, Health and Welfare Plans had been introduced by a Conservative government and had survived into the following Wilson administration. The ten-year plans had been introduced by Sir Keith Joseph, Secretary of State for the Social Services in the Heath government; and LAPS had been introduced by the Callaghan government.

Clearly, then, up to 1979 the thinking that had motivated the attempts to introduce a national planning system in the personal social services had spanned the party divide. Or perhaps there is a better way of putting it, one more in line with the thesis that planning was seen as a *managerial* solution to some of the problems of co-ordination and control which arise in the relationship between the central department and local authorities. Namely, that up to 1979 no minister responsible for the social services felt strongly enough about planning to block or oppose the successive efforts by *officials* to introduce a national planning system. For the initiative has always come from officials in the DHSS. There is no political kudos to be gained from setting up a planning system. But so far as many senior civil servants are concerned it could help to make their job a lot easier.

So what happened in 1979 was not just that the government changed; previous planning initiatives had survived elections and changes of minister only to fall at other obstacles. More significant was the fact that the change of government marked a fundamental ideological shift, a change in thinking. Instead of ministers being indifferent to planning – so indifferent as not to bother obstructing the initiatives of their officials – those same officials were now confronted by a government with a very clear view about planning, and one grounded in suspicion bordering on outright hostility.

The government does not like social planning for several reasons:

1   It thinks planning is a *waste of time*. If you believe, as important people in the government do, that a free market economy, if left to run itself without unnecessary state intervention, official regulation or red tape, will automatically tend to maximize national well-being, then you have no need of social planning.

2   It thinks planning is *dangerous* because it portends the managed society, and the managed society is inimical to individual freedom.

3   It believes that the ideology of planning is a breeding ground for *unsavoury ideas*. Social planning is the province of experts in the social sciences, and it is overwhelmingly those social scientists who are seen as hostile to the values of the market.

The character of the shift in ideas that has taken place is conveniently portrayed in the person of Sir Keith Joseph. Sir Keith was a senior minister in the 1970–4 Heath government which, in October 1970, published the White Paper on the Reorganization of Central Government. This White Paper announced 'a new style of government'. It promised greater efficiency in government as a result of more rigorous analysis and improved planning. To this end, among other things, Sir Keith Joseph, as Secretary of State for the Social Services, launched the ten-year plans which were intended as the start of a routine annual system of social services planning.

It would not be unfair to conclude, then, that in 1972, Sir Keith Joseph, marching in step with the Heath administration, was a planner. Yet by 1976, only four years after the ten-year planning exercise, Sir Keith had revised his views. Speaking at a meeting of the Bow Group in Norwich, in July 1976, on the theme of the Moral and Material Benefits of the Market Order, he asserted forcefully that:

> the blind, unplanned, unco-ordinated wisdom of the market is overwhelmingly superior to the well-researched, rational, systematic, well-meaning, co-operative, science-based, forward-looking, statistically respectable plans of governments, bureaucracies and international organisations preserved from human error and made thoroughly respectable by the employment of numerous computers. (Joseph, 1976)

The point here is not to show how one man changed his mind. The shift in Sir Keith Joseph's thinking is symptomatic of and partly responsible for the ideological lurch in the philosophy of Conservatism which Mrs Thatcher's government has generated. The sort of views Sir Keith expressed in his Norwich speech are now echoed in the actions and pronouncements of his Cabinet colleagues. But there is no surer sign of the Thatcher government's hostility to social planning than its pinched and repressive attitude towards information and statistics on the social condition of the nation, information that would assist in the measurement of social needs and the monitoring and evaluation of social policies.

A significant piece of evidence that lends support to this view comes from the House of Commons Social Services Committee, the parliamentary Select Committee which keeps an eye on the DHSS. In 1980 it recommended that 'the DHSS should give high priority to developing a comprehensive information system which would permit this Committee and the public to assess the effects of changes in expenditure levels or patterns on the quality and scope of services provided'. Roughly their argument was that cuts in spending were being made without anyone knowing what effects they were having (Social Services Committee, 1980).

In its reply the government referred rather mournfully to the 'great difficulties' there are 'at the national level in assessing the impact on services of changes in the level or pattern of expenditure' (DHSS, 1980b). Yet this claim was made *after* the local authority planning system had been suspended in 1979, and which had been geared to providing some of this information. In other words, the 'great difficulties' to which the government referred were of its own making.

They shelved the system which would have allowed them (and, of course, Parliament, the local authorities, pressure groups and the public) to monitor the effects of their policies on the personal social services. The suspicion lingers that they did not want to know, and probably just as important, did not want anyone else to know either. Added emphasis is given to this point by the fact that the only organization genuinely seeking systematically to monitor the national effects of the spending cuts on the social services – the Personal Social Services Council – was axed early in 1980 as part of the government's quango-culling exercise.

The 'cynical option' presents a disheartening picture in which the demise of LAPS is seen as just one more casualty of a systematic campaign by the government to reduce and restrict the amount and accessibility of information on the state of society, to censor what it can and to launder the rest, in order to mask or disguise the social impact of its economic policies.

The Softer Option

The 'cynical option' sets the apparent demise of LAPS in its wider context, showing how the suspension of national planning in the personal social services was motivated both by hostility to the idea of planning and by the political necessity of hiding from its critics the full social consequences of the government's economic policies.

Yet the initial decision not to ask local authorities to complete planning statements following the 1979 general election may also be seen as a prudent manoeuvre. Perhaps the DHSS was keen to shield LAPS from the cutting winds of the new political front. Possibly the suspension of LAPS was a protective measure.

After all, the new government was committed to 'rolling back the frontiers of the state' and to axing public expenditure. There was little point in getting local authorities to prepare plans for three years ahead when the public expenditure assumptions on which they would be based, derived from the previous Labour government's last Public Expenditure White Paper, were about to be drastically revised.

For this reason, there was a strong case for waiting until the new government had done its homework, published its own White Paper setting out its public spending plans, and then reintroducing LAPS. In this way, local authorities would be able to take account of the new economic climate in preparing their forward plans.

The DHSS had not forgotten the lesson of the 1972 ten-year planning exercise which had failed largely because it had proved so hopelessly out of touch with economic realities – a failure which had helped to bring planning itself into disrepute. If the new government is not very sympathetic towards planning anyway – so went official thinking in 1979 – better not run the risk of confirming ministers' prejudices by asking local authorities to draw up plans that are out of date before the ink has dried on them.

Accordingly, when informing the local authority associations that it would not be asking for planning statements in 1979, the DHSS indicated its intention of contacting them again in the autumn with advice 'as to how to proceed in the light of developments in relation to the subsequent planning period'.

Clearly, then, so far as the DHSS was concerned LAPS was not dead, but merely resting. This interpretation not only fits the facts, but also makes political sense. No matter what the ideological disposition of governments, the reality is that they cannot work effectively without information, and the information requirements of any government are particularly acute in fields such as the personal social services involving, as they do, 109 independent local authorities. The only way of obtaining a national picture of what is going on is by setting up some kind of information system.

This interpretation it seems is clinched by the fact that, as promised, the DHSS approached the local authority associations in 1980 with a view to reintroducing LAPS. But the approach backfired. The Association of County Councils opposed its reintroduction on the ground that the potential benefit to member authorities was outweighed by the efforts of completing the returns. The DHSS had run foul of the inertia inherent in local government which, like all bureaucracies and large organizations, is generally content to continue doing what has always been done but reluctant to start anything new or revive something once it has been abandoned.

Quite contrary to the cynical view of events presented earlier, this failure to resurrect LAPS was a genuine blow to the DHSS. As a senior official at the DHSS said, 'People have missed it now they haven't got it – even people who felt they could live without it.'

The information which LAPS provided for the DHSS began to be missed after the Thatcher government's first review of public expenditure. Nobody in the DHSS was in a position to say what impact the spending cuts were having on the personal social services. Were local authorities cutting the social services or were they making the required savings elsewhere in their budgets? No one knew.

In a desperate bid to fill the information gap created by the loss of LAPS, the DHSS asked the Social Work Service to use their regional offices to find out for them what was going on at local level. This exercise, first undertaken in 1980 and repeated in 1981, was a discursive affair which did not yield any information on individual authorities, such as LAPS had done, and which was largely impressionistic in style. Certainly, as officials at the DHSS readily admit, it was no substitute for LAPS. What had been lost was the quantitative information which LAPS produced.

There can be no doubt that the DHSS would like to see LAPS reintroduced, and the minister has specifically not ruled out the possibility of bringing it back. Indeed, this was one of the recommendations from a Review of Personal Social Services Statistics made by the National and Local Government Statistical Liaison Committee in February 1981. It is given extra drive by the success of the social services planning system developed by the Welsh Office which is still working smoothly. There has been a suggestion that the DHSS might be prepared to reduce the volume of other information it asks of local authorities in exchange for their agreement to the reintroduction of LAPS. And in 1982 the DHSS acknowledged they were exploring with the local authority associations the possibility of restoring some form of local authority planning/reporting system.

Reconciling the Options

Are these two explanations for the withdrawal of LAPS in 1979 as contradictory as they appear? Is it simply a case of choosing one or the other, or can they be reconciled?

It has been said already that information is necessary for the effective working of government. Broadly it is possible to identify six aspects of the work of the DHSS (or any government department) which it can only perform adequately if guaranteed a regular supply of information.

1 There are the requirements of day-to-day *accountability*, for example, dealing with Parliamentary Questions, answering letters, briefing ministers and senior civil servants, answering questions put by Select Committees. The information required for this purpose is often national aggregates and may involve trends or comparisons between authorities.

2 There are requirements springing from the *executive* responsibilities of the department, for example, the approval of local authority capital expenditure allocations and the calculation of the Rate Support Grant (RSG), both of which require detailed information about individual authorities.

3 There are the information requirements imposed by *statutory duties*, for example, specific obligations imposed by the Chronically Sick and Disabled Persons Act 1970 and the Children and Young Persons Act 1969 for central government to monitor local authority performance and to present reports to Parliament.

4   There are the requirements of *public expenditure planning* – in order to formulate the department's bid to the Public Expenditure Survey Committee for future resources for the personal social services, national trend information for all the major components of the personal social services by client group is required, and activity figures, staffing statistics, expenditure and unit costs are also employed. Much of this information is fed into the department's Programme Budget, which analyses expenditure by client groups, and forms an important source of DHSS input into the public expenditure planning process.

5   There are the information requirements of *policy-making* – a routine supply of trend information can help to give a general picture of a field in the light of which more specific and focused questions may be asked, and it can also be helpful in estimating the cost of proposed policy changes.

6   The department has a general role in *monitoring* the range of services and the performance of local authorities, and in *collecting and disseminating* such information for the benefit of people outside government.

Against this background the 'cynical' interpretation of the suspension of LAPS is shown to be based on too simple a reading of the direction and intentions of government policies, though correct in the overall judgement it presents.

The government is not against all information – only some. In particular, it is antagonistic to the sixth category of information described above; i.e. information collected for the purpose of monitoring and dissemination. Indeed, even here a qualification is necessary, for the government clearly believes that such information is highly desirable in the case of local government. The 1980 Local Government Planning and Land Act, for instance, requires local authorities to issue annual stewardship reports on the ground that, as the Minister of State for Local Government has declared, 'ratepayers are entitled to clearer information than they get at present and to information that gives them some chance of making comparisons and judgements on the performance of their authority.'

What the government is primarily opposed to is information designed to monitor its *own* performance, and the dissemination of this information to the wider public. That this is so is substantiated by the 1981 White Paper on Government Statistical Services, which bluntly states that 'Information should not be collected primarily for publication. It should be collected primarily because government needs it for its own business' (Cmnd 8236).

LAPS was quite compatible with this dictum and the thinking

behind it. It revealed the intentions, and monitored the performance, of local authorities, not central government. At the same time, it provided information which 'government needs for its own business'; in particular:

(a) LAPS yielded information on the services provided and the expenditure incurred by the personal social services which helped to meet the information requirements of DHSS client-based policy divisions;
(b) LAPS provided some of the personal social services input to the DHSS's Programme Budget, which is the main feature of the department's financial monitoring system;
(c) LAPS provided information which was used in calculating the annual RSG;
(d) LAPS was used to prepare the DHSS's bids for resources to the Public Expenditure Survey Committee.

By this reckoning the 'softer option' is probably correct in suggesting that the decision to suspend the 1979 round of the planning cycle was taken as a matter of temporary necessity. But it would be wrong to see this fact as invalidating the more cynical arguments presented earlier. What we have to do is to distinguish between different types of information. LAPS clearly belonged to that category of information which is useful to the central department. It helped to ease the problems of control, co-ordination, implementation and preservation which are a feature of the policy process in the DHSS. The 'cynical option' cannot be applied to information used for social monitoring which government needs 'for its own business'. What it does is provide an accurate and worrying account of the government's stance towards information of another sort: social reporting which might prove useful to independent critics of government outside official circles.

LAPS was not shelved because it was ineffective or because it asked the impossible. On the contrary, it provided information that was very useful to the DHSS and sorely missed when it was no longer available. After all, the DHSS is charged with a strategic role in relation to the personal social services. It is concerned with overall performance and with standards of provision; with significant changes over time in the balance between different forms of care; with the impact of changes in expenditure on the social services at the aggregate level; and with the interrelationship between the health and social services.

Without the kind of information LAPS gave, the DHSS found itself ill-placed to fulfil this strategic role. In this light, the reasons for its suspension must be seen as political not technical. The information it produced became too hot to handle for a government busy taking the axe to welfare spending while trying to hide the effects. The implication, that planning is a tender fruit sensitive to changes in the economic and political climate, is one which is discussed in more detail in Part II of this book.

Summary

There is 'no effective mechanism for determining coherent and consistent priorities in the field of social policy generally' (CPRS, 1975). This is the poverty of social planning. The reason such a mechanism or framework is lacking, says the incrementalist, is because planning by objectives is incompatible with the working of the policy process. Policy is not about final solutions. It is about moving from one problem to another.

The evidence from inside government tends to support this account of how things are done. For the rationalist, however, this only shows that we are ill-equipped to meet the challenge of governance in an increasingly complex society. The growth in the size of government, and the consequent fragmentation of powers, functions and responsibilities, has created problems of co-ordination that encourage a piecemeal approach to policy-making. At the same time, the growing complexity of the problems faced by government makes them harder to understand, which encourages a step-by-step, trial-and-error approach. Grappling instead of groping with these problems calls for better methods of social planning. First, though, we must get the measure of them; Chapter 2 addresses this task.

2 The social division of planning

'The nation has no organisation to help look at the great strategic questions that transcend the boundaries of individual departments.' (Mancur Olson, Deputy Assistant Secretary for Social Indicators, US Department of Health, Education and Welfare, 1969)

Chapter 1 described two models of decision-making and concluded that the incrementalist version offered the more true-to-life account of how government really operates. Lifting the lid on the inner workings of government reveals little that looks like rational social planning. There is no synoptic vision, no grand strategy, no systematic effort to explore what the future might hold. Progress is piecemeal and co-ordination poor. Problem-solving remains a hit-and-miss business. There is a surfeit of advice and a shortage of analysis. Hunch carries more weight than hard fact. The overall picture is one of individuals and departments each ploughing their own furrow and muddling through as best they can.

How far is the dismal state of social planning – the failure to co-ordinate policies in a coherent plan for social development – a result of 'tunnel vision' and an instinctive aversion to star-gazing among senior policy-makers and those whom they advise? This chapter sets out to explore the sociological roots of incrementalism inside government.

It is important to recognize at the outset that incrementalism, as defined in Chapter 1, is not just a way of working, but also a way of thinking. It describes both a technique for solving problems and a means of conceiving them. In looking at why incrementalism is so deeply embedded, therefore, we are not just concerned with what shapes the behaviour of policy-makers. We are also concerned with what shapes their perceptions of themselves and their world.

A plausible case can be made out that policy-makers think and act incrementally because of the kind of people they are and because their own experience teaches them that it pays. In other words, we might explain incrementalism in terms of the processes of professional recruitment and occupational socialization. Perhaps the civil service recruits new entrants who are predisposed to incremental ways, and thereafter rewards behaviour which corresponds to type. Perhaps those who lean towards a more radical or heretical approach are shut out or shunted into career sidings. Probably there is some truth in this explanation but it doesn't go far enough. It points to one reason why incrementalism persists within the government policy machine but it doesn't explain where it springs from in the first place.

In this chapter I shall argue that the origins of incrementalism are to be found deep within the structure of society and its network of institutions. In short, incrementalism prospers because of the institutional rigging that supports it and because of the institutional obstacles in the way of a more planned approach to the making of social policy. Fundamentally incrementalism is a product of what we may call the 'social division of planning' in society.

The social division of planning refers to those fissures within and between agencies, organizations and institutions which generally appear at the point where functions and powers divide and separate. It describes the fragmentation of responsibilities in a complex and structurally differentiated society. These fissures, as I've called them, split society, the state, institutions and organizations into countless separate constituencies, sometimes discrete and sometimes overlapping, each of them having command over different resources (both in kind and in quantity), a commensurate measure of power, a common interest grounded in their superordinate or subordinate position and a shared world-view to match. In this sense, the social division of planning is forged and shaped by the social distribution of power and the social division of labour in society.

In the realm of social policy the social division of planning makes it hard to see and deal with people and their problems 'in the round' (CPRS, 1975). It serves to compartmentalize our thinking and fragment our response to social needs in such a way as to induce and sustain a piecemeal approach to the making and execution of social policies.

The social division of planning leads directly to two general sets of problems which together comprise major obstacles to the development of a strategic approach to policy-making and a coherent framework for the determination of social priorities. These are: *problems of information*, which arise because agencies and organizations generally lack the knowledge they require about each other's plans and intentions adequately to integrate their services and activities; and *problems of collaboration*, which arise because organizations are generally dependent on others for the attainment of their own goals, yet lack the means of compelling them to adjust their policies and priorities to accord with their own plans.

Public Policy and Private Interests

The problems of information and collaboration presented by the social division of planning are clearly shown in one of the distinguishing characteristics of the mixed economy: the basic divide between a public sector and a private sector.

It is recognized in the higher echelons of British government that, in the words of a former Permanent Secretary at the Treasury, 'market behaviour has become a significant input in policy-making' (Wass, 1978). What happens in industry, or on the financial markets, may be beyond the control of government, but it can have far-reaching repercussions for the development of social policy. This is illustrated on the one hand by the growth in the 'company welfare state' of occupational benefits and perks (Field, 1981), and on the other hand by the 1976 sterling crisis and the subsequent cuts in the social wage and social services (Keegan and Pennant-Rea, 1979; Walker *et al.* 1979). Yet the interplay between government and the market is even more complicated than this suggests. For corporate decisions and market behaviour are not merely 'inputs' to the making of public policy. In an important sense they also 'invent the future' and so define the issues and problems with which policy-makers have to grapple (Kopkind, 1967; Sandberg, 1977).

Jones (1979), writing as a personnel executive with Lucas Industries, acknowledges the interest which big companies have in trying to shape the future to their own advantage:

> Those who have been involved in the preparation of (our) forecast are quite certain that, by making an informed guess at the future, Lucas businesses can be helped to prepare for that future and even to try and *influence it along lines favourable to the achievement of business objectives.* (emphasis added)

The point here is that, in what has been termed the 'contract state' where the government serves as a major market for the products of private firms, the efforts made by major corporations to manage their markets involve them in seeking to influence the behaviour of governments as surely as they seek to manipulate the behaviour of individual consumers. Obvious examples here arise in the fields of defence policy and procurement (Kopkind, 1967), and transportation, but others are not hard to find in the field of social policy. The influence of the tobacco companies on government attitudes towards health and smoking, the promotional activities of the pharmaceutical industry, or the impact which property developers and institutional investors have had on urban land use planning, especially 'green belt' policy and the balance between housing and office construction in the inner cities, all serve to make the point.

Indeed, housing provides a good example of the social division of planning between the public and private sectors. The problem of information has been spelled out by Richard Crossman, Minister of Housing in the 1964–6 Labour government: 'neither the Minister of Housing nor the Chancellor of the Exchequer has a really accurate picture of the private sector of housing with the result that the attempt to predict the figures far ahead is like a sweepstake' (Crossman, 1967).

Precisely the same difficulty was expressed, some fifteen years later, in 1980, by Michael Heseltine, Secretary of State for the Environment in Mrs Thatcher's first government. Giving oral evidence in response to a question from the House of Commons Environment Committee about whether he had made any assessment of private sector starts in the next couple of years, Heseltine replied:

> No, it would not be any good. We do not know. There is no way of knowing. If one likes to call in major builders as I do and ask how many houses are you going to start in 1982–83 they will say they do not know . . . There is no reason to suppose the Secretary of State by actually putting a slide-rule into a macro-economic calculation can get an aggregate figure when the individual building companies cannot give you an individual figure.

These two ministers, from different political parties, were speaking from opposing ideological points of view. Crossman was arguing that better information is necessary to plan housing properly; Heseltine was arguing that planning, or looking into the future, is no more than 'an exercise of academic curiosity' because the information on which to base decisions is lacking. Both, however, agreed about the nature of the problem.

Similarly, they saw the problems of collaboration in much the same way. Crossman (1967) noted how 'every Minister of Housing has been presented with an astonishing contrast between the public sector, which can be planned almost like a military operation, and the private sector, where production is at the mercy of market forces and interest rates'. More colloquially, Heseltine told the Environment Committee:

> There is not a building company in the private sector which will say, 'The Secretary of State has said there are going to be so many hundred thousand houses built this year. Therefore I must play my part'. If they adopted attitudes of that sort, more of them would have gone into liquidation than already have. It is because they have been wise enough to adapt to the market survey and their own economic resources that they have survived.

Other examples of the consequences for social policy of the social division of planning between the public and private sectors are easily found. As Rein (1977) has pointed out, for instance, 'something must be done about the low wage sector of the economy if we expect to solve the problems of work disincentives'. Simply trying to harmonize social security and taxation is not enough: 'Sooner or later the conflict between wage and benefit levels must be confronted.' Or again, the 'government of the NHS does not match the government of the health system if by the latter is meant the forces in our society that determine the pattern of disease and health' (Regan and Stewart, 1982). A government concerned to understand and redress the inequalities in health must reach out beyond the National Health Service (NHS) into the wider society where they originate. The recent boom in private residential care, especially for old people, has far-reaching implications for the management of local authority homes and also cuts across the government's own care in the community initiative. Each of these examples shows how the social division of planning often leads to an ill-coordinated or uncoordinated response to social problems where public policies and private interests pull in different directions.

Economic Management and Social Priorities

Another important manifestation of the social division of planning is the segregation of economic policy and social policy. We have squeezed economic and social policy into separate institutions of government and separate departments in Whitehall, and into separate compartments of our mind. In this way, social goals have been subordinated to economic objectives and social policy has been rendered subservient to the management of the economy.

This is shown most clearly in the system of public expenditure control where economic criteria effectively dictate social choices and priorities. Four aspects of the working of the public expenditure review (PESC) system serve to illustrate this point.

It is cost-oriented rather than needs-oriented (Townsend, 1980b). The system sets out to cost the spending plans of government departments, local authorities and nationalized industries as a basis for allocating resources between them in the light of the likely performance of the economy. It does not start from a definition of the goals or objectives of government policies and estimate what level of public expenditure would be required in order to attain them. As Ward (1983) has observed, PESC really only deals with expenditure 'whereas policy should be equally if not more concerned with the output of the public sector in terms of services provided and meeting social needs'.

This approach is well illustrated in evidence given by the Secretary of State for the Environment, Michael Heseltine, to the House of Commons Environment Committee in 1980. Invited to comment on how the cuts in the housing programme, announced in the government's White Paper on Public Expenditure, had been decided, the minister affirmed they were based on a view framed in discussions with the Treasury about 'what the country can afford' to spend on housing. They were not grounded on any assessment or forecast of housing needs over the period covered by the expenditure plans. In other words, housing policy and the size of the public housing programme were determined by the economic prospects of the country rather than the housing needs of the population. As Patrick Jenkin, the Social Services Secretary, put it in the House of Commons when acknowledging the dominance of economic criteria in the determination of spending priorities, 'in times of economic restraint we can only afford what we can afford'.

A second characteristic of the PESC system is that it is 'obsessed with an unreal concept of public expenditure' (Townsend, 1967). It focuses primarily on controlling the cash allocated for spending and deals only tangentially with the revenue forgone in the form of tax allowances (known as tax expenditures in the jargon of public finance). Yet for the Exchequer spending money and not collecting it amount to the same thing – a debit in the public accounts. Crucially, too, different groups in the population tend to benefit more from one or the other. In the field of income maintenance, for example, it is the poor who gain most from direct expenditure on social security, while the better-off gain most from tax expenditure in the form of reliefs and allowances. PESC thus separates the demands of financial management from the assessment of the distributional consequences of government spending decisions, another example of the social division of planning.

Thirdly, PESC encourages a narrow-minded approach to social policy by divorcing public expenditure decisions from developments in the private sector that also influence the distribution of resources and life-chances in society, again giving more weight to economic management than social planning. Thus, for example, while expenditure on the public welfare state is openly debated, carefully monitored and tightly controlled, expenditure on the 'hidden welfare state' of tax allowances, occupational benefits and the private market has grown unchecked, without any regard to the effects on social inequalities and the distribution of welfare.

Finally, the ascendancy of short-term monetary and economic considerations over longer-term social goals in the management of public expenditure is illustrated by two important technical adjustments to the PESC system made since the attack on inflation assumed overriding national priority after 1975. Up until then public expenditure allocations had been fixed in 'constant prices' showing the actual volume of resources (as opposed to the costs arising from inflation) committed to each spending programme. This was a way of ordering priorities among government policies in terms of their claims on national resources. However, as rising inflation pushed up the costs of labour and materials so the financing of the public sector, with its implications for taxation, became a fraught political issue. Inflation effectively increases the monetary cost (in pound notes) of financing any given volume of services. In 1974–75 the government overspent its estimates – the amount of money the Treasury had anticipated it would cost to pay for the public services the government had planned to provide – by almost a third, stimulating widespread fears that public expenditure was running out of control. The conviction grew that something had to be done to control the monetary costs (as opposed to the resource costs) of government policies: to bring the yearly bills into line with the ability to pay.

In 1976 cash limits were introduced for this purpose. Cash limits are essentially a mechanism for imposing a strict monetary discipline on public spending. They fix an administrative limit or ceiling on the amount of cash that the government will spend on certain services, or blocks of services, for the year ahead, irrespective of how inflation or the movements of wages and prices eat away at this figure in terms of what it will buy, and irrespective of any increase in the demand for these services brought about by social and demographic change. In other words, where there is an increase in prices or wages over and above that allowed for in the cash limit, the extra cost can only be met by a reduction in the volume of service or by making compensatory savings elsewhere. Equally, where demand for a cash-limited service increases more than was forecast, it can only be met by tighter rationing or by spreading the jam more thinly.

Cash limits were gradually extended to cover some three-quarters of government expenditure (including local authority current expenditure), and initially they were superimposed over the volume figures used in the survey. In 1981, however, the Chancellor of the Exchequer, after ridiculing constant prices as 'funny money', announced his intention of extending the logic of cash limits to the whole PESC process by abandoning the volume figures and constant prices and switching entirely to a cash-based system of expenditure control. Consequently, the 1982–83 plans were the first to be published which made no distinction at all between how much was to be spent and what it was hoped to buy with the money. They were the first to live up to the government's dictum that 'finance must determine expenditure and not expenditure finance'. As such, the system of cash limits and cash figures which now forms the basis of the PESC review process shows again how economic goals – in this case the imperatives of monetary policy and financial control – displace wider social objectives and distort social priorities. Unless allocations are made on a constant price basis, the actual effects of changing expenditure are unclear. Without other measures of public sector output, the only available indicator of what is happening to services is the volume of expenditure. With only cash figures to work on, it is impossible to determine whether a programme is receiving more or less resources year by year or how well it is doing relative to other programmes. If inflation changes significantly between reviews, then the volume of services which any given cash sum will finance also changes. Equally, if other factors affecting the real costs of providing services change (such as the number of eligible users or claimants), then the adequacy of any given cash allocation in relation to the needs it is supposed to meet will also change accordingly. All these limitations confound the task of planning to meet the needs of the community: they confuse and obscure the business of decision-making by making it impossible for ministers and policy-makers to see what they are getting for their money. For this reason, a cash-only review system 'cannot be reconciled with effective long-term planning and an ordered scheme of social priorities' (Society of Civil Servants, 1977).

Welfare as a Burden

The subordination of social goals to economic objectives is also induced and sustained by the deeply entrenched idea that social progress depends on economic growth. It is this view which underpins what Titmuss (1968) called the 'public burden model of welfare'. Although it appears in many guises, the gist of the idea is quite simple, as Royster (1975) illustrates:

> Britain, for those who would learn from it, offers a model study in how to bring to ruin a once vigorous nation . . . The formula is simple. You begin by putting upon a nation an economic burden it cannot bear. In Britain's case it was an all-encompassing welfare programme.

This analysis, and the assumptions on which it rests, have been incorporated into the thinking of the British Treasury (Townsend, 1980b) and accepted by successive governments (Abel-Smith, 1966; Glennerster, 1976; Peston, 1976). The 1979 Public Expenditure White Paper revealed precisely the same reasoning in only slightly less florid tones:

Public expenditure is at the heart of Britian's present economic difficulties. For a long time now the performance of the British economy has been deteriorating . . . Over the years public spending has been increased on assumptions about economic growth which have not been achieved. The inevitable result has been a growing burden of taxes and borrowing . . . If this continued, our economy would be threatened with endemic inflation and economic decline.

The implication is quite clearly that a sound economy is necessary to secure the welfare state: that what you spend has first got to be earned. For this reason, social goals are given second place to the pursuit of economic ends.

The presentation of welfare as a burden is an expression of the dominant ideology buttressing the role of the market in a capitalist economy. It is built into the Treasury's model of the economy (Ball, 1978). It is reinforced by the statistical conventions followed in the preparation of the national income accounts which measure only the inputs or costs of public services and not the value of their outputs (Glennerster, 1976; see also Chapter 3). It shows in the misrepresentation of the share of national output consumed by the public sector by the double counting of transfer payments in the White Papers on Public Expenditure (Holland and Omerod, 1979).

Yet the public burden model of welfare is based on a false premiss. In the real world there is 'no clear distinction between the economic problems and the non-economic problems of government' (Boulding, 1958) and the attempt to divorce them is bound to fail. First, this is because many economic objectives depend on appropriate social policies for their realization. For example, the acceptance by labour of the introduction of new technology in industry may depend on the provision of adequate retraining, redundancy or early retirement schemes for those whose jobs it threatens. Indeed, the link between economic and social policies was acknowledged in the Wilson government's 'social contracts' with the trade unions which traded improvements in the social wage for pay restraint. In 1974 food subsidies, a rent freeze and pension increases were provided in exchange for a voluntary incomes policy. A second social contract, signed in 1976, produced legislation on industrial relations, prices, taxes, nationalization, employment and training programmes and other areas of social policy in return for a tougher pay policy (Gough, 1979). Social policies do not just operate outside the market in order to offset some of the 'diswelfares' it produces. They also help to create the conditions which determine whether economic policies succeed or fail.

A second reason why economic and social policies cannot be neatly separated is because 'appropriate economic policies are needed to make the welfare state work' (Miller and Rein, 1975). Social policies aimed, for instance, at redistribution and the relief of poverty will not succeed unless economic policies are pulling in the same direction: they are insufficient by themselves to counteract the anti-egalitarian forces in advanced industrial economies (Rein, 1977) or to offset the growth of inequalities in the original distribution of income.

Broadly speaking, it is usual to distinguish three main spheres of government economic management (Ball, 1978). The government can, by its policies, seek to influence:

1   the uses to which the resources of the economy are put (as between public expenditure, private consumption, investment for the future, and overseas trade);
2   the distribution of rights to these resources (in the form of income and wealth) as between different groups or sections of the population;
3   the ups and downs in the level of economic activity including the level of employment, the rate of inflation and the balance of payments (a sphere generally described as 'stabilization policy').

The preoccupation of postwar governments with the pursuit of economic growth has led them to give most weight to the last of these three spheres of management – stabilization policy. The use and distribution of resources (spheres 1 and 2) have been largely determined by this objective. As a result, decisions about the division of the national cake, about who gets what, as expressed in decisions about public spending and rates of taxation, have been given second place to policies aimed at increasing its size. In other words, social policy has been reduced to a compensatory role in relation to the primary objectives of stimulating growth and controlling inflation, one of damage limitation. As such, it has proved quite unable to redress the inequalities generated by market forces and by macro-economic policies concerned more with increasing national output than with improving social well-being. Any serious attempt to reduce these inequalities in pursuit of a fairer society must entail giving more weight to redistribution as a goal of economic policy. The consequences of not doing so are amply illustrated by the persistence of widespread poverty and alienation in the face of generally rising living standards and, more particularly, by the emergence of the poverty trap, the expansion of the hidden welfare state and the growth of the black economy. As Crossman (1967) clearly saw many years ago, in the wake of the shocking discovery that penury had survived the coming of the welfare state, the 'war against poverty cannot be waged in isolation from the rest of our economic policy'.

The artificial segregation of economic and social policy has prevented us from seeing how they interlock. It has begotten a particularly narrow conception of the welfare state as serving only the poor by blinkering us to the redistributive effects of incomes policies, fiscal policies and occupational welfare. It is precisely this lack of a framework for comparing and assessing the impact of mutually interconnected policies that is a key characteristic of the social division of planning and a major reason for the piecemeal quality of public policy-making.

Departmentalism and the Policy Process

In 1925, Herbert Hoover, then Secretary of the US Department of Commerce, reported on the Federal government's custodianship of the nation's bears. Brown bears, he found, were under the jurisdiction of the Department of Agriculture, grizzly bears under the Treasury Department and polar bears were the responsibility of the Department of Commerce. The social division of planning is built into the structure of the modern state.

Different agencies, tiers and departments of government frequently share common or overlapping responsibilities in an area of policy. This is one reason why, for example, Britain's domestic fuel policy is 'divided, disconnected and disjointed' (Hencke, 1982). It is administered by three government departments (Energy, Environment and the Department of Health and Social Security); it is supplied by four separate industries (gas, electricity, coal and oil); and local authorities, charities and social securities pick up the bills for some of those people who cannot pay.

As the Central Policy Review Staff (1977) has pointed out, the fact is that 'government is plural, not singular'. For most practical purposes the concept of 'central government' is an abstraction which conceals the reality. In fact central government is more like 'a federation of separate departments' whose relations are typified more by competition than by co-operation, and whose instincts are to 'resist to the last any suggestion that they should relinquish some control over their resources or policies' (Dean, 1979). As a result, the development of a shared view on a common area of policy is a rare achievement and interdepartmental collaboration is the exception rather than the rule. In making and implementing policies, departments 'still act for most purposes in isolation from each other' (CPRS, 1977).

This compartmentalization of Whitehall makes it difficult for government to produce a co-ordinated response to problems or to formulate a collective view on priorities. It means that policy is generally conceived within administrative rather than functional boundaries. There is no effective mechanism for addressing those questions which transcend the boundaries of individual departments. In turn, this makes it hard for government to see and deal with people and problems 'in the round', another feature of incrementalism directly attributable to the social division of planning.

Much the same is true also of local government where the committee and departmental structure, with its ingrained traditions, loyalties and rivalries, tends to foster among members and officers alike a view of the authority as a grouping of 'separate firms operated by a parent company' (Bains, 1972). As the Paterson Report (1973) observed about Scottish local authorities, 'there is very little in the way of formal co-ordination across the whole range of an authority's activities'.

If departmentalism (the tendency to look at the world from behind one's own desk) is a major obstacle to strategic thinking in central and local government, its effects are also seen in the relationships between central departments and local authorities. Whitehall rarely speaks with one voice. Local authorities are prone to complain that poor co-ordination between government departments too often means that individually conflicting and collectively unrealizable demands are laid on them. There are many cases, for example, of local authorities being urged by ministers to improve their services while concurrent attempts are made by the Treasury and the Department of the Environment to reduce local government expenditure overall. At the same time, local authorities, and individual departments, vary greatly in their receptivity to influence from Whitehall. Local government in general is fiercely protective of its independence within the scope of the powers given by Parliament. Indeed, local authority autonomy represents another of those cracks in the structure of the state which give rise to the problems of information and compliance inherent in the social division of planning, and which contribute to social policy having more the appearance of a patchwork quilt than a seamless robe.

Failures of co-ordination, however, are not just a facet of relations between departments in central and local government or between central departments and local authorities. They also arise within departments. The House of Commons Social Services Committee, for example, has criticized the DHSS for its apparent lack of strategic policy-making and its failure to examine the overall impact of expenditure changes across the various services and programmes for which it is responsible. It went on 'to record its disappointment – and some dismay – at the continuing failure of the DHSS to adopt a coherent policy strategy across the administrative boundaries of individual services and programmes' (Social Services Committee, 1980). Two examples illustrate what the Committee had in mind –

both of them bearing on the interdependence of the health and social services:

1   The resources of the NHS are distributed according to a formula which seeks to take account of variations in need between different health regions. But as the Committee points out, this formula fails to take into account the level of complementary services provided in the community, and there are wide variations in the balance of services provided by the NHS and local authorities. The Committee questions the feasibility of planning services which, to some extent, depend on each other when expenditure decisions are taken independently.
2   The Committee criticizes the DHSS for planning cuts in the personal social services without attempting to assess their likely impact on the NHS or to estimate the extent to which they might result in a transfer of demands from the community services to the more expensive hospital sector.

The second example highlights the problems of information and collaboration presented by the social division of planning. The DHSS is unable to estimate the likely knock-on effects of reductions in social services spending, partly because it cannot foresee how far local authorities will implement any proposed cuts. Equally the DHSS is unable to estimate the likely transfer effects, partly because it lacks any reliable information about the substitutability of services and partly because it lacks information about local plans.

Social problems cannot be neatly pigeon-holed. They do not conveniently mesh with the structure of 'big government'. They spill over administrative boundaries and cut across lines of responsibility and command. Consequently, any effective response to the challenge they present almost always calls for co-operation between different parts of the government machine. Policy-making thus becomes, in part, the art of collaboration in dealing with the consequences of the social division of planning. The seeds of incrementalism are to be found in the failures of collaboration and the 'tunnel vision' they induce.

Collaboration and Interorganizational Relations

Thompson (1967) suggests that one organization is dependent on another to the extent that it relies on resources and services the other provides which cannot be obtained elsewhere. Following Blau (1964), dependence is sometimes presented as the obverse of power: 'A person who commands services which others need and who is independent of any at their command, attains power over others by making the satisfaction of their need contingent on their compliance.'

Power permits an organization to reach across agency boundaries and influence or dictate policies or practices in dependent organizations. Between these states of dependence and power are organizational relationships based on interdependence and reciprocity. Looking at organizations as boundary-maintaining systems, which seek to ensure their own survival and protect their own interests, collaboration may be viewed as one means by which they seek to manage their dependence. Within this framework, what are the motivations which frustrate or facilitate collaboration and under what conditions will it take place? The literature offers a wide choice of models which aim to answer this question of which three are particularly relevant here.

The *exchange model* conceives interorganizational relationships as a process of give and take. Organizations are basically goal-oriented and will collaborate voluntarily only when there is some mutual benefit to be derived from doing so: 'no goods or services are ever transferred without reciprocity of some kind being involved' (Levine and White, 1961). The currency of exchange is variable, with money, clients, services, skills and other less tangible commodities such as information or trust being bartered.

From this point of view, organizational interdependence may be seen as a predictor of collaboration (Litwak and Hylton, 1961–2). The more that organizations depend on each other in some way to accomplish their own ends, the greater their propensity or incentive to collaborate. In short, collaboration increases as autonomy decreases.

The exchange concept provides an understanding of the motivation for collaboration in terms of rational self-interest: organizations will only work together if they see it as being in their interest to do so. The exchange model recognizes that even where the sharing or transfer of resources may be desirable from the vantage point of the wider community, it will not take place without some form of coercion if one party is disadvantaged by the arrangement. Finally, the model acknowledges that collaboration is not a cheap option. It entails political and administrative costs which must be offset against the potential, though uncertain, benefits it might yield. Only if the investment promises a net gain to the organization will the risk be worth while.

The *political economy model* represents the pattern of interorganizational relations as a network of vested interests (Aldrich, 1972) whose participants are all busy pursuing the same ultimate aim of securing and maintaining an adequate supply of resources for their organization. Benson (1975) argues:

> Two basic types of resources are central to the political economy of interorganizational networks. These are money and authority. Organizational decision makers are oriented to the acquisition and defense of a

secure and adequate supply of these resources.

Authority is necessary to legitimate an organization's activities and money is necessary to fund them. Without both types of resources, the survival of an organization is threatened.

It is these fundamental considerations of resource acquisition which influence the sentiments and interactions of participants in the interorganizational network. They give rise to four basic 'action orientations' on which decision-makers draw in their dealings with outside agencies:

1 An inclination to protect and promote existing programmes, and to oppose any practices or proposals by other agencies which threaten to interfere with their fulfilment.
2 The preservation of the organization's sphere of operation.
3 The maintenance of a predictable supply of resources.
4 The defence of the organizational view on things, and a predisposition to dismiss outside definitions of problems and tasks which are seen as the prerogative of the agency.

According to Benson, the interorganizational network is in a state of equilibrium where there is agreement among the actors about the respective functions and spheres of operation of their agencies (what he calls 'domain consensus'); where participants agree about the definition of problems and tasks ('ideological consensus'); where they evaluate each other's work positively ('positive education'); and where working practices are closely integrated ('work coordination'). This state of equilibrium is characterized by 'highly coordinated, co-operative interactions based on normative consensus and mutual respect'. As such it defines the conditions for effective collaboration.

Benson argues that the precise balance to be found among these dimensions of equilibrium is determined by the underlying political and economic forces within the interorganizational network. For in the end administrators 'undertake or refuse to undertake co-operative ventures on the basis of reasonably careful calculations of costs and returns at the level of resource acquisition'.

Leach (1980) has partially reformulated Benson's model of the political economy by redefining the interorganizational network in terms of 'organisational interests'. Instead of pursuing money and authority, organizations are conceived as pursuing their own interests defined as 'those implicit, unstated aims of organisations which reflect the common interests of its members in terms of career prospects, status and power'.

According to Leach, the most fundamental organizational interest is survival. When it is not threatened, organizations mobilize to

protect their existing functions and associated resources. Having
secured the status quo, 'a search for sustained growth in activities
and resources' is often begun, the origins of which derive from the
interests of important people in the organization whose own prospects
and rewards are linked to the scale of their responsibilities. At the
same time, Leach argues, a number of second-order interests are
commonly pursued including 'the maximisation of autonomy' and
'the development of a favourable public image'. Pulling these various
threads together, he suggests:

> It is perhaps useful to picture. . .an organisation 'scanning its environ-
> ment', in search of opportunities to promote its interests and the existence
> of threats to these interests. Opportunities for growth in activities and
> resources will be taken so long as the perceived benefits are greater than
> the perceived costs. Threats to the survival, normal operation or autonomy
> of the organisation are met with 'dynamic conservatism', which operates
> in the form of strategies which embody the minimal compliance with the
> demand for change. In situations of enforced or voluntary inter-
> dependency with other organisations a similar range of strategies is
> employed, normally to 'maximise autonomy'.

The patterns of interaction and collaboration between organizations
are formed within this calculus of interests and strategies. The
interesting point about Leach's model is that by establishing a link
between the motivations of officials and the behaviour of organizations
he goes some way towards bridging the gap between the political
economy approach to interorganizational relations and the approach
of the third model reviewed here – the *economic model* of bureaucracy.

This model has emerged from attempts by economists to develop
an economic theory of the working of government and public
bureaucracy which will explain the supply of collective goods in the
same way as the theory of the firm explains the supply of private
goods in the market. It seeks to account for the output of public
services and the steady growth in the size of government in terms
of the purposive behaviour of individuals, in particular the motivations
and preferences of public employees. The key motivational assumption
is that public officials look after themselves.

For Breton (1974), 'bureaucrats seek to maximise the relative size
of their bureaus', for this is how they achieve the highest possible
incomes and prestige. Niskanen (1973) offers a slightly modified
version of this hypothesis when he argues that 'bureaucrats maximise
the total budget of their bureau'. They strive to do so, he suggests,
because their salary, perquisites of the office, public reputation,
power, patronage and the output of the bureau are all positively
related to the size of the budget they control; and because their
subordinates demand it (their rewards, opportunities and status are

similarly contingent on their office) and their masters expect the same.

Within this context, says Niskanen, 'the behaviour of bureaucrats and bureaus is primarily determined by the *incentives* and *constraints* specific to the bureaucracy'. The benefits and value of collaboration therefore will be judged, and action taken accordingly, in terms of whether it is likely to contribute to budget maximization or departmental growth rather than to the public interest or the general welfare.

Despite their major differences of approach, these three models of organizational behaviour and interaction hold similar implications about certain aspects of the process of collaboration:

1   They agree that collaboration is a self-interested process in which organizations will only participate if it suits their own ends, whether they are defined in somewhat reified terms like 'organizational goals' or, individualistically, in terms of the personal ambitions of office-holders.

2   They agree that the spirit of collaboration cannot be invoked by appeal to the public interest, and that organizations will not work together purely for the sake of the general welfare.

3   They suggest that the success of collaboration will be determined by the balance of incentives and constraints bearing on each of the parties.

4   They show the pursuit of narrow organizational interests to be rational in terms of an agency's survival and the security of its members.

5   They imply that organizations will generally seek to maximize their autonomy and minimize their dependency.

6   The exchange model and the political economy model in particular both attach great importance to the idea of 'domain consensus' as a prerequisite for successful collaboration. Without prior agreement between organizations on their legitimate spheres of operation and authority, relations will be stymied by persistent conflict over who does what.

The social division of planning creates relationships of power, dependence and reciprocity among organizations. The three models, described above, each throws some light on how these relationships unfurl and points to some of the factors that influence the outcome of collaboration. The next section draws on a case study of joint planning between the health and social services to illustrate the processes at work.

A Case Study in the Social Division of Planning
The development of more effective collaboration between the health and social services has been a prominent and consistent feature of national social policy under successive governments. Several factors help to explain the long-standing importance attached by government to the goal of better collaboration between health and social services authorities:

1   There is the interrelationship of needs in the community. The fact is that health and social needs overlap and shade into one another and are not divided into separate compartments.
2   There is the complementarity of services. The health and social services depend on each other in a host of ways which may lead to problems if their policies and priorities are not in step. Careful integration is seen as a prerequisite for the rational delivery of services.
3   There is value for money. Collaboration in resource allocation is held to be vital if costly waste and duplication are to be avoided; if economies of scale are to be achieved; if existing land and buildings are to be used effectively; and if better use of plant and equipment is to be obtained.
4   There are considerations of effectiveness. If the plans of each authority and the priorities they embody are not carefully aligned, then gaps and bottlenecks may arise to the detriment of the level and quality of services.
5   Effective collaboration is seen as a precondition of progress in the national strategy of developing community care which involves, among other things, shifting the balance of resources and responsibilities between the NHS and the personal social services.

Much of the early rhetoric of collaboration out of which national policy emerged was based on two key premises about the nature of the relationship between health and local authorities which together comprise what may be called a 'naïve position' on the challenge presented by joint care planning; they were:

(a) the *presumption of altruism* – the view that where benefits are to be had for patients and clients, then health and local authorities will collaborate purely for the good of the community they both serve;
(b) the *presumption of rationality* – the belief that authorities will collaborate where it can be shown they can achieve the same

ends more efficiently by working together than by going their own ways.

The reorganization of local government and the NHS in 1974 created new opportunities for closer liaison and greater co-operation. The new health and local authorities were organized into matching areas of administration. A statutory obligation was placed on them to collaborate so as to secure and advance the health and welfare of the people of their areas. The machinery for collaboration was established at local level.

Within this framework the experience of the next two years clearly showed that the invisible hand of altruism–cum–rationality was not enough to drive the motor of collaboration. Gradually perceptions of the issue and the difficulties it presented began to change as evidence of the lack of progress mounted. A more 'realistic stance' began to emerge as the realization spread that both health and local authorities are self-interested organizations which only co-operate when it suits them, or when they have to, and then very much on their own terms.

The Working Party on Collaboration between the NHS and Local Government (1973) stressed that the real objective is 'to secure genuinely collaborative methods of working throughout the process of planning', including 'the reallocation of the resources of both parties to conform to mutually agreed plans', in order to provide 'the most effective service for the community'.

This thinking was embodied in the first collaboration circular issued by the DHSS. Authorities were exhorted to sink their differences and work together for the common good:

> The aim of the collaborative proposals is to create an atmosphere of ready and informal co-operation at officer and member level so that the two sets of authorities can, despite their differing functions and structures, co-ordinate their services for the benefit of the people in their area. (DHSS, 1974a)

Although it was recognized that habits of joint working and joint planning would not develop without deliberate effort, the view from the centre was that the reorganization of the NHS and local government had created a climate in which they could flourish. Good communication between the health and social services was regarded 'as the single most important feature for bringing the two services into partnership' (DHSS, 1974b). Coterminosity of boundaries and the establishment of the Joint Consultative Committee (JCC) machinery, together with the appointment of specialist liaison officers at senior managerial level and the arrangements for cross-membership of local authorities on area health authorities (AHAs) were all seen to have created an organizational framework conducive to better communication. Accordingly it was expected that these arrangements for bringing the two sides together would eventually lead to effective collaboration as mutual understanding and confidence between them grew. Goodwill was the cement which would bind the partnership.

This analysis was soon shown to be faulty. Many areas encountered difficulties in setting up the JCC machinery, and others deliberately dragged their feet. Even those which responded positively were generally disappointed by the outcome of their efforts. As an advisory body only, the JCC lacked the power to turn decisions into actions. Consequently, it tended to become a forum where problems and grievances bearing on the two authorities were rehearsed rather than resolved.

The workings and procedures of local government were also frustrating to health administrators unaccustomed to a process of political decision-making and accountability. They tended to react impatiently to the inability of officers to commit themselves to a decision or policy, to the delay involved by reference back to the Committee and Council, and to the wasted effort when local politicians refused to endorse or sanction an agreement negotiated at officer level. At the same time, the managerial structure of the social services meant that the burden of extra work generated by joint planning fell almost entirely on the chief officer and a few members of the senior management team. When offset against its modest benefits, the administrative costs in terms of officer time were a disincentive to collaboration.

More seriously, however, it quickly became apparent to local authorities that the inducements to collaborate were skewed over-whelmingly in favour of health interests. The AHAs were critical of the deficiencies in social services which exacerbated the strain on their own resources or retarded their own plans. They sought to browbeat their local authorities into giving a greater priority to services for the elderly and mentally handicapped people, and into giving doctors a bigger say in who uses them (Booth, 1981a). In both these fields the efficient use of hospital beds and the rationalization of the hospital services depended on the adequate provision of residential and domiciliary services in the community. On the other hand, local authorities were not dependent on the health service in an equivalent way, and because they stood to gain so much less, their commitment was correspondingly lower. Indeed, most of them approached the business of joint planning reluctantly and many were obstructive. This conduct, in turn, bred impatience and resentment on the health side. Instead of generating an atmosphere of trust and goodwill, the new machinery produced only rivalry and suspicion.

This first and generally unproductive phase of relations was brought to a close by the growing recognition that the obstacles to collaboration were more serious and deep-rooted than had been initially suspected. The hope that the forces of altruism and economic rationality would be automatically released once the two sides began talking to each other was shown to have been naïve. Reality was more complicated, and the differences between health and local authorities in their organization, in the environment in which they operate and in their ways of working were discovered to be more troublesome than anticipated. Experience showed these differences to be:

(a) *political* – health and social services are subject to different kinds of political control and public accountability;
(b) *financial* – they are financed differently and have different budgetary processes;
(c) *organizational* – they operate with very different formal structures and administrative procedures;
(d) *professional* – they draw on different professional perspectives and traditions;
(e) *planning* – they face different demands on their resources, and have different perceptions of what are the most urgent problems; although the two authorities share a common concern for certain client groups, they rarely give the same priority to them.

Another lesson to emerge clearly was that the movement of cases between health and social services also involved the transfer of financial costs from one authority to another. At a time of growing financial uncertainty for local government, precipitated by the government's 'attack on inflation', authorities were ill-placed to meet the spending implications of a policy of community care.

In a bid to both protect social services budgets from the harsh consequences of expenditure cuts and to safeguard the priorities outlined in the 1976 Consultative Document (DHSS, 1976), Mrs Castle introduced her joint financing scheme for allowing health authorities limited use of NHS funds to support social services projects where the contribution in terms of total care is expected to be greater than if the same money had been spent directly on health services.

The introduction of joint financing changed the face of collaboration and joint planning. It altered the balance of incentives and constraints for social services authorities by bringing about a greater reciprocity in relations with AHAs. Initially, it provided a source of new money in a period of no growth and standstill budgets, so enabling an expansion of services which would not have taken place otherwise. Later, when the economic climate worsened, it provided a hedge against spending cuts and helped to cushion the social services from the more severe consequences of budgetary restraint. These benefits transformed the attitude of social services officers to collaboration and encouraged a more positive and forward-looking approach on their part.

At the same time, joint finance changed the pattern of dependence between the health and social services. With real benefits to be had by local authorities, collaboration was no longer the one-sided deal it had previously appeared. They became more receptive to the idea and prospects of using the joint planning machinery to get things done. This is not to underplay the difficulties and conflicts that were experienced in the early years of the scheme. But as the only source of money for growth in the social services, estimated at 0.5 per cent a year, joint finance was deemed to be worth the price of collaboration. As such, it gave AHAs a means of influencing local authority priorities. By offering financial support for some projects and schemes rather than others, they changed the balance of costs and benefits to local authorities of different paths of development, making some choices and options more (or less) attractive.

The success of joint financing exceeded all expectations for what had been a hurriedly devised scheme. What it showed most clearly was that authorities could be bribed into collaborating. They will only work together on their own terms which, broadly translated, means when they stand to gain (or lose something by not doing so). This lesson marked the shift to a more 'realistic' phase in national policy. Above all, joint finance taught that some sort of tangible inducement, in the form of a reward or sanction, which can be measured in terms of their own organizational interests, was an essential ingredient of any partnership between the health and social services.

At this point, a new problem emerged: how to finance collaboration if the only incentive is self-interest. The joint financing programme was too small to compensate local authorities for the full cost of the government's community care policies. Moreover, the detailed arrangements and working of the scheme limited the possibilities for expanding it much further. The tapering scale of (NHS) revenue support for projects made local authorities hesitant about over-committing their future resources at a time of great financial uncertainty. Also the scheme provides no guaranteed source of funds for major extensions of personal social services.

With these limitations in mind, the government declared that 'additional ways are needed of transferring resources to the personal social services to provide for people who would be better cared for outside hospital' (DHSS, 1981). A Consultative Document was published in 1981 inviting comments on six new suggestions for encouraging the transfer of patients from hospital to the care of social services departments, in addition to the extension of existing joint finance arrangements (ibid.). These suggestions were:

(a) lump-sum or annual payments by the health authority for each person discharged into the local authority's care;
(b) transfer of hospital buildings along with the people who no longer needed hospital care;
(c) pooling funds available for a particular client group;
(d) transferring funds at national level from the NHS to local government by an adjustment in public expenditure plans;
(e) earmarking NHS funds for use locally by social services departments;
(f) concentrating responsibility for particular client groups in one authority.

A characteristic of all these suggestions, which reflects the new 'realistic' stance on collaboration and joint planning by the central department, is the recognition they give to the self-interested motivation of both authorities, and the corollary that to be successful any scheme 'should contain some incentive for both health authorities and local government' (ibid.).

The response to these suggestions ruled out some on legal, administrative or financial grounds, but guidance on follow-up action was subsequently issued to health and social services (DHSS, 1983). It was decided to change the tapering arrangements for jointly funded schemes aimed at moving people out of hospital by extending the maximum duration of revenue support, so lengthening the time before the local authority has to pick up the bill.

Undoubtedly, though, the main innovation was the decision to allow health authorities to make lump-sum payments or continuing grants from their normal budget allocations to local authorities to pay for services which will enable people to move out of hospital into the care of the social services. The circular acknowledges that as such schemes gather momentum, then eventually a central transfer of resources will have to be made to accord with the permanent shift in the locus of responsibility. In the meantime the services to be paid for must be provided for identified individuals selected by 'joint assessment of a person's needs and of the most appropriate form of care for them'.

As well as building more financial bridges between the health and social services, so further interweaving their affairs, this proposal also promised to give the new District Health Authorities (DHAs) a great influence over the type and level of social services provided in their areas, and to give consultants in particular a bigger voice in who uses them. Once local authorities accept the bait of extra cash offered by this arrangement, they will be entrapped by legal and financial commitments into greater collaboration with DHAs at strategic, operational and case levels.

In trying to carry forward the achievements of joint finance, these proposals respect the fact that collaboration is not a free good for any of the parties, but a product which has to be bought and paid for by somebody. Whether they will succeed in producing a closer partnership between the health and social services is an open question. The story still has a long way to run, with no happy ending in sight. The 1982 reorganization of the NHS and the consequent loss of coterminosity in administrative boundaries certainly upped the ante in the collaboration stakes. Conflicts and disagreements over bridging arrangements for the transfer of hospital patients into the community are widespread. The signs are that 'district health authorities and local authorities frequently perceive the balance of incentives differently' (Wistow and Hardy, 1986). Some DHAs have taken their bat home and chosen to go it alone by opting to 'decentralize the hospital' and develop their own services in the community. Equally many local authorities have been dragging their feet, fearful that NHS bridging finance will be insufficient to meet the transfer costs accruing to them of caring for relocated patients. In the wheeling and dealing now going on about these issues both sides draw on a range of stratagems to protect their interests, including, following Lindblom (1965):

(a) *bargaining or negotiation* – through which each side seeks to reach agreement on a mutually acceptable trade-off;
(b) *persuasion* – by which one side tries to convince the other to accept its own definition of the situation;
(c) *compensation* – in which one side offers to reimburse the costs (financial or otherwise) of the other's compliance;
(d) *reciprocity* – a process of exchange from which both sides gain;
(e) *prescription* – in which one side defers to the other's authority or professional judgement;
(f) *manipulation* – in which the sides try to outmanoeuvre each other.

These stratagems indicate the variety of relationships subsumed under the notion of collaboration and the complexity of the process to which it refers. They show how the social division of planning between the health and social services leads to ways of working more suited to incremental progress than to fundamental change.

Summary

This chapter has argued that the incremental nature of public policy-making and the lack of any strategic framework for determining priorities in the field of social policy is a direct consequence of the social division of planning.

The social division of planning describes the fragmentation of powers and responsibilities in a complex and structurally differentiated society, and especially within the administrative apparatus of the state. It leads directly to problems of information and collaboration that hinder any sort of rational planning along the lines described in Chapter 1.

The chapter has outlined some key features of the social division of planning: the division between the public and private sectors, the artificial segregation of economic and social policy (as witnessed especially in the working of the PESC process of public expenditure control and in the public burden model of welfare) and the departmentalism within central and local government. The problems of collaboration presented by the social division of planning have been illustrated by a case study of the health and social services. The rest of this book focuses mainly on the problem of information.

3 Economic growth and social progress

'Growth rates of GNP are entirely valid and necessary economic indicators, but they are not adequate measures of the development of a nation.' (Robert S. McNamara)

In 1971 an interdepartmental Whitehall committee compiled a secret report on smoking and health. Almost ten years later it was leaked to the press. Its conclusions make depressing reading. A reduction in smoking would certainly lead to a parallel drop in invalidism and premature deaths but, the committee reasoned, such an improvement in the health of the nation would be undesirable. If two out of every five smokers kicked the habit, we should have to face the problem of caring for an extra 100 000 old people every year. Any savings in the costs of treating the victims of tobacco poisoning would be more than offset by the extra retirement pensions that the state would have to pay to the survivors. Moreover, the report went on, if people stopped spending so much of their income on a heavily taxed commodity like tobacco, they would have more money to buy other goods such as imported washing machines, video recorders and cars. Over a five-year period, a 20 per cent fall in cigarette consumption would produce a nasty deficit on the balance of payments. Therefore, on balance, the report argued that it would be better for the economy if people were left to smoke themselves into an early grave.

This cynical little story illustrates two points bearing on the theme of this chapter. The first lesson is simply that economics does not distinguish between what money is spent on. A pound is a pound whether it is spent on health or illness. This is most clearly seen at the macro-level where a billion pounds worth of exports goes down as a healthy plus in the national accounts whether it comes from the sale of arms or the sale of medicines: life and death are both valued on the same scales.

Another way of saying the same thing is that, for the economist, all pounds are worth the same (except perhaps in one respect, that private pounds are often seen as honest and productive, whereas public pounds are feckless and wasteful). A pound spent on medical care for someone suffering from a smoking-related disease or disability is the same as the pound in tax forgone from someone else who has given up cigarettes. This failure to differentiate what money is spent on is a habit of economists and a crippling weakness of economic analysis (Thomas, 1980).

A second lesson to be drawn from the thinking of those who calculated that it is better, for bookkeeping purposes, to allow a lot of us to kill ourselves before our time is that social policy is gravely subservient to traditional interpretations of what is good for the economy (Townsend, 1976). Narrow economic considerations too often dictate or distort social choices. The ascendancy of these attitudes in the conduct of our national affairs surfaces in all sorts of ways.

One example was cited in Chapter 2 as an expression of the social division of planning: the artificial segregation of economic and social policies. It shows also in the tendency for changes in the structure of taxation to be conceived solely in economic terms. Fiscal policy is used as a means of regulating the economy and the amount of taxes to be collected is adjusted to fit in with economic objectives. Tax rates are usually increased during inflationary periods and decreased when growth is low. In times of recession taxes on corporations and higher income groups are usually lowered more than those on lower income groups in order to expand investment and incentives. When inflationary pressures threaten, the tendency is to raise taxes more on lower income groups in order to reduce total demand since, taken as a whole, they spend more on consumption than higher income groups. In this way, the poor become the 'price-regulators of society' suffering unemployment in order to dampen prices. The social aims of progressivity and redistribution are thus 'sacrificed to political expediency and to national economic goals of stimulating growth or retarding inflation' (Miller and Rein, 1975). When Mrs Thatcher and her Chancellor, Sir Geoffrey Howe, put £3.5 billion in the pockets of the better-off by abolishing the 80 per cent tax band in the name of incentives, they gave no thought to the social costs of this measure in terms of the cuts in public services that helped to pay for it.

The ascendancy of economic ideas shows up clearly, too, in prevailing attitudes to economic growth which so often fail to address the question of 'growth for what?'. Why, as Abel-Smith (1966) asked, do we want economic growth if it is not to promote social ends? A rising national income has been too easily equated with improving national well-being. It has been forgotten that what goes into gross national product (GNP), not just its level or rate of growth, is important to individual welfare and the social health of the nation (Miller, 1975). The same GNP can have a very different distributional impact depending on the composition of the output, the way it is produced and the pricing of its components. The narrow-minded pursuit of 'growthmanship' has masked the real issue of what is being produced and distributed and with what physical and social effects (Miller and Rein, 1975).

From this point of view, economics is trapped in its own mathematical formulae. It must work with numerical quantities but not everything that matters can be counted. There is no room in the national income accounts for 'quality of life', for well-being or for deprivation. These accounts are a poor and inadequate measure of the condition of society. As Olson (1969a) says, they leave out most of the things that make life worth living such as the value of good health, safe streets, clean air, cultural amenities and stable institutions. The dethronement of GNP is an important challenge to social planners, and a necessary one if social development is to be given its rightful place on the political agenda:

> We accept too readily the precedence of economic institutions and the distribution of human resources in accordance with narrowly economic assumptions . . . If national progress were measured more against social objectives like the removal of poverty, the establishment of an effective system of civil rights, and the integration of racial groups, instead of the rate of economic growth, different priorities for political action would be produced. (Townsend, 1970)

But perhaps the surest signs of the ascendancy of economic criteria over social values in the setting of national priorities are the preoccupation of politicians with economic issues, the prestige enjoyed by economists as policy advisers within government and the scale of investment in economic information and analysis.

In contemporary Britain the central political issues are virtually all economic: 'There cannot be a politician alive who does not believe that successful economic management is itself a necessary, and probably sufficient, condition for electoral success' (Keegan and Pennant-Rea, 1979). An umbilical cord therefore binds politicians to economics. Indeed, in the USA the situation has advanced to the point where, increasingly, economists are becoming politicians. In the Carter administration there were no fewer than five economists in the Cabinet or holding Cabinet rank. As Galbraith (1978) has observed, a PhD in economics has replaced a law degree as the basic licence for practising the science and art of public administration.

These links were forged initially by the Keynesian revolution.

Classical economics had assumed the free market could ensure full employment. Keynes demonstrated the error of this view and showed how unemployment could persist indefinitely unless governments intervened to remedy it by the management of aggregate demand. His ideas led governments on both sides of the Atlantic, in the 1940s, to commit themselves to policies aimed at the maintenance of full employment. In this way, politicians assumed the responsibility for economic conditions which previously had been ascribed to impersonal market forces.

These new ideas were mirrored by parallel changes in the theory and practice of public budgeting. Traditionally budgeting and policy-making in the public sector were held to be radically different operations (RIPA, 1959). According to this convention, policy-makers decided what ought to be done and, as a separate exercise, finance or treasury officials decided how much the government could afford. The task of budget-making was to find a compromise between these two points of view (Smithies, 1968). This distinction between budgeting and policy-making only survived, however, in a world where the level of public expenditure was small in relation to national income. For then the problem of financing the budget was largely the political one of overcoming the reluctance of people to pay taxes. As government spending rose it became clear that the methods of financing public expenditure had marked effects on such things as the level of employment, income distribution and the rate of economic growth. This realization led to the prevailing Treasury view that 'finance must determine expenditure, not expenditure determine finance'. It also resulted in a shift of thinking away from the traditional demarcation between finance and policy to the view that, again in the words of the Treasury, 'finance is something integral with policy and cannot be disassociated from it' (Booth, 1979b). These two principles heightened the concern of politicians with the economic consequences of policy and effectively rendered social policy subordinate to the demands of the economy. The upshot has been that economic criteria have come to play an increasingly important part in political decision-making to the extent that, as Schonfield (1972) put it, 'social variables are often cast misleadingly in economic terms'.

These developments have prompted governments to call more and more on the advice of economists. In Western Europe and the USA economics more than any other social science discipline has gained the ear of policy-makers (ibid.). In 1961 there were only twelve economists in the central government in Britain and their numbers had barely expanded to twenty-five by 1964 (Keeling, 1972). Yet over the next ten years there was a fifteenfold increase in the employment of professional economists within Whitehall departments – a process of recruitment that has been sarcastically called Britain's 'economics miracle' (Booth and Coats, 1978). By the mid-1970s the economists had penetrated the prestigious second floor of the Treasury Chambers and even that part known as the Rotunda. Nowadays most major government departments employ a Chief Economic Adviser with the minimum status of Under-Secretary. This influx of leading academic economists has marked government service with a professional approval it does not have in other disciplines.

As their numbers have increased, so their role has changed. Professor Cairncross, who became the government's Chief Economic Adviser in 1961, was modest about the limits of his job: 'The principal task of an economic adviser is to prevent the government from making crashing mistakes' (quoted in Sampson, 1962). Certainly, it is important not to overplay their influence. Only in rare cases will a senior economic adviser change a minister's mind on a major issue of policy and, even then, only with the firm backing of top administrators, particularly the Permanent Secretary (Peacock, 1977). But economists have found their slot as organizers of economic intelligence services, as a conduit between policy-makers and the academic community, as monitors of the constant stream of outside advice which bombards ministers, as suppliers of the economic dimension to policy issues and, occasionally, as policy innovators.

Today any government will normally attempt to forecast the economic consequences of its policy proposals. In this way, economics often sets the actual terms in which questions of policy are posed (Schonfield, 1972). Moreover, this authority has come about despite the 'relative and surprising lack of success of economic theory in producing either reliable short-term or reliable long-term predictions' (Rothschild, 1982). As a former Permanent Secretary at the Treasury has observed, major uncertainties and controversies have arisen on some fundamental issues affecting the analysis of economic behaviour and economic policy but increasingly sophisticated technical analysis has not yet brought greater precision to forecasting or management (Wass, 1978). Faced with 'the challenge of uncertainty and ignorance', Wass calls for 'more, not less, research into the behaviour of the economy'. No one in the Treasury believes that economic policy can be run on the assumption that economic forecasts are going to be right. But everyone now accepts that forecasts are essential to the process of decision-making by setting a framework for exercising the art of judgement (Young and Sloman, 1984):

> Government without economists, or at least without the vision and the ideas of the economists, is a sad affair. It then becomes a blind beast plunging madly in response to pricks and jabs which it can neither avoid nor understand. (Boulding, 1958)

There is no clearer sign that 'nowadays the economic issues dictate all others' (*Guardian*, 12 March, 1981) than the lack of similar recognition given to the role and expertise of the social policy adviser in Whitehall, to the need for more, not less, social research and to the importance of assessing the social consequences of government policies. Without the ideas and vision of the social scientist government is still plunging wildly in the field of social policy.

Policy-makers are receptive to economists not only because they believe that economists have something useful to say, but also because economists have a demonstrable professional expertise or 'mystery' (Sharpe, 1978). In large part this mystery is based on postwar developments in national economic accounting, economic indicators and econometric modelling: developments that, according to Jackson (1980), amount to 'an "information revolution" of breath-taking proportions':

> Not only has the quantity of information greatly increased, but there has also been a concomitant improvement in quality and detail ... Furthermore, the economic 'articulation' of these statistics has been substantially enhanced in that the connections between related sets of data are now much more clearly set forth. (Jackson, 1981)

This facility for measuring 'manageable aggregates' of data (meaning the kind of information that people with power can use to manage change) is, Schonfield (1972) argues, 'the decisive difference between economics and the other social sciences as a policy-making instrument'; one 'which would alone justify the attention paid to it by policy-makers'.

Certainly, the richness and sophistication of our national economic and financial statistics present a striking contrast to the patchiness and rudimentary state of our social statistics. This uneven development is generally believed to stem from two characteristic features of economics which separate the discipline from its 'softer' stablemates in the social sciences. On the one hand, there is far greater consensus on the theoretical foundations and conceptual underpinnings of economic discourse. Economics draws on a comprehensive theoretical framework which, at least in principle, specifies the relationships between the key economic variables and aggregates. On the other hand, economics enjoys the advantage of dealing with things and quantities that can be measured using a single scale of value – money or relative prices. This has enabled a much greater degree of statistical and operational precision than is possible in the field of social policy, for example, where the relationships between key variables are frequently contested or frankly incommensurable. These two charac-teristics – a model of the economy and a method of aggregation –

have been instrumental in the rapid evolution of national economic accounting as compared with the retarded state of any equivalent form of social reporting.

National Economic Accounting

National economic accounting – the power and the glory of modern macro-economics – is 'a highly developed form of monetary bookkeeping on a nationwide scale' (Gross, 1965). The national accounts present a bird's eye view of the linkages between different parts of the economic system. They do so by means of a set of basic balances: total income must equal total output; savings must equal investment; inputs of materials, labour and capital must be accounted for in their use in outputs for the whole economy and for each industry; and payments to the rest of the world must equal receipts from the rest of the world.

The aggregation involved in the construction of these basic balances is made possible because monetary units are used to determine the relative weight or importance of one kind of output as against a different type of output. If the number of washing-machines has gone up by a million since last year, while the output of wheat has fallen by a million bushels, we need to know the relative importance of these two changes before any judgement can be reached about the movement of the economy as a whole. It would obviously be arbitrary to compare them in terms of the relative weight in tons of washing-machines and bushels of wheat. Instead the relative prices of these two commodities are used to make possible such a comparison in the national income and product accounts. By contrast, the 'weights' needed for aggregate indices of other social statistics are not available. There are no objective weights, equivalent to prices, that can be used to compare the relative importance of an improvement in health, an increase in social mobility, a decline in the divorce rate or a drop in crime. For this reason, it would be foolhardy to strive for a single index of Gross Social Product or Net National Welfare (US Department of Health, Education and Welfare, 1969).

Nevertheless, the elegance and technical ingenuity of the national economic accounts should not be allowed to deceive us into thinking they present anything like a true measure of individual welfare or national well-being. Indeed, even as indicators of national economic activity and performance their shortcomings are serious and manifold. Perhaps the most conspicuous is their failure adequately to record the costs and benefits of things that are not the object of market transactions. Three examples stand out as being particularly important.

The national income and product accounts fail to pick up those by-products of the process of production and consumption known in the jargon as 'externalities' or 'spill-over effects'. These come in two sorts. 'External economies' refer to the benefits which accrue to others aside from the immediate consumers of some goods or services. Health and education services, for example, produce benefits for society as a whole in the form of a literate, skilled and productive workforce. 'External diseconomies' refer to costs which do not enter into the internal costs of production, but fall on the wider community. These are illustrated by, for example, the harmful effects of smoking, the toll from road accidents and the damage caused by industrial pollution. Such externalities constitute costs and benefits that are not reflected in the market price of goods and services. For this reason, the market price of these goods and services is not a true measure of their marginal value to society. To the same extent, the national product accounts, which only record market transactions, are not a true measure of the value of national output. If as some writers argue (see e.g. Mishan, 1969) the costs of these external diseconomies are increasing faster than the output of goods and services, then economic growth may be accompanied by a reduction in the quality of life.

Another shortcoming of the national economic accounts is that they understate or misrepresent the value of public services to society. The output of public services is arbitrarily calculated in terms of the cost of their inputs. Thus, for example, in the case of the NHS its ouput is valued in terms of the costs of doctors' and nurses' salaries, the maintenance and building of hospitals, drugs and equipment, and so on, rather than its contribution to the health of the nation. There are two reasons for this practice. First, there is no price to serve as an index of value because public services are not marketed. Secondly, the output of public services is difficult to measure in money terms which is the only unit of value that can be accommodated within the framework of the national accounts. The consequence is that only spending on public services is recorded and not the benefits they produce. For this reason, public services cannot increase their productivity or the growth rate – not because they are incapable of treating more patients or teaching more children or satisfying people's wants, but because our statistical conventions debar them from adding to the value of the inputs they consume. As a result, the greater the share of final expenditure that is accounted for by the public services, the less relevance GNP growth has to individual welfare and the greater the possible misrepresentation of the rate of growth (Glennerster, 1976). Similarly, the effect of government policies aimed at the privatization of public services and the expansion of the private market in the provision of social care (as an alternative to statutory services) is to increase national output, even though nothing extra is being produced.

A third important defect of the national economic accounts is their neglect of the informal economy, for there are two economies (Shankland with Turner, 1984). The formal or officially enumerated economy comprises those economic activities which are counted, measured, taxed and statistically defined. Traditionally it encompasses all recorded monetary transactions in the primary, secondary and tertiary sectors. By contrast, the economic activities in the informal economy are officially uncounted and mostly unrecorded. They are not recorded because our present set of accounts only recognizes that human capital produces an output when its services are purchased in the market (Juster, 1973). Yet there exists a vast area of vital, wholly unpaid work on which even sophisticated Western societies are dependent as well as a huge range of essential or useful forms of human exchange which, although not marketable, are indispensable for the good life, or in some cases even survival. The concept of the 'dual economy' has arisen because it has become increasingly obvious that the officially enumerated economy, centred exclusively on paid employment, does not embrace all of economic life (Shankland with Turner, 1984); in short, that there is a difference between jobs and work. Jobs are paid employment in the formal economy, while work includes other forms of productive activity, mostly unpaid, much of it in and around the home. The same amount of time is spent in work at home as in paid employment but few economists have bothered to analyse how these hours in the informal economy are spent. Shankland with Turner (1984) spell out the puzzle:

> Only some eight hours of [a typical twenty-four-hour day] is spent in sleep. Those who are employed in the formal economy work nowadays at the most eight hours of the remaining sixteen; in any event this 'working population' constitutes only 26 million of the total population of 56 million. Only 58 per cent of the total population is of 'working age' (between 16 and retirement) and many of these are not recorded as formally working. What is everybody else doing? What, for that matter, is this 'working' population doing in their remaining eight hours not spent sleeping?
>
> Clearly formal 'work' only covers part of what can legitimately be called work, even for those in 'formal' employment, as not everything they do in the eight hours left to them could be called 'leisure'. For the remainder, mostly 'housekeepers', it is obviously absurd to consider most of their 'waking time' as leisure.

At the core of the informal economy is the domestic or household economy. It is the largest labour pool of all in which transactions are conducted almost wholly without cash. Its full-time workers are all 'housekeepers', mostly women, who cook, clean, wash, mend, rear children, look after granny and manage the household. Its part-timers are almost everyone else: those who, as well as sharing in the housekeeping, repair the car, fix the plumbing, put up shelves, paint the house and tend the garden in the evenings and at weekends. If these tasks were not done domestically, most would have to be paid for; only then would their value be officially recognized. The taxed income they generated would be counted and national output would increase. Hence the quip that when a man marries his housekeeper the GNP falls.

The size of the household economy is startling. Estimates in the USA put the value of household labour in 1968 as equal to almost half of total, after-tax labour income in the formal sector. The sum of women's imputed household wages alone was greater than the total amount paid in wages and salaries in manufacturing industry. In the USA the household economy is about a third of the size of the market economy and yields almost half the value of disposable income. Households are also responsible for capital investment on a vast scale. Most of it is in home ownership but increasingly, too, in other assets such as domestic equipment. It is about time that economists – mostly male – realized that washing-machines, etc. are capital equipment and perform exactly the same function as machines in factories, altering the capital–labour ratio so output is increased. As such – as one correspondent in the *Guardian* has indignantly observed – they should properly be included in the Gross Domestic Fixed Capital section of the national income tables: 'If I did the family wash by hand, I would not have to time teach economics and statistics; with a washing machine I both wash and teach' (Davies, 1982). Scott Burns (1975) has summarized the results of studies in the USA which attempt to put a price on the value of labour and capital assets in the home:

> If all the work done within the household by men and women were monetized, the total would be equal to the entire amount paid out in wages and salaries by every corporation in the United States. Similarly, the assets commanded by households, worth more than a trillion dollars, produce an annual return in goods and services almost equal to the net profit of every corporation in the United States. Very, very little of this appears in the conventional accountings for the gross national product. This is like assuming that something between a quarter and a third of our total economic product does not exist.

The informal economy, however, extends beyond the household. It also includes an army of people who are not recorded as 'active' in the labour force statistics, tax records or other official files, but who contribute vital services either voluntarily, as in the case of work for charities, community organizations, self-help groups and informal care networks, or for cash payments below minimum tax levels, as in the case of baby-sitters, gardeners, daily helps, handymen, delivery boys, etc. Many people, of course, have a foot in both economies.

The national accounts ignore the part played by this unmapped dimension of economic life in adding to people's security and well-being. Moreover, demographic changes, the impact of new technology, structural shifts in patterns of employment and government policies (for example, the emphasis on informal care by the community) are all tending to expand the informal economy. Consequently, as Shankland with Turner (1984) point out, it 'is increasingly dangerous and misleading to depend entirely on these official measurements of allegedly useful "productive" activity to regulate our national and international economic relations'. It is equally true that economic growth becomes ever more meaningless as an indicator of levels of living or the condition of society.

The informal economy must be distinguished from the 'black' or 'hidden' economy. The former, though uncounted, is entirely above-board and legal. The black economy, on the other hand, refers to the unlawful world of 'moonlighting', tax evasion and fiddling. It is made up of undeclared earnings in cash and in kind which avoid the tax net and, in consequence, fail to show up in the national income accounts.

Guesstimates of the size of the black economy, commonly based on discrepancies between surveys of people's income and expenditure, are inherently suspect and unreliable, varying as they do from a low of just over 1 per cent of GNP to a high of a quarter and more. The US Internal Revenue Service (IRS) puts the share of the black economy at somewhere between 5.9 and 7.9 per cent of the GNP. The IRS reckons that some 15–20 million Americans fail to declare income worth several hundred billion dollars, and that 4.5 million people live entirely on earnings from subterranean jobs. In Britain the last time the Inland Revenue put its finger to the wind it plucked out a figure of 2.3 million 'ghost' workers with undeclared income in 1978–79 totalling 7.5 per cent of GDP.

There is some dispute about the effects of the black economy. Some regard tax-dodging as a national disease threatening to undermine legitimate businesses, to erode the moral basis of the tax system and to hold down the social wage. For others, providing it can be kept within limited bounds, the black economy may reduce the disincentive effects of taxation, add to social relationships (especially by providing work for the unemployed), supplement the 'survival strategies' of the poor and facilitate some jobs that simply would not be undertaken at all if they were confined to the formal economy. There is also speculation about whether the black economy is growing. Most of the rather flimsy evidence suggests something of a boom fed by the expansion in self-employment, the growth in the number of small businesses, the rising level of unemployment, and the cuts in Inland Revenue staff and Customs and Excise officers. Whatever the reality, the fact is that all this underground economic activity produces income and output that appear nowhere in the national accounts.

Aside from these important omissions and shortcomings there are other reasons why national accounting variables expressed in monetary terms such as GNP or consumption per head do not provide an adequate measure of the conditions in which people live.

The national income and product figures make no distinction between the objects of production, yet the composition of the national product may considerably influence its effect on welfare. Some items that make up the national product have no, or very little, impact on the well-being of the population (Drewnowski, 1971). The classical example often cited is the pyramids: more up-to-date examples might include *Concorde*, nuclear weapons and the Humber bridge. One million pounds spent on perfumes or machine-guns is valued just the same as a million pounds spent on children's clothing or sewage disposal. All are assumed to contribute in equal measure to the satisfaction of human needs and all of these needs are assumed to be of the same order. Yet the market valuation of goods and services is not necessarily related to their welfare content. Clearly, there is likely to be a difference in the quality of life between two societies with the same objective levels of economic prosperity where one ploughs its resources into military spending (security against external threat), while the other gives priority to social expenditure (security against want). A more discriminating assessment of the consequences of different kinds of spending is required than can be gleaned from the national income accounts.

In the same way, the distribution of GNP may be as important as its level in terms of the effects it has on living standards. A society where most of the income and wealth is concentrated in the hands of a few will be a very different place in which to live than another, equally rich, but with a more equal pattern of distribution. In fact GNP measures generally obscure distributional effects by averaging.

For both these reasons, the structure of GNP – what is being produced and how it is distributed – is a crucial factor in determining the true results of development:

> The questions to ask about a country's development are . . . what has been happening to poverty? What has been happening to unemployment? What has been happening to inequality? If all three of these have declined

from high levels, then beyond doubt this has been a period of development for the country concerned. If one or two of these central problems have been growing worse, especially if all three have, it would be strange to call the result 'development', even if per capita income doubled. (Seers, 1969)

National accounting 'consumption' represents only the monetary value of resources available for the satisfaction of human wants. What is actually created with those resources should really be expressed in terms of social indicators that convey the conditions in which people actually live. The national income statistics are one kind of indicator: of the amount of goods and services at our disposal. But they tell us little about the learning of our children, the pollution of the environment, the quality of our culture or the toll of illness (US Department of Health, Education and Welfare, 1969). Quite apart from the economic challenge of producing goods and services is the social challenge of using those resources in ways which enhance individual welfare and lead to social growth and betterment (Drewnowski, 1971).

Finally, other commonly cited reasons for being wary of reading too much into the national income statistics, or relying too heavily on them as surrogate indicators of development, include:

1   Failure to distinguish adequately between income and capital when dealing with the depletion of national resources. Over-fishing and over-intensive farming show up as pluses for the GNP, in terms of the income they generate, rather than as a depreciation of natural capital. The accounts do not allow for the exhaustion of scarce mineral resources, nor for the wearing out of the fertility of agricultural land, the erosion of topsoil, the effects of acid rain on forests, the loss of fish stocks. They allow fully for the need to replace the North Sea oil rigs but not the oil. If full allowance was made for the depreciation of these 'gifts of nature', the national income would fall.

2   They ignore changes in the quality of commodities not reflected in changes in price. The issue is partly one of 'accelerated obsolescence', where manufacturers deliberately shorten the life-span of durable goods, such as motor cars, but it also includes improvements in quality such as has occurred in the package-holiday business.

3   They tend to ignore investment in people and institutions. These benefits are easily taken for granted in well-educated and stable Western societies but their value is more evident in newly industrializing or emergent countries. As President Kaunda of Zambia has declared, 'We need to remember that efficiency

cannot be measured wholly or even chiefly in terms of results that can be reduced to quantifiable terms. . .decentralization and the winning of power by the people. . .produce results in terms of human dignity and human self-fulfilment which are incapable of being expressed in any statistical form at all. Yet they remain things of profound importance in terms of the quality of life of our people' (quoted in Conyers, 1982).

4   There are significant dimensions of welfare that cannot be accommodated within an accounting framework that requires a single unit of measure (Juster, 1973). Important among these are subjective variables such as the feeling of security and of personal fulfilment, as well as more objective criteria such as social integration, family stability, crime, nutritional standards and health chances.

Irrespective of these shortcomings, the development of national economic accounting has provided an enormously fruitful conjunction of basic and applied research opportunities. It has allowed economists to work at the forefront of their own science – especially the articulation of macro-economic theory – while contributing in a very practical way to the understanding and everyday management of economic life. By these means, they have increased both their mastery and their prestige. One important offshoot of national income accounting has been the work on macro-economic model building.

Macro-Econometric Modelling

The publication of quarterly data within a national income accounting framework paved the way for macro-economic model-building. This involves the attempt to describe an entire economy in mathematical and statistical terms:

> A macroeconometric model is a mathematical representation of the quantitative relationships among macroeconomic variables such as employment, national output, government expenditure, taxes, prices, interest rates and exchange rates. Its equations comprise technical relations and accounting identities that reflect the national income accounting framework, and behavioural equations that describe the aggregate actions of consumers, producers, investors, financial institutions and so forth. (Wallis, 1984)

The first models were developed by the Dutch economist, Jan Tinbergen, in studies of the Netherlands and the USA; the first UK model was built in Oxford in the late 1950s. In the earliest studies all the calculations had to be done laboriously by mechanical means. This restricted the choice of methods to the simplest and limited the size and the range of applications of the systems. Subsequent advances in econometric techniques and computer technology have facilitated a gradual increase in the size of models and their degree of sophistication (e.g. in dealing with many non-linear processes) as well as enabling researchers to be more experimental in testing ideas. They have also reduced the cost of model-building, so allowing competing versions to be constructed for different purposes and in accordance with different views of the economy. It is now possible for econometricians to vary their forecasts according to different assumptions about events with great flexibility and to study policy alternatives involving the complex, dynamic behaviour of large systems of equations.

Many of these key equations are derived from macro-economic theory and established by historical data and by observation of the real world. Others – especially the behavioural relationships – are less well founded empirically and rest heavily on a-priori assumptions. Variations in these assumptions together with basic theoretical wrangles about how the economy actually works produce big differences in the behaviour of different models. There are six models in the UK, three quarterly and three annual ones, and each reflects the purposes and prejudices of its builders.

The three annual models are the Cambridge Growth Project (CGP), the City University Business School (CUBS) and the Liverpool University Research Group in Macroeconomics (LPL):

1 The CGP model is basically of the Keynesian type, giving only a minor role to the money supply and with primary adjustments to changes showing through quantities rather than relative prices. It is very detailed with almost 5,000 endogenous variables, 3,000 exogenous variables and around 16 000 behavioural parameters and co-efficients.

2 The CUBS model is small, with just under 130 variables and 10 behavioural equations, and differs from most of the others in its emphasis on supply-side factors in the determination of output.

3 The LPL model is built on monetarist foundations, in that higher monetary growth leads directly to an increase in inflation. Again, it is a small model with under 20 behavioural equations and just over 50 variables in total.

The three quarterly models are operated by the London Business School (LBS), the National Institute of Economic and Social Research (NIESR) and the Treasury:

1 The LBS model, like the other quarterly models, is built around the income–expenditure framework set out in the national accounts. It is often referred to as an 'international monetarist'

model because it gives the money supply a direct influence on the exchange rate. Also prices are given a greater role than in traditional Keynesian economics. The model comprises some 400 variables with over 160 behavioural equations.

2 The NIESR model is built on Keynesian specifications, being driven more by expenditures than by relative price factors. It distinguishes about 275 variables and incorporates some 90 behavioural equations.

3 The Treasury model is the biggest of the quarterly models. Its size – 700 equations and 1,000 variables – reflects its detailed treatment of the public sector. The model 'focusses on explaining the flows of expenditure by households, by firms and from overseas buyers which, together with government expenditure, determine the behaviour of the gross domestic product' (Ball, 1978). As with most of the models, its specifications are continually changing. In recent years, for example, changes have been introduced, in line with current political thinking, to give monetary factors a greater influence in the inflation process.

Even the largest models are an enormous simplification of the real world. Along with the fact that they are built on behavioural assumptions and econometric relationships, about which there is continuing disagreement among economists, it is not surprising therefore to find they come up with different answers when asked the same questions; nor is it surprising to find them biased towards the theoretical preoccupations of their originators or, in the case of the Treasury model, biased in support of the policy of the government of the day. As the Royal Society argued in their evidence to the Rothschild (1982) inquiry into the Social Science Research Council, the development of several different models of the economy lessens this danger: 'The fact that they may give different answers may be inconvenient, but at least highlights the uncertainties and may illuminate the nature of the problem even if the forecasts themselves are of limited or doubtful value.'

Certainly, the models have not displaced the role of judgement in the making of decisions about economic policy. Comparative assessments of their performance have shown them to be no more accurate in their forecasts than less formal methods, and the work of building larger and more complex models has not led to any improvement in their accuracy (MacRae Jr, 1985). What they have done is to reduce the purely subjective element in economic forecasting and to strengthen the empirical basis of policy analysis. These points are well illustrated by examination of the uses and limitations of the Treasury model of the economy.

The Treasury model now plays a central part in the formulation of economic policy. It is used to regularly monitor economic prospects; it provides much of the information on which the government's budget strategy is based; and it is used to produce the medium-term economic forecast which serves as the backcloth for the annual review of public expenditure.

Aside from its role in forecasting the future performance of the economy, the model also serves as a major tool of analysis for testing the likely effects of marginal changes in policy. Treasury boffins use it to simulate what might happen to the economy if the government chooses to pull some of the levers it controls or to assess what combination of policy measures seems most likely to keep the economy on an optimum course. By adjusting one economic variable, or some combination of variables, such as interest rates, the money supply, PSBR, taxation, public spending or the exchange rate, economists are able to forecast what the ramifications might be on the rest of the economy in terms of the effects on employment, prices, the balance of payments, output, and so on.

The model-builders have been attacked by those who argue that forecasting is either wholly unreliable or unnecessary, or both. The Thatcher government, which eschewed fine-tuning of the economy, did briefly consider abandoning what it held to be this mumbo-jumbo but found that it was technically necessary to go on forecasting in pursuit of its political aims. It is now generally recognized, as a former senior Treasury official put it, that 'the forecasts are essential to the process of decision-making within the government' (quoted in Young and Sloman, 1984). A former Permanent Secretary at the Treasury has likewise spoken up strongly in their favour, arguing that liability to error 'should in my view be a spur to more research and to attempts to understand better the working of the economy rather than a justification for abandoning forecasting' (Wass, 1978).

Those who use the forecasts have to learn how to handle them. They need to develop a feel for how far a forecast is sensitive to variations in its initial assumptions (e.g. to a rise or fall in the US growth rate) or to the departure of variables from their assumed path (e.g. the trend of import penetration), for always they are produced against a shifting world where relationships are apt to break down at any time and where, in any case, the number of relationships which are actually fully estimated is very small. Reading the forecasts is thus as much a matter of experience, judgement and art as of scientific expertise. A senior economic adviser at the Treasury has described the process in this way:

> If I wanted to know, for example, what the effect of changing tax allowances was. . . I would have to start from the forecast, that would give me a base. I'd have to formulate a rather precise question – it's very

important to ask the right questions if you're going to get a sensible answer – so I would have to ask the computer what would be the effect of changing tax allowances on the assumption, for example, that the exchange rate is free to float, on the assumption that the government is pursuing a fixed interest rate or a fixed money supply policy, on a range of assumptions about how the government behaves when the rest of the economy changes. We then do another computer run and it prints out a new version of the forecast, but most usefully it works out conveniently for us what the difference from the original forecast was. It will show the effect on output, on employment, on the PSBR, or on the exchange rate – and then typically I would sit and puzzle and decide whether I liked the answer and believed it. (Quoted in Young and Sloman, 1984)

For all its econometric sophistication, then, the Treasury model is only as good as the assumptions on which it is based. Like all such formal models, it presupposes theories of individual motivation and social action. After all, how the economy behaves is ultimately geared to how people behave as producers, consumers, workers, investors, etc. Yet these assumptions are seldom empirically grounded. Some are little more than guesses, and the track record of economic modellers is not good. As Boulding (1958) has tartly observed, 'The skill of the economist lies in the analysis of the behaviour of commodities and not the behaviour of men.' How, for instance, will people's expectations be affected by a change in fiscal policy? Do businessmen respond to financial incentives by working harder? Will a cut in marginal rates of taxation release an untapped fund of enterprise and entrepreneurial activity, as the 'supply-siders' believe, tempting the captains of industry to forsake the golf course for the boardroom? Or will the prospect of more cash for the same work incline them to opt for more leisure in order to enjoy their increased rewards – to spend more time on the golf course? Clearly, the effect on output of a cut in marginal tax rates on higher incomes will vary according to the motivation and behaviour attributed to company executives. The difficulty for the modellers, as Professor James Meade has pointed out (Rothschild, 1982), is that they 'can only form a "hunch" on observations about behaviour in different circumstances, an introspection as to what is a probable human reaction, and an organised "gossip" with those who are likely to be affected'. Despite the numbers, the differential equations and the control-engineering jargon of economic modelling, the 'same basic uncertainty will inevitably remain'.

It is also the case that, for all its statistical complexity and size, the Treasury model is still 'limited in the goals it can deal with and the information that it can include' (Ball, 1978). Like all models, it was designed for a purpose and its building involved a process of selection as to the variables and relationships to include or to exclude.

Although adjustments have been made to its specification, the Treasury model developed out of traditional Keynesian thinking and its main emphasis is on the goals of stabilization policy. It was designed mainly to assess the performance of the economy in terms of the level of economic activity; in terms of its potential for economic growth. As such, the model ignores 'the effects of macro policies on other goals such as income distribution, the sharing of economic power or the general quality of economic life' (Ball, 1978). While the Ball Committee, set up to investigate the scope and limitations of economic modelling, recognized that these issues 'weigh heavily with a country's citizens and are much affected by the economic policies of government', it acknowleged that macro-economic models 'do not encompass these areas'.

This is another example of how economic goals, narrowly viewed, are given precedence over social issues. The fact is that the Treasury model, which supplies much of the information on which government economic strategy is based, is blind to the social implications and effects of macro-economic policies; it simply does not take them into the reckoning. Thus, for instance, like the other forecasting models, it does not look beyond the rate of inflation to its more fundamental effects on, say, the distribution of income, the living standards of different sections of the population or the social and regional distribution of employment.

There is no need to stress the point that there is no computer model of society equivalent to the Treasury model of the economy to supply this missing information on the social consequences of government policies. Social forecasting, to the extent that it is undertaken at all, is an altogether more primitive art than economic forecasting. Indeed, not only are policies framed without heed to their fundamental social effects, but social policies too are generally cobbled together without the same kind of searching analysis that goes into economic decision-making.

Undoubtedly part of the reason for this state of affairs derives from the scientific strengths of economics when compared with the other social sciences, from its theoretical coherence and the fact that it commands a method of aggregation. But this is not the whole story.

Official Statistics and Government Priorities

Official statistics are not gathered merely out of a sense of curiosity, nor is the elaborate machinery needed to collect and process them set up simply out of a vague desire to know. Statistical data about society and the economy are themselves social products: usually of major and costly social undertakings. As such, they generally reflect something of their origins in the history and organization of government, and in the priorities that have informed the behaviour of governments (Townsend, 1976).

By this line of reasoning, the relative surfeit of information about the state of the economy by comparison with the paucity of information about the state of society is no mere accident or oversight. It must be seen as yet another expression of the paramount importance of economic affairs in the cut and thrust of political life, a preoccupation that has led to a huge financial and intellectual investment in the development of economic intelligence services without any matching investment in social indicators or statistics. There are few powerful voices in government prepared to argue that the shortcomings in our knowledge about the working of society should be a spur to more research in the way Sir Douglas Wass, Permanent Secretary at the Treasury from 1974 to 1983, responded to criticisms about the limitations of macro-economic modelling. The tendency is for people who matter simply to shrug their shoulders.

Some statisticians have spoken out. From inside the Government Statistical Service, Cunliffe (1980) has argued that the lack of an adequate theoretical framework for linking social statistics has not arisen because of any shortage of social theories, but because they have not been stiffened by adequate statistical support. She suggests that the Central Statistical Office (CSO) should divert some of the millions spent on the Business Statistics Office into original fact-finding work in untapped areas in the social field:

> As the task of Government is to govern people, our statistics must increasingly consider the science of people. Economists, I suggest, play an elegant game which is frequently disrupted by the apparently wicked behaviour of human beings. Our statistics are frequently torpedoed by apparently errant humans and their behaviour.

She cites as an example the predictions of the school population based on the birth rate of legitimate children, when increasing numbers are born out of wedlock; and which ignored the effects of the pill and of abortion. The failure of people to behave as expected 'pushed the economics of education almost over the cliff'.

The response to this stance, when not dismissive on scientific grounds, often points to bureaucratic reasons for the fragmented and underdeveloped state of social statistics. In particular, it is argued that social policies, and consequently social statistics, are more departmentalized than their economic counterparts and that systematization has been inhibited by the failure to make data linkages between departments (Moser, 1980). In other words, that since social statistics depend substantially on administrative sources, their integration has been frustrated by the social division of planning. One of the factors that supposedly stands in the way of progress is political sensitivity about confidentiality constraints which, it is said, has even ruled out feasibility studies to explore methods and safeguards (ibid.). Whether such sensitivities are genuine or merely a convenient pretext for masking less scrupulous motives must be questioned. Enough work has been done in other countries to show how easily the confidentiality and anonymity of individual information can be protected. When combined with other recent evidence about the government's pinched and repressive attitude towards the production of social information, the suspicion grows stronger that the real reason is a desire to conceal.

A sheaf of examples helps to substantiate this point and to highlight the political resistance to social monitoring and social reporting:

(a) There was the decision, taken in 1979, to abandon Programme Analysis and Review (PAR) which was the government's main instrument for monitoring spending programmes.

(b) In 1981 the decision was made to cut the staff of the Home Office Research Unit by 40 per cent and to focus its work more narrowly on the short-term policy requirements of government.

(c) On coming to office the Thatcher government abolished the Standing Commission on the Distribution of Income and Wealth, the Centre for Environmental Studies, the Personal Social Services Council and the Supplementary Benefits Commission (which under its chairman, Professor David Donnison, had done much to bring attention to the realities of poverty in Britain – see Donnison, 1982); it broke up the social research division in the Department of the Environment; also a sustained attack was launched on the Social Science Research Council heralded by a disproportionate cut in its research budget relative to those forced on other research councils.

(d) There was the decision to publish government statistical reports only where the revenue from sales covers their full costs. The effect has been to price most official publications giving information on the state of society out of reach of all but the most dedicated readers and to seriously jeopardize the continuation of some important series including, for example, *Social Trends*, which has had to be reduced in size in order to maintain its viability.

(e) Also there has been a change of policy regarding government sponsorship of social research, marked by a switch from programme funding (the financing of independent units responsible for determining their own research priorities) to project funding in order to enforce tighter specifications on the kind of research done and to tie it more closely to government policy. This was accompanied by a tightening-up of departmental control over the publication and dissemination of the results of government-sponsored research projects (Willmott, 1980).

Alongside these overt acts of suppression – justified in the name of value for money and cost-consciousness – are signs of greater political interference in the presentation of statistics and in decisions about what should or should not be published.

Perhaps the most revealing insights are provided by the 1981 White Paper on Government Statistical Services which announced cuts in the staff and administrative costs of government statistical services of a quarter over the period up to 1984. Its proposals were based on the recommendations of review teams under Sir Derek Rayner, who was appointed by the Prime Minister specifically to investigate the scope for economies in departmental statistical work. The Rayner exercise amounted to a systematic and deliberate onslaught on the supply of official information with social statistics carrying the brunt of the attack. The welter of specific recommendations, for instance, included:

(a) curtailing the role and hiving off much of the work of the Social Survey Division of the Office of Population Censuses and Surveys (OPCS) (involving reductions in the scope of the Family Expenditure Survey and the General Household Survey – which a former Director of the Central Statistical Office described as the two centre-pieces of social statistics – see Moser, 1980);
(b) abandoning the mid-term Census planned for 1986;
(c) stopping work by the CSO on wealth distribution;
(d) cutting back the sample size of the annual income survey;
(e) terminating the series of Statistics of Education;
(f) reducing the scope and volume of information on the personal social services collected by the DHSS from local authorities;
(g) making more extensive use of press notices in place of 'compendia of descriptive statistics'.

The 1981 White Paper was more than just a pruning exercise. It was a radical attempt to redefine the role and responsibilities of the government in the statistical field. Government, it declared, should not act as a 'universal provider' of statistical intelligence, nor should information be collected primarily for publication. On the contrary, information 'should be collected primarily because government needs it for its own business' and then no more 'than is essential to the efficient discharge of its functions'.

This stance breaks with a tradition that stretches back well into the nineteenth century when the Blue Books began to provide an impressive and reliable portrait of the social condition of Britain. As Marx observed in his preface to the first German edition of *Capital*:

> The social statistics of Germany and the rest of Continental Western Europe are, by comparison with those of England, wretchedly compiled . . . We should be appalled at the state of things at home if, as in England, our governments and parliaments appointed periodically commissions of inquiry into economic conditions; if these commissions were armed with the same plenary powers to get at the truth; if it was possible to find for this purpose men as competent, as free from partisanship and respect of persons as are the English factory-inspectors, her medical reporters on public health, her commissioners of inquiry into the exploitation of women and children, into housing and food.

The Blue Book tradition imbued official attitudes to social statistics well into the second half of the twentieth century when the same concerns for accuracy, reliability and integrity became part of the ethos of the newly formed Central Statistical Office (CSO) after the war. Most recently, the introduction of the annual series *Social Trends* by the CSO in 1970 may be seen as part of the same legacy.

Social Trends was designed to bring together in an integrated manner information on related aspects of social life and conditions, 'the sole objective being to throw light, by figures and frank commentary, on major social issues of the day' (Moser, 1980). As an annual report on the state of the nation, concerned with the quality of life in all its guises, the series followed in the footsteps of the pioneers of social monitoring and measurement. It also aimed to create and develop public opinion. A former editor stressed the importance of this role:

> The most important point, however, when considering an audience for *Social Trends*, is the belief that democracy requires an informed public opinion. The numbers involved may be quite small, but it is nevertheless of immense importance that there should be really well-informed people outside the circles of official administration. (Thompson, 1978)

The 1981 White Paper deliberately turned its back on arguments of this sort, and on the objectives which originally inspired the publication of *Social Trends*. Statistics were to be collected for the benefit of government only, not in order merely to keep the public informed or supplied with the information necessary to judge its performance. Indeed, the effect of the proposals is precisely to cover the traces on the social impact of government policies by censoring the information that would enable people to measure their social consequences (Booth, 1981b). As Townsend (1981) has commented, by restricting the flow of information, the 'Government's proposals seem designed to reduce knowledge of social conditions and reduce too the chances of government policies being criticised on grounds of failure to meet needs'.

This break with an honourable tradition of social reporting was marked by a shift in the editorial aims of *Social Trends*. The introduction to the 1982 issue declared flatly that it was, first and foremost, 'a descriptive brief *for government* about broad changes in society' (emphasis added). For this reason, it added, it had been arranged to correspond with the administrative functions of government. The emphasis on its role in highlighting major social issues of the day for an audience outside the circles of official administration had gone. From now on it was to offer no more than a 'window through which Parliament and the public can see the sort of data which are available to government' (but, perhaps, no more than are good for them to see).

In his 1979 Presidential Address to the Royal Statistical Society, Sir Claus Moser, who had served as head of the Government Statistical Service under three Prime Ministers and was responsible for starting *Social Trends*, reflected on the issue of integrity as it bears on the production of official statistics. He listed a number of principles which had to be protected in order to preserve the credibility of governments (Moser, 1980), every one of which has been ignored or traduced in the aftermath of the 1981 White Paper and the new ground rules it introduced. Moser argued as follows.

Figures should be published in full (subject only to secrecy constraints), with their form, method of calculation and publication, and their analysis and interpretation, determined on statistical rather than political grounds.

This maxim has been effectively supplanted by the new Rayner principle that information should not be collected primarily for publication, and further undermined by the political restraints of cost-cutting – especially the requirement that statistical publications should pay for themselves.

There can never be justification for knowingly manipulating figures.

The official monthly unemployment statistics have been redefined sixteen times since Mrs Thatcher came into office. Reports also suggest that ministers are dissatisfied with the way the figures detailing the extent of poverty in Britain are collated and that a change in the definition of the official poverty line is planned (Taylor, 1986).

*There can never be a case for withholding the publication of a regular
series for non-statistical reasons, and an unwillingness to disclose known
figures, or to select what is published, should be regarded as tantamount
to a breach of propriety.*

For the first time since 1911 the Office of Population Censuses and
Surveys dropped the details showing the differential death rate
between the social classes from its 1986 decennial report on
occupational mortality, even though the statistics were available.
Similarly, a DHSS-commissioned survey revealing what has happened
to children's diets since the government abolished nutritional
standards and price controls in the 1980 Educational Act was withheld
from Parliament until a copy was leaked to the press. A request by
the researchers to have more of their data processed by the OPCS
in order to establish why children from deprived families had such
poor nutritional levels was refused on the ground of cost (Veitch,
1986). In 1985 a table showing the unemployed were more vulnerable
to illness than those in work was removed on the insistence of
ministers.

*Delaying the publication of figures for non-statistical reasons is a harmful
practice detrimental to confidence.*

Figures from the 1984 Census of Employment showing the regional
disparities in the distribution of employment and the impact of job
losses in creating a 'two nations' divide between the north and south
were suppressed for political reasons and were not published until
1987. Likewise, when the findings of a study on the closed shop,
carried out by Professor Gennard of Strathclyde University, failed
to justify the measures taken against it in Mr Tebbit's Employment
Act, its publication was delayed until after the legislation was safely
on the statute-book.

*Interference with statistical methods or operations should not be tolerated
under any circumstances. The methods, concepts, standards, definitions
and all other aspects of statistics, surveys and censuses should remain the
professional province of the statistician.*

Following the Rayner reviews, the sample size of the annual income
survey and the General Household Survey was substantially reduced,
though no estimates were given of the effects of the changes on
sampling errors, nor of how they might affect the analysis and
presentation or comparability with earlier surveys. In both cases the
changes were made on financial rather than statistical grounds. Or

again, when researchers carrying out work for the Department of Employment concluded that Wages Councils did not price workers out of their jobs, as ministers claimed, another unit was set up in the Department to prove the opposite (Taylor, 1986).

The failure to adhere to Moser's principles of integrity is not the fault of professional statisticians. It has come about because of deliberate political interference in the work of the government statistical services. This interference has been justified in the name of efficiency – the overt rationale of the Rayner reviews. But its effects go far beyond mere cost-cutting. By redefining its role as primarily the servant of government, the Government Statistical Service has been effectively politicized. Moser had no doubt that the duty of government statisticians was to deploy the vast range of information they command 'to the benefit of the entire community'. They must serve many different communities: regional and local authorities; the business community; trade unions; the market research and advertising world; academic scholars and researchers; the media; and, of course, the public and their representatives in Parliament. The 1981 White Paper formally repudiated these wider responsibilities and passed over the claims of these user communities: official statistics should serve only the needs of government. This new guiding principle opened the door to the political meddling in the statistical services which has followed.

The impact of the Rayner reviews is, perhaps, most clearly revealed by examination of one Whitehall department. The DHSS Study Team submitted its report in June 1980. It identified a list of the main purposes for which statistical information was used by the DHSS:

(a) for fulfilling the requirements of public accountability through Parliament;
(b) for promulgating policies and informing decisions;
(c) for managing and allocating resources;
(d) as a substitute for action;
(e) as a defence or protection against allegations and complaints;
(f) to support policies already hallowed;
(g) as insurance against the day when it might be needed;
(h) as a shield against serious analysis;
(i) because the DHSS ought to know something about a topic;
(j) because it always has been collected.

In reviewing this range of statistical work, the Study Team applied three criteria to judge whether it should be retained, altered or discontinued: whether the information is actually used by the DHSS;

IF...
Steve Bell
OLD YOUNG'S ALMANACK FOR 1987
I FEEL A MYSTIC THROBBING IN MY FINGERTIPS! BRING ME THE FACTS! BRING ME...
...THE FIGURES!! LISTEN!! THE FIGURES ARE SPEAKING!!
1468
COLLAPSE OF MANUFACTURING INDUSTRY
POVERTY
NHS IN A SHIT-CREEK MINUS PADDLE SITUATION!!
DEAD BABIES
SUICIDES
CRIME
HUMAN MISERY
PUBLIC SERV-ICES IN TATTERS
EDUCATION WRECKED
WE'RE NOT LISTENING TO THAT KIND OF DEFEATIST CLAPTRAP!!
NO! NO! YOU'RE LISTENING TO THE WRONG FIGURES!! LISTEN TO THESE!!! NNNNNNNNNN!!
DOUBLE DINNERS!
VASTER ACCUMULATION OF WEALTH THAN EVER BEFORE
SALES OF HE-MAN FIGURES UP BY 500%
1200% INCREASE IN DICKHEADS WITH CAR TELEPHONES
MASSAGE MASSAGE
AND THIS IS THE CLINCHER!! NNNNN...
ENTIRE NATION'S YOUTH DISAPPEAR ONTO MICKEY MOUSE TRAINING SCHEME!!
YOUTH UNEMPLOY-MENT? WHAT YOUTH UNEMPLOYMENT??
YOU'VE NEVER BEEN SO WELL OFF!!
HOW ABOUT ANOTHER SMALL WAR? OR EVEN A LARGE ONE?
...SO YOU'LL NEED A FEW MORE SERVANTS, WON'T YOU?
© Steve Bell '86

if so, whether the purpose for which it is used is necessary; and if it is necessary, whether the information is essential to its performance. Finally, having assessed what was essential, a decision was taken on whether the costs of collecting the information were justified by the benefits obtained, 'bearing in mind the over-riding need for economy' (DHSS, 1980). The Study Team had no illusions about the significance of their exercise. They acknowledged it was not just the cost of providing information that was under scrutiny. As their Report makes plain, 'when costing information, in this case a wide range of social statistics, the price tag is in part attached to the democratic right to know'. On this basis the Study Team proposed cuts in statistical work estimated to bring savings of over £2 million by 1984 (compared with expenditure in 1979) and to reduce the number of statistical staff from 517 to 322 over the same period.

The effects of such cost-consciousness on its proposals were, as the Study Team recognized, 'unquestionably rigorous'. In future, MPs will have to be referred repeatedly to published sources instead of having their questions answered by the DHSS. Select Committees and Royal Commissions may have to obtain their own information where it is not available already within the DHSS, and may have to work without some of the accumulated trend data that has been available before. The Public Accounts Committee may have to accept that staff and resources are not available to provide some of the information it requests. Researchers, too, would be hit. The Study Team recommended that the DHSS should not continue to collect information primarily because it is a potentially valuable source of research material.

Looking at the implications of the Rayner proposals for statistics on the personal social services in particular, the National and Local Government Statistical Liaison Committee (1981) concluded that they would deprive local authorities of aggregate comparative information about key service activities and prevent the effects of new policies initiated by central government from being monitored effectively. These observations are especially telling in the light of the frequently repeated exhortations by the House of Commons Social Services Committee for the production of a more sophisticated statistical information system covering the personal social services, and its criticisms of the government's current inability to make serious assessments of local authority service provision (Social Services Committee, 1982).

Two features of the Rayner scrutiny of DHSS statistical information stand out and illustrate the government's sparing regard for social reporting and for the traditions of the Government Statistical Service. In preparing their Report, the Study Team only consulted with the DHSS's Statistics and Research Division and with some of its in-house customers from the policy branches. In other words, the review took place largely behind closed doors. There was no attempt to garner the opinions of important users and suppliers of information outside the central department in, for instance, Parliament, the NHS or local authorities. Although to cite just one example, the Association of Metropolitan Authorities had already made plain its view that 'constructive dialogue about the significance and relevance of national policies to local needs is inhibited by the paucity of useful and valid comparative data'. Nor was any attempt made to sound the views of the wider community of users in professional associations, voluntary organizations, pressure groups, trade unions or the academic world. While quite consistent with the Rayner principle that information should only be collected when it is necessary for government business, this inward-looking approach altogether ignores the requirements of democratic accountability and the responsibility of government in an open society to nourish an informed public opinion.

At the same time, the review – in line with its remit – only looked at what cuts should be made in departmental statistical work. It failed to address the question of how the work might be improved and strengthened so as the better to meet the needs of its users. Undoubtedly there was plenty of scope for pruning and streamlining. But equally there was room for expansion and innovation. In 1981, for example, the House of Commons Social Services Committee called on the DHSS to extend its work on the comparative analysis of the performance of local personal social services and to make such information public. The blunt fact is that the review was guided primarily by political rather than statistical considerations: its aim was not to improve the standards of the statistical service, but to fulfil the overriding political compulsion of cutting costs.

The Rayner scrutinies and the 1981 White Paper are important because they demonstrate how little importance is attached to social statistics within government. Even the DHSS Study Team seemed slightly taken aback to find that 'very few people identified the need to keep the public informed as a general duty of a large Government department concerned with a wide range of social provision'. Inside the corridors of power the instinct for secrecy prevails. In the world outside there are no powerful constituencies of users to protect social statistics from neglect or manipulation. It is this lack of political muscle that largely accounts for the relative underdevelopment of social statistics and indicators: they have too few friends in the right places. The result has been that economists have established almost a stranglehold on policy analysis inside government, so allowing the inherent limitations of a purely economic frame of reference to go unchallenged or unchecked. In this way has social planning been shut out, and social policy subordinated to the demands of economic management.

PART II
EXAMPLES:
CASE STUDIES IN
POLICY RESEARCH

4   The age of analysis: PPBS in US federal agencies

'I hope that in future the Congress will no longer be as impressed with sociological assertions as it has been in the past. The judgement of politicians is at least as meritorious as the pronouncements of social scientists.' (Admiral Hyman G. Rickover)

The date is 25 August 1965, the venue a White House press conference. President Johnson is announcing his decision to order the installation of a Planning–Programming–Budgeting System (PPBS) throughout the Executive Branch in these words:

> This morning I have just concluded a breakfast meeting with the Cabinet and with the heads of federal agencies and I am asking each of them to immediately begin to introduce a new and very revolutionary system of planning and programming the budgeting throughout the vast federal Government so that through the tools of modern management the full promise of a finer life can be brought to every American at the lowest possible cost.
>
> Under this new system each Cabinet and agency head will set up a very special staff of experts who, using the most modern methods of program analysis, will define the goals of their department for the coming year. And once these goals are established this system will permit us to find the most effective and the least costly alternatives to achieving American goals.
>
> This program is designed to achieve three major objectives: it will help us to find new ways to do jobs less expensively. It will insure a much sounder judgement through more accurate information, pinpointing those things that we ought to do more, spotlighting those things that we ought to do less. It will make our decision-making process as up-to-date, I think, as our space-exploring programs.

Once in operation, the President went on to say, the system will:

(1) Identify our national goals with precision and on a continuing basis.
(2) Choose among those goals the ones that are most urgent.
(3) Search for alternative means of reaching those goals most effectively at the least cost.
(4) Inform ourselves not merely on next year's costs, but on the second,

and third, and subsequent years' costs of our programs.

(5) Measure the performance of our programs to insure a dollar's worth of service for each dollar spent.

'Our judgement', declared the President, 'is no better than our information. This system will present us with the alternatives and the information on the basis of which we can, together, make better decisions.' Under questioning, enthusiastic government officials told reporters that shortly it would be possible to establish with confidence the relative pay-offs of, say, building a dam in Florida or improving Indian schools or eradicating syphilis.

Two months later, in October 1965, the Bureau of the Budget issued advice to all federal departments and agencies on the setting up of the PPB system, and instructed them to establish an adequate central analytical staff whose head should be directly responsible to the head of the agency or his deputy. These offices were charged with the task of undertaking the hard analysis that would provide a quantitative basis for decisions about goals and priorities.

So began the most ambitious and far-reaching attempt to apply the methods of systematic analysis to the business of policy-making ever attempted by any national government. By making full use of techniques such as cost–benefit analysis, operational research and systems analysis, PPBS promised to rationalize the process of policy-making in the federal government by injecting hard information on the costs of alternative programmes and on their effectiveness in achieving desired objectives. In this way, it was hoped, objective criteria of efficiency and effectiveness would take over from political wheeling and dealing as the basis for decisions about resource allocation, so improving the value for money from federal spending and the success of government in dealing with the nation's problems.

Over the next two years there was a massive recruitment of specialist analytical staff to work on the PPB system, representing a huge investment of intellectual capital. An official survey showed that, in its heyday, about 1,600 full-time staff were employed on the PPB system in twenty-one federal agencies with another 2,100 engaged part-time on the system (Marvin and Rouse, 1969). Annual expenditure on in-house and contract services for policy analysis rose to about $60 million (Carlson, 1969). These facts alone single it out as the largest ever attempt by a government to harness the social sciences for a civilian end. Yet by 1969, PPBS was dead. As one influential commentator has observed, 'I left Washington in 1965 full of enthusiasm about it, and when I came back in 1969 it had disappeared' (Moynihan, 1970b).

The PPBS experiment repays careful study for the unique insight it offers into the uses and limits of analysis as a tool for decision-making in a political bureaucracy. One of the reasons why it provides such an illuminating case study is that so many of the key participants went straight back to their university departments (or to the Brookings Institution) on leaving Washington to write up their experiences. As a result, there is an abundance of inside evidence on the workings and outcomes of the experiment, including a massive three-volume compendium of expert testimony compiled by the Joint Economic Committee of Congress (1969; see also Haveman and Margolis, 1970). The remainder of this chapter seeks to draw out the important lessons from the rise and demise of PPBS.

The ABC of PPBS
The groundwork for the development of programme budgeting techniques was undertaken in the 1950s by the RAND Corporation. Over many years RAND analysts, working under contract to the US Defense Department, had been researching the application of new and developing methods of systematic analysis to the solution of defence problems. There they might have rested but for the appointment of Robert MacNamara as Secretary of Defense in 1961. MacNamara faced the task of imposing some kind of co-ordinated control over the separate armed services. Two problems in particular stood out: the fact that choices were having to be made between vast, and vastly expensive, new weapons systems without any knowledge of their long-term consequences for future expenditure; and the lack of co-ordination in military planning where the initiative lay with the service chiefs.

In an effort to overcome these problems, which had dogged successive Secretaries of Defense since 1947 when the Office was created, MacNamara appointed a former RAND employee, Charles Hitch, as his Comptroller with instructions to introduce programme budgeting into the department in time for the 1963 fiscal year.

MacNamara met with what is generally held to have been outstanding success in his use of programme budgeting as a means of enforcing central direction over the defence establishment, often in the face of bitter opposition from the top brass in the Pentagon, breaking with the incrementalism of the annual budgetary cycle and transcending the divisions between the services. For the first time the biggest business in the world had a comprehensive, department-wide plan extending more than one year into the future relating defence spending to national security objectives. Also for the first time since the Office was created the Secretary of Defense was in a position to carry out his responsibilities under the National Security Act to exercise 'direction, authority and control over the Department of Defense' instead of playing second-fiddle to his military bigwigs.

MacNamara's achievements did not go unnoticed across the Potomac. President Johnson was about to launch his 'Great Society' programme, a bold and sustained legislative attack on the burning social issues of the day. He saw in MacNamara's success a way of overhauling the organization and working of the federal government to speed the way for his social reforms, and of bringing the same kind of coherence and purpose into the direction of social policy.

The PPB system had been conceived as an aid to decision-making and a framework for planning. As a process it involves 'identifying end objectives, designing alternative ways of achieving these objectives, and choosing among them on the basis of systematic analysis' (Novick, 1968). As a system PPB is made up essentially of five steps or tasks (Schultze, 1968):

1　it requires that the goals and objectives of government activity be spelled out clearly;
2　it sets out to analyse the output of government policies and programmes to see how far they meet their objectives;
3　it aims to measure the total costs of programmes over several years ahead;
4　it calls for the analysis of alternative ways of achieving the same objectives in order to identify the most effective or efficient course of action;
5　it entails that these techniques and procedures be established as a systematic feature of the annual budgetary process.

This last step — the programming phase — is the crucial one. It provides the critical link relating planning to budgeting, and aims to ensure that analysis becomes an integral part of decision-making.

Broadly, then, the hallmarks of PPBS are its adherence to a rational mode of problem-solving; its stress on the role of analysis as opposed to trial and error; the emphasis it puts on analytical criteria of effectiveness and efficiency as against political criteria of compromise and consensus in the making of decisions; and its stress on long-run planning rather than muddling through.

Under the guiding hand of Johnson's Budget Chief, Charles Schultze, the PPB system slowly took shape in the giant federal bureaucracy despite the reticence of many agency heads. Although it was subject to almost continual modification and amendment in its detailed operation, the four main elements at the core of the system, around which it was built, remained the same. They were:

1　*The program structure*, which grouped together the functions and activities of agencies contributing to the same objective, so that they could be discussed as one block of expenditure; e.g. all the separate services and activities contributing to the prevention and control of disease or income maintenance or the care of the aged were amalgamated into the same program category. The main purpose of the program structure was to enable better analysis of agency programmes by making it possible to link cost and output information, by highlighting trade-offs and alternatives, and by identifying gaps.

2 *Program memoranda*, which were drawn up every year for each of the separate groups of activities identified in an agency's program structure. The program memoranda presented the agency head's spending proposals for the next year's budget. As well as spelling out what the agency planned to do, the program memoranda also had to show why by relating the proposals to agency objectives in a measurable way, outlining the alternatives that had been considered and comparing them in terms of their costs and effectiveness. Program memoranda were designed to ensure that decisions were made on the basis of evidence, after consideration of alternatives, and that the choices were deliberate rather than accidental.

3 *The program and financial plan* for each federal agency laid out the projected costs and benefits of its programmes over the next five years. The plan was supposed to be updated and rolled forward every year. It was intended to relate annual budget allocations more closely to longer-term plans and priorities.

4 *Special analytical studies* were commissioned when a proposal for major new legislation was put foward. The studies were intended to identify the purposes, costs and pay-offs of the proposed legislation, and to investigate whether the same objectives could be achieved more effectively or efficiently in some other way.

The PPB system was devised as an approach to decision-making which aimed to make as explicit as possible the costs and consequences of major choices and government actions and to encourage the systematic use of this analysis in the making of public policy by linking it directly to the budgetary process (Carlson, 1969). It set out to tackle the incrementalism, rooted in the annual budgetary cycle, by extending the time-horizon for expenditure planning. It also promised to bridge the social division of planning created by the departmentalism and fissiparous tendencies of government agencies. There were, for example, no fewer than forty-two federal departments, agencies and bureaux spending funds on education, while the health budget was spread over thirteen agencies and seven Cabinet departments (Garrett, 1972). By bringing together all these expenditures and the activities they financed, in the program structure, PPBS held out the prospect of improved collaboration and better co-ordination in the pursuit of common objectives. No wonder that excited policy analysts greeted its introduction as 'potentially the most significant management improvement in the history of American government' (Gross and Springer, 1967).

The PPBS record

How far did PPBS live up to its promise? Did it succeed in bringing about a more rational and co-ordinated approach to planning? What does the initiative teach us about the value of research and analysis in the making of policy?

Only one thing is certain: there are no easy answers to these questions. Indeed, the answers you get depend in part on whom you ask. Some emphasize the successes, some the failures and, in both cases, the opinions of commentators tend to be coloured by their own role in the drama. The reality is also blurred by the exaggerated expectations that were generated by the selling of PPBS.

In the face of these uncertainties Carlson (1969) put forward three criteria for evaluating the achievements and failures of PPBS: did it work as intended, was it better than what went before and was the analysis it produced useful or would it have been done anyway?

On the first of these criteria the evidence shows that PPB, *as a formal system*, was at best only partially successful and certainly failed to match the aims of its theorists. But, then, these aims were rather ambitious: to establish 'a decision process in which choices would be based on the results of analysis' (Haveman, 1970) instead of the political arts of advocacy, negotiation and bargaining.

The attempt to tie policy analysis into the hectic and complex budgetary process proved to be impossible (Glennerster, 1975). Steeped in its own long-standing traditions and routines, the practice of budgeting was incompatible with the task of analysis. The strict deadlines and procedural constraints of the budget cycle simply led to unsatisfactory and superficial work that tarnished the reputation of the PPB-ers. Moreover, the politicians were not enamoured by the virtues of analysis. The congressional committees, which examine and authorize departmental appropriations, viewed the PPB system with suspicion as just another smart dodge by the Executive to try and outsmart the Legislature. Time and again they defied the logic of analysis in order to do right by the interests they represented (Garrett, 1972).

The quality and utility of the program structures developed by the agencies varied widely in terms of their attempt to classify expenditures by objectives. Generally, however, they did present a helpful way of looking at agency activities for analytical purposes. As a result of this approach, the US Federal Budget has become 'a document far more illuminating on what the government is doing, and why, than anything produced by the government in Britain' (ibid.).

The program memoranda, too, were of very uneven quality. Some made a genuine effort to link spending proposals to agency objectives in the light of a consideration of alternative policy options. More often, however, they turned out to be 'descriptive, verbose, non-analytic accounts of existing and proposed programs with an impassioned plea for funding' (Carlson, 1969).

Similar shortcomings were also evident in the program and financial plans (PFPs) prepared by the agencies. In the early years these turned out to be little more than lengthy 'wishlists' of what the agencies would like to spend over the next five years regardless of financial constraints. More discipline was eventually introduced but even so the PFPs were usually prepared in haste, and based more on guesswork than analysis.

Overall, then, the formal structure of PPB, conceived as a new system of decision-making in which intuition gave way to analysis, stuttered briefly and then stalled. Design faults that had not been evident on the drawing-board confounded the system engineers in the Bureau of the Budget. The PPB system generated more work than could be done well, and more than the bureaucracy could digest. It asked more from analysis than it could deliver. It made budgeting more complicated than it already was by grafting new methods on to old practices. And it ran up against the instinct of politicians to be more responsive to their own constituencies than to the advice of experts. As a result, instead of transforming the system, the system transformed PPB by re-shaping the ideal to fit the world of experience.

If PPBS did not work as intended, what about the second of Carlson's criteria of evaluation? Was it better than what had gone before? Once again, the balance-sheet shows both gains and losses.

There is no doubt that PPBS forced many agencies to look systematically and critically at what they were doing and why. It stimulated a heightened awareness of the strengths and weaknesses of agency programmes and a greater receptivity to possible alternatives. In so doing, it mounted a challenge to the traditional view that spending makes good things happen and spending more money makes better things happen. The quality and relevance of official information also improved with more emphasis than before being given to collecting data that was useful for planning as opposed to simply good housekeeping.

At the same time, there were many in government who remained sceptical of the new ideas and lukewarm, if not openly hostile, to their implementation. Some top officials, firmly embedded in key posts, who had built their careers on their grasp and understanding of the established rules of the game, reacted defensively and sometimes obstructively to the innovations, seeing in them a threat to their own position and authority. These anxieties were magnified by the suspicion that the new system being thrust upon them marked a significant increase in the level of Presidential intervention in departmental affairs, and by the arrogance of the whizz-kids recruited to run the analytic offices whose overblown opinion of their own importance caused friction with operating officials.

A lot of agencies succeeded in charting their way through these initial fears and rivalries, and in reaching a concordat between the roles of generalist administrator and analytic expert, by acknowledging the simple fact that sound judgement is usually enhanced when it is supported by good analysis. Even so, problems remained. By throwing more light on choices and alternatives analysis tended, in many instances, to sharpen conflicts about ends and means where ambiguity had minimized them in the past (Keeling, 1972). Also it turned out that the exponents of PPB 'misjudged the capacity of the bureaucracy to produce analysis and of the polity to use it' (Schick, 1971). Many of the questions thrown up by the policy process were beyond the formal techniques of quantitative analysis and, in any case, the agencies had little interest in objective fact for its own sake. Their instinct leaned towards the legitimation and continuation of their existing programmes or the justification of their proposals for new ones. Analysis was harnessed to these aims and transformed, at the hands of agency management, into just another tool of advocacy. Indeed, by requiring quantitative statements of goals and quantitative reporting on how well they were being met, PPBS probably increased rather than decreased the dishonesty of budget submissions and annual reports (Salasin, 1973b). In the competition for resources, agencies could not afford to be too frank about their performance or reveal too much of their own hand. The rectitude of analysis had to give way to the reality of expedience.

Overall, then, it is hard to escape the view that the long-term impact of PPBS was slight. Certainly, it did not succeed in establishing itself as a new structure of decision-making. In this sense, the question of whether or not it represented an improvement on what went before is misplaced. In 1969 a survey of sixteen federal agencies concluded that 'the planning, programming and budgeting functions are not performed much differently . . . than they were before the introduction of PPB' (Harper, Kramer and Rouse, 1969). Schick

(1971) similarly concluded that 'decisions continue to be made in the pre-PPB fashion . . . there are few traces of planning and systems analysis in the annual budget cycle'. But at a more modest level PPBS is generally credited with having brought about some improvements in the working of big government. Even the most traditionally minded officials began to show a greater fluency in the language of priorities. It encouraged the examination of a wider range of alternatives than are normally encompassed by the political process. It introduced a new set of participants into the policy arena, labelled 'partisan efficiency advocates' by Schultze (1968), who, from their base in the analytic offices within agencies, promoted the cause of value for money in decision-making. There was a pay-off, too, in terms of open government as a result of the clearer specification of policy objectives and outcomes and a marked improvement in the quality of information on the operation of programmes.

Also, and this leads us on to a consideration of Carlson's third criterion, PPBS undoubtedly created a climate more receptive to the use of analysis and more heedful of it than in the past. How useful most of the early analytical work was is another matter.

The new breed of policy analysts who flooded Washington to staff the PPB offices were quickly charged with opportunism, of trying to 'solve what problems they can, not the problems that most need to be solved' (Thompson, 1969). In the main, this charge amounted to an accusation of manipulating the research agenda to match their methodologies. Some critics detected more chronic signs of 'numerophilia' in the analyses: a predilection for neglecting relevant variables that are not cardinally measurable (Spengler, 1969). Certainly, the more successful examples of programme analysis tended to come from agencies responsible for the management or production of physical assets and resources, such as transportation, water and aerospace projects, where their objectives are more easily defined and the costs and benefits are more easily measured. Fewer examples are available from civil agencies running social programmes whose goals are often contested and diverse and, as we shall see, whose benefits are frequently incalculable or incommensurable.

Moreover it was soon found that PPBS imposed heavy systems costs that detracted from the aims of analysis (Schick, 1971). The formal structure of the PPB system, with its paraphernalia of documentation and deadlines, got in the way of good analysis. The link between policy analysis and budgeting, which constituted the core of PPBS as a system of decision-making, was designed to ensure that research did not languish on the sidelines, but was translated into action through the expenditure process. In the event, the marriage turned out to be unworkable. Policy analysis cut across budgetary traditions and institutional loyalties, while budgeting made good policy analysis impossible because of the time constraints it imposed (Wildavsky, 1970).

The quality of the analysis done also suffered as a result of the across-the-board introduction of PPBS. Sam Cohn, the top permanent official at the Bureau of the Budget in 1967, reflected some ten years later that the Johnson administration had 'tried to push if off too fast, on every agency at once. It was too advanced for the clerks who had to do the work' (quoted in Garrett, 1980). Hundreds of analysts were needed when there were almost none to be had either in the government outside defence or in the private sector. Consequently, the existing talent was spread very thinly and, to make up the deficit, large numbers of established staff were literally reclassified as 'policy analysts' without any training (Marvin and Rouse, 1969). The upshot was a paucity of good analysis, a surfeit of mediocre work and a gift to those who sought to rubbish the effort or who disliked having someone looking over their shoulder.

None the less, the army of analysts did still make their mark. As Alice Rivlin, a respected Assistant Secretary for Planning and Evaluation in the Department of Health, Education and Welfare during this period later remarked, the PPBS experiment led to 'the acceptance of analysis as part of the decision process and of the analyst as a participant at the decision table' (Rivlin, 1971). Interestingly, this appraisal echoes that of Charles Schultze, cited earlier, from his desk at the Bureau of the Budget.

The rise of the professional policy analyst also created a more competitive market for information. Statistical data assumed a new importance as a key input to the policy process, and consequently came under more rigorous challenge and scrutiny than before. Flawed information and argument was more quickly exposed and more heavily penalized. Noticeably the competition and bargaining for resources both within and between agencies focused much more explicitly than before on the performance of their programmes. In this sense, the introduction of analysis may be said to have injected a new discipline into the discussion of expenditure plans and priorities. Although the power of analysis as a tool of decision-making was undoubtedly oversold, it did in this way – as a stimulus to critical thinking – help to raise the level of debate (Williams, 1983).

The story of PPBS is largely a story of frustrated hopes. On each of Carlson's three criteria of evaluation its small achievements are overshadowed by larger disappointments. One important qualification, however, is necessary to this summary verdict. There were big differences between federal agencies in the effort they put into trying to make the PPB system work. Most commentators agree with Marvin and Rouse (1969) that the single, most important factor in the development and intregration of PPBS within agencies was the attitude of the agency head. Drew (1967), for instance, concluded that: 'How well PPB has worked, agency by agency, has depended more than anything on how seriously the man at the top has taken it, how hard he worked to attract good people to do the job, how much he lent his authority to the adoption of a system of hard analysis.' Other facilitating factors included having an executive with an aggressive interest in promoting PPBS to lead the central analytic unit, a sufficiency of qualified analysts to staff it and a belief that PPB was likely to be of use to the agency and not just the Bureau of the Budget.

With these points in mind, it seems only fair that in seeking to assess the contribution which systematic analysis made to policy-making we should look at an agency which really tried to make a go of PPBS. By common consent the one place where it did take root in a significant way was at the Department of Health, Education and Welfare.

PPBS in HEW

President Johnson had appointed William Gorham, a 36-year-old economist and veteran of the Defense Department's managerial revolution, as his Assistant Secretary for Program Coordination in 1965, with instructions to establish the PPB system in the Department of Health, Education and Welfare (HEW). With the active support of the Secretary of HEW, John Gardner, Gorham assembled a trio of talented deputies and an enthusiastic team of twenty-five top-flight economists, mathematicians and sociologists (described in the department's newsletter as 'young, rapier-witted, and brimful of ideas and good humor'). While taking to heart Secretary Gardner's dictum that HEW should be 'an organization that leaves nothing unexamined', Gorham and his staff understood the limits of analysis, 'we aren't about to replace judgement, common sense, and compassion':

> PPBS does not guarantee that our choices will always be logical or that decisions will always be made quietly and rationally in full light of all the facts. Some decisions may fly in the face of the most careful studies. Tradition and public sentiment will continue to have their say, and many decisions will continue to be non-economic. But PPBS will mean that fewer decisions will be made in the dark. (Secretary's Letter, 1967)

Despite the strength and quality of the analytic staff in HEW, PPB soon ran into problems which forced even its most thoughtful practitioners into a considerably narrower view of what was possible (Drew, 1967).

Some of these problems were of an organizational kind. There seems to be a definite limit on the capacity of organizations to make use of research and analysis, especially when it is critical of the status quo. Certainly, the development of PPBS incited a running 'conflict between those who ran programs (and believed in them) and those who analyzed the programs (and whose job it was to be sceptical of them)' (Williams and Evans, 1969). These frictions in the system between the analytical staff and the operators of programmes were underestimated. As it turned out, the politics of analysis – in essence the clash between methodology, bureaucratic inertia and professional self-interest – loomed much larger than was imagined at the outset.

But the problems of PPBS in HEW went deeper than this. William Gorham has subsequently identified four major obstacles they encountered in trying to harness research to policy (Gorham, 1967).

First, they met with a 'technical problem of absence of data'. Most health, education and welfare services aim to change the lives of people in some way. In order to estimate their effectiveness, it is necessary to know what actually happens to the recipients or consumers. But this sort of information was simply not available from routine administrative statistics. As one practitioner ruefully observed:

> Those who picture Washington as one mass of files and computers containing more information than they would like will be comforted by the experience of program-planners in attempting to evaluate on-going programs. Whatever the files and computers do contain, there is precious little in them about how many and whom the programs are reaching, and whether they are doing what they are supposed to do. (Drew, 1967)

Moreover, it was found that the costs of collecting the sort of information needed to judge the effectiveness of the programmes often turned out to exceed any likely savings accruing from the more efficient use of resources. One result of this lack of data was that analysts tended to allow the form of available statistics to shape the way they conceived and approached problems.

The second obstacle cited by Gorham was a conceptual one. Technical problems of data collection aside, it was 'far from obvious how the benefits of most health, education and welfare programs should be defined'. The orthodox answer of the economists, of course, was by putting a money value on the services either by estimating their effects on the future income of recipients or by assigning shadow prices purporting to show what consumers would have been prepared to pay for them on the open market. But this approach implies that an increase in the national income is an overriding goal of social policy, and fewer and fewer people were prepared to accept economic growth as an indicator of social well-being. However, once the analysts moved away from making dollar estimates of the benefits of social programs, they found themselves in a never-never land having to set values on things like self-reliance, personal independence, contentment, the pleasures of clean air, access to outdoor recreation, security, and so on (Rivlin, 1971). Unable to count anything anymore, suddenly nothing seemed to add up.

These problems merged with the third obstacle mentioned by Gorham. Even if the analysts were able to identify and measure the benefits of individual programmes, they could not always be measured in the same units once a monetary scale of value was abandoned. This made impossible the task of comparing the relative worth or effectiveness of different programmes by objective analysis and so vitiated some part of the promise of PPBS.

The fourth and final difficulty referred to by Gorham is that, all other obstacles aside, the analysts always come up against the fact that the benefits of different programmes go to different people. Should equal benefits to different individuals be weighted equally? Is a day-nursery place worth the same to a working mother, a single parent and a housewife with a large family? Is an hour of home-help time worth the same to a fairly active but socially isolated old man as to an infirm old woman with an attentive family and supportive neighbours? And if not, how should the benefits be weighted? There is no objective welfare function by which to compare gains and losses spread among different people, and no scientific way of determining how the marginal loss of a pound by one person compares with the marginal gain of a pound by another. The kind of analysis called for by the PPB system came unstuck in the face of the fact that 'Outside of the political process, there is no agreed upon way of comparing and evaluating the merits of different programs for different people' (Wildavsky, 1968).

As William Gorham himself eloquently testified later before the Joint Economic Committee of Congress when it investigated the contribution of economic analysis to national policy-making:

> The benefits of health, education and welfare programs are diverse and often intangible. They affect different age groups and different regions of the population over different periods of time. No amount of analysis is going to tell us whether the nation benefits more from sending a slum child to preschool, providing medical care to an old man, or enabling a disabled housewife to resume her normal activities. The 'grand decisions' – how much health, how much education, how much welfare, and which

groups in the population shall benefit – are questions of value judgements and politics. The analyst cannot make much contribution to their resolution. (Quoted by Wildavsky, 1970)

Gorham's assessment of the lessons of PPBS is echoed by another high-ranking practitioner of HEW, his deputy in charge of program analysis, Alice Rivlin, who later went on to become Assistant Secretary for Planning and Evaluation in the Department. Reflecting afterwards on her experience at HEW, from a vantage point in the Brookings Institution, Rivlin (1971), attempts to sum up the contribution that analysis made to social policy decision-making. She arrives at four broad conclusions, two favourable and two unfavourable, which she believes convey what was learned. First, she argues, considerable progress was made as a result of the work of the policy analysts in identifying and measuring the social problems in American society. Similarly and also on the positive side, systematic analysis led to a better understanding of the distributional consequences of social programmes. On the other hand, little progress was made in comparing the benefits of different programmes; and finally, little was gained in terms of knowing how to produce more effective health, education and welfare services.

Put to the test, analysis failed to do all that was asked of it, but then experience showed that too much had been expected. PPBS had been conceived as a new system of decision-making in which the choices between competing claims on resources would be based on rational analysis of their costs and benefits rather than the calculus of political advantage. In the event, instead of analysis taking over from politics as the basis for allocating resources, it was politics that took over analysis. Slowly the proponents and practitioners of PPBS scaled down their aspirations as the dream began to fade and the limits of analysis were exposed.

Analysis, it was said, cannot perhaps replace politics, but it can facilitate better political decisions. It is a method of investigating rather than solving problems. It may not provide the answers, but it does illuminate the questions. It reveals – even if it does not resolve – the choices that have to be made. Such compromises were part of the new realism that came with the loss of innocence.

If ultimately PPB as a system demanded too much from analysis, none the less it did reveal how useful analysis could be. This, as Rivlin (1970) has stressed, is the message from HEW:

I fail to see how a Secretary of Health, Education and Welfare who wants to do a good job can get along without planning ahead, evaluating the effectiveness of programs, analyzing alternatives carefully, and making decisions in an orderly way in the light of maximum information. It does not matter what he chooses to call it, but he badly needs the basic tools of PPBS.

Analysis cannot provide all the answers, and the 'traditions and sentiments' referred to by Gorham may loom larger in the making of policy than rationalists might wish, but in the end 'it is better to have some idea of where you are going than to fly blind' (Rivlin, 1971).

The Limits of Analysis

By 1968 the clouds were gathering and the forecast for PPBS looked glum. It had been introduced at a time of unparalleled optimism and national self-confidence. President Johnson had pledged his administration to the goal of moving 'beyond opportunity to achievement'. In a declaration of faith equal to Kennedy's promise to land a man on the moon in ten years, he felt able to announce, in 1964, that 'for the first time in our history, it is possible to conquer poverty'. All that was required to master the hard-core social ills, and fulfil the promise of social betterment, was the intelligent application of money and know-how (Schick, 1971). The Great Society programme and the War on Poverty were the political expression of these hopes. The PPB system by applying the methods of the social sciences to the expenditure process provided the tools for the job. Or so it was thought.

In the event, things turned out very differently. Riots in the ghettos, crime in the streets, protests on the campuses and increasing evidence of the persistence of widespread poverty, ill-health and under-attainment, despite the vast sums of money spent on remedial social action programmes, undermined confidence in the capacity of big government, and political leaders, and fostered a growing feeling that 'nothing works'. Disillusionment set in. On top of which the escalation of the Vietnam War began to eat away at the 'fiscal dividend', slow down the economy and push the budget out of balance. By 1968 the country was running a $25 billion deficit, the scope for innovation and social growth had vanished, and the axe was beginning to rise over social spending. Austerity undercut the need for analysis (Engquist, 1970). Time was running out for PPBS.

During his 1968 Presidential campaign Richard Nixon, fastening on the mood of the times, threatened to kick the whiz-kids out of government. After his election, the PPB system, so closely associated with the Johnson administration, was 'de-emphasized' (as the White House put it), fell into disuse and was gradually dismantled. Analysis was unhitched from the budgetary process, its scope was curtailed and PPB documentation was abandoned. The formal death notice

was conveyed to agencies on 21 June 1971 in a memorandum from
the Office of Management and Budget. A fitting obituary was
provided by Elliot Richardson, Nixon's Secretary at HEW from 1970
to 1972:

> It is important to have fully and clearly in view the limitations of a
> purely rational process for allocating resources. What we need to do in
> substance is to make the decision process – the difficult choices among
> competing claims – as conscious and articulate as possible while
> recognising at the same time that in the end feelings, attitudes and values
> must have ultimate and controlling weight. (Quoted in Glennerster, 1975)

The age of analysis covered only a few years, though its style
dominated much of the decade (Schick, 1971). Richardson's quote,
however, bears witness to the fact that in the end those 'traditions
and sentiments' about which Gorham warned in the early days of
PPBS in HEW finally won the day.

By 1972 the only traces of the PPB era left in Washington were
the analytic offices and their teams of staff lodged in the agencies.
They survived because they had proved useful to agency heads in
monitoring the work of their departments, and in helping them to
argue a better case in congressional committees. But the focus of
their work had shifted: the emphasis was no longer on analysis, but
on evaluation. This, however, leads us into the subject-matter of
Chapter 6.

PPBS and PAR

The PPBS reorganization attracted worldwide interest and a flurry
of observers from other countries. The Treasury sent its emissaries
to Washington; and so, too, did the Conservative Party. During his
unsuccessful 1966 election campaign Edward Heath had pressed the
need for a reform of the government machine in order to cut out
waste and inefficiency. In the years of opposition that followed, while
preparations were being made for the next general election, this
theme was honed into a major pledge to introduce a 'new style of
government' in Britain, one firmly based on the principles of rational
public administration (Heath and Barker, 1978; see also Chapter 8).

The party spent a great deal of money developing its proposals.
Two specialist groups – the Conservative Systems Research Centre
and the Public Sector Research Unit – were set up to sift the detail
and evaluate the options. Teams of businessmen were brought in to
advise on management techniques. The Conservative Research
Department, assisted by a number of keen, forward-looking back-
benchers, tackled much of the spadework, including long study tours

abroad looking for ideas. One of the gems that caught their eye was PPBS.

All these preparations paid off in the aftermath of victory in the 1970 general election. Within four months of assuming office the new Heath administration had published its White Paper on the Reorganization of Central Government (Cmnd 4506). As Heclo and Wildavsky (1981) have commented, it is unthinkable that the reforms would have gone so far so quickly if the civil service had not been inclined towards similar ideas and had not been working along the same lines.

The pedigree of the aims and changes put forward in the White Paper is apparent from the reasoning behind them and the language in which they are couched – their line of descent runs directly from PPBS. But there is no starry-eyed acceptance of all the baggage associated with programme budgeting in the USA, no attempt to institutionalize an entirely new system of decision-making. The mistake of trying to fly too high had been well learned. What was proposed was nearer to PPB – without the 'S' – the formal system of programme structures, programme memoranda, output budgets and other gadgetry. In essence, the White Paper accepted the premiss on which PPBS was built, that analysis has a crucial role to play in any rational system of decision-making, but avoided the attempt to couple it with the budgetary process in the way that had proved its undoing in Washington.

This is not to say that the government or Whitehall eschewed the idea of budgetary reform. There were pressures for change on this front too. For example, in 1971 the House of Commons Expenditure Committee argued that: 'proper discussion about the Government's plans . . . requires information about the outputs which projected . . . expenditures are expected to provide and how this provision relates to policy objectives.'

This kind of management accounting was simply not possible within the budgetary and supply framework that existed. But the Treasury was chary of going too far down this road too fast. They had seen the dangers on the other side of the Atlantic. The best approach was to proceed gradually and with caution. Accordingly a few interested departments – the Department of Education and Science (DES), Home Office and DHSS among them – were encouraged to carry out feasibility studies aimed at linking expenditure to service outputs and to try their hand at programme budgeting (Banks, 1979; Garrett, 1972). If the effort came to nothing, then little would be lost. But no attempt was made to pursue such reforms systematically on a government-wide scale.

The commitment to analysis, however, was altogether less half-hearted. The White Paper spelt out the thinking clearly:

> The basis of improved policy formulation and decision-taking is rigorous analysis of existing and suggested government policies, actions and expenditure. This analysis must test whether such policies or activities accord with the Government's strategic aims and, indeed, whether they are suitable for government at all. And it must test whether they are of greater or lesser priority than other policies or activities at present carried out, or likely to be proposed in the future; what is the most efficient means of execution; and whether their long-term effects are likely to accord with Government priorities and policies as they develop. (Cmnd 4506, para. 7)

The mechanism for achieving these aims was a new system known as programme analysis and review (PAR).

A PAR was designed to provide more and better information in support of departmental submissions to the annual public expenditure survey (PESC). PESC sets out to relate government spending plans to projected resources in line with the Treasury's medium-term economic assessment. It was conceived as a system of expenditure planning and financial control (Wright, 1979). As such, it was deficient in at least two respects. It did not require departments to provide explicit statements of the objectives of their spending proposals in a way that would allow ministers' plans to be tested against government strategy; nor did it call for the detailed analysis of existing programmes to show how they were working and how they compared with alternative ways of pursuing the same ends. PAR was intended to strengthen PESC by improving the background analysis for expenditure decisions 'while avoiding the problems of analytical over-kill encountered by the practitioners of PPB in American federal government' (Garrett, 1972). As one Treasury expert is quoted as saying, 'PAR is like programme budgeting without a programme budget' (Heclo and Wildavsky, 1981). The link between PAR and PESC provided the channel through which the results of analysis were fed into the expenditure process. Essentially the PAR cycle began each year with ministers agreeing the topics for study in consultation with the Treasury and the Central Policy Review Staff (a new analytic unit set up in the Cabinet Office following publication of Cmnd 4506 – see Chapter 8). The aim was to review some ten or twelve major expenditure programmes each year. The individual departments concerned took the lead in conducting the reviews with the Treasury and CPRS advising on their scope and methodology, setting the timetable and appraising the drafts. There was no fixed format for a PAR, but the sort of questions usually asked of any particular programme included: 'why are we doing this?'; 'is it working OK?'; 'are there better or cheaper ways of doing the same thing?'; and 'is it receiving the right kind of priority?'. Again showing its grasp of the lessons of PPBS, the Treasury did not press for anything grand or ambitious in the way of defining objectives or measuring outputs or calculating comparative social returns. The line was to stick with the doable and, given that few departments had any professional analysts, the quality of analysis produced was often rudimentary.

Although there was no fixed format, a PAR analysis did usually follow certain common steps or guidelines (ibid.). First, departments would be expected to assess the trends and determinants of expenditure in the chosen programme area. Secondly, they would be asked to take stock of the resources already allocated to the programme. Thirdly, how they are made up in terms of, for example, manpower costs, capital investment, debt charges, etc. Fourthly, they would have to evaluate how far the programme was meeting the needs it addressed and how, if at all, these were expected to change in the future. Finally, a PAR would be expected to consider how things might be done differently and to spell out the choices open to ministers. When completed, generally after twelve months or so, the PAR report was submitted to the appropriate Cabinet committee where it was discussed in time for any policy changes to be fed into the summer PESC operation.

How did the softly-softly approach to the introduction of analysis in Whitehall fare by comparison with the fanfare and hullabaloo in Washington? Did modesty reap more than razzamatazz? The answer is almost certainly no, and probably a lot less. Before going on to look at the impact of the PAR system, however, caveats are necessary.

The task of reviewing PAR is not unlike reviewing a closed book, for none of the reports was ever published. The obsessive secrecy that envelops all levels of government in Britain, and none more so than Whitehall itself, resulted in PARs being treated as internal working documents and classified as official secrets. When the House of Commons Expenditure Committee asked to see PARs on higher education and school expenditure, as part of an investigation of policy-making in the DES, it was refused. The quality of the analysis that went into the reports is, therefore, unchartered. Hearsay suggests they varied from being 'excellently reasoned' to 'hopeless', though in most cases it seems they were technically unsophisticated documents with an emphasis on discursive rather than empirical reasoning (ibid.; Garrett, 1980). These facts point to why, in exploring the uses of analysis in the policy process, the focus in this chapter has been mainly on the US experience of PPBS. The greater openness of government in the USA, the freer exchange that exists between the academic community and government and the less deferential approach of American journalism have all helped to provide a measure of information and insight that is simply not available in this country.

A second caveat, also relevant to the points made above, puts a question mark over just how far the PAR system really did inject more 'rigorous analysis' (Cmnd 4506) into the process of policy formulation. Certainly, it is doubtful whether what passed for analysis in Whitehall bore much resemblance to its namesake in Washington. Whatever went into a PAR was agreed by the mandarins who had always worn the 'thinking-caps' in Whitehall departments. There was no new recruitment of specialist, trained analytical staff to match the influx into federal agencies. There was no investment in new methodologies or technical expertise as happened with PPBS. There was no attempt to harness the social sciences to the making of policy as in the USA. The job was done by those whose role had always been to offer advice; people with a classical frame of mind whose analytical strengths were more likely to be logical than empirical. The lurking suspicion is that in practice instead of representing a new departure, PAR became a special form of gamesmanship in the Whitehall community.

PAR's first main achievement was to survive a change of government in 1974 – a vulnerable time for all new ideas and especially when they are unloved. And no one was very fond of PAR. Parliament wasn't really interested because it was denied access to the reports. So far as most of the departments were concerned, PAR was either close to what they did already or a nuisance foisted upon them from outside. Either way they stood to gain little from their involvement or to lose a lot by exposing their programmes to more detailed scrutiny from the Treasury. The result was a scepticism, shading into distrust, of the formalities of the PAR system.

As Ashworth (1982) observed from his perch in the CPRS, the 'difficulty has been to find a device (or a set of devices) whereby enthusiasm for the review process can be kept alive and periodically rekindled'. This problem was lessened so long as government spending was on the up and up. For then PARs could be used to add some analytical muscle to the departments' spending bids. But from about 1974, as economic prospects blackened, the control of public expenditure became the key target of economic management. The PESC system moved from being an instrument of planning to an instrument of control (Wright, 1979). As the demands of crisis management became ever more pressing, so the attention of government shifted away from the luxuries of analysis and review to the more immediate, short-term preoccupations of survival (Gray and Jenkins, 1983b). In this climate, as spending gave way to pruning, the incentive for departments to play 'PARlour' games was lost. Their only protection against the increasingly piratical raids from the Treasury was to close the hatches.

Over this period the PAR system fell by the wayside to have its place taken by a new creature – the 'efficiency review'. The efficiency review was born of straitened times. Its purpose was to cut costs, to yield savings, to make economies in the name of value for money. Unlike analysis, it faced only one way: it did not look for what more should be done, only at what could be done for less.

Following the 1979 election, Mrs Thatcher appointed Sir Derek Rayner, of Marks & Spencer, to lead a team of Whitehall wastesavers, sometimes styled 'Rayner's Raiders'. They were charged with conducting *ad hoc* efficiency audits in departments, focusing on particular activities or functions, with the sole aim of identifying ways in which they could be carried out more efficiently, more effectively and at less cost (Richardson, 1982). Their arrival signalled the passing of PAR and the analytic tradition to which it belonged. In 1979 Mrs Thatcher formally abandoned the PAR system.

The Lessons of Analysis
In their different ways both PPBS and PAR may be seen as attempts to institutionalize analysis in the system of government. What do they tell us about the role of analysis in policy-making, the limits within which it works and the conditions necessary for it to flourish?

Many of the most important lessons, especially from the PPB era, have an almost naïve ring about them, as if those involved should have known better from the start. They reflect their times and show up best against this background. For the age of analysis was a spin-off from the optimism brought about by economic growth. It emerged from the belief that sustained prosperity, which for the first time seemed to be within reach, would deliver the means of solving the major problems facing society. The old ideological conflicts, born of scarcity, would disappear and so, too, would the old adversarial politics to which they gave rise. The new challenges would be largely technical ones in the face of which the politician would give way to the expert. (Addressing a White House Conference on National Economic Issues in 1962, President Kennedy declared, 'The fact of the matter is that most of the problems, or at least many of them, that we now face are technical problems . . . they deal with questions which are beyond the comprehension of most men, most governmental administrators.') It was this faith in the ability of the expert that led to the rise of analysis.

The optimism of the 1960s has faded and gone along with PPBS. So, too, has the faith in the expert. But some of the lessons remain as a warning to any social scientists who think they can succeed where the politicians and administrators have failed. Broadly they may be summarized as follows:

- analysis is no substitute for political judgement;
- political judgement often involves considerations beyond the scope of analysis;
- many imponderables are involved in the making of major decisions and analysis cannot provide all the answers;
- analysis has its uses but is not easily integrated into bureaucratic routines;
- analysis is rarely worth while unless it is understood and wanted by its clients;
- analysis tends to serve as an instrument of advocacy in the highly charged political environment of government;
- analysis only thrives in periods of relative affluence, not austerity.

5 Social indicators and the Mondale Initiative

'The fact is that neither the President nor the Congress nor the public has the kind of broad-scale information and analysis needed to adequately assess our progress toward achievement of our national social aspirations' (Senator Walter Mondale, 1967)

The 1960s were a bad decade for the American Dream. The early hopes of Kennedy's 'New Frontier' and Johnson's 'Great Society' were soon dashed by domestic crises. The Vietnam War added shame to the disillusionment. Somehow American society seemed to have lost its way.

Yet only a few, short years before the outlook had been so very different. The ending of the Cold War following the Cuban missile crisis switched the focus of attention to domestic issues. The success of the Civil Rights movement in enforcing desegregation showed there was a mood for reform. Kennedy's promise to land a man on the moon within ten years reaffirmed the belief in American technology and the capacity for problem-solving (badly dented by the launch of the first Sputnik in 1957). And a booming economy promised to deliver the resources for ensuring a better life for all. It appeared as if the will, the means and the way were prepared for social advance. Faith in the potential of government to steer society along the path of social progress was firmly in the ascendant (Aaron, 1978).

The scene was all set when President Johnson walked on to the stage following his landslide victory over Barry Goldwater in 1964. The 89th Congress, elected with him, provided the biggest Democratic margins since 1936: a huge 295–140 majority in the House, and a 68–32 majority in the Senate. Johnson quickly saw that what he called the 'Great Congress' presented a unique opportunity for attacking the social problems disfiguring American society – an opportunity which might be lost with the next congressional elections in 1966. He immediately declared a War on Poverty and embarked on a massive programme of social legislation to expand health, housing, education and training, and to increase transfers in cash and in kind. His aim was to create the 'Great Society' in which 'the least among us will find contentment and the best among us can find greatness'.

The vision was short-lived. The ambitious new programmes failed to bring the expected returns. The problems proved more intractable than had been foreseen; they refused to go away. Finding solutions was harder than enacting Bills. Under the spotlight of congressional attention and academic scrutiny, problems that had first seemed manageable grew in size and complexity. Instead of changing for the better, it began to seem to many legislators and critics, on Capitol Hill and beyond, that 'society is crashing about our ears'.[1] Under pressure, the consensus that sustained the Great Society programme started to crumble.

During the mid-1960s the gap between the economic achievements and the social aspirations of American society appeared, if anything, to be widening. What stuck in the craw was that a country with a GNP equal to the total of the rest of the world should continue to display unmistakeable signs of social underdevelopment. Moreover, the symptoms pointed to a deepening malaise. Among the more telling of these were: the rediscovery of poverty as a structural feature of contemporary society condemning fully a quarter of the population to subsistence living; the revelation that millions of Americans were suffering from malnutrition, hunger and even starvation; the burning of the ghettos in a wave of riots from Watts to Newark; rising crime rates; the despoilation of the physical environment; child mortality rates that were higher than many less affluent nations (the USA ranked only fifteenth in the world league table of infant mortality); and the disaffection of youth signalled by turmoil on the campuses and anti-war protests on the streets.

This accumulation of troubles presented what many saw as 'the most mystifying fact of our time': 'Why is the richest, best educated, most technically advanced nation in the world unable to eliminate poverty, keep babies from dying, teach its children to read, or get the traffic moving?' (Rivlin, 1972). Society seemed to be coming apart at the seams, yet no one knew why or what to do:

> Yesterday I was in Detroit, and I felt like I was coming into Saigon as I had done a year earlier. There were the same puffs of smoke. You had the same edgy sense that you were safe but not quite sure you were safe. And just as there, you have the feeling that we are a great and a powerful nation, but at the same time we are awfully puny, because here, despite all our wealth, we had as serious a social disruption as this country has ever seen, and we just do not know what we are dealing with. (Senator Walter Mondale)

The conclusion was reached that such impotence was the result of ignorance: 'we have a crisis of understanding rather than a crisis of resources' (Mondale, 1972). Surely, 'there must be more peaceful and precise ways than riot to measure the state of our social health' (Mondale, 1967). Certainly, the irony of a society in which some men were mobile enough to travel in space while others lacked the mobility to travel out of their ghetto did not pass unnoticed. More, it seemed, was known about extraterrestial mobility than about intrasocietal mobility. The 'luxury of such relative ignorance' could no longer be afforded. What rendered such a rich nation so puny was, more than anything, that its government was continually being caught on the hop: 'Just as we once floundered in the area of economic policy for lack of hard factual information, so today we are floundering in the area of adequate social policy due to lack of hard factual information' (Whitney Young, National Urban League).

The 'fundamental inadequacy' of the information on which social policies and programmes were based meant that:

> national problems go nearly unnoticed until they are suddenly forced upon us by some significant development . . . We desperately need ways to monitor our social health and to identify such problems before they destroy our society. (Senator Walter Mondale)

A forceful case in point was the sudden official discovery of starvation in Mississippi. Irrefutable testimony of the existence of hunger and malnutrition was introduced into the record of hearings before the Senate Subcommittee on Manpower, Employment and Poverty, in 1967, by doctors working in the Mississippi Delta. They were followed by a parade of public officials who, shamefacedly, had to admit their ignorance of the situation. Information was readily available on how many soya beans were grown, on how much was spent on the direct commodity distribution programme, on the cost of the food programme, and so on, but no one, it turned out, knew the extent or degree or distribution of hunger in America. The Secretary of Agriculture, who ran the food programmes, did not know; the Surgeon-General of the United States did not know; the Director of the Office of Economic Opportunity, who co-ordinated the War on Poverty, did not know; and the Secretary of Health, Education and Welfare did not know.

A year later, in April 1968, a privately sponsored Citizens' Board of Inquiry published an independent report on *Hunger and Malnutrition in the United States*. Using national data, area studies and case histories, the report estimated that 10–14 million Americans were going hungry. It was pilloried for its supposedly exaggerated conclusions but, in the same month, CBS aired a documentary, *Hunger in America*, showing the crippling effects of undernourishment on children in Alabama, on pregnant women in San Antonio and tenant farmers in Virginia. The film's narrator, Charles Kuralt, closed with the simple hope that 'the most basic human need, food, might someday become a human right' in the land of abundance.

Under this sort of pressure the US Government Public Health Service was authorized to conduct a national nutrition survey. The results, based on a study of thousands of families in the bottom quartile of the income distribution in ten states, indicated that hunger and malnutrition in America were 'as severe as in some of the poorer nations of the world'. This finding prompted Senator George McGovern to exclaim, 'we have our own Biafras'.

Thirty-four per cent of pre-school children examined were found to exhibit serious anaemia, and growth retardation was common. Vitamin A deficiency, unknown to any child who simply drinks enough milk, afflicted 33 per cent of children under 6. In Texas goitre, a disease that can be prevented for a fraction of a penny per person per year and thought to be extinct in the USA, was by World Health Organization (WHO) standards endemic. Children were discovered with rickets, scurvy, beriberi, marasmus and kwashiorkor – diseases common in Third World countries and usually associated with famine.

These shocking facts emphasized the gulf separating the promise of full opportunity held out by the Great Society programme and the realities of poverty, deprivation and powerlessness into which so many people were born. They were also seen as revealing the seriousness of the 'domestic intelligence gap'. The federal government did not know enough about the condition of society. Consequently, it was forced by its own ignorance into a hand-to-mouth posture, leaving unforeseen problems to blow up into crises before anyone realized what was going on.

As well as allowing policy-makers to be upstaged by the process of social change, the lack of adequate information about the state of society meant that programmes were generally devised and operated on the basis of myth and ignorance: 'hunch, intuition and good intentions have been the heavy artillery of social problem-solvers to a far greater extent than anyone has recognised' (Mondale, 1970).

Joseph Califano, for example, a one-time special counsel and adviser on domestic programmes to President Johnson, once described as Johnson's tsar for domestic policy, recounted how he had once asked the Secretary of Health, Education and Welfare, Wilbur Cohen, how many people were on welfare and who they were. Since several billion dollars were being spent on welfare programmes, he expected the information would be readily available. So also did the Secretary, who promised to send it over as soon as he returned to the office. In the event, it took the Department of Health, Education and Welfare (HEW) more than a year to unearth the statistics. As Cohen remarked later: 'Unfortunately, most government statistics are by-products of the needs of accounting and administrative routine, and thus tell us more about the operation of government than the condition of society' (Cohen, 1968).

Federal agencies certainly generated masses of information – about 400 million dollars worth in the mid-1960s – but very little threw any light on the purposes of their activities or the success with which they were being pursued ('it is worth about 4 cents when it is all done because nobody looks at it'). A new distinction between 'hot' and 'cold' facts entered the federal lexicon: 'hot facts' were those that penetrated, revealed and illuminated policy choices, 'cold facts' were those produced solely for the sake of bureaucratic housekeeping. Joseph Califano illustrated the power of hot facts by recalling how President Johnson had asked for statistics on infant mortality: 'The very day the President received the infant mortality statistics which indicated that more than a dozen countries had a lower infant mortality rate than the US . . . he decided that the federal government would embark upon a major child health programme.' Other factors, of course, played their part and, quite probably, were more influential in precipitating the final decision to aim at reducing the rate of infant mortality from 25 to no more than 16 deaths per 1,000 births. The point is that the hot facts about child mortality, unlike the routine outpourings of government, were the stuff of action.

The organization of government statistics to meet the requirements of administrative accountability and bureaucratic control had other consequences which also reduced their usefulness for the purpose of informing policy-making. It meant that they tended to be insular, fragmented and self-serving: insular because they only took an agency perspective; fragmented because they failed to link up; and self-serving because they were designed and collected by administrators primarily for their own use. New sources – and new kinds – of information were called for that would provide 'the "hot data" to help us understand our society and what we must do to make it more effective than it is in meeting this Nation's human problems' (Senator Walter Mondale).

A third factor also contributed to the ignorance, and hence the impotence, of government in the field of social policy. Government was ill-prepared to meet the future impact of social change, ill-informed about the present state of society and also incapable, or so it seemed, of learning from the past. Billions of dollars were spent on social programmes but pennies, if anything, on finding out what they accomplished. Moreover, what evaluative research was done tended to be the monopoly of the executive branch; of those who had a vested interest in the running of programmes. Too often 'the executive is exposed to the temptation to release only those findings that suit its purposes; there is no-one to keep them honest' (Moynihan, 1967).

These problems were made worse by what Bunker (1978) called a deficit in 'institutional memory':

> The government is prevented from learning from experience because it has no adequate and organized way of recalling what it has tried and what were the results. Similarly it has no systematic and functional way of finding out what questions it has asked and what the answers were.

What was required was a new emphasis on evaluation, instead of trial and error, by social scientists whose own careers were not tied to the success of the programmes, whose findings would be disciplined by public scrutiny, and who would act as a knowledge bank for government.

The Social Indicators Movement

If the mounting evidence of the federal government's failure to deal with the problems of a rich but troubled society showed that it was labouring with inadequate and insufficient information, then the yoke of ignorance was, for many, tightened by the way economic values displaced social values in the determination of policy. PPBS, for instance, was criticized for giving too much weight to economic indicators at the expense of non-monetary costs and benefits.

At the heart of the matter was the widespread and growing conviction that 'our ability to measure social change has lagged behind our ability to measure strictly economic change' (National Commission on Technology, Automation and Economic Progress, 1966). The same report, in a chapter on 'Improving Public Decision Making', continued: 'The American commitment is not only to raise the standard of living, but to improve the quality of life. But we have too few yardsticks to tell us how we are doing.'

Whereas economics had succeeded in developing an enormous array of statistical indicators for measuring ups and downs in the economy, for judging its performance and for forecasting the future, there existed no equivalent indicators for assessing social progress. In the area of social policy 'basic and cumulative information is sorely lacking, as is the knowledge needed to analyze and measure change' (National Academy of Sciences, 1968).

The quantity and quality of economic information both had increased the control which government exerted over the management of the economy and increased its accountability for the handling of economic affairs. It had also brought vast numbers of economists into the inner circles of government. However, a strong lobby of opinion now began to form around the idea that the power and sophistication of national economic accounting had contributed to the rise of 'a "New Philistinism" that expresses national goals and performance in dollar sign figures' (Gross, 1965):

> If we examine the President's major policy documents, particularly the Economic Report and the Budget Message, we find practically no information whatsoever on 'social structure'. We find that the major indicators deal not with how good but with how much, not with the quality of our lives but rather with the quantity of goods and dollars. (Gross, in the Preface to Bauer, 1966)

Economic indicators had come to exert such a seductive influence that people tended to equate a rising national income with improving national well-being. Yet the Johnson years showed that a wealthy society was not necessarily a fair, healthy, stable or integrated society. Economic growth was not a surrogate for social development and fewer and fewer people were prepared to regard it as an overriding objective. But equivalent ways of charting the social health of the nation were not available. As a result, monetary information of lesser significance tended to displace qualitative information of greater significance, leaving economic criteria to dictate social choices.

In 1962 the Behavioral Science Subpanel of the President's Science Advisory Committee had called attention to the great advance over the past generation in the quantity and quality of information about the economy and the effective use now made of it in formulating national economic policy. 'Similar benefits', the panel concluded, 'would flow from a corresponding advance in the quantity and quality of information about non-economic aspects of behaviour'. In the era of the Great Society, and the aftermath of Watts, this argument found a new resonance and a more receptive audience; it chimed with the times:

> There is no question in my mind that we, as a nation, need new tools to assess our efforts and progress in the area of social reform and to arrive at a better understanding of these efforts and the state of our social health as a nation. We need a clear and precise picture of how well we are doing in our efforts to provide a decent life and full opportunity for all Americans, and we do not have one. (Whitney Young, National Urban League)

A set of social indicators was needed 'for taking the nation's pulse' which measured what the national income statistics left out (Olson, 1969a).

The social indicators movement began as a reaction against the almost total reliance on economic information as a basis for policy decisions. It was carried forward by an alliance of interests. Within the social sciences community a major investment in social indicators was seen as a way of eliciting support for basic and applied social research. If a political market could be created for such information, other social scientists might be brought in from the cold and follow the economists in getting a slice of the action. As Schonfield (1972) observed, 'If there is one thing that could help to relate social science research more closely to public policy, it is the rapid development of efficient social indicators.' From a humanist perspective they also promised to bring people back into the reckoning and to offset the 'econocentrism' so deeply embedded in the policy process.

In the political arena social indicators attracted many friends with different motives; on Capitol Hill some Congressmen saw in them a way of strengthening the arm of the Legislature against the Executive. They suspected that their dependence on information supplied by the Executive branch left them open to manipulation by the federal bureaucracy:

> When the executive branch approves the position we are supporting, we are immediately supplied with voluminous, sophisticated, computer-supported information. When they don't, we don't get any information. The computers have selective 'paralysis'. (Senator Walter Mondale)

By providing an independent accounting of the social state of the nation, a system of social indicators might greatly improve congressional scrutiny in the field of social policy much the same as economic indicators had done in the field of economic policy.

Social indicators also found favour among the strong liberal coalition of social reformers in Congress. They saw them as the keystone of a system of social reporting on the condition of society. As such, they would increase the visibility of social problems; keep them on the political agenda; raise public awareness of the need to do something about them; increase the accountability of the executive for the operation of its social programmes; and lead to a more rational determination of social priorities.

This last consideration links with a third axis of support for the social indicators movement; those who believed in the need for rationalizing the policy process by putting it on a more scientific footing. This grouping itself spanned a wide range of thinking. At one end were politicians and academics who thought that government was not making enough use of social science knowledge. They had no illusions about the shortcomings of the behavioural sciences, but they were equally sure about the far more damaging consequences of ignoring them:

If we want to navigate a satellite or produce a new drug or a new hybrid, or even explode a nuclear weapon, we do not call in the old wives. In social systems the old wives, or at least their husbands, are called in all the time. Creating a peaceful world, abolishing slums, solving the race problem, or overcoming crime and so on, are not regarded as suitable subjects for scientific technology but are regarded as fields where a pure heart and a little commonsense will do all that is really necessary. (Boulding, 1967)

The social sciences could help to temper intuition with understanding. At the same time, just as with economics, greater recognition of their role would stimulate their development and so increase their usefulness. Social policy and the social sciences would feed off each other.

On the other wing, there was a breed of enthusiasts, somewhere between politicians and technicians (labelled 'technopols' by some), who dreamed of using social science instead of pressure politics to solve the nation's problems (Kopkind, 1967). Their aim was to build on the achievements of macro-economics in the management of the economy by developing similar tools for the management of society. Social indicators were part of the instrumentation of the managed society. They were to provide the feedback to ensure that society was kept on its pre-set course.

Given its cosmopolitan roots, it is perhaps not surprising that the social indicators movement should have branched out in a number of directions. Broadly the movement was made up of four cross-currents (Gross and Straussman, 1974).

Social Accounting
The initial response to the challenge of developing social indicators was to think in terms of a system of social accounts, analogous to the national income accounts, which would indicate the social costs and social benefits of investment and services – a sort of balance-sheet of the effects of social change on society. It quickly became apparent, however, that our understanding of the workings of the social system was altogether inadequate for this task. The basic theoretical requirement for a system of social accounting is the ability to define the relationships between the input of social resources and the output of social welfare. Such a causal model of society is still beyond the horizons of the social sciences (Schonfield, 1972).

Goaded by the criticism that the national income accounts were inadequate as a measure of welfare, notably because they missed out those costs and benefits not fully reflected in market prices, many economists tried to adjust gross national product (GNP) by incorporating these externalities such as household work, leisure, pollution, etc. Practically, however, there are no limits to what the national accounts can be made to absorb, and these efforts also ran up against the absence or unreliability of measures and time-series data about these non-monetary aspects of life. In the end, the conclusion was drawn that the aim of devising a grand, all-purpose measure of net national welfare was unrealistic.

Future Planning

A second strand of the movement viewed social indicators as tools that would help to establish social goals and priorities. It was the province of the futurists: those interested in 'anticipating the future' for the purposes of societal management. Its origins may be traced to President Eisenhower's Commission on National Goals which, in 1960, published a report, entitled *Goals for Americans: Programs for Action in the Sixties*. It was carried forward by a 'Commission on the Year 2000', set up by the American Academy of Arts and Sciences in 1965, with a remit to probe the future for major structural changes and problems that would be coming to a head at the turn of the century and to propose strategies for coping with them (Bell, 1967). Further impetus came in 1967 from two special volumes of the Annals of the American Academy of Political and Social Science devoted to 'Social Goals and Indicators for American Society'.

Future planning reached its zenith in 1969 with the creation of President Nixon's short-lived National Goals Research Staff (NGRS) in the White House. The NGRS was 'a small, highly technical staff, made up of experts in the collection, correlation and processing of data relating to social needs, and in the projection of social trends'. Its functions were to include: forecasting future developments and assessing the longer-range consequences of present social trends; measuring the probable future impact of alternative courses of action; estimating the range of goals that might be attainable in the light of the availability of resources and the likely rate of progress; and developing and monitoring social indicators that reflect the quality of American life and the direction and rate of its change.

President Nixon summed up the thinking that led to the creation of the NGRS in these words:

> We can no longer afford to approach the longer-range future haphazardly. As the pace of change accelerates, the process of change becomes more complex. Yet at the same time, an extra-ordinary array of tools and techniques has been developed by which it becomes increasingly possible to project future trends – and thus to make the kind of informed choices which are necessary if we are to establish mastery over the process of change. (Nixon, 1969)

The first assignment of the NGRS was to address itself to the question 'of what kind of nation we want to be as we begin our third century'. To this end, it was instructed to prepare a public report, within a year, illuminating the possible range of national goals for 1976. Thereafter it would report annually.

The NGRS only just survived long enough to submit its first report (NGRS, 1970). From the outset it had been overshadowed by more pressing political imperatives of the Nixon administration and its director had been preoccupied with other responsibilities as a member of the White House staff. But its fate was sealed by the savaging of its first report by the press. The *New York Times* dismissed it as a 'disappointing evasion of responsibility' which spelled out neither goals nor priorities and showed only that the NGRS 'was either misnamed or misdirected or both'. The NGRS was summarily abolished in 1970, ending the political flirtation with future planning.

Within this tradition, then, social indicators were the technical means of mapping the future, of enhancing social prediction, and of measuring progress towards the realization of politically defined, social goals.

Societal Monitoring
This third branch of the social indicators movement focused on the development of indices for assessing the state of society and for evaluating the impact of social programmes. In this sense, social indicators were conceived as aids to policy-making and problem-solving. Potentially they were seen as serving two purposes: increasing the *responsiveness* of government by providing advance warning of encroaching problems, by identifying unmet needs and by measuring the effects of innovations and changes in policy; and improving the managerial *effectiveness* of government by strengthening the oversight of programmes and providing feedback on how well they were working.

Unlike the advocates of social accounting, those who pressed the use of indicators for societal monitoring harboured no ambitions about aggregating them into a single measure of the quality of life. Instead they envisaged a range of separate, quantitative indicators each measuring an aspect of the state of society: health, housing, education, transportation, law and order, the environment, social mobility, etc. A sensitive social indicator should tell whether, in the area to which it refers, things are getting better or worse and to what degree.

The intellectual origins of societal monitoring go back to the 1920s and 1930s. An extensive, empirical analysis of US trends was first conducted following the 1920 Census. In 1929, President Hoover commissioned a group of social scientists, with a research staff headed by the sociologist William Ogburn, to study the feasibility of a national survey of social trends. As part of this work, Ogburn's team produced a series of thirteen monographs reviewing different sectors of US life, each presenting much original data and analyses. The Research Committee's report, *Recent Social Trends in the United States*, published in 1934, was immediately recognized as an important landmark in the application of statistical reporting. Although the report was eclipsed by the Great Depression, as interest in emerging social trends gave way to the more immediate and pressing concerns of economic stabilization, it nevertheless had a lasting influence in the applied study of social change. Many of the authors who contributed to the report, notably Ogburn himself, continued to research and teach in the field and their work inspired a future generation of social scientists who themselves had reached positions of influence by the 1960s.

Indeed, it was one of the contributors to *Recent Social Trends*, Thomas J. Woofter who, while working in HEW, advanced the idea of publishing key statistics on what was going on in the health and welfare field. This initiative eventually led to the publication, beginning in 1960, of the Department of Health, Education and Welfares *HEW Indicators* and its annual supplement *HEW Trends*. These two series aimed to monitor both the operation of public programmes and the changing backcloth of national needs. As well as presenting tables and graphs (modelled on the Council of Economic Advisers' *Economic Indicators*), they also included review essays, trend analyses, details of forthcoming legislation and appraisals of individual programmes. Both publications were widely used and praised by HEW administrators, scholars and members of Congress. In 1967, however, they were discontinued in order to shift resources into a still more ambitious and comprehensive attempt at social monitoring announced by President Johnson the previous year.

In a Message to the Congress on Domestic Health and Education, in March 1966, the President instructed the Department of Health, Education and Welfare to investigate the possibility of developing a wide-ranging system of social indicators to complement the economic indicators already available:

> Through the programs entrusted to its care, the Department of Health, Education and Welfare exercises continuing concern for the social well-being of all our people . . . To improve our ability to chart our progress, I have asked the Secretary to establish within his office the resources to develop the necessary social statistics and indicators to supplement those prepared by the Bureau of Labor Statistics and the Council of Economic

Advisers. With these yardsticks, we can better measure the distance we have come and plan for the way ahead.

HEW was given this task partly because, under Secretary John Gardner, it had attracted a lot of support and respect for the quality of its work on PPBS and partly, too, because of its experience in producing *HEW Indicators* and *Trends*.

Within HEW, responsibility for this new assignment was delegated to William Gorham, Assistant Secretary for Program Co-ordination, who was also in charge of PPBS. He quickly organized a Social Indicators Panel, composed of about two dozen scholars and data experts from universities, research institutions and other government agencies, and asked Daniel Bell, the Harvard sociologist and 'end-of-ideology' theorist, to serve with him as the Panel's co-chairman. Gorham and Bell outlined the guiding aims of the initiative in a working memorandum to the Panel:

> No society in history has, as yet, made a coherent and unified effort to assess those elements in society which facilitate and which bar each individual from realizing his talents and abilities, in order to allow him to find a job, or establish a career commensurate with his talents, to live a full and healthy life equal to his biological potential, to establish the conditions for an adequate standard of living which allows him to live in a civilized fashion, and which provides a physical and social environment which enhances his sense of life. We believe that these are aims implicit in the American purpose. We believe that the means of realizing these are possible. If it is agreed that this is an appropriate and adequate focus, the function of the Social Report would be to provide a continuing assessment of our abilities to realize these aims. (Quoted in Gross and Springer, 1967)

It was left to Gorham's successor, Alice Rivlin, and her deputy, Mancur Olson, under a new Secretary of HEW, Wilbur Cohen, to see this project through to completion with the publication, on the last day of the Johnson administration in 1969, of *Toward a Social Report* (HEW, 1969).

Toward a Social Report was presented as 'an attempt on the part of social scientists to look at several very important areas and digest what is known about progress towards generally accepted goals'. It was a slimmed-down version of twenty-three essays, prepared by scholars and experts for the Social Indicators Panel, each of which set out to summarize the state of knowledge about social trends in American society. The published report focused on the following areas: health, social mobility, the physical environment, income and poverty, public order and safety, learning, science and art, and participation and alienation.

The report's drafters stressed that it was not to be seen as the end of the road, but only the first step down a long path; much more work still needed to be done. Nevertheless, they concluded, the development of social indicators could improve public policy-making, if not by making the hard choices the nation must make any easier, then at least by ensuring they were not made in ignorance of the nation's needs.

Despite its optimistic tones, and the generally welcome press it received, *Toward a Social Report* marked something of a watershed in the social indicators movement. For what it left undone actually revealed the difficulties and dangers of social monitoring. It showed, for instance, that the government did not routinely produce the sort of information required for social monitoring; and that the kind of statistics needed could not be obtained as a by-product of current accounting or administrative procedures. Most official statistics only measured the inputs of resources – in terms of money spent, people employed or places available, etc. – rather than the outputs of programmes in terms of their effects on health, crime, educational attainment, and so on. The requirements of social monitoring could not be met simply by an expansion of existing statistical efforts; they called for new ideas about what ought to be collected and new methods for closing the 'domestic intelligence gap'.

At this point, however, the deficiencies of official data began to merge into deficiencies of social science theory. It was by no means clear what social indicators should measure, how to construct them or how to interpret them. Take crime, for instance. Social theory offered no clear-cut definition of criminal behaviour; no principles for weighting, say, crimes against the person as against crimes against property; and no ready answer to the question of whether, for example, an increase in recorded offences represented a genuine rise in criminality, changes in law enforcement practices, the emergence of new norms of behaviour or simply the effects of shifts in the composition of the population.

Even if these problems of measurement and interpretation could be overcome, and many optimists believed the social sciences would rise to the challenge, there were still others to contend with just as serious. One of the chief selling-points of social indicators was their supposed usefulness as aids to policy-making. By measuring how national well-being was changing, it was thought they would enable better evaluation of the impact of public programmes. *Toward a Social Report* cast doubt on this promise by showing that it was not possible to distinguish between changes in a social indicator due to the effects of government programmes and those due to extraneous variables. Health and life expectancy, for example, depend not only on public health programmes, but also on private medical expenditures, the standard of living, working conditions, the quality of nutrition, and so on. Without precise knowledge of the relationship between these variables, it simply is not possible to untangle the reasons behind any changes in health indicators. The fact that ultimately there was no way of linking social indicators to what the government does seriously undermined their practical worth (and, incidentally, led to a growing interest in social experimentation as a way of getting round some of these difficulties – see Chapter 7).

Finally, the snowballing of official interest in social indicators gave many social scientists cold feet. They feared a government take-over of the movement; and feared, too, that they themselves might be turned into little more than 'market researchers of the welfare state' (Gouldner, 1970) – paid technicians in the service of state power. These worries assumed many guises. If social indicators were tied too closely to the needs of government, it was argued, they could easily become social vindicators: manipulated for short-term political ends; infused by administrative values; embodying only official perceptions and definitions of social needs; closing off the possibility of new insights into national problems; and reflecting the bias of existing institutions. In short, they could be monopolized by ruling élites for the purposes of social control.

These concerns produced something of a rift between those who saw social monitoring primarily as a tool for policy-making and those who saw it, in more scientific terms, as a way of getting to grips with the changes going on in American society. Moreover, whereas the former were now less sure of the practical utility of social monitoring, the latter were more conscious of the risks of it being abused. One result was that this branch of the social indicators movement lost a lot of its steam in the 1970s. Another was that the focus of attention shifted more towards social reporting as the last of the major cross-currents that made up the social indicators movement.

Social Reporting

Social reporting is best seen as a response to the dangers of social indicators becoming a 'one-way flow of information' (Zapf, 1976) in favour of the government, and the risk of them being captured by powerful interests within the policy system. In particular, social reporting aims:

- to prevent the monopolization of data by official users and interpreters;
- to avoid the 'hardening of categories' (Gross and Springer, 1967) around official definitions of needs and problems;

– to insulate social indicators from political interference or manipulation.

Like the other branches of the social indicators movement it, too, is concerned with measuring the impact of social change on society. But social reporting differs in two respects: in its approach to the construction of indicators, and in its handling of their interpretation and presentation.

Social reporting starts from the premiss that the business of constructing social indicators 'is not a task for government alone' (National Commission on Technology, Automation and Economic Progress, 1966). An 'intellectual market' needs to be created for indicators research, much as exists in the field of national economic accounting, which draws on multiple sources of ideas for their development, multiple sources of data, and which is attuned to the needs of multiple users (not just those inside government). Ensuring that social indicators are designed as part of an open process of critical research and enquiry offers at least some protection against them being hijacked by vested interests.

Social reporting insists on other safeguards against the abuse of indicators. The agencies whose activities are to be monitored should not be involved in decisions about what data to collect or even, ideally, in the process of data collection itself. If indicators are to serve as objective and reliable measures of what programmes are accomplishing, of how policies are working, of whether things are changing for the better or worse, then they must be independent of those who have a stake in the facts they reveal. Government cannot be entrusted to report impartially on its own activities and nor can administrators be left to evaluate their own programmes. The responsibility for the formulation of social indicators must be separated from the responsibility for the formulation of policy. A second line of defence is to ensure that the process of interpretation is not hogged by government, through its ready access to the press and television, and twisted to serve its own political ends. An independent and authoritative forum needs to be created, comprised of outside experts with standing and respect in their own professions, whose function would be to produce a social indicators report based on their non-partisan reading of the evidence.

The production of social reports – 'on where we are and where we're going' – is the essence of social reporting. They are seen as the vehicle for a periodic stocktaking and *public* accounting on the changing state of society: providing a regular assessment on the progress being made towards the achievement of social goals. A system of public reporting is intended to increase the visibility of social indicators, so strengthening their role in the making of policy

(Gross and Straussman, 1974), to increase the accountability of the Executive by closer monitoring and more careful scrutiny of its work, to arouse public awareness of social issues and to generate ongoing public debate about priorities and directions for the future.

All these cross-currents within the social indicators movement – social accounting, future planning, social monitoring and social reporting – came together in a fascinating and revealing snatch of legislative history best described as the Mondale Initiative.

The Mondale Initiative

During the late 1960s and early 1970s, Walter Mondale – the later, weary loser to Reagan in the 1984 Presidential election – served as a tireless advocate on Capitol Hill for the social indicators movement. So much so that, as an energetic freshman in 1967, he was quickly tagged the 'Senator for the State of Social Science'. As a *Washington Post* columnist mockingly observed, 'Fate has endowed Mondale with reverance for the social sciences, and Fate has not been moderate.'

The lessons of Johnson's Great Society programme had convinced liberal opinion in the Senate that government was not up to the challenge of the times. Looking around for an answer to what had gone wrong, these liberals latched on to the analysis offered by the social indicators movement, namely:

- government's ability to manage the course of social change had lagged seriously behind its capacity for managing the economy;
- social goals had been displaced by the short-sighted pursuit of narrow, economic objectives;
- social programmes often failed because not enough had been invested in finding out how to make them work;
- governments had failed to harness the potential of the social sciences, with the exception of economics, by using their knowledge in the making of policy.

It was Mondale who seized the moment to act on these ideas. The fact is, he argued, 'neither the President nor the Congress nor the public has the kind of broad-scale information and analysis needed to adequately assess our progress towards achievement of our national social aspirations'. As a matter of practical politics, the passage of legislation requires a constituency. But where, he asked, is the constituency of legislation that looks to the future? To build such a constituency, 'we must look to the social scientists themselves'. Just as economic expertise has become an essential factor in the management of the modern economy, so too should other social scientists be brought into the forefront of national decision-making, and into the highest councils of government, to help deal with the pressing social problems of the day.

Over the past two decades, Mondale reasoned, 'we have developed the sophisticated capability to register every quiver in the US economy'. As a result, economic policy is 'now shaped on the basis of hard, factual information, and our economy is doing far better than it has ever done before'. The same cannot be said of social policy and social planning:

> For when we come to debate the dimensions of our social ills and the effectiveness of efforts to alleviate them, promote individual opportunity, or enhance the quality of American life, we often lack the kind of hard data and analysis provided by the Council of Economic Advisers and the various economic indicators that have been developed.

Another obstacle to effective social planning was 'the complexity of interagency co-ordination' (what I have called the 'social division of planning' – see Chapter 2). Mondale cited a survey by the *Washington Post* which had counted 300 federal programmes dealing with education, poverty, the physical environment and community development. Responsibility for administering these programmes was scattered across 150 major bureaux and offices in Washington and 400 regional and sub-regional offices in the field. In education alone, 10 departments and 15 agencies ranging from the Department of Justice to the Department of Housing and Urban Development exercised operational responsibility. 'Bureaucracy is burgeoning', he concluded. Better information was required in order to 'help the administration coordinate its attack on massive social problems'.

In setting out to correct the faults which 'hobble our efforts to plan and coordinate', Mondale took his cue from the example of economics: 'For just as we thrash around in the area of social policy today, so too did we thrash around in the area of economic policy before 1946 – making decisions on the basis of untested theories and inadequate information.'

In 1946 Congress had enacted the Employment Act which, among other things, established the Council of Economic Advisers and required the President to deliver to Congress an annual report on the progress of the economy during the past year and on prospects for the year ahead. It also created the Joint Economic Committee of Congress whose public hearings subject the President's annual Economic Report to critical analysis by the nation's leading economists. These measures are generally credited with giving economists the ear of policy-makers and with putting economics in the centre of the political stage. More specifically, it is widely held that they sensitized the nation to the importance and effects of changes in economic growth; demonstrated that the economy could be managed and so built up public support for government intervention; and paved the way for a dramatic improvement in the techniques of macro-economic analysis and accounting. Mondale was convinced that comparable arrangements were called for to help the President achieve his social goals. 'Evaluation of our social progress', he argued, 'should equal the present evaluation of our economy'. A view lampooned by one sceptical commentator as implying that what stands between society and happiness is an insufficiency of information (Will, 1976).

In February 1967, Mondale introduced his Full Opportunity and Social Accounting Act (S.843) backed by a group of ten liberal co-sponsors including Senators McCarthy, Muskie and Kennedy. Its purpose was simple: 'I would hope', Mondale told the Senate, 'that this act might accomplish in the area of national social policy what the Employment Act of 1946 has accomplished in the field of economic policy.'

The proposed legislation declared social accounting a national goal. It was designed 'to give us a clear and precise picture of how well we are doing in our efforts to provide a decent life and full opportunity for all Americans'. With this end in view, the Act provided for:

1 The establishment of a Council of Social Advisers, modelled on the Council of Economic Advisers, to assist the President in the formulation and direction of national social policy.
2 The submission by the President of an annual Social Report to Congress, prepared by the Council of Social Advisers, and comparable to the annual Economic Report.
3 The creation of a Joint Committee of Congress to review the President's annual Social Report just as the Joint Economic Committee exercises oversight in the field of economic policy.

These proposals were designed to fulfil six main objectives:

1 To provide an arm's length perspective on the nation's social needs and conditions, free from the vested interests and 'tunnel vision' of federal agencies and pressure groups.
2 To bring the expert knowledge and prestige of prominent social scientists to bear on the task of developing social information and the tools of social measurement.
3 To create a highly visible, public forum for the discussion of social goals and priorities capable of attracting the attention of the nation and with direct access to the President.

4   To ensure that the analyses and recommendations which emerge
     are subject to the review of the legislative branch, the academic
     world and the private sector.
5   To develop effective social indicators for identifying social needs
     and for illustrating the progress – or lack of it – being made in
     meeting them over time.
6   To provide a framework for improving the co-ordination of social
     programmes.

The Council of Social Advisers (CSA) would serve as a 'social
statistical agency' for analysing and monitoring social conditions in
the USA and reporting factually on those conditions to the President,
the Congress and the country at large. Its principal task would be
the development of a system of social indicators adapted to this
purpose. The CSA would be headed by three of the nation's 'most
gifted and respected social analysts', appointed by the President and
confirmed by the Senate, and staffed by 'a number of America's
brightest young social scientists'. Alongside its responsibilities for
data-gathering and social monitoring, the CSA would also develop
priorities and recommend the most efficient way of allocating national
resources as well as conduct special impact studies into the social
consequences of government programmes and policies. It would
provide a funnel through which the findings of social science research
would be directed to the government instead of disappearing into
academic journals beyond the ken of policy-makers. At the same
time, it would 'integrate, co-ordinate and systematize the now
discordant efforts of social planners within the federal government'.
Finally, the Council would advise the President on the preparation
of the annual Social Report.

The annual Social Report would assess the overall progress and
effectiveness of federal efforts to promote the general welfare. It
should delve deeply into aspects of life that are only briefly touched
upon in the President's State of the Union message which has to
deal heavily with economic policy and international affairs. 'At a
time when there is much emphasis on the quality of life', Mondale
said, 'the annual social report would measure it with facts and
figures, putting flesh on what are now usually only abstract
suppositions'. Broad coverage, historical perspective, frank assessment
and a prescriptive scope would be paramount (Shostak, 1978). It
would report and analyse trends of the past year, as measured by
social indicators, and would set out goals for the future and a policy
for achieving them. The aim was greater public disclosure of
information to increase public awareness:

Requiring the President to report annually on such areas as education, health, housing, alienation, political participation, personal security, and social mobility would do far more than assure the publication of CSA findings and recommendations. It would guarantee such societal knowledge visibility of the sort that only Presidential involvement can generate. (Mondale, 1970)

In short, the Social Report was intended to present a detailed public accounting of social progress open to review and analysis by the Congress and by the American people as voters and citizens.

A Joint Committee of Congress, composed of eight members from both the House and the Senate, was to lead this review of the Social Report. It would conduct public hearings, calling on the testimony of independent experts and file a report containing an appraisal of each of the main recommendations made by the President in his Social Report. Such a public and critical examination of its work on social trends would help to keep the CSA on its toes and, in the longer run, elevate the level of its analysis in the same way as the measurement of the economy has been enhanced by the hearings on the Economic Report. A Joint Committee on the Social Report would also serve an educational role. Lebergott (1965), for example, describes how the Joint Economic Committee has become: 'the nom de plume of the world's largest class in economics in which astute and overworked Congressmen and Senators take turns in being pupils and instructors to most of the Nation's economists.' Finally, a Joint Social Committee might overcome the history of mistrust towards social scientists on the part of some members of Congress. This attitude, Mondale reasoned, had come about for a variety of reasons. It was based partly on unfamiliarity, partly on poor communications, partly on the fact that many Congressmen regarded themselves as successful practitioners of applied social science because they had won elections and partly on an instinctive wariness about the political backlash from social science findings. A forum such as a Joint Committee could help to break down these barriers and prejudices by creating a working alliance between policy-makers and social scientists.

Mondale had high hopes that the proposals embodied in his Full Opportunity and Social Accounting Act could 'begin to elevate social policymaking in America to new levels of sophistication' (Mondale, 1970) by unlocking 'the enormous potential of the social sciences to assist the Congress and the Executive in developing and administering public policy'.

The attempt to 'apply non-economic measures to the quality of life in America could have a revolutionary impact on government'. Equally, 'it will have no less impact on the social sciences':

There is every reason to believe that the social sciences – like economics since 1946 – will be greatly stimulated by enactment of the legislation. Such legislation may prod many social scientists into devoting increased attention to social problems that have specific relevancy to government. Instead of concentrating solely on research and comment, they will become active participants in policymaking. (Mondale, 1968b)

Such a prospect stirred one commentator to remark that, in years to come, 'the Ninetieth Congress, opening in 1967, may be viewed as the place and time of the take-off point for the underdeveloped social and behavioural sciences' (Brayfield, 1967). Mondale himself was aware of the uphill climb before this point could be reached. He warned against expecting sophisticated social indicators to be developed overnight and against expecting evaluation and analysis straightaway to bear the stamp of certainty. It took the Council of Economic Advisers many years of experimentation (and many chairmen) to establish its role – some say not until it had won the confidence of President Kennedy. A slow evolution 'will be even more necessary when we are dealing with elusive social values' (Mondale, 1968b). The fact that the social sciences have not yet developed the methodology for the task is not a good reason for holding back. It was the creation of the Council of Economic Advisers that stimulated economists into developing their accounting instruments and indicators. Likewise, a CSA would thrust responsibility on other social scientists and they, too, will not shun the challenge.

The Full Opportunity and Social Accounting Act was referred for hearings before the Committee on Government Operations at which the testimonies of social scientists, present and former government officials, businessmen and prominent journalists were received. These hearings revealed a groundswell of support for his initiative and, for Mondale, bore out much of his thinking. In particular, they buttressed his views that:

1 the nation lacked a comprehensive information base upon which major decisions in social affairs could be made;
2 what information was available was not sufficiently precise, consistent or systematic to allow rational judgements about the gaps between present programmes and urgent social needs, or even to measure satisfactorily the impact of those programmes;
3 significant improvements were possible in the collection, analysis and interpretation of social data and in the development of predictive tools needed to establish social priorities;
4 the enactment of his legislation would provide the institutional and procedural framework for co-ordinating attempts to measure

the nation's social health, stimulating the development of social indicators, focusing public attention on social problems and providing policy-makers with the information and analysis needed to make rational allocations of resources.

Mondale's proposals received a further boost from two important reports published in 1969. A survey of the outlook and needs of the behavioural and social sciences by the National Academy of Sciences and the Social Science Research Council (1969) solemnly warned that 'We are living in social crisis'. It went on to say that the social sciences, though providing no easy solutions in the near future, 'are our best hope, in the long run, for understanding our problems in depth and for providing new means of lessening tensions and improving our common life'. On this basis, it recommended: 'that substantial support, both financial and intellectual, be given to efforts under way to develop a system of social indicators and that legislation to encourage and assist this development be enacted by Congress.' In the same year the National Commission on the Causes and Prevention of Violence issued its final report with the conclusion that the major threat to the security of the nation came from internal conflicts within society rather than the menace of foreign aggression. 'The time is upon us', it declared, 'for a re-ordering of national priorities.' Resources should be reallocated to deal with social problems. In aid of this task the Commission recommended that: 'consideration should be given to establishing a counterpart to the Council of Economic Advisers to develop tools for measuring the comparative effectiveness of social programs, and to produce an "Annual Social Report" comparable to the present Annual Economic Report.'

Against this background Mondale reintroduced his Bill to the Senate in 1969 as the Full Opportunity Act (S.5) where it was referred for further hearings before the Labor and Public Welfare Committee. The Bill was amended in Committee. The proposal to establish a Joint Committee on the Social Report was deleted and an amendment from Senator Javits was passed to set up an Office of Goals and Priorities Analysis within Congress. The Office would be directly responsible to the Congress, and would have the job of conducting a 'continuing nonpartisan analysis of national goals and priorities'. It would produce an annual national priorities report for examination by the Joint Economic Committee of Congress. The change watered down Mondale's original Bill by removing the forum designed to bring the proposed Social Report into the public spotlight. It may be seen as a flanking move by the powerful Joint Economic Committee who were keen to avoid anyone else digging in their patch. As such, it was probably a necessary concession made in order to safeguard the proposed Council of Social Advisers.

The Bill, as amended, was twice passed by the Senate (in 1970 and 1972) but never reached the floor of the House of Representatives and so failed to earn congressional passage. It was last recommended to Congress by Mondale in 1974, though staffers updated the Bill in the summer of 1976 after a leading journalist cited it as Mondale's outstanding Senate venture (Shostak, 1978).

It would be mistaken to conclude that the Mondale Initiative was a failure simply because his Bill was never enacted. The social indicators movement on Capitol Hill generated a considerable head of steam and its influence may be detected in several subsequent developments that carry the stamp of ideas voiced originally – and persuasively – by Mondale and his supporters. Both the Johnson and Nixon administrations pledged themselves to further the development of social monitoring. Various federal agencies experimented with their own version of a social report. The Office of Management and Budget launched a triennial publication series of national social indicators, in 1973, presenting selected statistics on social conditions and trends in the USA. The 1974 Congressional Budget Act required the House and Senate Budget Committees to study ways of developing 'techniques of human resources accounting'. Also in 1974 most congressional committees were required to undertake systematic, long-range, social science studies of future national problems and of the future implications of current social problems (ibid.). But all these efforts have been scattered and piecemeal, and Mondale had warned that 'no good can come from continuing to make decisions based on the chance availability of unconnected social measurements and evaluations' (Mondale, 1972). His purpose had been to create a structure for bringing together these 'disparate and disconnected impulses . . . into some sort of comprehensive, systematic enterprise'. Why did his initiative fail in these terms?

There is no simple answer, but a hotchpot of reasons. The Executive branch responded to protect its virtual monopoly of evaluative research. The President's minders were opposed because it might give ammunition to his critics. Sectional interests inside federal agencies mobilized to protect themselves from the closer scrutiny that social reporting would permit. Sociologists reacted with hostility to the prospect of getting into bed with government. Economists sought to preserve their stranglehold on policy analysis. And Congress indulged its mistrust of the underdog and liberal leanings of social scientists. In each case, of course, their arguments were dressed up for appearance's sake.

Both the Johnson and Nixon administrations, while endorsing the aims of Mondale's Bill, opposed the establishment of a Council of Social Advisers within the Executive Office of the President, and for the same reason. It would duplicate and so confuse existing responsibilities. In particular, it would overlap with the role of the Council of Economic Advisers. No meaningful division could be made between social and economic affairs anyway. Better, therefore, to extend the remit of the CEA and to leave the Office of Management and Budget with the responsibility for collecting social statistics and developing social indicators. Underlying this public response were the growing strains on the economy caused by the Vietnam War and the pressures to restrain federal social spending. The White House was not inclined to see a new lobby set up arguing for more spending on social problems, acting pesky, embarrassing the President with evidence of unmet needs and the shortcomings of his social policies, and raising public expectations.

Schneider (1974) argues that conservative resistance in Congress was primarily responsible for the demise of the Mondale Initiative. With the passing of Johnson's 'Great Congress' conservative control, based on a coalition of Republicans and Southern Democrats, especially in the House, was re-established from 1967 onwards. This coalition, which in any case tended to oppose liberal legislation aimed at extending the reach of the federal government, reacted vigorously to Mondale's ideas which were seen as leading down the anti-libertarian path towards the managed society. These fears were also deepened by mistrust of the social sciences and of the values they embodied. As Boulding (1967) observed: 'It could well be that the kind of knowledge which would result from taking the social sciences seriously would turn out to be more threatening to traditional values and institutions even than the H bomb and bacteriological weapons.'

In this sense, social science presents much more of a danger to the politician than the physical sciences or even economics. In the case of the latter it is easier to keep scientists on tap but not on top. They are merely the servants of values upheld by the dominant institutions in society. The social sciences are different. There is often 'a deep conflict between the values which are created and sustained by folk images of the world and the values which both create the social sciences and are fostered by them' (ibid.). Herein lie the origins of conservative scruples about the social sciences in general, and Mondale's proposals in particular. But a final point tipped the balance. In facing up to the nation's social problems, Mondale implied that social scientists could succeed where the politicians had failed. Even some of the more liberally inclined members of Congress were not prepared to give the future over to the social scientists.

The federal establishment came out squarely against Mondale's proposals mainly on the grounds that mirrored the objections of the White House. They would lead to an overlap of functions between the proposed Council of Social Advisers and the Council of Economic Advisers, further complicate the organization of the Executive Office, duplicate much that was already being done in this area within departments and bring about an unhelpful distinction between social and economic policy. The Department of Health, Education and Welfare was especially forceful in its criticisms. The 'very, very limited state of our knowledge about the working of society', brought home by the preparation of *Toward a Social Report*, had convinced HEW that a Council of Social Advisers would be premature because it could not 'pronounce without dispute as the CEA does'. Again, though, behind the officialese lurked other, more self-serving considerations. As Mondale remarked, 'most of the information we obtain in Congress is dependent upon the candour of the affected agency to tell us all the facts'. So far as federal departments were concerned that is just how they wanted things to stay. They had no wish to see anyone snooping into their activities except on their own terms.

Much of the opposition within Congress was led by Senator Proxmire, chairman of the Joint Economic Committee and the political voice of professional economists. They were antagonistic to Mondale's proposals, seeing them as possibly diluting their own influence and eroding their status as the pre-eminent policy advisers to government. Gerhard Colm, the Chief Economist with the National Planning Association in Washington, DC, warned that he could 'only foresee friction if there were two different groups of advisers to the President, and similarly in the Congress'. Most economists believed that the same objectives could be accomplished just as well by action through the Council of Economic Advisers – by including among its members economists with a broad perspective on social affairs, or by recruiting social policy specialists on to its staff. Some played with the notion of a joint Council of Social and Economic Advisers as a sort of last-ditch compromise. Mondale retorted that little would be gained by shoe-horning a few, token social scientists into the hidebound CEA whose own track record showed that the assessment of social needs was obviously a fifth wheel to its main preoccupations.

Other economists stooped to ridicule, scoffing at the absurdity of thinking that a Council of Social Advisers could hope to monitor the changing state of society in the same way as the CEA monitored the economy. One Washington economist conjured up the following parody of a day in the CSA:

> Dan Bell is idly watching the Dow-Jones societal wire (formerly the business wire): 'Consumer Indignation Index down .04 percent . . . Black Power Ratio steady (two percent drop in hair-straightener sales offset by two percent rise in empty seats at Miriam Makeba concerts) . . . Participatory Democracy Determinant drops slightly (collapse of antifluoridation organization in West Texas) . . . Gross Social Product extrapolated in 789 by December 31.' Suddenly Bell calls excitedly, 'Mike, Bert, come here quick. The Native Restlessness Index has hit an all-time high!' The Advisers go into special session with their staff, then report their conclusions and recommendations to the President . . . He activates the National Guard and calls a White House Conference. (Quoted in Kopkind, 1967)

Funny, perhaps, but really an undercurrent in a powerful tide of opposition strong enough to prompt one insider to say of Mondale's Initiative: 'The economists killed it.'

There is, however, an equally persuasive case for the argument that it was the social scientists themselves who ultimately scuppered Mondale's hopes. Jealous of their self-styled role as critics of the social order, and fearful of incorporation by the state, they retreated into their ivory towers. Springer (1970) summed up these doubts: 'If social reporting is to become a major enterprise in our federal government, social scientists may very well become so linked to (governing) elites that they will become indistinguishable from them.'

When Mondale first introduced his Bill in 1967 it received the collective endorsement of the social science community. Three years later this support had crumbled. This change in the mood of social scientists reflected the loss of faith, within American society, in government as a force for good (Aaron, 1978): a reappraisal brought about by the Vietnam War (and eventually sealed by Watergate). Thus, Green (1971) spoke for many social scientists when he urged them to oppose all efforts to institutionalize social reporting and data collection at the Presidential level and to lobby against the proposal for a Council of Social Advisers. Similarly, Miller (1974) touched a nerve when he urged social scientists to develop their own 'counter-indicators and counter-analyses' to offset the efforts by government and so prevent the monopolization of knowledge.

The instinct to keep government at arm's-length was justified by a battery of arguments: some intellectual, some ideological and some unashamedly pragmatic. The intellectual critique argued that the social indicators movement was based on a false premiss: that the failure to solve persistent social problems was a result of an insufficiency of information. This technocratic explanation, which reduced politics to an exercise in managerial rationality, was simply wrongheaded. Rule (1978) summarizes the opposing view:

> a close and critical look at the array of 'social problems' in America today shows that few of them represent authentic 'problems' in the sense of conditions equally undesirable from all political and social standpoints. Quite the opposite: conditions like pollution, racism, poverty and the like are basically oppositions of interest – not social problems but social conflicts, overt or concealed.

The ideological critique called attention to the disturbing prospect that the co-option of social scientists into the service of the corporate state might lead to an official social science with a one-sided, 'topdog' perspective on society. Herbert Gans expressed these misgivings among liberal sociologists in testimony before a 1967 Senate subcommittee on Mondale's Bill:

> I am particularly concerned that the development of social policies and social indicators could be monopolized by those groups in American society which are affluent and powerful enough to gather information and make their points of view heard, and that groups in the society which are politically unorganized, weak or nonvocal will be left out. Social-economic accounting could become a decision-making system by which the technicians and the most powerful agencies in American society would control the information and other inputs into the accounting apparatus, determine what social indicators and what criteria for benefits and costs will be established, and thus influence the choice of objectives and Government programs to realize their vested interests. This would 'disenfranchise' millions of citizens, particularly those who now have difficulty in being heard in Washington.

Lastly, the pragmatists warned of the hidden hazards which the glare of publicity accompanying involvement in the policy-making councils of the nation, especially a Council of Social Advisers, might bring. Looking back, Etzioni (1977) comments:

> high-level representation has been in disfavor among social scientists because they believe that the 'high visibility' would make them into the whipping boys of Congress . . . Hiding behind the backs of the economists or natural scientists is therefore considered prudent.

For those who believed such prudence to be a virtue the idea of an 'invisible college' of social science mandarins quietly serving policy-makers in the anonymity of departmental policy shops was altogether more appealing.

Lessons of the Mondale Initiative

Mondale's grand vision of building a constituency that looks to the future around social scientists foundered on the humdrum realities of power. The lessons are manifold but best revealed in the story as it has been told. A few, summary observations, however, perhaps deserve emphasis:

- social science knowledge without a concomitant power to act is politically threatening to government;
- there is no ready-made market for social science findings within the policy process;
- social scientists are deeply ambivalent about their relations with government and there is a well of mistrust among politicians towards social scientists;
- in the maelstrom of the policy process all social science is politically charged.

[1]Unattributed quotations in this chapter are taken from the *Congressional Record*, 1967–1971, mainly from hearings and debates on s. 843 and s. 5.

6 Evaluation research in the policy process: federal lessons from US experience

'though it is hard to be against evaluation in principle, it is easy to be unenthusiastic about it in practice' (Laurence E. Lynn, Jr, Assistant Secretary for Planning and Evaluation in the US Department of Health, Education and Welfare 1971–3)

The age of analysis, which opened in the USA with the rise to prominence of McNamara's systems engineers in the Department of Defense, and took off with the introduction of PPBS, was brought to a close, as we have seen in Chapter 4, by the Vietnam War, domestic turmoil, and a loss of faith in government. In the ensuing crisis of confidence evaluation research gained a hold in the policy process.

The shift from analysis to evaluation was symptomatic of the creeping disillusionment that marred the last years of the Johnson Presidency and ushered Nixon into the White House. During the mid-1960s when resources were plentiful and optimism was high, public confidence in the efficacy of government action soared. Politicians and policy-makers, too, looked to the future with buoyant hopes and promises of a better life for all Americans. These rising aspirations found legislative expression in Johnson's 'Great Society' programme: an unparalleled outburst of social reform aimed at making a reality of the dream of full opportunity.

By the end of the decade the bubble had burst. The Great Society programmes had yielded little more than a harvest of disappointments, sinecures and red tape. The social problems they had set out to address stubbornly persisted or even grew worse. Public officials and their political masters despaired of the effectiveness of service programmes (Rein and White, 1977a). The policy community in Washington was swept by the conviction that 'nothing works'. On top of everything else the 'fiscal dividend' from economic growth dried up and social expenditure plummeted as the spiralling cost of the Vietnam War ate away at the federal budget. In this changed –

and altogether more gloomy – climate policy-makers lost both the will and means to launch new initiatives. The emphasis switched from innovation to retrenchment, from 'future planning' to retrospection. A period of stocktaking began which paved the way for the emergence of evaluation as an adjunct of policy.

The first inkling of this mood-swing came in early (1967 and 1968) congressional amendments to some of the basic Great Society legislation. These required the US General Accounting Office (GAO) to review how far the programmes authorized by these keystone Acts were achieving their intended objectives. This process of performance review and audit gradually extended as disenchantment deepened. The major impetus towards evaluation, however, came from the Nixon administration whose legislative and budgetary stance favoured consolidation more than the breaking of new ground.

The differences between analysis and evaluation are tied to the policy-making contexts in which they thrive (Schick, 1971), and to different models of the working of the policy process. Analysis, as the PPBS experiment showed, is essentially a forward-looking activity in which research is used as a tool for identifying the best way of achieving defined objectives. It is about finding answers to the question of how we get from where we are to where we want to be. In this sense, as Chapter 4 points out, analysis is a feature of the rational model of policy-making. Evaluation, on the other hand, looks to the past by using research as a source of feedback about the impact of policies and the performance of programmes. It is a way of finding out what works and what doesn't work and so of keeping policy-makers in touch with their successes and failures. As such, evaluation is closely linked with the incremental approach to policy-making (Bulmer, 1985) where the emphasis, as Chapter 1 shows, is on learning from mistakes.

The switch from analysis to evaluation therefore may be seen as indicative of a realignment of perspective within the policy community, a change of outlook caused, in large part, by a change in the underlying state of the economy. When economic prospects are rosy and the public purse is flush, policy-makers can afford to plan ahead and to risk new ventures. At other times, when the economic climate is gloomy and resources are tight, horizons are shortened, enterprise flags and caution prevails. These different contexts encourage a different approach to policy-making and resource management (one geared to anticipating change, the other to careful housekeeping) and so tend to impose different criteria of policy relevance on the social sciences.

The failure of so many of the Great Society programmes had by the late 1960s provoked widespread scepticism about the capacity of government to match promises with performance. Moreover, the tightening squeeze on social spending had increased the perceived costs – both in opportunity terms and in political terms – of policy failure (Rossi and Wright, 1977). In the face of these pressures, demands for greater accountability mounted within Congress, especially from the conservative elements who ran the powerful appropriations committees. One expression of these demands was the call for evaluation to be built into the policy process – if necessary as a legislative requirement (Rein and White, 1977a). In the cold light of experience it was a call which liberals dared not oppose.

What is Evaluation?
Before delving into the history of evaluation research in US federal agencies, and exploring what we can learn from it about the place of research in policy-making, it is necessary first to prepare the ground by clarifying what we are talking about.

Rutman (1984a) has defined evaluation research as 'the use of scientific methods to measure the implementation and outcomes of programs for decision-making purposes'. Programmes, he adds, are interventions or activities mounted to meet some recognized social need or to solve an identified problem. Programmes embody ideas about means of achieving desired objectives. How ideas get implemented and their impact are the dual concerns of evaluation research.

The evaluator and the analyst stand with their backs to each other, looking in opposite directions. Policy analysis is usually biased towards change: it focuses on the examination of new proposals and initiatives, on highlighting gaps in policy and on weighing up what more needs to be done. With evaluation the bias runs the other way – towards the review of existing activities.

Evaluators operate with what Schick (1971) has called a 'show-me attitude' that puts the burden of proof on those who wish to see a programme continue. The presumption is that programmes should demonstrate clear-cut benefits to justify their funding. These different orientations help to explain the ups-and-downs in their fortunes. Analysis was suited to the forward-looking 1960s. Evaluation emerged as the dominant theme of the more reflective 1970s.

Within these rather broad parameters, evaluation research may take different forms reflecting different purposes. It is too easy to think of evaluation just as a one-shot effort to determine whether or not a programme is working. Generally speaking, evaluations fall into four main categories (Evaluation Research Society, 1980):

1   *Front-end or context evaluations* – these take place before a

programme, or project, is started in order to estimate needs, operational feasibility, financial costs and other such factors bearing on its design and start-up.

2   *Formative or process evaluations* – these focus on *how* a programme, or project, is working with special attention to the ongoing processes of implementation and service delivery.

3   *Impact or outcome evaluations* – these are concerned with how *well* a programme, or project, is working in terms of achieving its desired effects.

4   *Programme monitoring* – this includes a range of activities from periodic checks on compliance with policy to the routine tracking of services and the counting of clients.

In addition to these four mainstream categories, there are two secondary types of evaluation:

(a) *Evaluability assessments* – these aim to ensure *credible* and *useful* evaluations by determining, in advance, before resources are committed to the job, what purposes they are intended to serve and how, if at all, these aims can best be met (Rutman, 1984b).

(b) *Evaluation audits* – these are independent reviews or appraisals of evaluation studies aimed at assessing their quality and methodological soundness for the sponsor or end-user and verifying the reliability of their findings. They may take a variety of forms ranging from professional critiques of evaluation reports; reanalysis of original data; or even the collection of new information. In some cases they may involve bringing together and comparing the results from a number of different studies. Whatever the approach, the intention is to provide the user with a check on the adequacy and credibility of the evaluation (Hudson and McRoberts, 1984).

Evaluation research may serve a variety of purposes. It may be commissioned in the interests of political or bureaucratic account-ability. In this case, the concern is with establishing whether a programme is working according to plan and whether the results justify its continued support. It may be used as a tool of management. The main issues here relate to the measurement of performance with the emphasis on improving the economy, efficiency and effectiveness of programmes. Finally, evaluation research may be undertaken in order to improve understanding or add to the stock of knowledge about the state-of-the-art in different fields of policy and practice. From this point of view its immediate practical utility is less important than its longer-term contribution to new thinking and developments.

Alongside these explicit uses there are also a number of covert reasons for doing evaluation. It may be undertaken to whitewash – or to undermine – a programme, to avoid or postpone action, as a token response to pressure or for the sake of political positioning. (The covert functions of policy research are discussed more fully in Chapter 9.) These different purposes – both overt and covert – all have a bearing on decisions about the organization, design and execution of evaluation studies. Indeed, the history of evaluation research, as will be shown, is partly about how its practitioners learned to adapt their methodologies to meet the criteria of policy relevance.

The Upward March of Evaluation

The big challenge facing the incoming Nixon administration, especially in the health, education and welfare fields, was whether some way could be found of reorienting the federal budget towards new priorities at a time when its total growth was severely limited (Schultze *et al.*, 1970).

Nixon was anxious to distance himself from the failures of the Johnson era. At the same time, he was hemmed in by the fiscal consequences of war and inflation and by the steady rise in 'uncontrollable' (i.e. demand-led) expenditure on such things as social security, public assistance, Medicare and Medicaid. In the non-defence area approximately nine out of every ten dollars spent by the federal government in 1971 were determined by statutory entitlements and irreversible administrative actions taken in previous years (ibid.).

Offsetting the fiscal effects of these 'uncontrollables' while making a little room for new priorities and holding the budget within tolerable limits necessitated cuts in existing programmes. To be sure, doubts had arisen about the effectiveness of many of these programmes, and some were ill-adapted to the changing pattern of needs, but most had developed their own vociferous and entrenched lobby on Capitol Hill and in the field. Unseating them promised to be a hard fight. Planning a coherent strategy for even the 'controllable' programmes became extremely difficult.

In this context it is not surprising that demands should grow for greater accountability of public programmes, for closer scrutiny and more rigorous challenge of their performance and for better services for fewer dollars. These pressures were increased by public demands for more information on the effectiveness of tax-supported programmes, which erupted in some places as 'taxpayers' revolts' (Mushkin, 1973; Chadwin, 1975). Evaluation was conceived as one way of responding to these budgetary and political quandaries.

At bottom, the Nixon administration was a coalition of people who had cut their teeth in the Kennedy–Johnson era and of problem-solving Republicans. Both of these groups accepted the need for an interventionist stance on the ground that there were some problems which only the federal government could tackle. Equally, both were chastened by past mistakes and concerned to ensure that what the federal government did it should do well. Evaluation neatly fitted this posture.

Carried along by these currents, then, evaluation came to mark the style of government in the early 1970s. One of the important early moves by President Nixon was the establishment of the Office of Management and Budget (OMB) within the Executive Office of the President. The OMB explicitly harnessed the evaluation function to the budgetary process. In his reorganization message on 12 March 1970 the President declared:

> The new Office of Management and Budget will place much emphasis on the evaluation of program performance; on assessing the extent to which programs are actually achieving their intended results, and delivering the intended services to the intended recipients. This is needed on a continuing basis, not as a onetime effort.

Nixon's public support for evaluation as a tool of management hardly wavered throughout his time in office. His 1974 Budget Message to the Congress, shortly before his humiliating resignation under threat of impeachment following the Watergate scandal, promised that:

> Increased emphasis will also be placed on program performance. Programs will be evaluated to identify those that must be redirected, reduced or eliminated because they do not justify the taxes required to pay them. Federal programs must meet their objectives and costs must be related to achievements.

Initially, however, for evaluation to take off, it had to be installed at the agency level within the federal government where the major programmes are managed. This meant building from scratch. An extensive survey of federal-level evaluation, conducted by the Urban Institute in 1969, found there was no system for planning, executing and using evaluation studies: 'The most impressive finding about the evaluation of social programs in the federal government is that substantial work in this field has been almost non-existent' (Wholey *et al.*, 1970). As a result, with uncertainty about the effects of past and present programmes, 'it is difficult if not impossible to be efficient in planning or in allocating funds to future programs'. One testimony to the rapid progress made in developing evaluation research is that, less than three years later, these same authors, having revisited the scene, were moved to the view that subsequent advances would certainly prevent anyone from drawing the same conclusions in 1972 (Buchanan and Wholey, 1972).

There was a dramatic expansion of funds for federal non-defence evaluations from less than $20 million in fiscal year 1969 to at least $110 million in fiscal year 1972 (GAO, 1973). In response, executive agencies set up new evaluation offices and also began to contract out a great deal of work. In the social policy field more money was budgeted for evaluation than ever before with a 30 per cent increase in funds between 1971 and 1973 alone. A 1974 telephone survey of federal departments by the General Accounting Office reported a 500 per cent rise in expenditure on evaluation research between 1969 and 1974 (Rein and White, 1977b). The 1975 Congressional Sourcebook on federal programme evaluations contains 1,700 citations of evaluation reports issued by eighteen executive branch agencies and the GAO between 1973 and 1975 (Richardson, 1982). Moreover, the evaluation bandwagon was not just a federal phenomenon. In 1970 no state legislative had a full-time staff responsible for the evaluation of programme effectiveness. Less than five years later, a dozen had committees, commissions or auditor's offices working in this area with more appearing by the month (Chadwin, 1975).

This huge investment created a buoyant market. Evaluation research became big business. Private research firms grew fat on the steady flow of government contracts. Several universities set up evaluation institutes. 'Think-tanks' and individual consultants entered the arena. A specialist literature began to emerge. When *Evaluation* magazine was launched in 1972, the anticipated readership was 5,000 at the most. Two years later it had climbed to 30,000. The Evaluation Research Society was formed in 1976.

A number of factors – aside from White House patronage – contributed to the snowballing of evaluation. One of the most crucial was the backing it received on Capitol Hill during what was a period of heightened Executive–Legislative tensions when, once again, Congress was mindful of its loss of power to the Presidency and to the federal bureaucracy (Chelimsky, 1978). Evaluation came to be recognized in Congress as a means of increasing agency accountability by strengthening Legislative oversight of the Executive.

Congressional support for evaluation showed itself in two main ways. One was the increasing tendency for evaluation requirements to be written into new legislation. Although the details often varied, it became common for authorizing legislation specifically to set aside funds for evaluation; to spell out measures of effectiveness; sometimes to lay down methods of data collection and analysis; to specify reporting dates; and to assign responsibility for conducting the evaluation and disseminating the results (GAO, 1973). Another was the growing involvement of the General Accounting Office in the evaluation of federal programmes.

The GAO is the investigative arm of Congress and acts as its watchdog over federal spending. Created in 1921 as a non-partisan agency within the Legislative branch, it is responsible for reporting on the economy, efficiency and effectiveness of government operations (Staats, 1973). The GAO is headed by the Comptroller-General of the United States, who is appointed by the President for a single term of fifteen years and cannot be removed by him.

It was the Comptroller-General who, in 1972, issued a letter to congressional committee chairmen strongly recommending the insertion of evaluation requirements in new or re-enacted legislation. Two years later, GAO was formally directed by the Congress to 'review and evaluate' the results of federal programmes at the request of either House, any Legislative committee or on its own initiative. The aim was to give Congress access to information equal to that produced by the Executive. The effect was to create a big new market-place for evaluation and to draw the GAO more and more into this kind of work as an extension of its traditional auditing and accounting functions. By 1977 approximately 40 per cent of all GAO resources were devoted to evaluation-type activities – equivalent to an annual commitment of 1,700 staff-years.

The impetus towards evaluation was also boosted by the availability of trained personnel who had learned their trade as policy researchers back in the days of PPBS. As a result of their earlier experience, these people brought with them a more sophisticated appreciation of the inner workings of government which helped to establish their credibility and the usefulness of evaluation research in the eyes of decision-makers.

By the mid-1970s evaluation was an established part of the Washington scene and well embedded in the management process of most federal departments. So much so that an Evaluation Interagency Group had been formed, bringing together federal agency evaluation directors and representatives of GAO and OMB to identify common problems, share information and experiences, and improve the conduct of evaluations.

The broad-brush account sketched out so far has linked the rise of evaluation to broader political and economic currents in a society struggling with the disenchantment brought on by 'Great Society' blues and the after-effects of a costly and shameful war. Government needed to rehabilitate itself by proving its competence: evaluation was part of the therapy. The period illustrates how the kind of social science called for by government is related to the policy context. To complete the picture, however, it is helpful to look at how evaluation took root in one agency. Because the approach followed by the Department of Health, Education and Welfare (HEW) was one of the best conceived and most thoroughly developed in the federal government, it serves as a useful example (Lynn, 1972).

Evaluation in HEW

Prior to 1968, there was no involvement of top HEW Secretarial staff in programme evaluation. Few programmes had money allocated for this purpose in the legislation, meagre funds were available and little evaluation was done. What work did go on was largely administered by the front-line agencies in the field without Secretarial guidance. In other words, the position in HEW matched precisely that described at the federal level by Wholey *et al.* (1970) when they bemoaned the lack of a comprehensive evaluation system.

The seeds of change, however, had already been sown. William Gorham, the first PPB chief in the department (see Chapter 4), had started to write an earmark for evaluation into HEW appropriations. Generally this meant that up to 1 per cent of the funds authorized to be spent on a programme were set aside to be used for evaluation. This ploy turned out to be something of a 'sleeper'. In the early days it yielded only small amounts of money most of which either went to the field agencies running the programmes or went unused, because there was no system for managing them.

As the interest in evaluation grew, in response to mounting public and congressional concern about the effectiveness of social programmes, so too was more attention given to ensuring that legislation included this earmark. Gradually the sums available from these set-asides began to swell. Some framework was needed for seeing they were not frittered away.

It was soon recognized that it did not make sense to leave the field agencies with the responsibility for evaluating their own performance. In any case, few programme managers or agency heads were inclined to do so. A system for co-ordinating and directing the department's evaluation efforts was needed at Secretarial level. Accordingly, under HEW Secretary Robert Finch, the Office of the Assistant Secretary for Planning and Evaluation (OASPE) was charged with improving the quality of its evaluation research and seeing that it related to central policy concerns. To this end, 25 per cent of the evaluation set-asides were to be retained each year for spending at the discretion of the Assistant Secretary for Planning and Evaluation. The other 75 per cent of the funds went to the field agencies who were required to submit annual evalution plans to the OASPE for review and approval.

Big money was at stake. In 1972 the '25 per cent moneys' alone brought in $9.1 million for use by the OASPE in evaluation. Altogether HEW had some 40–50 million dollars for evaluation research in that year and employed about 125 professional evaluators (Lynn, 1972). The bulk of the work was contracted out to universities, research institutes and private firms. These in-house evaluators were mostly occupied in drawing up project specifications and monitoring the contracts. It was here that the cracks in the system first started to show.

Laurence Lynn, Assistant Secretary for Planning and Evaluation at HEW from 1971 to 1973, has summed up the lessons of these early efforts to weave evaluation into the fabric of social policy-making (Lynn, 1973). On the positive side, he argued, HEW experience had demonstrated the following.

It is possible to institutionalize evaluation in a large, complex bureaucracy. Funds were routinely appropriated for the purpose; an administrative apparatus had been set up to direct their use; and the results of evaluations were fed into the policy-making process in the department.

Objectively developed and useful evaluations can be produced by such a system. Although examples of self-serving studies were not uncommon, the visibility created by an evaluation staff in the Office of the Secretary, along with evaluation offices in the programme agencies, guaranteed enough accountability to ensure that the forces favouring objective evaluation survived agency instincts for self-justification.

At the same time, certain limitations or obstacles to the effective use of evaluation had also emerged. Among the most important were the following.

The availability of funds and the existence of a broad organizational commitment are not enough to ensure a good evaluation programme. Evaluation calls for really good practitioners inside the agency and a number of factors worked against getting the right people in the right places. For a start, there were not enough of them. The best ones, with a heightened sense of relevance, tended to get drawn into immediate policy issues. Competition for staff positions offering better prospects of career progression meant that evaluators soon moved on leaving their offices understaffed or lacking experience.

Political considerations affected the conduct of studies. In HEW, their influence was most noticeable on the selection of evaluations to be done and on the dissemination of results. The coalitions of support that create and sustain programmes typically showed scant interest in risking potentially dangerous or embarrassing evaluations. Where they were agreed, it was sometimes because they had been subtly rigged; and when tough-minded findings did emerge, it was not unusual for them to be suppressed, laundered or ignored.

The impact of evaluation on policy proved to be disappointing. In these early years there was a general lack of confidence in the findings of evaluation research. This was accentuated by the fact that the political process often kept alive programmes that evaluation had shown were not working. The alliances of interest between officials, legislators, organized pressure groups and segments of public opinion, on which all programmes were founded, often formed a tough, protective skin that was hard to penetrate.

Finally, according to Lynn, HEW probably spent too much money on evaluation and put too few resources into the oversight of this investment (Salasin, 1977). The upshot, all too often, was poor-quality work, stuff that was not worth the time and attention of policy-makers and did not really deserve to be read by anybody. As Secretary Elliot Richardson said about the early progress of evaluation efforts in HEW, 'Too much money has gone into poorly conceived projects, too few of the results have been rigorously assessed, and our means of disseminating the worthwhile results have been too feeble. This means we know less than we should, that we're less sure of what we know, and that too few people share the knowledge we do possess' (quoted in Lynn, 1978b).

These comments point to a stark truth. Having got off the ground, evaluation ran into some stormy weather and began what turned out to be a bumpy ride.

Evaluation at the Crossroads

It was not long after the idea of evaluation gained widespread currency that suspicions arose about the quality of the coin. Policy-makers began to suspect it was debased. Practitioners, drawn into the booming evaluation industry by the free flow of research funds, complained they were being short-changed.

The nub of the trouble was that evaluation research seemd to be failing to live up to its promises (Freeman, 1975). Its impact on the policy process and programme development was meagre when compared with the amount of money and effort it was swallowing. As Robert Bruce, Assistant Administrator for Program Planning and Evaluation in HEW, admitted: 'We might as well be candid: federal program evaluations so far have been largely ineffective.' While almost everyone agreed that evaluation was essential for the sound management of public programmes they also had to concede that it was only sporadically and inconsistently used for this purpose (Buchanan and Wholey, 1972). Decisions continued to be hastily made on the basis of impressions, scanty information and 'seat-of-the-pants' wisdom rather than firm knowledge of the relationship between programme inputs and their outcomes (Bruce, 1972).

Imperfections in the new market for evaluation research started to show on both the demand side and the supply side. Four, in particular, stood out (Wholey *et al.*, 1970):

1 *Organizational inertia* – agencies tended to resist change, whereas evaluation often revealed it was necessary.
2 *Lack of dissemination* – too often the results of evaluation studies failed to reach the relevant decision-makers, were not presented in a form they could use and were not followed through.
3 *Methodological weakness* – shortcomings and deficiencies in the conduct of studies prompted policy-makers to rely instead on their own instincts; part of the problem at this time, as Mushkin (1973) noted, was that 'the methodology of evaluation is still inadequate to serve as an overall policy guide'.
4 *Design irrelevance* – too many studies lacked any conceivable policy pay-off; in many instances it seemed as though researchers were more interested in upholding academic traditions than in addressing the operational needs of policy-makers (Lynn, 1973, 1978b).

These 'market imperfections' took on a different hue for the producers and the consumers of evaluation research. What social scientists saw as a 'crisis of underutilization' was seen by policy-makers as a problem of the relevance and utility of their research.

The Crisis of Underutilization
In a three-year period up to 1974 over 1,000 evaluations were conducted in the education field alone. Yet, as Marvin and Hedrick (1974) reported at the time, 'we have found that the results of these evaluations are often not used by the Congress or the agencies when they make major decisions concerning program alternatives'. This was the crisis of underutilization.

For the shoals of social scientists sucked into the evaluation net by the lure of ready funding and political influence it was all a bitter disappointment. The research was being done; it was just not being used. They concluded that the policy process was impermeable to research or incapable of acting on its findings. A whole library of books appeared exploring the obstacles to the application of research (see Chapter 9). In the case of evaluation several front-runners emerged for the bogey prize.

The hot favourite was the 'iron triangle': the relationship between congressional committees that pass, bureaucracies that administer and constituencies that benefit from federal programmes. The 'iron triangle' embodies the most powerful vested interests at the core of the American political system. By closing ranks around pet programmes, it was usually strong enough to avert the threat of evaluation or fend off the impact of negative findings. As a minor but typical example it was not uncommon for evaluators to have difficulty in arranging for the publication let alone the use of evaluation results because middle management officials in the congressional liaison bureaucracy feared upsetting a delicate friendship with a key legislator or disrupting a committee deliberation (Lynn, 1973).

Another consequence of such legislative politics was to channel evaluation research into programmes that did not have a high political profile, were less well entrenched in the bureaucracy and lacked well-organized constituencies. New and marginal programmes were therefore more vulnerable to selection for evaluation, while the hardy perennials – irrespective of performance – tended to escape close scrutiny by the sheer weight of tradition (Weiss, 1973a). In the event, then, evaluation itself also came to be marginalized, focusing less on the big spending programmes and more on the loose change from the federal purse.

The effects of legislative politics on the use of evaluation were compounded by the workings of the bureaucratic machine. Government agencies are not organized merely around the pursuit of their programme goals. Other considerations, too, have a bearing on the way they operate. As with all formal organizations, time and effort has to be invested in ensuring their own survival and maintaining their autonomy. For any agency this means, among other things, securing both the necessary support to legitimate activities and an adequate supply of resources to fund them (see Chapter 2). Inevitably therefore agency officials are engaged in a far wider range of tasks than merely goal attainment. They have to recruit and train staff, keep up morale, promote their agency's image, handle external relations, fight their corner in the annual budget round, manage the housekeeping, deal with trouble-shooting, and so on. Against this background the raw programme aims of the agency are not usually the dominant or the most pressing concerns on the administrator's mind.

As a result, administrators and officials tend to see things from a very different perspective from that of the evaluator. Quite apart from the basic point that practitioners, at all levels, have to believe in what they are doing while evaluators have to doubt, they also tend to locate issues in a different frame of reference. Evaluators focus on programme goals, while administrators see them through the filter of wider system objectives. At bottom, what we meet are two types of rationality: a bureaucratic model of rationality, and a scientific model of rationality (Weiss, 1973b). These two models, as experience showed, do not always gell. Evaluators generally failed to credit administrators with any points for effectiveness in the politics of organizational survival. Equally agency officials and programme managers were disinclined to view evaluation findings as conclusive, or even to act on them, when they ignored this dimension of their work. In the conflicts that resulted as administrators mobilized to defend their programmes and researchers fought for the integrity of their data, evaluation lost much of its cutting-edge.

In these battles the typical response of agency partisans to an unfavourable evaluation was simply to shoot the messenger. They were assisted in this ploy by tacky methods and slippery programmes. When it came to the crunch, weaknesses in research design or execution invariably presented a loophole though which programme sponsors could crawl to escape a critical appraisal. As Williams and Evans (1969) noted, 'we have never seen a field evaluation of a social action program that could not be faulted legitimately by good methodologists, and we may never see one'. Even the best evaluations left room for enough uncertainty to preclude cut and dried answers, and programme staff were well-placed to use their first-hand knowledge to expose this haziness. Also, of course, the programmes themselves did not stand still: they presented a moving target. Evaluations take time, and in that time programmes may be modified, adapted or changed. It was not unusual for evaluators to be outflanked or to have their work debunked by the simple riposte: 'Things aren't like that any more.' Like generals, they too often found themselves equipped for fighting the last war.

This point links with the last main reason why evaluations were so often disregarded. They accepted too readily bloated promises and political rhetoric as authentic programme goals. Consequently, the sins of the programme were often visited on the evaluation (Weiss, 1973a).

Social programmes are rarely furnished with clearly defined and unambiguous goals. This is a mark of the process of coalition-building through which policy is formed. Policy-making is about securing agreement between people and groups with different values and interests. It means finding a compromise between the competing claims and the conflicts of purpose which fuel the political process. One way of coping with these is by vagueness and ambiguity. Leaving policies open to a variety of interpretations defuses opposition and wins over support. It also allows for a measure of flexibility in dealing with the unforeseen problems and special cases arising from their implementation. For this reason, too, formal statements of objectives frequently bear little relation to what happens on the ground where policies are often reformulated, from the bottom up, by the actions and decisions of street-level bureaucrats (Hill, 1982). As Weiss (1973b) has said, 'What the Congress writes into legislation as program objectives is not necessarily what the Secretary's Office or the director of the national program see as their mission, nor what the state or local project managers or the operating staff actually try to accomplish'.

Faced with the task of sifting the real goals from the window-dressing, researchers not unusually ended up by evaluating a programme against meaningless criteria. One reason for the generally negative pall of evaluation results was that, at least in the early days, evaluators uncritically addressed only the official programme goals. Administrators were quick to point out that these did not accurately describe what they were trying to do. Indeed, this lack of clarity rendered evaluation a hostage to the problems of the setting with poorly designed and managed programmes, beset by disruptions and makeshift changes of plan, tending to produce bad evaluation studies.

Another reason for the negative thrust of most early evaluation research was because its practitioners were misled by inflated official promises into using rough-hewn measures of programme impact. As a result, their instrumentation was often too blunt to pick up more subtle effects. These crude criteria of success and failure were also generally insensitive to the fact that programmes may also have multiple benefits and beneficiaries. As Abt (1979) has pointed out, there are usually between ten and twenty major programme constituencies – ranging from the Presidential administration, through the legislature and federal bureaucracy to state and local government agencies and user groups – who each have legitimate and disparate views of the costs and benefits to be addressed. Given these deficiencies, it is not surprising therefore that evaluation studies were given little weight in the calculus of decision-making unless they happened to drift with the tide.

In short, the major problems of evaluation research were vague goals, strong promises and weak effects (Rossi and Wright, 1977). Together these conspired to frustrate the good intentions of evaluators and the hopes of decision-makers. Unless success in evaluation could be linked with success in the competition for money and status, government departments would have few incentives to take it seriously (Schick 1971). With most evaluations apparently showing that nothing worked, these incentives were lacking and, accordingly, evaluation research itself went largely unused.

In the face of these frustrations, and the sense of wasted effort, many social scientists packed their bags and returned to their campuses. Their conviction, that having done what they regard as a good piece of work it should be acted on by the decision-maker, was attacked by Lynn from his eyrie in the evaluation office of HEW as 'the worst form of arrogance' (Salasin, 1977). Others stayed on and took his advice that they needed 'to attain a much more sophisticated sense of what the political process is all about'. Looking back over their recent experiences, these evaluators began to face up to:

1 the power of vested interests, especially professional lobbies, to rubbish findings that threaten their position;
2 the 'tunnel vision' that characterizes any role in an organizational hierarchy;
3 the self-serving arguments that are used to legitimate existing policies and practices;
4 the selective perception of administrators and practitioners when evaluating their own work.

All these factors, they saw, had to be taken into account in conducting evaluation research because of their implications for the study design, the methods of data collection, the kind of analysis undertaken and how the results are presented. At this point, the vision of the researcher shifted more closely into line with the perspective of the policy-maker.

The Crisis of Relevance

If growing disgruntlement within the social science community signalled the end of the honeymoon for evaluation, similar feelings of estrangement also affected the other partner to the marriage. The policy community began to doubt the value of much of the work being done. Federal officials openly questioned whether evaluation research generated much useful knowledge or whether what was produced justified its cost. A 1976 report from the Federal Council for Science and Technology warned of the 'indications that too little social R & D is relevant to policymaking and that too much research, even if relevant, is not available to and utilized by the appropriate decision-makers'. Again, in the same year, the National Research Council, following a review of applied social science research, concluded that the quality of the work, on average, 'is relatively undistinguished with only modest potential for useful application'.

The problem, in short, was one of utility: too much research lacked policy relevance. One reason, already mentioned, for this state of affairs was that the system of research management in federal departments was slipshod and ineffective. Evaluation had taken root and grown so fast it had become potbound. Too few officials involved in contracting for evaluations were well-versed in research methods or capable of giving proper guidance and direction to the contractor. Even fewer had the time to keep a close eye on the contractor's work when most of them were administering, on average, half a million dollars worth of new grants and contracts each year. When asked what was the greatest problem in gaining the maximum benefit from HEW's huge investment in evaluation, Lynn responded bluntly that it was shortage of the right people: 'People to conceive of a good evaluation agenda . . . people to monitor work, people to be concerned about the work once it was done, and to worry about its dissemination and its use' (Salasin, 1977). Without adequate contract monitoring, the private research firms who quickly moved into the booming evaluation market enjoyed a heydey of easy pickings for often shoddy work, earning themselves a reputation as 'beltway bandits' (from the location of their offices on the inner ringroad, or beltway, around Washington).

But this was by no means the whole story; managerial failings and the commercial instincts of private research contractors were not the only reasons why so much evaluation research lacked application. The cloistered outlook of academic social scientists was also to blame. Attracted into the evaluation field by the harvest of grants, these researchers proceeded to translate the government's problems into academic problems and to answer the questions that interested them instead of those that occupied their sponsors. Far too much of their work was structured by the incentives within the academic community rather than the requirements of policy-makers. Locked into an environment where scientific values hold sway, they generally chose to put their own integrity as social scientists first by showing more concern for the opinions of their peers about the quality of their research than for those of their customers. Consequently, criteria of scientific merit and technical adequacy consistently outweighted criteria of utility in the design of their evaluations. When these are the standards by which the reputation and career prospects of academics are assessed, it is perhaps not surprising that they should have opted for the pursuit of scientific rigour before policy relevance whenever the two came into conflict. As a result, a good deal of the evaluation research they produced was scientifically elegant but indigestible: it outran the comprehension of policy-makers or their capacity to use and apply it successfully. As the volume of these studies accumulated, so their deficiencies became more evident (Booth, 1986; Patton, 1984):

1. Social scientists tended to conceive problems and issues too narrowly in terms of their own disciplines.
2. Statistical analyses were often too complex and sophisticated, with quantitative methods overplayed and data too reified.
3. Evaluators relied too heavily on the 'mysticism of the scientific priesthood' to establish the credibility of their data. In technical terms too much emphasis was placed on content, construct and predictive validity at the expense of simple face validity. The plausibility of data to its users is just as important as its scientific robustness.
4. The pursuit of methodological precision often upped the cost of evaluation without commensurate returns in utility. Options on rigour had to be more thoroughly explored: how much is enough? How much can be afford? (Rutman, 1984a)
5. The focus of academic evaluators was frequently on understanding rather than action. Many of their studies seemed more geared towards producing publishable results and contributing to their own disciplines than towards producing solid policy pay-offs.
6. Evaluations rarely came to any clear-cut conclusions or made firm recommendations. More often, they were indecisive and hedged by all sorts of qualifications and reservations.
7. Scientifically tight evaluations take time and often outstretch the urgency of decisions.
8. Evaluation reports were generally too long, jargon-loaded, over-technical and plainly written for other researchers to read rather than policy-makers.

Spurred on to think afresh by these sorts of criticism, leading figures in evaluation circles, like Marcia Guttentag, a Harvard professor and first president of the Evaluation Research Society, began to argue that the application of research models developed for other purposes had led to many of the difficulties in producing useful evaluations. Guttentag (1978) suggested that experimental designs either force a set of assumptions on programmes or change them to fit the constraints of the model; anthropological research produces descriptive information but cannot be generalized so as to inform policy decisions; and economic analyses focus mainly on programme inputs and outputs while neglecting process variables.

At this point, the concerns of social scientists about underutilization and the worries of policy-makers about lack of relevance started to merge into a shared conviction. The requirements for effective policy research (aimed at improving decision-making) are not the same as the requirements for good academic research (aimed at advancing knowledge). Fundamentally *these different tasks call for a different science*. Enlivened by this insight, practitioners set about unscrambling this new paradigm.

New Standards for Evaluation Research

The turning-point in the development of evaluation research was marked formally by a series of congressional hearings on programme evaluation held by the Senate Committee on Human Resources on 6 and 27 October 1977. At these hearings expert witnesses from within and outside the federal government testified on past and current evaluation activities, and on evaluation's potential as an aid to policy-making.

Witnesses were generally agreed that evaluation had an important role to play in government, but not the one originally envisaged in the springtime of the Nixon administration. Then the hope had been it would help to weed out those programmes that were not working. In the event, this emphasis on impact or outcome evaluation turned out to have been misguided. Outcome studies proved to be not only methodologically knotty – because of the problem of isolating programme effects from effects due to other uncontrolled variables – but also politically friable. Experience had shown, most witnesses concurred, that evaluation was more likely to be useful as a tool of management: in answering questions about what happened rather than about what worked. As Henry Aaron (1978), Assistant Secretary for Planning and Evaluation at HEW, averred, 'evaluation by itself rarely will enable the decision-maker to determine whether a social program should continue or be terminated'. A point echoed in the testimony of Eleanor Chelimsky (1978), later to become Director of GAO's Program Evaluation and Methodology Division, who added that while evaluation cannot in most cases provide definitive conclusions on the ultimate worth of a programme, it can yield essential information about its operations. In short, the thrust of expert opinion was that context, process and monitoring forms of evaluation – where the aim was 'to illuminate the situation, not to dictate the decision' (Cronbach *et al.*, 1980) – were by far the most worth while.

Witnesses were emphatic, too, about one other point. Evaluators should apply themselves to the task of developing a set of common standards for the conduct of evaluation studies. Guidelines were needed to codify the practice of evaluation that were not tied to traditional disciplinary research, but that were responsive to the needs of programme managers and policy-makers.

Both the research fraternity and the policy community rose to this call by setting out to define new criteria of significance by which evaluations might be judged: criteria distinct from those applied to scientific research and which embodied the essential qualities of good policy research. Cronbach *et al.* (ibid.) summed up the drift of this thinking: 'Scientific quality is not the principal standard; an evaluation should aim to be comprehensible, correct and complete, and credible to partisans on all sides.'

In 1980 the Evaluation Research Society (ERS) produced a set of 55 standards for evaluation practice, organized in the form of simple admonitory statements into six sections covering the following phases of work:

1 *Formulation and negotiation* – this section specified twelve standards designed to ensure that before a project starts all those involved should have a clear, mutual understanding of what is to be done, how it is to be done and why, and an appreciation of possible constraints or impediments.

2 *Structure and design* – while acknowledging that factors apart from methodological requirements necessarily influence evaluation design, this section listed six standards aimed at ensuring the methods adopted matched the purposes of the study.

3 *Data collection and preparation* – this section laid down twelve standards for ensuring that data collection procedures are adequate for the job and carried out according to a sound plan of work.

4 *Data analysis and interpretation* – nine standards were issued stressing the importance of justifying the methods of analysis used, describing them explicitly and spelling out their limitations to the target audience.

5 *Communication and disclosure* – good communication, the ERS emphasized, is essential to a well-executed evaluation and should not be equated solely with the production of a final report. Ten standards were defined for ensuring that findings are presented clearly, fully and fairly.

6 *Utilization* – although utilization can never be guaranteed, it will be more likely if careful attention is given to the information needs of the potential users of the results during all phases of the evaluation. Six standards were set down for practitioners to follow in feeding evaluation results into the policy process.

The ERS standards represented an important step forward in that almost for the first time they openly acknowledged that the challenge of producing information useful for policy-making makes evaluation different from traditional academic research. By showing that successful evaluation designs depended on answers to several questions aside from the issue of technical adequacy, they loosened the grip which ivory-tower methodologists had long held over the practice of evaluation research. Among these several questions are (Patton, 1984):

Who is the information for, and *who* will use the evaluation findings?
What kinds of information are needed by its end-users?
How will this information be used and for what purposes?
When is this information needed?
What resources are available to conduct the evaluation?

The answers to these sorts of question have as much bearing on the evaluation design, the kinds of data collected and the methods used as other more scientific considerations. In short, methodological rigour is not enough to ensure a good evaluation: sometimes a judicious trade-off between rigour and relevance may be called for in the interests of effective policy research (Booth, 1986).

Less than a year after the publication of the ERS guidelines, a high-powered Joint Committee on Standards for Educational Evaluation released its own long-awaited report on the same theme. The result of five years' work by a seventeen-member team appointed by twelve professional organizations, with input from hundreds of practising evaluators, the report dramatically reflected the ways in which the practice of evaluation was changing.

The Joint Committee on Standards for Educational Evaluation (1981) defined good practice in terms of four important features: utility, feasibility, propriety and accuracy, *in that order*. As the chairman explained (Stufflebeam, 1980), their rationale was that an evaluation should not be done at all if there is no prospect of its being useful; that it should not be done if it is not feasible on political, practical or cost grounds; and that it should not be done if it cannot be conducted fairly and ethically. Only after it has been demonstrated that an evaluation will be useful, feasible and properly conducted should attention be given to the matter of its technical adequacy.

These four key attributes of an evaluation were each elaborated in terms of a set of standards which practitioners should follow:

1 The *utility standards* are intended to ensure that evaluation research serves the practical needs of its users and that it will be 'informative, timely and influential'. They call for the clear identification of the end-users and of their information needs; responsiveness to their interests; clear and understandable reports; specific recommendations; timely completion; and follow-through of the results to maximize their impact.

2 The *feasibility standards* are intended to ensure that an evaluation will be 'realistic, prudent, diplomatic and frugal'. They call for

research methods that are adapted to the setting; attuned to their political context and endorsed by those affected; and cost-effective in the sense of being worth the effort.

3 The *propriety standards* are intended to ensure that evaluations are conducted legally, ethically and with due regard for the welfare of those involved in or affected by them.

4 The *accuracy standards* deal with issues such as the soundness of the information, sources of data, validity, reliability, data control, the use of statistics, the analysis of qualitative information, the drawing of conclusions and objective reporting.

The important point about these standards, as with those produced by the ERS, is that they represent a genuine attempt to articulate a set of criteria for judging 'policy-driven research' which is different from the criteria applied to 'internally driven science' (to use a distinction employed by Kogan and Henkel, 1983). Quality is not seen primarily as a methodological issue. Whereas, in the past, an evaluation was rated as good if it followed the rules of scientific method, under the new standards it also must be useful, understandable, relevant and practical (Patton, 1984). Trow (1984) has summed up the difference:

> Perhaps the most important distinguishing characteristic of the policy analyst as contrasted with the academic research social scientist in the university is that he or she is trained, indeed required, to see and to formulate problems from the perspectives not of the academic disciplines but of the decision-maker. In his work he accepts the constraints and values of the decision-maker – the political pressures on him, the political feasibility of a proposal, its financial costs, the legal context within which it will operate, the difficulties of implementing it, of shaping organisations, and of recruiting, training and motivating people to work in the service of its purposes.

Meantime, back in the agencies, federal evaluation officials, too, had arrived at the conclusion that it was a mistake to apply the same tests of relevance to knowledge-building research and to policy-forming research. Evaluation, they had learned, did not have to be authoritative to be useful. This put a new gloss on things. For so long as the worth of an evaluation had been measured by its methodological precision the social scientists had called the tune. The new standards of utility and responsiveness shifted the initiative into the departmental policy shops. Two agencies which took the lead in developing new approaches to the management and practice of evaluation, from the inside, were the US General Accounting Office (GAO) and the Department of Health, Education and Welfare (HEW).

Inside the Agencies

A survey by the Office of Management and Budget showed that in 1977 over $243 million was channelled into programme evaluation by the Executive branch. About 70 per cent of this money went into studies done under contracts or grants. In the human resources field alone nearly $140 million was spent on evaluation research. By 1980 there were 1,300 full-time professional evaluators employed in 164 federal departments and agencies with 2,362 active evaluations on their books (Hudson and McRoberts, 1984).

In the face of this burgeoning level of activity the GAO, the congressional watchdog over federal spending, decided that more should be done to ensure the accountability of evaluators for the quality of their work. In the words of the Comptroller-General, 'those who evaluate must also be evaluated' (GAO, 1978). Too often there was a worrying gap 'between our ability to evaluate programs and our ability to manage these evaluations so that their results directly aid decisionmakers and properly inform the public'. The GAO pursued a two-track response to this problem. It set out to strengthen congressional oversight procedures by establishing a disciplined process for agencies to follow in monitoring, evaluating and reporting on how their programmes are working to Congress; and it introduced a management system designed to measure and improve the quality of evaluation research.

The oversight procedure was intended to enhance the usefulness of evaluations to Congress and its committees by ensuring that they:

- addressed the relevant questions that congressional decision-makers wanted answering;
- used measures or indicators of performance that were acceptable to congressional interests;
- produced information and findings that were perceived as trustworthy by their end-users; and were reported in a form that the Congress could understand.

Under this procedure the Congress when enacting authorizing legislation would spell out what it expects the programme to accomplish, and what questions it wants the agency to answer about the workings of the programme. The agency would then seek to translate these oversight concerns into practical criteria for guiding their evaluation of the programme, having regard to what is feasible in research terms and in terms of resources, and then submit their proposals to Congress for approval. Having thus agreed an evaluation plan, a timetable for the work and reporting arrangements would be finalized (GAO, 1977).

The internal management system introduced by GAO was based on the principles of evaluability assessment and developed over a period of years. It was conceived as a response to the need for tighter control over the rapidly growing evaluation industry. The GAO set out to define a set of standards that evaluations must meet 'to achieve the high quality necessary to make them useful' (GAO, 1978). The following minimum criteria were specified:

relevance – evaluations must provide the information needed by a variety of audiences, especially decision-makers, and must answer the right questions at the right time;

significance – the information must tell users something new and important; it must go beyond what is already apparent to them;

validity – the evaluation must provide some indication of how confidently the measured effects can be attributed to the programme; as a general rule, the evidence must be sufficient to persuade the well-informed reviewer;

reliability – the evaluation must show that the conclusions are not based on chance or inconsistent measurements;

objectivity – evaluators should not expect users to accept the study results on faith; they must be reported in a clear, complete and unbiased manner;

timeliness – the information must be available in usable form when decisions have to be made.

These criteria were operationalized in the form of a checklist for use by evaluators, sponsors and decision-makers in planning an evaluation, and afterwards in assessing the quality of the final study. The checklist comprised a series of fifty questions organized into five sections referring to different phases of the evaluation project from its initial planning, through data collection and analysis to reporting and dissemination of the results.

As time went on, and the expertise of the GAO in the management of evaluation increased, this system was gradually refined and simplified. In their original form the standards embodied in the checklist applied mainly to impact evaluations. The shift towards process and other types of evaluation prompted modifications to the approach while sticking to the principle that quality calls for more than just a sound methodology.

Most of this development work was carried out within the Program Evaluation and Methodology Division of GAO. Under the energetic leadership of its director, Eleanor Chelimsky, the review system was streamlined, and the emphasis put on two basic components of quality: technical adequacy and usefulness (Chelimsky, 1983).

The technical adequacy of an evaluation was defined in terms of its design, execution and reporting. The key issues were judged to be: the appropriateness of the design for answering the questions posed in the study; the feasibility of the design, or how well it was executed, given time and cost constraints; and the absence of major conceptual errors, inappropriate methods of analysis or improper conclusions and inferences (see also GAO, 1984).

The usefulness of an evaluation was defined in terms of four factors: its relevance, timeliness, presentation and impact. The notion of relevance refers to how well a study meets the information needs of its users. Timeliness means delivering the findings when they are most likely to be of help to the user. Presentation is a matter of how successfully the results are communicated to users. Lastly, the impact of a study is assessed on the basis of direct evidence of its actual use.

The GAO system of evaluation planning and review bears witness to the new realism that had crept into the field. As Chelimsky (1983) put it: 'Technical adequacy alone does not ensure usefulness.' Evaluators had to earn their keep and this involved listening more carefully to their paymasters. Usefulness could not be taken for granted; it had to be planned for and built into the design of studies as an essential aspect of evaluation methodology.

Similar concerns about quality and accountability arose at about the same time in HEW. With the third largest budget in the world behind those of the entire US government and the Soviet Union, HEW had invested heavily in evaluation. In 1980, for example, the department planned to spend $55 million on evaluation studies. Yet only the previous year a Senate Appropriations Committee report had expressed concern about the value of much of this work:

> The Committee is unaware of any significant program improvements that have been brought about by the Department's large annual investment in evaluation... It seems as though, year after year, the same programs get re-evaluated, yet never change. (Senate Report 96-247, 13 July 1979)

As a response to these criticisms, the department undertook a review of the reasons for the past failure of evaluation to affect programme performance. Typical causes of failure that were identified included (OASPE, 1980):

1 inadequate definition of the programme or problem addressed by the programme;
2 insufficient understanding of the links between programme activities and their anticipated results;
3 lack of management willingness or ability to act on the basis of evaluation information;

4   conflicting demands and expectations imposed on evaluators by programme managers, policy officials and other users;
5   an organizational structure for evaluation that was too decentralized.

To overcome these problems, the department established its own process of evaluability assessment and review, centred in the Office of the Assistant Secretary for Planning and Evaluation, with the purpose of injecting greater accountability into the management of evaluation research. The process was made up of three stages (OASPE, 1980, 1981).

Stage 1 involved the preparation of an evaluation plan or strategy. This meant defining realistic, agreed-upon and measurable objectives and performance indicators for the department's programmes, and specifying the intended uses of evaluation information. Stage 2 comprised an internal review of individual evaluation studies at several phases of their development, designed to cull any projects that seemed unlikely to produce useful information. The new process was also intended to ensure that:

(a) projects furthered the agency's management and evaluation strategy;
(b) the questions addressed in each study were answerable;
(c) the methodologies were appropriate to the task;
(d) the intended use of the studies was clearly and specifically identified;
(e) the expected value of the study justified its cost.

Stage 3 called for monitoring of the uses of completed evaluation studies. All evaluation offices were required to institute a follow-up procedure to determine with primary intended users:

(a) the extent to which the evaluation met the specific information needs of the HEW staff member requesting the study; or
(b) the extent to which it influenced the design or performance of the programme; or
(c) the extent to which it affected the attitudes, opinions, or positions of those involved in debate on a specific policy issue; or
(d) what other information needs or purposes, if any, the evaluation served.

The feedback from this procedure was collated by OASPE into an annual report on the uses of completed evaluation studies and transmitted to Congress each year.

Once again, as in GAO, usefulness is the touchstone of quality and the key to accountability in the system of evaluation assessment and review. All HEW evaluations are required to demonstrate their relevance to departmental decision-making or programme management. In this context, one important measure of their usefulness is consumer satisfaction.

An interesting manifestation of this concern for utility is the recent development within HEW of the short-term policy evaluation (Brush, 1983) and programme inspections (Kusserow, 1986). These are designed to avoid the most serious drawbacks of traditional evaluation research, i.e. time, length and high costs. Their keynote is responsiveness to the pressing information needs of top decision-makers. When even the process of reaching a contractual agreement can take six to eight months, full-scale evaluations often cannot be done inside the deadlines imposed by the legislative and budgetary cycles. Moreover, the further into the future the research is located, so the less related it is to immediate issues and the more remote its usefulness and the smaller its current constituency (Lynn, 1978b). Short-term evaluations and programme inspections were devised to meet the need for disciplined, focused and quick-turn-around reviews of programme performance.

Their methodology is based on two simple premises. First, that partial information available at the time the decision must be made is better than no information or late information. Secondly, that accuracy has to be defined relative to the questions being asked and the problems faced. Only marginal adjustments call for precise measurement (Hope, 1978). Normally it is not necessary to wait for all the facts to come in, for definitive answers, before arriving at an informed decision. In driving to Scotland, it is enough to know that you begin by heading northwards without having precise compass bearings to follow.

These two premises led to the notion of 'good enough' research: research that did not necessarily meet scientific standards of admissible evidence, but which provided *enough* information with a *sufficient* level of confidence to illuminate the options and choices facing the decision-maker.

Thus short-term evaluations and programme inspections are generally carefully designed to answer specified, clearly defined questions, determined by the information needs of policy-makers, usually within three weeks to six months. The emphasis is on them being quick and timely with data collection methods adapted to meet the constraints of the policy process. Where this involves shortcuts, these are acknowledged. They call for the active involvement of end-users in all stages of the project: from the beginning phase when questions are formulated; through the design phase when decisions are made about what sort of information should be collected and how much; to the end phase when recommendations are drawn up with a weather eye on what is politically feasible and implementable. Final reports, generally supplemented by personal briefings and presentations, are short (rarely more than twenty pages), readable (jargon-free and short on technical detail) and targeted to managers. They begin with a one-page executive summary highlighting the most important findings, and usually conclude with a schedule of follow-up action. Though a recent innovation, the new form of 'rapid evaluation' and the related notion of 'good enough' research seem likely to find a growing place in the repertoire of evaluation techniques.

The Prospects for Evaluation

All in all, the history of evaluation in US federal agencies, particularly GAO and HEW, must be seen as a story of the successful application of research to policy. What began as a phenomenon of hard times has survived through changes of administration and changes in the political and economic climate. Indeed, evaluation has done more than just survive; in many ways it has prospered. Even the 'New Federalism' of the Reagan years which has transferred many social programmes to the states, and which might have been expected to reduce the demand for national evaluations, has not significantly dinted the level of output. The 1984 *Directory of Federal Evaluations*, issued by the US Comptroller-General, lists 1,676 evaluations conducted by federal agencies in fiscal year 1983. The previous six volumes together abstract 11,420 evaluation reports completed in the ten years up to 1982. The 926-page 1985 edition of the *Compendium of HHS Evaluations and Relevant Other Studies*, produced by the Department of Health and Human Services (formerly HEW), describes 1,843 studies completed over the previous decade. This is a prolific rate of activity by any reckoning.

One reason for this record of accomplishment is that evaluation has successfully adapted to its habitat – the Washington jungle. In doing so, compromises have had to be made, some more than many critically minded social scientists were prepared to countenance. Evaluations, it has been learned, have to be designed around the user's information needs and not the knowledge-building aims of the research community. They are also most likely to affect decisions only when the researcher accepts the values, assumptions and objectives of the decision-maker (Weiss, 1975) and abandons the stance of critical detachment. New criteria of policy relevance have ousted academic criteria as the standards for assessing evaluation quality. The price of usefulness has been a downgrading of scientific excellence. In return, the rewards for these sacrifices have not been great: evaluations have been shown to influence fine-grain programme decisions but for the big policy issues research has remained marginal (Abt, 1976). It is not surprising that in-house evaluators and private research firms working for contracts have found it easier than academic social scientists to make these adjustments. The overriding lesson of the evaluation saga, however, is one that Merton (1959) anticipated long ago: research must accept 'new criteria of significance' if it is successfully to enter the policy arena.

7 Field experimentation in social policy

'We must help create a political climate that demands more rigorous and less self-deceptive reality testing. We must provide political stances that permit true experiments, or good quasi-experiments.' (Donald T. Campbell)

Evaluation research, as we have seen in Chapter 6, took hold during Nixon's spring-cleaning of the 'Great Society' programmes, and thereafter established itself as a badge of good housekeeping.

An important task facing any incoming administration is to mark the break with its predecessor by setting its own stamp on the times. Evaluation answered the need for economy and style. Initially it was seen as a way of 'new-brooming' the failed policies of the Johnson era: of finding out what worked and what didn't, of sorting out the best and discarding the rest. The evaluation researcher was cast in the role of political hatchet-man (Weiss, 1973b). Later when the administration had to live with its own reputation, evaluation was embraced as a useful managerial device: a means of keeping tabs on the executive, of checking whether programmes were meeting their objectives and of relating their costs to achievements.

Looking back, things never worked out quite so neatly. Evaluation did not easily fit the mould into which it had been cast. In practice, it proved to be too blunt an instrument for settling the fate of programmes, and for two reasons. First, evaluation studies rarely produced definitive evidence about programme outcomes. They were dogged by the methodological problems created by vague goals and weak effects. Even when positive measures of impact were obtained they usually could not be attributed unambiguously to the programme because of the impossibility of controlling for all the extraneous variables. Secondly, the ultimate decision about whether programmes should be continued or terminated was invariably taken on political rather than empirical grounds. It was the strength of their constituency, not the findings of research, which sealed their future. In this political scrimmage over resources, evaluations were frequently hijacked for partisan ends and badly mauled in the process

– especially when threatened interests mobilized to rubbish an unfavourable study.

The politics of evaluation research eventually forced a reappraisal of its role in the policy process, and precipitated something of a split in the evaluation movement. The early emphasis on impact studies had produced a shower of negative findings, so feeding the view that 'nothing works'. This was politically embarrassing (encouraging a loss of faith in government), practically unhelpful (offering little guidance to federal policy-makers) and factually dubious (given the methodological weaknesses of the studies). For evaluation to survive it obviously had to offer more than cold comfort to its sponsors and users. This challenge led to a conflict among its practitioners between the claims of rigour and the claims of relevance.

The proponents of relevance took their cue from policy-makers. Above all else, evaluation research must aim to be useful and tackle only what is feasible. For the most part, impact studies designed to assess whether a programme was working had met neither of these two criteria. Accordingly, it was argued, evaluators would do better to focus on process issues with a managerial pay-off: to answer questions about what happened rather than about what worked (Weiss and Rein, 1970). In the end, as we have seen in Chapter 6, this camp won the day. But not without a fight.

The proponents of rigour stuck firmly to the principles of the scientific method as the only proper foundation for evaluation research. The reason why so many studies had lacked application was because they were flawed. The answer was not to abandon the quest for reliable information about the relationship between programme inputs and their outputs, but better research designs. Technical problems, such as whether a programme is achieving its intended results, require technical solutions. A hard-nosed, empirical approach to programme development and evaluation would also transform policy-making by putting it on a more scientific footing. The main technical resource in the arsenal of the advocates of rigour was the method of social experimentation.

The Method of Social Experimentation

Social experimentation was an attempt to extend the logic of the laboratory into the field. It was promoted as a 'radical new strategy of social reform' (Rivlin, 1971), aimed at resolving the fundamental dilemmas of policy-making:

1   The uncertainty of knowing beforehand whether new policies or programmes will achieve their intended results.

Figure 7.1: Archetypal schema of the experimental design

	Experimental group	Control group
Pre-test measure (before treatment)	A_1	B_1
Post-test measure (after treatment)	A_2	B_2
Outcome measure	$A = A_2 - A_1$	$B = B_2 - B_1$

Final treatment effect $= A - B$

2　The difficulties of establishing afterwards whether they have been successful or not.
3　The bias towards self-justification which works against the righting of wrong decisions and so increases the risks of innovation.

Experimentation was seen as a way of tackling these dilemmas of reform and innovation by the simple expedient of 'suck it and see' – but under strictly controlled conditions. These conditions were modelled on the classical design for true experimental, laboratory research.

Experimental designs are used to infer causal relationships. They seek to estimate the effects of some treatment or intervention on a target group or outcome variable. This is done by assigning subjects to two groups: an experimental group and a control group. A pre-test measure is taken of the dependent variable (the one which might be expected to change after treatment) in order to establish a baseline against which the outcome may be compared. The experimental group is then exposed to the treatment, while the control group is not. After the treatment, a post-test measure is taken in both groups using the same instruments as before. The pre-tests and post-tests for both the experimental and the control groups are finally compared to identify precisely what, if any, changes might be attributed to the treatment as measured by differences in the recorded outcomes between the two groups. Figure 7.1 presents an archetypal schema of the experimental design. Experimental designs can be classified into two main types depending on how assignment to treatment occurs: randomized experiments and quasi-experiments.

In randomized experiments the subjects are assigned to the experimental or control group in such a way that each person has an equal chance of being selected for either group. The purpose of this procedure is to ensure that the two groups are comparable in every respect except for the treatment they receive. Random methods of assignment mean they will differ from each other only by chance. As long as the sample size is adequate the groups may then be considered equal and alike for the purposes of comparison. Whatever differences in outcome appear between the pre-test and the post-test measures of the experimental and control groups may therefore confidently be attributed to the effects of the intervention or treatment.

Another method of achieving comparability is by matching pairs of subjects on the basis of their relevant characteristics and then assigning them to the experimental or control group by random methods. The result of matching should be the same as for random assignment enabling the effects of the treatment to be isolated.

In quasi-experimental designs the researcher is unable to regulate who receives the treatment. In other words, the assignment of subjects is not random, usually because individuals select themselves for treatment or because officials act as gatekeepers. The same basic framework of before-and-after testing, however, is maintained. There are many sorts of quasi-experimental methods but, broadly speaking, they may be divided into time-series designs and non-equivalent group designs. The time-series design involves taking a series of measurements before, during and after the experimental treatment or intervention (e.g. a behaviour modification programme), and by comparing the trial and before-and-after measures (say, frequency of absenteeism from school), identifying any change or rates of change in the subjects' behaviour (truancy). The non-equivalent group design involves taking pre-test and post-test measures of both a treatment group and a comparison group whose characteristics resemble but are not strictly equivalent to those of the experimental subjects. Because random selection is lacking from both these methods, it cannot be supposed that any observed change in the outcome as measured is due to the treatment: rival explanations cannot properly be ruled out and therefore valid inferences about causation cannot be made (Mark and Cook, 1984). In line with the convention adopted by Riecken and Boruch (1974) true social experiments will here be regarded as those where provision is made for the random assignment of subjects to treatment and control groups. Quasi-experimental trials of new programmes including those lacking controls will be called 'demonstration projects'.

Social experimentation, however, was more than just a rigorous approach to evaluation. For many of its more vociferous advocates it also represented a new, scientific approach to policy-making.

One of the chief obstacles to producing better social services, so they argued, was the adversarial system of politics and the partisan loyalties it generated. People are pushed in advance into taking up positions for and against any proposed reforms, which are always packaged as if they were certain to be successful. When changes are carried through, politicians are obliged to stand by their efficacy and uphold the correctness of their own decisions. Administrators are debarred from admitting their failures in order to avoid embarrassing their political masters and jeopardizing their own reputations and careers. Such a system is not conducive to honest evaluation, social learning or effective problem-solving because it cannot tolerate facing up to mistakes.

A new political posture was needed, or so the argument ran: one which fostered new ideas without the excess of commitment that 'blinds us to reality testing' (Campbell, 1969). A simple shift that would help to make this possible was to acknowledge the essentially risky nature of policy-making and the possibility of failure while stressing the importance of the problem and the need to carry on searching until an answer was found. In other words, 'to shift from the advocacy of a specific reform to the advocacy of the seriousness of the problem' (ibid.). Experimentation offered a framework for rejigging the policy process along these lines. It would have the effect of removing issues of effectiveness from the political arena into the zone of science where they could be resolved by systematic investigation instead of by the decibel count. By setting up a controlled trial, politicians would be able to demonstrate their determination to tackle a problem without the risks of backing an untried solution. Equally, trapped administrators would be freed from the straitjacket of past commitments and airy promises and encouraged to look for new solutions where previous ones had failed. In this light, experimentation can be seen for what it was: a scientific version of incrementalism, trial and error under laboratory-like conditions. In Campbell's influential vision of 'the experimenting society' (Salasin, 1973) programmes would be devised 'using the best of science' and retained, modified or discarded on the basis of hard-headed analysis of their effectiveness.

Examples of Field Experiments

The Office of Economic Opportunity (OEO) emerged as an experimenting agency under the Nixon administration. In 1968 – the last year of Johnson's Presidency – its research budget was slightly over $7 million. By fiscal year 1971 this sum had risen to

$23 million with roughly two-thirds of the funds being allocated for field experiments (Williams, 1980). Conveying something of the size, scale and variety of this work is not easy. Social experiments ranged widely in their contexts, their character and their complexity. Boruch (1974) provides an illustrative bibliography of randomized field experiments for programme planning and evaluation; Riecken and Boruch (1974) list a selection of abstracts of social experiments classified by programme area; and Gilbert, Light and Mosteller (1975) attempt to assess and rate a series of social innovations on the basis of the results of controlled field trials. The following examples have been chosen because they are widely known, fully documented and models of their type. A detailed account is also given of one demonstration project in order to point up how it differs from a social experiment.

The Manhattan Bail Bond Experiment

The Manhattan Bail experiment is worthy of mention as a pathfinding project. As a forerunner in the field of social experimentation, its success laid the foundations for the growth of interest in this method of evaluation.

The project was initiated by the Vera Foundation, New York University School of Law and the Institute of Judicial Administration in 1961. It evolved out of serious and long-standing concerns about the working of the bail system. Bluntly the evidence pointed to the fact that bail was being misused. Committing magistrates were manipulating the system to punish defendants, to keep them off the streets, to aid the prosecution and to appease the public. Bail was being set too high and with little regard for the person's financial circumstances. It was known that defendants released before arraignment were less likely to be convicted or, if convicted, to be sent to prison. Consequently, the system discriminated against the poor, flouted the presumption of innocence and cut across the principle of equality under the law. The Manhattan Bail Project was set up to see whether arrested people could be successfully paroled without bail pending trial on the basis of verified information about their backgrounds.

The Vera Foundation developed a set of criteria for judging from interviews with defendants whether to recommend their release prior to arraignment. As part of the experiment, all those thought suitable for parole were randomly split into two groups: an experimental group who were recommended to the court for release without bail, and a control group for whom no recommendations were made. The outcomes for the two groups were compared in terms of whether parole was granted by the court, the dispositions of the cases, sentencing and default rates.

The results were conclusive. During the first year of the experiment the court accepted the recommendation for release without bail in 60 per cent of cases. Over the same period only 14 per cent of defendants in the control group were paroled by the court. In other words, four times as many people were paroled as would have been without the verified information about the defendants' backgrounds obtained from the interviews by Vera staff. Between 1961 and 1964 less than 1 per cent of the experimental group failed to turn up for trial, showing that the relaxation of the bail requirements did not produce unacceptable default rates. Indeed, the evidence suggested that there were fewer parole-jumpers than bail-jumpers. Analysis of the final dispositions in the experimental and control groups revealed that 59 per cent of the parolees in the experimental group were found not guilty as against only 23 per cent of the control group. And finally, the study showed that, even when convicted, defendants released without bail were less likely to be sent to prison than those detained pending trial. These findings confirmed the suspicion that a person not in jail at the time of trial stood a better chance of receiving a favourable disposition, and so demonstrated the injustices in the working of the bail system.

Following the experiment, the New York Probation Department extended the Vera programme throughout the city. Similar projects were launched in other areas and gradually the idea of pre-trial release was taken up nationwide. Many of the innovations first tried in the Manhattan experiment were subsequently incorporated in the 1966 Bail Reform Act. Quite apart from the substantive issues with which it dealt, however, the Manhattan Bail Project may in retrospect also be seen as a test of the validity of social experimentation itself to which its results gave an enormous stimulus. A full account of the project can be found in Ares, Rankin and Sturz (1963) and Botein (1965).

The New Jersey Income Maintenance Experiment

The New Jersey Income Maintenance Experiment was the first, large-scale social experiment carried out in the USA. It was set up to test the idea of tackling poverty through a system of negative income tax.

A negative income tax is a cash-transfer system of income support. It works by making payments to families whose income falls below the poverty line. Broadly the system operates by linking two variables: a guaranteed minimum income and a tax rate. The 'guarantee level' is the amount paid to an individual or family with no other income and is defined as a percentage of the poverty line adjusted for family size. The tax rate is the rate at which that amount is reduced as other income rises. Consider, for example, a negative income tax scheme providing a guarantee level of $3,000 and a tax rate of 50 per cent. At zero earned income a family's cash payment would be $3,000. The tax rate of 50 per cent means that for every dollar earned the payment is reduced by 50 cents. Thus for earned income of $1,000 the transfer payment is $2,500 (the guarantee of $3,000 minus 50 per cent of the earned income or $500). Similarly, where earned income is $5,000 the family would receive $500 ($3,000 minus 50 per cent of $5,000). At incomes of $6,000 a year and over no payment would be made: the individual moves from being a tax recipient to being a tax-payer.

Obviously different combinations of guarantee levels and tax rates will produce different schedules of payment that decrease as income rises. Other things being equal, the higher the guarantee level and the lower the tax rate, so the more generous will be the resulting cash transfers.

The New Jersey experiment was designed to test the effects of such a scheme on the socio-economic behaviour and lifestyles of the poor and to provide policy-makers with estimates of its administrative costs and operational feasibility. Most importantly, the experiment set out to test whether a system of direct cash payments to poor families reduced their incentives to work in line with the assumptions of economic theory and the fears of politicians.

The experiment began in 1968 and ran through until 1972. It covered a target population of intact families with a total income not exceeding 150 per cent of the poverty line. Eligible families were identified by means of a large household survey. Over 1,200 families spread across five communities were enrolled in the experiment and randomly assigned to one of eight treatment groups or a control group. The treatment groups were defined by various combinations of different guarantee levels (ranging from 50 to 125 per cent of the official poverty line) and different tax rates (varying from 30 to 70 per cent). The control group consisted of families who did not receive any payments.

Families in the experimental groups reported their earnings each month, and these statements provided the basis for calculating their entitlement under the appropriate schedule of payments. The only condition for receiving the payments was that the family filled out their income report form. Prior to their enrolment in the programme, and thereafter, at three-monthly intervals throughout the three years of the experiment, all the families in both the treatment and the control groups were interviewed in detail. These interviews were the main source of data from the experiment and provided information on such things as employment, expenditure and consumption, debt accumulation, health, household composition and fertility, social behaviour, leisure activities and psychological adjustment. These data were then analysed along with the monthly earnings reports to determine whether those receiving payments changed their working patterns or lifestyles compared with the equivalent families in the control group.

The main findings of the experiment were that there was no substantial withdrawal from work on the part of those receiving income support. The benefits they obtained represented a net increase in family income, allowing greater command over material goods and services and enhancing their economic well-being. The payments, however, did not appear to have any systematic effect on recipients' health, self-esteem, social integration or perceived quality of life. A full account of the experimental methods and results is provided by Kershaw and Fair (1976) and Watts and Rees (1977). A shortened version is given by Kershaw (1972).

The Californian Parole Survival Experiment

In the 1960s the Californian Adult Authority (the agency responsible for prisons) had introduced a voluntary group counselling programme in most state prisons. The purpose of the scheme was to help prisoners develop an understanding of the motivations that had led them into criminal activity. It was hoped that this would improve their ability to rehabilitate to civilian life and so increase their chances of succeeding on parole.

The construction of a new prison provided an opportunity for running a controlled trial of the counselling programme. The architectural design of the prison which had been built as four relatively self-contained units or 'quads' facilitated an experimental approach. It was unlikely that there would be any serious contamination of the results as a consequence of spillover effects between the inmates in the separate quads. Also the random assignment of subjects was made possible as part of the process of filling the new prison.

With the support of the prison authorities, two of the four quads were designated as experimental units. Their inmates were to receive different forms of counselling. A third quad was designated to serve as the control where no counselling would be given to the prisoners. The fourth quad was reserved as a special unit for prisoners who presented exceptional problems of behaviour. As new inmates were referred to the prison those who were not creamed off into the special unit were randomly assigned to one of the other three quads.

When prisoners from the experimental and control groups were released on parole, their records were monitored for a period of two years after release for evidence of adjustment to civilian life. No differences were found between those who had received counselling and those who had not and the group counselling programme was judged a failure. For a full account of this experiment, see Kassebaum, Ward and Wilner (1971).

The Sesame Street Experimental Evaluation

The American 'War on Poverty' attached a high priority to the role of education in breaking out of the paradox of poverty amid plenty. Yet it was clear that the schools alone could not meet this challenge. The children of the poor mostly arrived at school age seriously deficient in their ability to profit from formal education and already significantly behind their contemporaries. Some other means had to be found of narrowing the 'academic achievement gap' between those from economically disadvantaged homes and those from better-off homes, and of ensuring that all children were enabled to develop their full potential. Pre-school education was seen as a vital part of the solution on the ground that it is during the early years of a child's life when environment has the strongest impact on development. It was within this climate that many pre-school initiatives, including *Sesame Street*, were launched.

Sesame Street was a television series aimed at entertaining and teaching all children between the ages of 3 and 5 but particularly disadvantaged pre-schoolers. Produced by the Children's Television Workshop (CTW) whose funding came half-and-half from government (mainly the Office of Education) and private sources, the series combined a carefully planned educational programme, designed on the basis of extensive research to stimulate intellectual and social growth, with slick attention-holding techniques (fast movement, variety, humour, slapstick, animation). Originally broadcast across the nation for one hour a day during the school week, the five shows were later run consecutively on Saturday mornings during its highly successful first year in 1969 when it met with zooming popularity and widespread critical acclaim. In its second season *Sesame Street* went on the air twice a day in many areas and, in later years, even more frequently.

In the early stages of programme development CTW contracted an independent research organization to evaluate the impact of *Sesame Street* in terms of the series' own goals. The evaluation strategy aimed to discover whether viewers learned more than non-viewers; whether children watching the show at home or in pre-school classrooms learned more; what were the characteristics of those who benefited the most (in terms of their age, sex, socio-economic class, extent of viewing and intellectual ability); and what elements of the series seemed to be the most effective in stimulating learning.

The evaluation design involved selecting two groups of children from five different locales spread across the USA: an at-home group and a pre-school group. The pre-school group comprised classes of children attending kindergartens or nursery schools. These classes were randomly assigned to an experimental group, who were encouraged to view the programmes, and a control group of non-viewing classes. The at-home group of children were obtained from the same neighbourhoods by means of house-to-house canvassing. These children were then randomly assigned to an experimental (viewing) group and a control (non-viewing) group. The encouraged-to-view group was told about *Sesame Street*, given publicity material, and paid a weekly visit by trained staff during the morning telecasting time. The control group did not receive this treatment. Overall almost 1,000 children took part in the study.

A variety of measuring instruments was used in the evaluation. A battery of nine, separate pre-tests and eleven post-tests were employed to measure the educational effects of *Sesame Street* in terms of the areas of knowledge and learning covered by the programmes. Additional information was also obtained on the viewing habits of the children and their home backgrounds.

The results of the evaluation were clear. Children who viewed learned. This learning could not be attributed to the effects of normal growth, IQ, previous achievement or socio-economic status. Moreover, high-viewers learned more than low-viewers. The programme benefited children of between 3 to 5 years old from ghetto communities, middle-class suburbs and isolated rural areas. It was not only effective with all groups, but equally effective with them all. In terms of its own educational goals *Sesame Street* was adjudged a success. For a fuller account of the *Sesame Street* evaluation, see Ball and Bogatz (1970), Bogatz and Ball (1971) and Cook *et al.* (1975).

The Alum Rock Education Voucher Demonstration

The Alum Rock voucher project is an example of a large-scale social demonstration. A demonstration is more of a prototype than an experiment, in that unlike the latter it does not apply scientific controls for the measurement of programme effects (such as random assignment to treatments or the selection of matching groups). In this sense, it is more correctly seen as a trial run than a controlled trial. A demonstration may be used when the conditions for a true experiment cannot be assured. For example, when there are no clear criteria of success; when the likely outcomes cannot be specified in advance; when unanticipated developments are likely; when objectives might change in the light of experience or other circumstantial factors; when the researchers cannot guarantee continuity of methods of treatment; and when interest focuses as much on process as on end-results.

In autumn 1972 the Alum Rock Union Elementary School District in San Jose, California, was chosen as the site for the first evaluation voucher demonstration. Voucher plans were designed to introduce a market mechanism into the educational system. Although many variants of the scheme have been proposed, they all basically involve tying school finances to student enrolment. Parents are given credits or vouchers, equivalent to the cost of their child's education, which they use to pay the schools of their choice. Schools survive only if they receive enough income in the form of vouchers to meet their outgoings. Additional 'compensatory' vouchers may be allocated to disadvantaged children in order to give them more 'purchasing power' in the educational market-place.

Proponents of the scheme have argued that with schools dependent on these funds for their survival, they will become more responsive to the needs of parents and students. In this way, vouchers will encourage parental interest in education, promote educational innovation and diversity, and improve the quality of schooling. Opponents of the scheme have claimed that vouchers could foster segregation by race and class, undermine professional tenure, destroy the democratic values embodied in the public school system and encourage hucksterism in the schools.

In the late 1960s the Office of Economic Opportunity (OEO) began investigating vouchers as a means of improving the educational opportunities of poor families. In 1970 OEO agreed that a voucher demonstration should be tried and a year later authorized feasibility studies in four school districts. Only Alum Rock agreed to participate. After twelve months of negotiations, a model outline for the demonstration project was finally settled and granted federal support for five to seven years. The main features of the model were that the demonstration would initially involve public schools only, with six of the district's twenty-four schools participating (covering 4,000 of the district's 15,000 students); each participating school would diversify into at least two 'mini-schools' offering distinct educational programmes; and the district would provide the basic voucher from its current income with OEO providing a compensatory voucher for disadvantaged children. The OEO granted the district $1.5 million dollars towards the first year of operation in 1972–3 and also awarded the Rand Corporation a contract to evaluate the demonstration and the policy issues it raised.

The Alum Rock model, then, comprised only a set of general rules waiting to be worked out and, in some areas, modified as the project was implemented. Within the broad outline agreed the approach was one of 'feel as you go'. This alone ruled out a more formal experiment along the lines described above. The important variables were either unknown or uncontrolled.

At the outset the RAND researchers set about collecting evidence on the effects of the demonstration on the education of students, the cost and efficiency of the schooling process and the relationship between citizens and their schools. Subsequently, during the first year of the project, a fourth important category of effects emerged: the effects on the roles of professionals and on patterns of school decision-making.

During the first year data were collected on the range of educational options, the exercise of parental choice, parental satisfaction, school governance, the organization of classroom instruction, the role of teachers and administrators, educational costs and resource use, the distribution of students by ethnicity and socio-economic status, and student achievement. A variety of methods was used including social surveys, personal interviews, observational techniques, achievement testing and the analysis of official records and statistics. Much fuller data were gathered for voucher schools than for non-voucher schools, and for the (post-test) period after the project had started than for the (pre-test) period before it began.

Almost as soon as the project got under way a conflict flared up between the principals of the participating schools and the internal evaluation staff. Arguing that the release of test data and a uniform evaluation strategy would inhibit diversity among the mini-schools, the principals insisted that student test scores should not be released for two years and that the evaluators should be barred from imposing any evaluation requirements on the mini-schools. The principals won on both counts giving them substantial *de facto* control over the conduct of the evaluation during the first year.

The success of the voucher model requires that: a truly diverse set of options be created of which parents are made aware; parents have the right to transfer their children to preferred options; the size of schools should be responsive to parental demand; and funds actually follow the students. In the event, the diversity of the educational programmes offered by the mini-schools was real but limited. At the beginning of the school year mini-school sizes were adjusted to accommodate the choices of parents, but thereafter the schools were generally unwilling to expand in response to parental demand. In several cases, where demand was enough to support expansion, mini-schools declared themselves 'temporarily closed' to further enrolment. Several factors worked to influence this decision including weak financial incentives, professional norms against competition, faculty cohesiveness, concern to maintain the quality of teaching and space considerations.

A voucher system is supposed to give parents greater leverage over the schools through the exercise of choice. The first year of the demonstration saw little change in the low level of participation by parents in the school system. They showed little inclination to transfer their children between schools, generally opting for and sticking with the one nearest their home, and were not encouraged to change by principals or teachers.

Overall the evaluators concluded that the voucher scheme in Alum Rock was not sufficiently competitive in its operation to ensure school responsiveness to parental choice. This was partly because the parents were not given enough economic power, but partly too it was because the teachers were successful in preventing such competition which they saw as unethical and unprofessional. Rather than competing against one another, the six voucher schools co-operated against the central administration which was trying to implement the elements of a market system. For this reason, the researchers argued, the demonstration did not really serve as a full-blown test of the original voucher model. Contrary to initial expectations, the major discernible effect of the first year of the demonstration was not upon parents' behaviour or students' academic achievement, but the roles of teachers. Voucher schools gained new autonomy, teamwork within the schools improved and teachers' control over the curriculum and the use of discretionary resources increased. Whether these changes would eventually uplift the quality of education and the relationships between parents and the schools remained an open question.

Some time has been spent outlining the Alum Rock experience because it well illustrates the fundamental differences between a demonstration project and a true social experiment. At the outset the evaluators were unable to foresee what the effects of the project might be; their task was to find out. As a result, they were not in a position to pre-select the criteria of success. Instead of using carefully honed measures of outcome, they had to trawl for evidence. Moreover, they lacked control over most of the important variables including the way the scheme (technically speaking, the treatment) was implemented. No one knew exactly how to transform a school system in line with market principles. Accordingly as problems arose and were overcome the model changed. The inability of the evaluators to manipulate what was happening is nowhere better shown than by the success of the school heads in circumscribing their research strategy. Finally, as has been seen, it was not possible to obtain equivalent data for non-voucher schools, or for voucher schools in the pre-demonstration period, that would serve as a baseline for making comparative judgements about the scale and ramifications of the changes wrought by the scheme. In short, the lesson from Alum Rock is that a demonstration, unlike an experiment, presents the researcher with a moving target. A fuller account of the first year of Alum Rock is provided by Weiler (1976). Wortman, Reichardt and St Pierre (1978) present a secondary analysis of the data using a quasi-experimental design.

Experimentation: Paradigm or Pitfall

The purpose of experimentation 'was to pursue technical solutions to technical problems through social scientific techniques' (Higgins, 1980). By turning the real world into a laboratory, its advocates hoped to produce more precise and trustworthy information on the effectiveness of social services, so improving its usefulness for policy-makers. The formula was simple: hard facts cannot be ignored. This was a purist view of the relationship betweeen research and policy, one in which research generates knowledge that impels action. It was also a politically naïve view.

Weighing up the lessons of the experimenting years, and the value of an experimental strategy, Rivlin (1973) identifies a series of dilemmas that dogged most of the work done:

1 *Design dilemmas* often arose from the conflict between the desire to obtain valid, reliable results and the need to produce them quickly and economically.
2 *Implementation dilemmas* arose as people learned that while the tightly regulated experiment may produce more clear-cut answers, it may also be an unreliable predictor of what will really happen in a messy world.
3 *Evaluation dilemmas* arose because of the conflicts between involvement and objectivity, and between the goals of the programme and the requirements of the experiment.
4 *Timing dilemmas* arose because results were often wanted quickly, yet good experiments take time. Pressures to release data early, so risking false conclusions, were counterbalanced by the dangers of seeing the analysis through, but not having the findings available when they were needed.
5 *Moral dilemmas* focused on the issue of whether it is ethical to experiment with people in ways that might disadvantage them,

and on the equity of deliberately creating inequalities for experimental purposes.

6 *Dilemmas of confidentiality and openness* clustered around the issues of how to protect the privacy of the participants in the experiment and how much they should be told about the reasons for the experiment, bearing in mind that such knowledge might influence their behaviour and bias the results.

Design Dilemmas

The design dilemmas struck at the heart of the experimental method. After all, its selling point was that policy-makers could bank their reputations on the results. If experimental designs could not be guaranteed to hold up in practice, then this claim rang hollow. In fact experience showed there were inherent difficulties in the method which rendered it unsuitable for the evaluation of broad-aim, social action programmes (Weiss and Rein, 1970).

It proved difficult to select satisfactory criteria of success. The aims of social programmes were often only vaguely formulated, if at all; articulated in different ways by different sets of interests; and changed or were re-interpreted over time. This made it difficult to know what baseline data to collect and how to measure the changes that followed. Experimenters often responded by imposing their own narrow criteria on the programme, measuring what they could count and ignoring any unanticipated consequences (whose importance frequently rivalled and sometimes outweighed the initial aims). In this way, they were often unwittingly led into misrepresenting the programme's true impact.

In *field settings the situation is essentially uncontrolled.* Random assignment is not enough to control for the effects of exogenous variables. Field experiments were limited in their scale by their cost. Usually they were carried out within an institution or a local community. These institutions or communities were rarely randomly selected: they had to be willing to host the experiment, and this willingness distinguished them from other places or locales. Consequently, there was no way of being sure that the results were not influenced by special characteristics attached to those sites or that the results would be the same if the experiment was repeated elsewhere or on a larger scale. In other words, experimentation rarely allowed for confident generalizations to be made about the operation of a full-blown programme (Rossi and Wright, 1977).

Even when experiments were conducted in a variety of locations, in an attempt to control for such context variables, they met with another problem: *they could not ensure the treatments were standardized.*

As Edwards and Guttentag (1975) say, 'it is certainly nonsense to assume that some program, implemented in different ways by different people in different places, is a single entity simply because it is called by a single name and perhaps funded from a single source of money . . . such variations make the experimental approach to evaluation difficult to apply.' Experimenters were pushed into assuming that what actually took place was what was supposed to take place.

A last and important shortcoming in the experimental design itself is that it was shown to be *seriously limited in the information it could produce for policy-making*. The science got in the way of the sense. The demands of rigour and precision obliged the experimenters to focus on tightly defined questions about measurable variables using carefully calibrated instruments to collect quantitative data that could be statistically tested. Policy-makers just wanted to know what happened. They were not interested merely in how far a programme had achieved its goals, but in what forces had shaped its development, what opposition it had encountered, the reasons for its success or failure and any unanticipated consequences it may have had. Broad-brush matters such as these did not fall within the ambit of experimental designs and reduced their utility accordingly.

Furthermore, the results from experiments turned out to be much less convincing and authoritative than their advocates had promised. Few produced completely unambiguous findings; many encountered problems of execution so serious they had to be converted into quasi-experiments; while others (especially the larger, more high-profile ones) provoked furious controversy among social scientists about their methodological adequacy, leaving policy-makers no wiser about the validity of their conclusions. A common problem was 'experimental mortality'. High drop-out rates in a lot of studies, especially among non-captive subjects outside of institutional settings, and among the control groups, undermined their statistical foundations. At this point, design difficulties began to merge into Rivlin's second category of implementation dilemmas.

Implementation Dilemmas

One of the major threats to the integrity of an experiment was failure to adhere to the design (Riecken and Boruch, 1974). Such hiccups arose, as Marris and Rein (1967) have pointed out, because the demands of action and experimental research are not at all the same and their claims are hard to reconcile. Research calls for a clear and unwavering purpose, and a clear definition of the means by which it is to be pursued – which then must be exactly and consistently followed, without revision, until the experiment has been completed. Action, on the other hand, is tentative, non-committal and adaptive. It is responsive to changes as events proceed. Their different bearings make it difficult for each to be carried out as part of the same operation. The testing of social action programmes in the field generally imposes a more explicit and rigorous definition of means and ends than administrators in charge of running them can comfortably sustain.

Experience of social experimentation repeatedly showed that, as the a-priori ideas of action programmes were put to the test of a field trial, the expectations, convictions and knowledge of programme managers and their staffs altered considerably, with the understandable result that they pressed for or introduced changes in how things were done (Riecken and Boruch, 1974). As soon as staff discovered better ways of running the project or serving their clients they tended to adapt their procedures, methods and techniques accordingly. It was almost impossible to combine good, flexible management on the one hand, with scientific, controlled research on the other.

In the frequent battles that broke out between administrators and researchers the former usually won the day. When all was said and done, they had their hands on the wheel and, so it seemed, common sense on their side. It was not easy to argue that what managers clearly saw as a failure in a programme should not be corrected until the experimental results had verified their judgement; or that a potentially successful programme should be allowed to crash in the interests of science for want of a bit of tinkering. The cost of common sense, however, was the loss of experimental rigour.

Evaluation Dilemmas

Conflicts between researchers and administrators were also a feature of what Rivlin called the evaluation dilemmas accompanying social experimentation. Objectivity required that the research side of an experimental programme should be detached from its operational side. The evaluators could not effectively wear both hats. This split often grew into a breach. Field staff whose first loyalty was to the programme showed a lack of commitment to the research effort. Evaluation staff, locked in their eyries away from the scene of action, were insulated from what was happening in the field. Research directors chafed at the inconsistency and incoherence of much that was done in the front line. Programme managers cavilled about the theoretical preoccupations of the research team and the methodological constraints placed on their day-to-day work. Misunderstandings flourished in the cross-fire.

Two particular consequences had worrisome implications for the validity of evaluation findings (Weiss and Rein, 1970). First, there were the likely effects on the reliability of records maintained for research purposes by uncommitted field staff who neither appreciated nor valued their importance. Secondly, there was the danger of goal displacement, where field staff chase the outcome indicators chosen by the researchers to measure the programme's success. In other words, the very act of operationalizing the programme's aims carried with it the risk of influencing the behaviour of field staff and so thwarting the experiment.

But the problems of evaluation went deeper still. The mounting of an experiment is a political act, not primarily a scientific decision. It involves a big commitment of resources, so it must deal with a policy issue in which its sponsors already have a substantial political investment. Its implementation often affects local alliances, awakens public interest and creates its own constituency of support. In short, as Thomas (1985) has observed, its 'very existence contains the seeds of its continuation'. Bernstein and Freeman (1975) take the same point a step further by suggesting that many experiments were set up as a pretext for obtaining funding for the operating programmes. In such cases the evaluation components were little more than superficial trimmings added on so as to appease the doubters.

Following through this line of reasoning, the bigger experiments – and many, such as the New Jersey Income Maintenance Experiment, were very big indeed – should also properly be regarded as programmes in their own right. That is to say, they lived or died in the world of politics more than in the world of science (Yarmolinsky, in Abt, 1976). Considerations of legitimacy, feasibility and support were as crucial as those of impact and effectiveness, if not more so, in deciding their eventual fate. For this reason, in many cases, the validity of a social experiment turned out to be almost irrelevant in predicting whether its policy recommendations would be adopted. Social scientists were misguided in assuming that more sophisticated, and technically sound, research would necessarily lead to greater utilization (Higgins, 1980).

Timing Dilemmas

Another obstacle to the use of experimental results for policy-making, as Rivlin noted, was timing. The basic dilemma is brought about because experimentation is a lengthy business. The New Jersey Income Maintenance Experiment, for instance, lasted six and a half years from the award of the contract to the submission of the final report. To be useful, therefore, experimentation should really be concerned with policies that may appear on the political agenda of the future – probably well beyond the political horizon of most governments (Rossi, 1975). Few administrations would be prepared to back a hunch about priorities so far ahead. What happened instead was that politicians rarely financed an experiment until the problem it addressed landed on their doorstep, or rarely took seriously a new proposal unless there was a chance of doing something about it soon. So, often, the same political conditions that made it possible for federal agencies to fund a field experiment of an innovative policy were also the ones that favoured the introduction of the policy itself (Rossi and Wright, 1977). In such cases the pressures were for quick results. The danger was that the experiment would not be finished before the proposal was enacted.

Once again, the New Jersey Income Maintenance Experiment is a case in point. The Office of Economic Opportunity (OEO) had first advocated a national, negative income tax in 1965 but had been unable to persuade the President to legislate. The OEO therefore decided to fund a project with the intention of producing hard evidence about its feasibility that could be used to bring politicians and the public around to the idea. In 1967 a grant was awarded to the Institute for Research on Poverty at the University of Wisconsin and, after a year spent on design and planning, the experiment began in mid-1968. Knowing the negative income tax (NIT) concept was controversial, the OEO had, from the start, proceeded cautiously and fully expected it would be many years before convincing evidence emerged.

In September 1969, however, political reality caught up with the experiment. President Nixon submitted legislation to the House of Representatives proposing a new Family Assistance Plan that included a negative income tax for families with children. The investigators were invited to testify before the House Committee in its hearings on the Bill. They had planned to wait until the end of the experiment before releasing their findings and, at this stage, with data not yet available, they were unable to be very specific in their testimony. But the pressure to produce results intensified. Powerful voices wanted to know why, after two years of research and $5 million worth of federal funds, the researchers could not find anything useful to say on the questions interesting the Committee. The project staff, too, were anxious to contribute to the debate and, in February 1970, the decision was made to issue a report based on a preliminary analysis of the early data.

This report was greeted with enthusiasm by supporters of the legislation and intense criticism from its opponents. The General Accounting Office wrote a hard-hitting, critical appraisal of the OEO report and made plans to undertake their own re-analysis of the data over the heads of the experimental staff.

Meanwhile the House passed the Family Assistance Act and the Senate Finance Committee began public hearings on it immediately. The researchers were plunged into a further round of controversy about the adequacy of their data. The rumpus only subsided when the Act was killed in the Senate, in December 1970, and the NIT plan was pushed on to the back-boiler.

This episode neatly illustrates the problems of timing. The scheduling of experiments rarely geared with the timetabling of decisions. Unless they were very fortunate, experimenters often had to choose beween the imperatives of science and those of policy. The former option risked missing the boat. By grabbing the moment to inform decisions, however, they risked invalidating the experiment. This conundrum showed once again that policy usually would not wait on definitive research.

Ethical Dilemmas
Moral dilemmas are not unique to the method of social experimentation; they arise in all forms of social research. Indeed, it can be argued that the ethical problems of experimental evaluation largely mirror those of social reform itself because it amounts to no more than a controlled trial of a new programme (Riecken and Boruch, 1974). As such, whatever 'price' an experiment imposes on those subjected to it may unknowingly be paid anyway if the programme is implemented without testing (National Academy of Sciences/Social Science Research Council, 1969).

Nevertheless, in order to justify experimentation in the eyes of sponsors and the wider public, its practitioners have had to accommodate their moral qualms about some features of the method. Broadly these concerns fall into four categories:

1 Concerns about the possible *manipulation* of experimental subjects or, more sinister still, about the manipulation of the method itself by establishment forces seeking ways of regulating the lives and opinions of citizens. British criticism of *Sesame Street*, for instance, expressed fears on this last point.
2 Concerns about the possibility of exposing people to *damaging or detrimental treatments* for experimental purposes.
3 Concerns about the *fairness* of experimental programmes where the benefits are arbitrarily denied to some of the participants in the trial.
4 Concerns about the effects on recipients of *withdrawing* the benefits of the programme once the trial is completed.

Such ethical issues could place political limitations on the use of the experimental method. Random assignment to treatment and control groups was not always easy to justify. Government officials risked public censure for allocating scarce resources on the basis of chance rather than by some more acceptable criterion such as need or merit or even 'first come, first served' (Rivlin, 1971). Deliberately treating one group differently from another group could easily provoke a backlash from those who felt they were getting the raw end of the deal.

Moreover, because ethical considerations prevented the withholding of existing services for which people were eligible, experimentation could only be used for field testing add-ons or innovations. It was not a method for evaluating the status quo. Governments not interested in innovation were unlikely to be interested in experimentation.

But perhaps the most serious ethical dilemmas had to do with issues of confidentiality and openness. Social experiments may be more vulnerable to threats to the confidentiality of their data than other kinds of social research (Riecken and Boruch, 1974). Operating at the cutting edge of new ideas in social policy, they were often caught up in political controversy and legal argument. In these battles the status of the data could be seriously challenged.

The New Jersey Income Maintenance Experiment ran into just such problems. Shortly after the experiment began, the county welfare authorities started looking into the misappropriation of state welfare payments by families receiving overlapping benefits under the NIT plan. Legal proceedings were instituted which rumbled on for the better part of two years, culminating in a four-month grand jury investigation. In the process the experimenters were subpoenaed to produce the confidential records of some of their families (a case eventually resolved out of court), and later a number of families were wrongly pilloried in the local press as welfare frauds. As the researchers concluded, these happenings 'illustrate the potential vulnerability of any social experiment to the antagonism of local officials' (Kershaw and Fair, 1976).

This, however, was not the end of their troubles. Following the critical GAO audit of the preliminary findings from the experiment (see above), the Senate Finance Committee asked to look at individual family files. Doubting the figures, they wanted to add them up for themselves. The research staff offered the information in a form that did not identify individual families, but this was not good enough. The Committee wanted case histories. At one point it seemed as if the families themselves might be called upon to testify. In the end, only GAO support at a crucial Committee hearing saved the experiment from having to fight a congressional subpoena for individual records. Kershaw and Fair (ibid.) cite this episode as a warning of what can happen 'when an experiment becomes politically relevant on the national level and is thrust into the spotlight of political debate'.

The issue of openness presents a different sort of dilemma. It is generally held that, on ethical grounds, social experiments using people as subjects should only proceed with their informed consent. They should not be deceived about the purposes of the experiment or their part in it. Such awareness, however, raises difficulties for the researcher. People who know they are being watched may behave differently. This brings into play a host of familiar threats to the working of the experiment. Among the more important of these are:

1 *Hawthorne effects*, where the subjects make special efforts to live up to the expectations of the researchers.
2 *Placebo effects*, where the subjects act as if the idea being tested were true, so turning it into a self-fulfilling hypothesis.
3 *Volunteer effects*, where subjects, knowing the purpose of the experiment, either selectively decline to participate or, later, selectively withdraw, so destroying the comparability of the experimental and control groups.
4 *Sabotage effects*, where subjects deliberately behave in a way contrary to that expected or seek to manipulate the outcome for their own ends.

Problems of this sort once again throw doubts on just how far the results of an experimental programme provide a valid basis for predicting what would happen if it was extended to cover the country. While technical methods can be found for mastering these effects, they all tend to increase the complexity, the cost and the length of experiments, considerations which themselves were powerful drawbacks to the widespread use of experimentation.

The Politics of Rigour
By the late 1970s the palmy days of social experimentation were over. The method continued to attract its advocates but their toehold in the world of policy grew steadily more precarious. Their ranks were filled mostly by scholars who wrote textbooks on evaluation rather than by people who practised it for real. Among this latter group methodological virtuosity was not an end in itself.

By 1978, Boruch *et al*. were able to list over 300 experimental trials of novel social programmes. Enough had been learned to show that policy-making could not be turned into a laboratory science, and that the ideal of an 'experimenting society' was no more than a pipe-dream conjured up by social scientists blinkered to the realities of power. As Riecken had observed (in Abt, 1976), it may be only when an innovative programme is one to which relatively few people are willing to give serious consideration that an experiment can be run without it being captured by political forces. In other words, experimentation works best in scientific terms under conditions when it is least likely to command support or attention. Once again, it was found that the requirements of methodological rigour are not easily reconciled with those of policy relevance.

Experimentation was always a gamble, and a costly one to boot. So many unforeseen factors could derail even the most carefully planned experimental design that the quality of the information eventually produced, often after years of research, rarely justified the effort. Experience showed that field experiments are only feasible and worth while where (Rossi, 1975; Heclo and Rein, 1980):

1 the programme under trial is a simple one with clearly defined aims;
2 there is a need to establish its effectiveness;
3 the inputs are specific and measurable;
4 people can agree on how the outcomes should be measured;
5 randomization is both politically feasible and administratively possible;
6 ethical objections do not intrude;
7 non-cooperation or attrition can be kept within acceptable bounds;
8 the results are likely to be useful and timely.

These limitations show that experimentation was oversold as a strategy for social reform. Too few innovatory programmes met these guidelines for it ever to play a significant role in policy development.

On balance, it must be concluded that experimental designs did not stand up well to the buffetings of the action setting. They were too fragile to take the knocks. This is not to say that field experiments were a waste of time. There were tangible returns in the form of administrative knowledge. They helped to link policy abstractions with practice complexities; created opportunities for trying out new services without having to make long-term commitments; and stimulated innovation. But all these benefits could be had in other ways: by demonstration projects, pilot schemes, simple field trials or case studies. The extra costs of scientific rigour added too little in the way of usable knowledge. Policy-makers kept the kernel and shed the husk. This was the undoing of experimentation as a method of evaluation.

8 The Central Policy Review Staff and JASP

'I created it [the CPRS] for a number of reasons, but first and foremost so that the government strategy could be continuously reviewed and regularly reported upon.' (Mr Edward Heath)

'The abolition of the CPRS . . . was a sad blow by prejudice against enlightenment.' (Lord Bancroft)

There is no place on earth where the professors have reigned like the USA (Moynihan, 1970b). For over thirty years they have moved freely among the corridors of power, been listened to with respect and enjoyed a privileged access to the inner sanctums of decision-making within the federal bureaucracy. Even now, when the folksy fundamentalism of Reaganite politics has spread a mistrust of 'clever-dicks', their influence is still something to be reckoned with in the policy process. You can't afford to buck the guru: better to have him strapped in the saddle than making his noise outside the corral.

The situation in the UK could hardly be more different, where the academic expert is lucky to get a foot in the door, and then only at the tradesman's entrance. When 364 of the country's leading economists signed a round-robin letter in 1981 criticizing Mrs Thatcher's economic policies, she felt secure enough to tell them all to go back to school and not to meddle in things they didn't understand (Crawford and Jacobs, 1981). Sir Keith Joseph showed a similar disdain for the academic community when he insisted that the SSRC (subsequently the Economic and Social Research Council) drop the world 'science' from its title.

The conclusion is inescapable: by comparison with the USA, the ruling echelons of British society are much less receptive to the potential contribution of social science to public affairs (Bulmer, 1978). There are many reasons why this is so: reasons of history, tradition, sentiment and polity among them. In the UK the party whip gives authority, and weight of numbers legitimacy, to government actions. Whitehall secrecy stifles the free flow of ideas and information. A permanent civil service encourages inward-looking attitudes and the closing of ranks against outsiders. The cult of the generalist still permeates the higher ranks of officialdom. The more overtly ideological character of British politics is less conducive to the use of social science research. (Significantly, as Cherns (1986), has pointed out, social science flourished best in the period of Butskellite consensus.) Also a strong anti-intellectual streak in British society has cultivated a distrust of the expert and contributed to a certain standoffishness among its scholars. These and other traits have helped to give British government an old-fashioned look in terms of its use of hard-edged research for policy (Williams, 1983).

As the Organization for Economic Co-operation and Development (OECD, 1980) has remarked, the USA is 'the country which has been most ambitious and systematic in its efforts to develop social science research of relevance to the problems of society and the urgent concerns of government'. This is why Part II of this book has looked across the Big Pond to see what can be learned about harnessing research to policy-making. The fact is that, in this country, examples are hard to find, and what there are tend to be poorly documented.

None of this should be understood as saying that government in Britain has been untouched by the outpourings of social science research. Such an idea would plainly be silly. The real point is that few serious attempts have been made systematically to integrate research into the policy process at an institutional level. Whether the research commissioned by government departments and agencies ever percolates through into decisions remains, as Thomas (1985) has shown, a hit-and-miss affair. Equally, although every social policy department in Whitehall now has its own research unit, these are commonly divorced from the line functions of the agency, occupying a marginal position on the organizational chart.

Drawing on US experience, Williams (1971) argues that a central analytical office deep within the bowels of an agency will not have much impact on policy. If it is to be given a chance of working effectively, such a unit must be tied into the mainstream of activity within the agency. At a minimum, this calls for recognition on the part of the agency head of the importance of analysis; a direct link into the decision-making and implementation process; the status to go with the role; and enough staff to support the workload.

These requirements echo conclusions reached earlier by the US National Academy of Sciences (1968) in an influential report on *The Behavioral Sciences and the Federal Government*. Three sets of conditions, it said, appear to be necessary for the effective use of the knowledge and methods of the behavioural sciences in government:

1 An understanding by top administrators of the nature of the behavioural sciences and of their relevance and potential contribution to the work of their agency.
2 A professional environment to attract social scientists into government, along with incentives and opportunities for the development of research.
3 A strategy for research to give it cohesion and purpose and to relate it to the agency's policy concerns and programme operations.

As Gray and Jenkins (1983a) make clear, these preconditions have not been met in British central government where the forces of bureaucratic politics have remained stronger than the organizational need to learn.

There are, therefore, real difficulties in finding homespun examples to set alongside the case studies from the USA. One, however, which fits the bill is the attempt during the 1970s to mend what Lord Hunt, formerly Sir John Hunt, Secretary of the Cabinet from 1973 to 1979, has described as the hole in the heart of British government – the lack of any mechanism for providing a strategic overview of policy (Hennessy, Morrison and Townsend, 1985). The prosthesis implanted in Whitehall to remedy this ailment was the Central Policy Review Staff (CPRS). This chapter looks at the history and working of the CPRS, paying particular attention to its efforts to develop a trans-departmental approach to social policy.

Compared with the US studies, there was no huge influx of specialists, no massive injection of funds, no ambitious overhauling of bureaucratic machinery, no fascination with new methodologies. Yet the aim was bold enough: to challenge the 'adhockery' and short-sightedness of government. This is why the CPRS warrants our attention.

A New Style of Government

The CPRS was Edward Heath's baby. 'I want to see a fresh approach to the taking of decisions,' he said, in a personal foreword to the 1970 Conservative election manifesto. Within four months of coming to office he had presented to Parliament a White Paper on the Reorganization of Central Government (Cmnd 4506). Its proposals were designed to carry out this pledge, and to bring about a new style of thinking in Whitehall.

The White Paper pointed a finger at crucial defects in the collective mechanism by which public policy was made and carried out. These were of two sorts: there were defects in the *structure* of government which worked against a strategic approach to policy-making and the definition of objectives; and at the same time, there were defects in the *methods* by which collective policy decisions were taken.

Here, again, we can see evidence of the social division of planning, and of the twin problems to which it leads: problems of collaboration and problems of information (see Chapter 2). The structural division of responsibilities between Whitehall departments creates problems of collaboration that make joint working the exception rather than the rule, and give rise to a piecemeal approach to policy-making. Equally because information is departmentalized, it is not possible to take a strategic view of government policies to see how they link together.

Part of the answer proposed in the White Paper was a functional reorganization of government departments. This involved the creation of 'super-ministries' based on the grouping together of functions within unified fields of policy. Thus, for example, the child-care responsibilities of the Home Secretary were to be transferred to the Secretary of State for Social Services in order to match, at ministerial level, the integration of the personal social services carried through at local authority level following the report of the Seebohm Committee. Bigger conglomerate departments would be better placed to deal with issues of policy in the round, and have fewer excuses for squabbling among themselves. They would also lead to less work being referred to interdepartmental Whitehall committees – the forum for dealing with issues spanning more than one department. This would lighten the load on ministers, enabling them to take a more synoptic view of policy. Also it would result in more decisions being taken on the basis of analysis rather than compromise. At any rate, this was the reasoning behind the proposed aggregation of functions in large departments. In the event, things didn't quite work out this way.

In many ways, the 'super-ministries' proved to be unwieldy, even unmanageable. The Department of Trade and Industry, for example, was subsequently dismantled and split into three. The pressures of running them certainly made it no easier for ministers and top management to rise above the press of daily business. To the extent that neighbourly conflicts between departments were reduced, family rows tended to increase. And the hope that giant departments would pull together better has been shown to be misplaced by, for example, parliamentary criticisms of the continuing failure of the Department of Health and Social Security (DHSS) to adopt a coherent policy strategy across individual services and programmes (Social Services Committee, 1980). This, however, is looking ahead. In 1970 the promises seemed real.

Another White Paper recommendation was for radical improvements in the information system for ministers. Improvements that would help them in exploring major policy options, in assessing the relative priorities of departmental policies and programmes, and in relating their plans to overall government strategy. The policy apparatus as it stood was deficient on all these counts. Ministers did not have before them, at the time when decisions had to be taken, the kind of analysis they required. A system was needed to ensure they were presented, collectively in Cabinet and individually within their departments, 'with well-defined options, costed where possible, and relating the choice between options to the contribution they can make to meeting national needs.' (Cmnd 4506, para. 3)

These ideas were the pickings brought back by Heath's emissaries from their study of the planning–program–budgeting (PPB) system in the USA and reformulated by the civil service machine. The new system for providing more and better information which they ushered in came to be known as programme analysis and review (PAR) whose story has already been told in Chapter 4.

A third, and for us here, the most important proposal advanced by the White Paper was for the establishment of a 'central capability unit' whose job would be to provide a strategic perspective on government policy. Edward Heath's vision was of a unit 'whose role was to remind a Prime Minister and Cabinet harried by day-to-day problems of government that they had a collective, strategic view formed while they had been in opposition and to which they should cleave' (Ashworth, 1982). The reality was that however well defined the government's strategy when it entered on its term of office, there was no central, co-ordinating machinery for rolling it forward year by year, monitoring the actual outturn, and modifying it where necessary (Plowden, 1973b). The formal, constitutional position – laid down by the Report of the Haldane Committee on the Machinery of Government in 1918 – is that these functions are performed by the Cabinet. The practice is somewhat different. The Cabinet now is largely preoccupied with managing the government's legislative programme and with the political task of maintaining the government in Parliament. Ministers are too burdened with administrative duties to devote much time collectively to the formulation of longer-term policy. Cabinet committees, each concerned with a separate area of policy, have been used increasingly as a means of coping with the workload. These have served to maintain the principle of collective responsibility on which Cabinet government is based but only by fragmenting the management of its affairs.

Something needed to be done to reinforce the centre. The creation of a new unit in the Cabinet Office specifically charged with helping ministers to develop and hold to a more corporate approach was seen as a first step towards counteracting the social division of planning within government. The basic purposes for which it was set up were spelt out in the White Paper as follows:

- to assist ministers in working out the implications of their basic strategy for policies in specific fields;
- to establish the relative priorities to be given to different parts of the government's overall programme;
- to identify areas of policy in which new options and choices could be exercised;
- to ensure that the underlying implications of alternative courses of action are fully explored and analysed.

The name given to this new unit was the Central Policy Review Staff (CPRS).

The Central Policy Review Staff

The CPRS was modelled on the lines of a think-tank. Edward Heath wanted to call it just that but his Cabinet Secretary, Sir Burke Trend, demurred because the title would not look seemly on headed notepaper. The press sided with the Prime Minister and popularly referred to it as the Think Tank anyway.

Certainly, it met with two of the characteristics of a think-tank. It shared the same commitment to objective, interdisciplinary research and analysis; and it had the same sort of critical mass of full-time, professional staff (between fifteen and twenty). On the other hand, the CPRS did not have quite the same freedom to carry out studies on topics of its own choosing and to publish the results; nor did it look to a variety of funding agencies for research contracts. It was a creature of government bound by Whitehall conventions. Unlike the classic think-tank, it had to please its masters. As will be seen, this was always a delicate and, ultimately, a deadly responsibility.

The broad remit of the CPRS was to work, under the supervision of the Prime Minister, for ministers collectively, for the Cabinet and the government as a whole. In this sense, it was clearly a 'staff' rather than a 'line' unit. The CPRS did not act in a policy-making capacity. It could not impose goals on ministers, nor did it exercise any direct executive authority. Its purpose was to help and to encourage ministers to approach issues in their role as members of the government instead of simply defending their own departmental territories and interests. This meant tackling two problems (Plowden, 1973a):

1   The under-briefing of ministers on issues outside their sphere of responsibility. Traditionally, when claims on resources are

put forward in Cabinet, the only arguments presented are the partisan cases submitted by the protagonists.

2 The tendency for decisions to be taken seriatim, in isolation from each other, and without full understanding of how they overlap or their likely consequences.

The CPRS set about these problems in a number of ways as its work programme shows.

Collective Briefings
The CPRS saw the papers prepared for discussion in Cabinet and in committees and could prepare its own brief for ministers on any issue raised in them. The main aim of collective briefs was to set issues in a wider context, bring out their longer-term implications, and show their ramifications for related areas of policy. They were intended to prevent Cabinet discussions from degenerating into arguments between a few ministers with a departmental axe to grind while the insufficiently briefed majority, unaware of the broader issues at stake, looked on in silence (Ashworth, 1982). The CPRS briefs were not always reactive and sometimes raised issues which seemed in danger of being neglected in order to put them on the political agenda.

Strategic Reviews
At regular intervals the CPRS attempted to take stock, across the board, of what the government was doing; to assess progress in the light of objectives; to anticipate problems looming in the shorter and longer term; and to clarify the priorities ahead. These reviews were intended to provide ministers with a framework for thinking about their work and about the government's strategy in a non-departmental way.

Special Studies
The CPRS maintained a rolling programme of in-depth studies on which it reported to ministers. At any one time, it was normally involved in two or three such projects whose topics were either suggested by ministers or approved by them. Normally these studies focused on issues which cut across departmental responsibilities or were central to the government's strategy or called for a second opinion to set against an entrenched departmental view. Some of this work was commissioned from outside consultants. The main criteria for choosing topics for detailed study were that they should be of interest to more than one department, fairly long term, and not under review elsewhere in government.

Programme Analysis and Review (PAR)
This hefty slice of CPRS work has already been discussed in Chapter 4.

Other Activities
Members of the CPRS were also involved in a variety of *ad hoc* tasks: following up ministerial decisions, ferreting information out of departments, keeping tabs on policy developments, co-ordinating interdepartmental activities, trouble-shooting on sensitive issues. Though not directly related to its mainstream responsibilities, this work was important in preserving links with the Whitehall network and its grapevine, in keeping attuned to political sensitivities and in avoiding the danger of being wrongfooted or upstaged by events.

The composition of the CPRS reflected its need to work with the existing machine while contributing something new to it. About half its members were career civil servants on secondment from their departments. The other half were outsiders recruited from universities, the City, industry, local government and international organizations. The staff, who averaged, in number, about fifteen, usually stayed between two and three years.

In order to operate effectively in Whitehall, the CPRS had to keep on the right side of departmental officials. It depended heavily on them for information, and for access to ministers. Any number of traps could be sprung in the Whitehall undergrowth by hostile officials who wanted to make it look foolish. At the same time, the rationale for the existence of the CPRS was that it should say and do things beyond the compass of ordinary civil servants. Somehow a middle way had to be found between playing patsy with the system and upsetting the apple-cart. An over-willingness to please would simply lead to the CPRS reproducing the same kind of lowest-common-denominator advice it was meant to counteract. Confrontational tactics, on the other hand, would invite retaliation from the big departments, and they outgunned the CPRS on all fronts.

These considerations played a large part in shaping the work of the CPRS. The longer term was a focus where critical thinking could be indulged without the same risks of ruffling departmental feathers. The longer term was no one's province in Whitehall. Departments were always up to their eyes in the crises of the moment, and ministers were preoccupied with their reputation in the here and now. But there were dangers for the CPRS in simply annexing the longer term. Ministers might easily lose interest in a unit whose gaze was fixed beyond the political horizon. There was no way of mortgaging relevance: the CPRS had to be useful in the present if it was going to be useful at all. In any case, issues could not be so easily pigeon-holed. Today's pressures merge into tomorrow's problems. Short-run decisions have long-run repercussions. The CPRS could not vacate the short term entirely without cutting itself off from most of the action.

The danger of being drawn too deeply into the day-to-day business of government, however, was of staff spreading themselves too thinly and producing shoddy, shallow work. As Heclo and Wildavsky (1981) have said:

> The CPRS must try to produce advice that is relevant to the interests of ministers (so they won't ignore it), timely for the processing of decisions (so it won't be lost in the rush), accurate in its facts (so as to avoid ridicule), original in policy design (so as not to duplicate the work of departments), and brief in compass (so ministers will read it).

This was a tall order for less than two dozen people at the best of times. Doing it in a rush, for snap deadlines, and a changing array of topics, was impossible. In the short run the constraints of timeliness always threatened to drive out rigorous analysis. In order to find the space in which to work, the CPRS had to create an early-warning system about issues likely to be coming from departments for decision in Cabinet, and a set of rules or principles for selecting those on which to prepare a collective briefing for ministers.

The early-warning system was the Whitehall grapevine. The people who knew better than anyone else what was likely to be coming up on the agenda were departmental officials. The CPRS therefore put a lot of effort into maintaining good channels of communication with departments.

Keeping up good relations in this way had implications for the choice of topics for analysis. Aside from avoiding those with only minor resource implications, with little strategic significance or where the outcome was a foregone conclusion, the CPRS also sought to avoid stepping on the toes of departmental officials. In general, this meant that it tried to steer clear of challenging departments on their own ground, and to hold back from seeking to influence a minister on an issue in which his department was already interested (Plowden, 1973b).

There were pragmatic as well as diplomatic reasons for this posture. Departments could muster much larger resources, had more expertise and easier access to information in their own fields of policy than the CPRS. Against such odds, a CPRS brief was unlikely to prevail, and might look distinctly weak and superficial. Equally, no minister would ever contemplate allowing the CPRS – or any other body – to insinuate itself between himself and his top officials and drive a wedge between his view and his department's. To do so would be to threaten the relationship which sustained him in office.

These facts of life all helped to make interdepartmental issues attractive candidates for CPRS attention (Plowden, 1981). Interdepartmental issues are ones for which no single minister or department is responsible. As such, they avoid the pitfalls encountered in trying to invade departmental territory. As Heclo and Wildavsky (1981) have pointed out, interdepartmental issues come in several types:

1   There are issues that span the entire range of government operations yet have no sponsoring department (e.g. the administration of research or the use of computers or the control of red tape).

2   There are issues that once were the province of an individual department but since have acquired a wider political profile (e.g. fuel and energy policy).

3   There are issues that cut across the boundaries of several departments but which no one owns (e.g. family policy, or the welfare of children).

The third category of trans-departmental or cross-departmental issues offered a particularly happy hunting-ground for the CPRS. It was a legitimate area of interest, consistent with the oversight purposes for which the CPRS had been set up. It allowed for intervention in a wide sweep of government programmes. It avoided putting individual departments on the rack – apparently singling them out for criticism or seeming to tell a minister how to do his job. Lastly, the focus on cross-departmental issues protected the CPRS from charges of replicating the analytical work already going on in departments. In other words, it provided scope for originality, for doing something new, which in the end was important to the credibility, even survival, of the CPRS itself.

For the most part, then, the work of the CPRS was concerned with the larger picture and the longer view. Indeed, some of its more spectacular 'own goals' – like its Review of Overseas Representation (cf. Hennessy, Morrison and Townsend, 1985) – came when it deviated from this game plan. Certainly, these were the characteristics of one of its more important and longer-lasting initiatives: the attempt to develop a joint approach to social policy (better known, inevitably, in Whitehall as JASP).

The CPRS and JASP

The CPRS had been created to add some analytical muscle to the process of working out government priorities, to try to ensure these priorities were reflected in decisions, and to offset the fragmentation of policy among different departments and agencies (Plowden, 1987). JASP grew directly out of these aims. It was an attempt to apply these principles in the field of social policy generally.

Social policies had comprised a sizeable chunk of the workload of the CPRS from its earliest days. About five or six people were normally occupied in this field, though given the CPRS house-rule that people should carry a mix of types of work, none of them was full time. The reasons for this commitment are not hard to find. Social policies figure high on the political agenda, consume a large share of public expenditure, involve several government departments and are dogged by problems of co-ordination. They were therefore an ideal target for a trans-departmental approach to policy analysis. The CPRS saw clearly the need for a new and more coherent framework for the making and execution of social policies:

> Our hypothesis is that few of the most important social problems fall within the responsibilities of a single government department. Each department will recognise only a part of the total problem and will tend to define it differently in terms of its own limited perspective, formulating its objectives accordingly. Thus, while the policies and programmes of individual departments may be seen to be both appropriate and effective in terms of their own objectives, from the client's viewpoint the result is often a set of inconsistent or conflicting policies, which may be inefficient or at worst may tend to aggravate their situation. (CPRS, 1973)

This piecemeal approach produced patchwork services. It led to gaps and imbalances in provision, conflicts of objectives and missed opportunities for making trade-offs between different programmes. Unless a better basis for determining social priorities could be found, the CPRS argued, the structure of social expenditure was likely to become increasingly arbitrary and its effects ever more capricious.

So saying, the CPRS set about selling to ministers the idea that a more analytical approach to policy-making was needed to help them resolve the difficult choices imposed by resource constraints. In 1973 a ministerial group agreed that the CPRS should press ahead with its proposal.

So began the first major foray by the CPRS into the interdepartmental jungle. It set about the task with bags of confidence, grand ambitions and an almost swashbuckling vigour. The aim was to devise a comprehensive analytical framework for showing how the policies and programmes of different departments interlocked, so that spending decisions would no longer have to be taken in isolation from each other.

With the help of McKinsey's, the management consultants, the CPRS spent the better part of 1973 working on this new framework.

By the autumn it was ready for presentation to ministers. The way forward, the CPRS proposed, lay in adopting a 'client-group approach' to the analysis of trans-departmental affairs and a process of 'social audit' for monitoring the distributional impact of government policies. The *client-group approach* was conceived as a way of looking at the interrelationships between government programmes in terms of their cumulative effects on social problems and social needs. A *social audit* was a process of review and appraisal aimed at monitoring the progress being made towards the achievement of government objectives for different client-groups and identifying opportunities for improvement.

Little more is known about the CPRS proposals. A number of working papers were produced, demonstrating how the framework might be applied to particular client-groups but these were never published and remain classified state documents. (Another example of the difficulties in learning from the past which secrecy imposes.) From what insiders have reported, however, it is clear that the approach was grounded on a rational model of the policy process (Plowden, 1987). It was a serious attempt to overhaul the system of resource allocation on schematic lines.

In the event ministers would have nothing to do with it. They sent the CPRS away to think again, to talk some more with departmental officials and to come up with something less ambitious. Departments had thrown up their hands at the prospects of the extra work they saw coming their way. In briefing their ministers, officials had pointed out that the approach called for a vast input of information, much of which was not routinely available, and some of which raised serious and unresolved problems of measurement. In short, the whole approach was overdone and just too speculative. Ministers would be ill-advised to invest in proposals where the pay-off was so uncertain.

Ministers also had reservations of their own. The framework was too complicated for easy management, too disciplined for their own comfort and too far removed from the world they understood. It threatened to swamp them with more information than they could assimilate and extend the hold of civil servants over the levers of policy. All in all, as one key participant in this abortive exercise has observed, it was 'both too transparently "rational" in its approach, and too little concerned to develop consensus at the level of the permanent bureaucracy' (ibid.).

Somewhat chastened and with its credibility dented, and departmental suspicions aroused about its ambitions, the CPRS withdrew. Obviously a different tack would have to be tried. Clearly, it could not afford to fail again.

Edward Heath's decision to call a general election in February 1974 provided something of a breathing-space for the CPRS. At the same time, the oil crisis threatened to transform Britain's economic prospects and added a new urgency to the CPRS's position that a more coherent mechanism for planning social priorities was needed. The resignation in October 1974 of Lord Rothschild, head of the CPRS since its inception, also helped to clear the decks for a new approach. Lord Rothschild's style and influence were stamped all over the failed 'client-group' initiative and it was largely he who had drafted the report for ministers. His replacement by Sir Kenneth Berrill, formerly Chief Economic Adviser to the Treasury, and a man with little personal interest in or experience of the social policy field, left the JASP team in the CPRS with more room for manoeuvre and the opportunity for a fresh start.

There was to be no repetition of past mistakes. This meant not trying to do too much too quickly. Thinking in terms of an overarching framework for looking at social policies across the board had proved to be too big a step; a more modest approach was required. Trying to impose a system of collaboration on departments had only provoked their resistance; a more consensual approach was required to carry them along. Seeking to bounce departments out of their inertia had only served to magnify it and make them more wary of change; a more gradual approach was required. It seemed, then, that a more rational approach to social planning would have to be brought about by incremental methods.

Accordingly the CPRS team decided to home in on a limited number of specific areas where a joint approach looked promising and likely to yield positive results. In developing this idea, they deliberately worked very closely with the Cabinet Secretariat and with individual departments. Sir John Hunt, the Cabinet Secretary, agreed to convene and chair a committee of Permanent Secretaries to oversee progress and smooth the way. Throughout 1974 an exhaustive series of bilateral discussions was held by the CPRS with departments to identify a list of useful and acceptable topics for inclusion in a programme of action. In addition, each department was asked to nominate someone who would act as a permanent liaison with the CPRS. From time to time these representatives were brought together as an informal group to advise the CPRS on how its ideas were shaping up. Finally, extensive use was made of the help of experts from outside government in an attempt to ensure that what proposals emerged were not unduly constrained by political and bureaucratic niceties. All this behind-the-scenes bustle finally came to a head in May 1975 when the Cabinet endorsed the rolling programme of work proposed by the CPRS and agreed to the publication of its report entitled *A Joint Framework for Social Policies* – JASP was back on the agenda.

'There can never be', the CPRS contritely acknowledged, with half an eye on its earlier failure, 'a "total social strategy" in which every existing policy and every new decision is related to every other.' There are no instant solutions for putting right the defects in social policy-making. Changes must be manageable and will take time to follow through and implement; progress must be cumulative. Above all, if a more collective approach is to succeed, departments and ministers 'must be prepared to make some adjustments, whether in priorities, policies, administrative practices, or public expenditure allocations'. With these caveats out of the way, the JASP report went on to outline a package of proposals for improving the co-ordination of services and the ways in which decisions on social policies are made. This package included:

1   The setting up of a 'strategic forum' of senior ministers in the social policy field, meeting every six months or so, to take a longer-term view of social priorities.
2   A regular 'forward look' exercise, surveying likely forthcoming developments in social policy with the intention that the CPRS would identify with departments those issues likely to be coming up in the next twelve months. So forewarned, ministers would be able to consider these impending decisions together, instead of separately as they arose, and to weigh up the relative strengths of their claims on resources.
3   Specific studies of major problem areas and of a selected social group to see how policies interact in practice and to pinpoint the gaps, overlaps and inconsistencies which arise; and studies of longer-term social trends which are likely to have a significant effect on the demand for services in the future.
4   Improvements in social monitoring, aimed at building social statistics more firmly into the policy-making process.

This package was not seen by the CPRS as an integrated whole whose elements would stand or fall together. On the contrary, the idea had been to try, quite deliberately, a number of different ways of encouraging joint working in Whitehall in the expectation that some might succeed where others failed. The way forward would be to build on what worked. Once again, the scars left by the humiliation of the earlier client-group approach are evident. This time the CPRS was spreading its bets. How well did this approach fare and how successful were the various elements in the package?

The 'strategic forum' made little impact on governmental thinking and ministers soon grew bored of it. Meetings, initially held at six monthly intervals, became steadily less frequent. Its essentially deliberative role did not satisfy ministers' appetites for action. Dwelling reflectively on the longer term seemed like a distraction when their boxes were full of matters calling for urgent decisions. What agreements they might reach in principle tended to be breached as soon as some practical departmental issue put them to the test. Also, importantly, no linkage was established with the PESC process. Consequently, there was no mechanism for feeding guidelines on social priorities from the ministerial group into decisions about the allocation of resources. It thus became little more than a talking-shop, a forum for 'paper-planning' where ideas were aired without concurrent power to affect events. When Mr Callaghan became Prime Minister, he handed over the job of chairing the group to Shirley Williams, in her capacity as Paymaster-General, so effectively sealing its fate. Without the authority of the Prime Minister, there was nothing to combat the departmental instincts of the other ministers. Shortly afterwards it ceased to meet. In 1979, Mrs Thatcher did away with it altogether.

The failure of the 'strategic forum' to maintain the interest of ministers in JASP was probably a major blow to the cause of interdepartmental co-ordination. Without a firm lead from ministers, and especially the Prime Minister, it was almost impossible for the CPRS alone to keep up the momentum against the force of departmental inertia. This fact probably played a large part in the CPRS's own decision to pull out of JASP.

The CPRS produced a number of specific studies of trans-departmental issues as part of its JASP work programme. A report was submitted to ministers on aspects of financial poverty. Other studies included working relationships between central government and local authorities, the social aspects of housing policy, services for the disabled and services for children with working mothers. A major review of the implications of demographic trends for the social services was also published.

Most of this work was well received and aroused a great deal of interest outside government. The studies themselves were acknowledged as dealing squarely with important issues. But it is hard to detect any tangible sign of their impact. Analysis alone was not enough to trigger action. It needed a hefty political shove. Yet by the time most of the studies were published, ministers had already lost interest in JASP. In another sense, too, the moment had passed. The axe was looming over public expenditure. The price demanded by the International Monetary Fund (IMF) for bailing out Britain's economy after the 1976 sterling crisis was the pruning of the welfare state. Certainly, there would be no new money to fund trans-departmental initiatives. And with their own budgets under threat, departments were becoming steadily more edgy, introverted and defensive. The likelihood of them countenancing any adjustments in their public expenditure allocations, such as the CPRS had warned would be necessary if JASP was to work, had all but vanished. Under pressure from tightening resource constraints it was competition rather than collaboration which rose to the surface. For these reasons, the CPRS's special studies fell on stony ground.

Perhaps the most exciting and far-reaching proposal in the JASP report was for improvements in the quantity, quality and relevance of social statistics. A more coherent approach to social planning, the CPRS argued, demanded better social information on the state of society, on the impact of government policies and on how they affect different groups in the population.

The CPRS's recommendations were greeted enthusiastically by the Central Statistical Office (CSO) whose head, Sir Claus Moser, had long been keen to establish a more integrated framework of social data (Moser, 1980). A Social Group of senior statisticians was set up within the CSO, on the same lines as the existing Economic Group, to co-ordinate this work. One of its tasks was to improve the analysis of the distributional effects of government policies and of the changing situation of different groups and subgroups in society.

Another task was to link social statistics more effectively with the policy-making process. To this end, the CSO Social Group began compiling a periodic series of Social Briefs similar in their conception to the fortnightly economic reports circulated to senior officials by the Economic Group. These Social Briefs presented information on a range of specific topics, such as the effects of population change on jobs and housing, the geographical distribution of the poor or trends in education. Most of the statistics were shown in the form of diagrams with the main features highlighted in a brief commentary. Their purpose was to make such information more accessible and more palatable to ministers and senior officials, to persuade them of its value, and to sharpen their understanding of the links between social policies. Originally these briefs were classified but later ones were released.

It would be unrealistic to expect any immediate or dramatic changes to have resulted from these modest improvements in the presentation of social statistics. They were no more than a start on the long road towards developing a trans-departmental information base for social policy. What was needed was time (to sort out the measurement problems), resources (to fund the statistical work) and political commitment (to sustain the effort).

In the event, none of these was forthcoming. As the Callaghan government approached the back end of its term, workaday issues such as JASP faded from the scene. The workings of the policy machine are only ever of interest to governments with a long stretch ahead of them and things to accomplish. As election time draws nearer the politics of survival take over.

Mrs Thatcher's triumph at the polls in 1979 put the lid firmly on any further work on social monitoring. She instinctively recoiled from anything which smacked of social planning. The machinery of government held no fascination for her as it had done for Edward Heath and Harold Wilson. As a politician she was interested in the substance rather than the process of policy-making. Certainly, the JASP work on the distributional effects of public policies was of no consequence for a government pledged to rolling back the frontiers of the state. As a result, shortly after Mrs Thatcher entered office the Social Group in the CSO was disbanded and the Social Briefs were discontinued. This was a foretaste of the broader assault on social statistics that was to follow (see Chapter 3).

The JASP work programme within the CPRS, launched by the publication of *A Joint Framework for Social Policies* in 1975, lasted for about two years. Early in 1977 the JASP team proposed to their colleagues that the time had come for them to move on to new pastures. Sir Kenneth Berrill, head of the CPRS, did not demur, nor did anyone else. There were no objections either from any of the departments involved in JASP when the suggestion was conveyed to them. Work continued on bits of the programme. The CPRS itself had some unfinished special studies to complete. The Social Group in the CSO went on producing Social Briefs. The 'strategic forum' still existed on paper. But these activities no longer hung together. When the CPRS pulled out, JASP ran into the sand.

A number of considerations prompted the CPRS to withdraw. JASP was taking up a lot of time and the feeling began to grow that perhaps the CPRS had bitten off more than it could chew. The managerial demands of keeping up the momentum of the programme were also threatening to divert the CPRS from its analytical work. Persuading departments to undertake a great deal of work which they would not have done for themselves was a continual strain. Finally, it was concluded that the effort being invested in JASP had begun to outweigh the value placed on it by ministers. All the signs pointed to the fact that the CPRS would serve its own interests better by re-directing its resources into work which ministers regarded as more important. As Lord Hunt has since commented, 'Few ministers wholeheartedly supported JASP and certainly some saw it as an intrusion into their own bailiwicks' (Hennessy, Morrison and Townsend, 1985).

Few, if any, traces of JASP now remain. The forces stacked against it – departmental traditions, ministerial indifference, the economic climate and the CPRS's lack of clout – proved in the end to be overwhelming.

The End of the CPRS

After Mrs Thatcher became Prime Minister the role of the CPRS changed dramatically. Most informed opinion had expected she would abolish it immediately as nothing more than a refuge for failed ideas. However, she was persuaded to keep it going on a trial basis in case it might prove useful.

Its workload altered substantially to reflect Thatcherite preoccupations. Within a year it had virtually been transformed into an advisory unit on economic and industrial policy with a special interest in nationalized industry finance. The social policy slice of its activities withered into insignificance, and it became less and less involved in public expenditure issues – two fields which had comprised a major part of its work since its creation (Hennessy, Morrison and Townsend, 1985).

All this time its life hung on a thread. As a self-confessed conviction politician Mrs Thatcher never really had much use for policy analysis; the strategic purpose for which the CPRS originally had been created did not accord with her vision. It became steadily more dependent on issues thrown to it, bone by bone, by the Prime Minister. One of these was its undoing.

Just before the 1982 summer recess, the Cabinet asked the CPRS to review the options for cutting public expenditure as a proportion of gross domestic product over the period up to the end of the decade assuming nil or low economic growth. Its report was put before a Cabinet meeting on 9 September. Among the options spelled out were replacing the NHS with a system of private health insurance, de-indexing all social security benefits so allowing their real value to fall, ending state funding for higher education, increasing the teacher–pupil ratio in schools and introducing an educational voucher scheme. A week later the substance of the report was leaked by *The Economist* (18 September 1982) – just in time for the story to dominate the party conference season. In the uproar that ensued Mrs Thatcher publicly disowned the report which she described as 'politically inept'. Her ministers spent the next few weeks frantically denying that they intended dismantling the NHS and bulldozing the welfare state. A Downing Street inquiry failed to uncover the source of the leak. The finger pointed to some disaffected Cabinet 'wet' but rumour also implicated the CPRS itself.

The episode rankled the Prime Minister and helped to convince her that she could live without the CPRS. Immediately after the 1983 general election, Mrs Thatcher proposed its abolition to her new Cabinet. Not a single minister spoke up in its defence (Hennessy, Morrison and Townsend, 1985). On 16 June the Downing Street press office announced its demise.

If the CPRS's passing was a touch inglorious, what can be said about its record? In the very early days Lord Rothschild asked his new team to let him have their thoughts on what they should be doing. One of them, Robert Wade-Gery, a diplomat on loan from the Foreign Office, produced a checklist that was adopted as a kind of unofficial charter (ibid.). It read as follows:

– sabotaging the over-smooth functioning of the government machine;
– providing a synoptic view of policy;
– supporting those civil servants in Whitehall who are striving to retain their creativity and to avoid being totally submerged in the bureaucracy;
– seeking to devise a more rational system of decision-making between competing programmes;
– advising the Cabinet collectively, and the Prime Minister, on major issues of policy relating to the government's strategy;
– focusing the attention of ministers on the right questions to ask about their colleagues' business;
– bringing in ideas from the outside world.

How far did the CPRS succeed in living up to its own expectations?

As leaven in the Whitehall dough, the CPRS had little influence and brought itself a lot of trouble. Basically it lacked the muscle to transform bright ideas into practice. There was no minister to speak for it in Cabinet. What authority it enjoyed was derived almost entirely from the Prime Minister. For this reason, the relationship between the head of the CPRS and the Prime Minister was absolutely crucial. Only under Edward Heath and Lord Rothschild was the partnership strong enough to sustain the CPRS as a source of grit in the machine or a base for piratical adventures into the affairs of departments. As one insider is quoted as saying, 'You could ring up anyone, in any department, and demand information, backed by Rothschild's authority and close links with the Prime Minister. Later on you had to become circumspect, and go through all the formalities' (Hogg, 1982). Even then, however, in what many of those involved later fondly regarded as 'the good old days' there were limits to how far critical reasoning could be pushed. Following a speech to the Agricultural Research Council in September 1973 in which he warned that Britain could be producing about half the output of France or

Germany by 1985 unless the British people were made aware of the dangers and of the need to change their ways, Lord Rothschild was given a sound dressing-down by Mr Heath for publicly dissenting from the government's official line that Britain was on the threshold of a superboom.

In later years challenging the complacent nostrums and encrusted habits of masters and mandarins, without the same Prime Ministerial backing, became a much more dangerous business. Also, after Rothschild, none of the subsequent heads of the CPRS really had the temperament for taking on the permanent bureaucracy. Their inclination was to work with the grain.

As Chief Scientist within the CPRS from 1976 to 1981, Professor Ashworth has looked back over his spell in the Cabinet Office and commented: 'a think-tank that does not think the unthinkable from time to time is useless' (Ashworth, 1982). Maybe, but every time the CPRS stepped too far outside the reach of conventional wisdom it was firmly slapped into place. Indeed, as the example of the ill-fated review of public spending illustrates, it was eventually the sin of saying what is best left unsaid that contributed to its ultimate fall. Apparently the choice, in Professor Ashworth's terms, was between being unwanted or being useless.

On the second of Wade-Gery's tasks the CPRS undoubtedly did make a genuine effort to break away from the compartmentalized nature of social policy-making. The failure of JASP was a major blow to these hopes. It showed that the pressures on departments to go their own way were stronger than the inducements for them to work together. The only incentive the CPRS could offer for greater collaboration was extra work. Two other lessons also stand out. As Isserlis (1984) has suggested, there is 'an important political limit to the utility of the kind of policy advice that is formed and proffered and considered otherwise than in fairly close and continuous relationship to current operational necessity and to the experience and responsibilities involved in meeting it'. Also as Blume (1982) has pointed out, there is no customer in Whitehall for research or policy analysis that transcends administrative boundaries or is not rooted in departmental concerns except, in principle, the Cabinet. Unless ministers collectively demand it, there is no one else who will. The JASP episode demonstrated their lack of interest.

Turning to the third item on the CPRS shopping-list, it is arguable that instead of supporting creative civil servants the CPRS merely siphoned them off into a backwater. Over its life somewhere around sixty-five up-and-coming officials passed through its ranks. Yet this interpretation is too cynical. After the creation of the CPRS, there followed a marked strengthening of departmental research and planning units and of the quality of analytical work and forward thinking within departments (Isserlis, 1984). Whether this improvement was a response to the example set by the CPRS, a defensive manoeuvre or just coincidence it is hard to say, but the effect was to inject more resources into policy analysis, to give it a higher profile and to make decision-makers more aware of its uses. This may be counted as a modest success for the CPRS, though ultimately it probably made its own job more difficult and, to some extent, undermined the justification for its own existence.

The CPRS worked long and hard to fulfil its fourth mission of bringing about a more rational approach to decision-making between competing programmes but without making much headway. Most of the spadework went into the system of programme analysis and review (PAR), already discussed in Chapter 4. PAR was a procedure for evaluating individual policies and programmes, usually defined in budgetary terms, as part of the annual public expenditure survey. Broadly PAR involved reviewing the scale and content of particular spending programmes, analysing the policy options, relating them to expenditure constraints and, where possible, to the government's wider objectives.

PAR turned out to be indigestible. Departments would not swallow it: they were adept at deflecting PAR studies away from their mainstream programmes on to marginal activities or twisting them to serve their own ends (Heclo and Wildavsky, 1981). The Treasury was wary of CPRS involvement in what it saw as being its own patch. Parliament was denied scrutiny of the reports (which made it easier to bury them). Ministers, adhering to the convention of not meddling in each other's departmental affairs, passed over the opportunity PAR offered of taking a collective view on priorities. Finally, technical difficulties relating to the evaluation of programme outputs proved a major stumbling-block to the development of comparative measures of effectiveness.

Gray and Jenkins (1983c) have argued that 'all analysis and evaluation requires a regular discipline, a recognised methodological and organisational framework, and a political commitment to make it effective'. It was for want of these features that PAR – and with it the CPRS's attempt to introduce a more rational system of decision-making – drifted on to the rocks.

Aim number five in the CPRS's unofficial charter was to provide collective advice to ministers on policy and strategy. The two main channels it used for this purpose were 'strategy reviews' and 'special studies' (see above).

Up until about 1973 strategy meetings were held every six months when the whole Cabinet met together at Chequers or No. 10,

Downing Street to assess the government's overall progress assisted by presentations and papers from the CPRS. A parallel series of meetings with the same agenda was held separately for middle-ranking and junior ministers. As Lord Rothschild explained at the time, the aim of this exercise was 'not to get executive decisions, but rather to encourage all ministers to think more broadly than they can do in their departments or at interdepartmental meetings' (quoted in Pollitt, 1974).

The enthusiasm for these meetings began to tail off as the Heath government lost its bearings in the face of the oil crisis, the miners' strike and the slump in the economy. When Harold Wilson succeeded as Prime Minister after the 1974 election, he immediately set up a new Policy Unit in Downing Street, under Dr Bernard Donoughue, to beef up his sources of political advice. The days of the CPRS, a Tory creation, seemed numbered. In fact the axe did not fall, but the Policy Unit slowly annexed the ground formerly covered by the CPRS strategy meetings and these eventually ceased. Later when James Callaghan became Prime Minister, only the No. 10 Policy Unit was invited to contribute to collective strategy discussions.

The value of the CPRS 'special studies' is hard to assess since only some were published, while even the existence of others has been kept secret. From what can be seen about half a dozen such reports were produced, on average, each year and their quality and impact varied widely. There were disasters, like the infamous *Review of Overseas Representation*, whose savaging by the Foreign Office and its allies did lasting damage to the credibility of the CPRS (see Hennessy, Morrison and Townsend, 1985), and like the similarly ill-fated review of public spending, already mentioned. On the other hand, a well-received report like *The Future of the British Car Industry*, with its far-sighted analysis of overcapacity, was simply ignored by the Wilson government when it stepped in to save Chrysler in 1975. Most of the studies probably fell somewhere between these two poles and may safely be accounted as sound but shelvable.

Sir Douglas Wass, a former Permanent Secretary at the Treasury, argued in his Reith Lectures (1983) that the CPRS embarked on many studies which would have been done better by departments with their greater expertise. His views have been echoed by officials who served in the CPRS (Hennessy, Morrison and Townsend, 1985). They remember being spread too thinly, having too little time, dealing with issues about which they had no specialist knowledge, and producing too much superficial work as a result.

Moving on, the method chosen by the CPRS for keeping ministers alert to the wider implications of everyday business (its sixth aim) was the system of collective briefing. Lord Rothschild set great store by the preparation of collective briefs. Such briefs, often less than a page long and sometimes written at very short notice, usually consisted of a series of questions that ministers might like to ask in Cabinet on agenda items outside their departmental domain. Their purpose was to ensure that individual decisions were not taken on a case-by-case basis, but discussed in the light of the government's overall strategy.

There is no evidence that the CPRS succeeded in generating a demand among ministers for briefing of this kind. Ministers preferred to trust their departmental advisers and were reluctant to stray from under their umbrella. Moreover, digging in someone else's allotment is asking for trouble. It risks making an enemy of a colleague whose support might be needed in the future. For both these reasons, it 'is hard to think of a single Cabinet decision which would have come out differently if the collective briefs had never existed' (*New Society*, 1 November, 1979).

At the same time, the system of collective briefing may have done something to whittle away ministerial support for the CPRS. It is quite possible to make enemies of the entire Cabinet by doing just one thing that angers each of the ministers personally, even though they approve of everything else that does not affect them directly (Heclo and Wildavsky, 1981). As Ashworth (1982) has commented from his own experience as a former CPRS member, 'on any one issue there will be at least one minister who will not regard the CPRS brief as a help to good government and, in time, all ministers (including the Prime Minister) can be expected to harbour the thought that the CPRS has outlived its usefulness'.

The last objective in the hidden charter was to bring in outside ideas. For most of its life about half of the staff was made up of Whitehall regulars for the very good reason that their knowledge of the civil service and the inner workings of Whitehall was an invaluable asset. The tenure of most incomers was too short for them to learn their way around effectively without nursing. In the social field the JASP initiative did draw on a network of academic social scientists. The CPRS was helped in commissioning people to prepare papers by the Cabinet Office Social Research Co-ordinating Unit. This was a small staff of social scientists whose role included maintaining contacts with the research world (Blume, 1982). The closure of the Unit in 1977 – at the same time as JASP also folded – deprived the CPRS of one of its main links with the social science community. Thereafter as the emphasis within the CPRS shifted more towards economic issues and away from social affairs, its motive for sustaining these links also waned. Under its last two heads, Robin Ibbs (of ICI) and John Sparrow (from the merchant bankers Morgan Grenfell), relationships between the CPRS and social policy analysts outside government virtually ceased.

Last Words

The Central Policy Review Staff was created as an analytical base at the centre of government to bridge the social division of planning. The conclusion to which this chapter leads is that it failed. The clearest example of this failure is when JASP succumbed to the wiles and power play of the spending departments. What is less certain is whether this came about because too much was asked of analysis or because too much was asked of the CPRS. On this point three last observations are worth making.

First, the CPRS was kept deliberately small. Supposedly this was to encourage an *esprit de corps*. Lord Rothschild is rumoured to have kept its size down so that all its members could sit round his conference table. His successor, Sir Kenneth Berrill, also believed in keeping it lean. Other key people have argued that this was a mistake. Sir Douglas Wass, for instance, and Sir John Hoskyns, one-time head of Mrs Thatcher's Downing Street Policy Unit, who believes it could easily have numbered between eighty to 100 people, both feel it was not big enough for the job it had to do. As one CPRS member mused reproachfully: 'The British believe in mobilising extremely small numbers of people to deal with very large problems' (quoted in Heclo and Wildavsky, 1981).

Secondly, a great deal of the work undertaken by the CPRS did not really qualify as analysis. As Peter Jay (1972) has commented, much of it was about what might be expected from a good newspaper leader-writer. The collective briefings for ministers, often produced at very short notice, were especially prone to the 'well-known vices of instant punditry'. Even a lot of the longer term stuff is better described as advice rather than analysis (see Chapter 1) and distinguishable from the normal Whitehall variety only by the absence of any departmental view.

Finally, the CPRS never really sorted out whether its role was to provide technical analysis or political advice. Certainly, its members moved in a more overtly political environment than all but a handful of the most senior civil servants (Pollitt, 1974). Yet as Ashworth (1982) has said, it was actually set up to provide intellectual support to the Cabinet and was ill-equipped to give political advice. The dilemma was that ministers have to deal with problems which always have a political dimension and they were frequently tempted to expect the CPRS to respond in kind. Williams (1980) has pointed to the dangers that can arise:

the policy analyst who . . . has a technical role can become too political. The critical point is that technicians . . . should operate as much as possible within the confines of their techniques, and do what they do best. There are boundaries which if exceeded . . . threaten to diminish the usefulness of the technical function for the organisation it is intended to serve; and over time, if not to lessen the analyst's influence, to misshape the desired function.

This is not a bad epitaph for the CPRS.

PART III
THREADS:
RESEARCH, POLICY
AND PLANNING

9 Research and policy-making: the uncertain connection

'Social scientists typically provide three rather different kinds of assistance to policy makers: knowledge, legitimation and partisanship.' (Suzanne Berger, 1980)

The time has come to pick up some of the threads running through the case studies in Part II. What do they reveal about the interlacing of research and policy? This chapter focuses on the utility of research by drawing on two decades and more of evidence from the case studies to throw light on its role in the policy process and on the use made of it by policy-makers. Again looking back over the lessons contained in the case studies, Chapter 10 examines the characteristics of policy-driven research linking the discussion to the themes outlined in Part I of the book.

Government and Social Science

In 1968 the US National Science Board set up a Special Commission on the Social Sciences charged with making recommendations for improving the nation's use of the social sciences. Its report, published by the National Science Foundation in 1969, concluded that crucial opportunities for exploiting the best of social science knowledge were being missed. Moreover, the Commission warned, it must be doubted whether 'this country can successfully solve its challenging and diverse social problems unless it draws upon the increasing capabilities of the social science community'. Full advantage must be taken of its strengths. Accordingly at all levels in the federal government where major policy is made, 'social scientists should be deeply involved' (National Science Foundation, 1969). At long last, declared Peter Rossi (1969), social science has come on centre-stage in American society: 'Decades of being poised in the wings waiting for cues and polishing lines are over . . . No longer do sociologists have to disguise themselves to obtain civil service ratings.'

It is a remarkable testimony to this faith in the potential of the social sciences (and the openness of American government) that inside ten years substantial progress had been made towards this objective. By the mid-1970s, Lynn (1977) reports, research brokers were fixtures in virtually every federal agency. Professors and researchers from the world of social science were regularly appointed to Cabinet posts. The staff of government bureaux and congressional offices had been beefed up by the recruitment of specialists with the ability to read, criticize and evaluate research reports. Also the Congress had begun to develop its own cadre of trained policy analysts and social scientists.

Yet all was not well. Unrest was spreading among both sides of the partnership between social science and government. Research by Caplan (1975) among senior policy officials in federal agencies showed a high level of interest in and receptivity to social science information but little evidence that it had any impact on decision-making. Seemingly research was getting through but going unheeded. For social scientists the blockage was in the workings and constraints of the policy process. Whether or not their work was used in any given instance appeared to depend upon the outcome of political competition among different vested interests (National Science Foundation, 1969). As Niskanen (1975) observed:

> You can provide information about improved opportunities and about errors that are being made from now until kingdom come, and unless somebody somewhere has an incentive to correct those and has the opportunities to do so then providing more information serves very little purpose other than embarrassing people, and frankly making them mad. Sometimes embarrassment itself will have some effect, but my impression is that Congressmen and most appointed officials have a very high tolerance for embarrassment if their fundamental interests lie elsewhere.

For policy-makers, on the other hand, the fault lay in the research. There was too much shoddy work and too little with any potential for useful application. When called upon, social scientists had failed to deliver. After interviewing a range of federal officials, *Fortune* magazine reported that, 'No-one in government is much tempted by the fruits on social science's tree of knowledge' (Alexander, 1972).

Both the users and producers of research began to think that the attempt to manufacture socially useful knowledge to order – to treat the acquisition of knowledge like any other government procurement

– had come unstuck (Lynn, 1978b). A 1976 report from the Federal Council for Science and Technology warned of the 'indications that too little social R & D is relevant to policymaking and that too much research, even if relevant, is not . . . utilized by the appropriate decision-makers'.

These criticisms provided ammunition for those conservative politicians who were instinctively hostile to the social sciences. In the first budget of his incoming administration President Reagan proposed lopping 75 per cent off the share of the National Science Foundation's budget allocated to social research on the ground that it was 'relatively less important to the economy'. Only a concerted campaign by the social science associations persuaded the Congress to reduce the cut to 26 per cent.

By comparison with the USA, as Bulmer (1978) has pointed out, 'the ruling echelons of British society are certainly much less receptive to the potential contribution of the social sciences to public affairs'. Chapter 3 of this book has offered ample support for this view. Nevertheless, the record of government/social science relations in Britain has many parallels with American experience.

In 1965 the Heyworth Committee recommended greatly increased government spending on social science, and the establishment of a Social Science Research Council (SSRC) to manage these extra funds. Such an investment the Committee declared, 'will in the course of time be more than repaid by the improvement in the efficiency of the national economy and in the quality of our national life'.

Coinciding with the expansion of higher education inspired by the Robbins Committee (1963), the Heyworth Report sparked off a rapid growth in the social sciences and of government support for social science research. In the ensuing decade the number of undergraduates reading sociology in the universities trebled (Smith, 1975), and the teaching staff increased correspondingly with the creation of twenty-eight new departments and thirty new chairs (Abrams, 1981). The expansion of sociology in the universities was soon matched by polytechnics, colleges of education and other institutions of higher education. Membership of the British Sociological Association doubled every two or three years. There was also a big rise in the number of full-time research occupations. Smith's survey (1975) showed that by 1973 over 200 organizations employed almost 900 sociologists as research workers, a third of them working in government agencies.

As in the USA, the political impetus for this growth stemmed from the conviction that social science could strengthen the government's arm in dealing with the problems of an increasingly complex society. Certainly, the financial basis for the expansion of social research after 1965 came from the injection of government funds. Addressing the SSRC Council in 1969, Mrs Shirley Williams, then Secretary of State for Education and Science, pointed out how 'it is still commonplace for major decisions about social programmes to be taken without preliminary research and without any attempt afterwards to evaluate the results of those programmes' (Williams, 1969). Modern government needed better guidance. Harnessing the potential of the social sciences by integrating research into the making of policy promised just that. Here was a role for the social science community that would justify the confidence in it shown by government and repay the investment in its development.

These hopes were short-lived. Only ten years later the Secretary of State for Education, Sir Keith Joseph, was slashing the social science research budget and seriously toying with the idea of abolishing the SSRC altogether. Between 1979 and 1982 under his stewardship the SSRC's expenditure was cut by 24 per cent in real terms. Postgraduate training awards were pruned 'to a painful and undesirable extent' (Rothschild, 1982). Sociology alone saw a reduction in the opportunities for postgraduate research of over 50 per cent in the five years up to 1980. The Association of Learned Societies in the Social Sciences (1986) concluded that 'a state of crisis exists' in the relations between the social sciences and the government. While Macrae, writing in 1961, was able to announce with wide-eyed zeal that 'sociology had arrived' and become 'a word of virtue and of power', the talk twenty years on was of its collapse (Abrams, 1981): as Marsland (1983) declared, 'sociology's failure is a taken-for-granted fact of Britain's official recent past.'

The reasons for this turn-about in fortunes are diverse and tangled. Fearful of co-option, many social scientists sought to preserve their critical independence by 'standing aloof from the state' (Stacey, 1971). They were not prepared to compromise what they saw as the essentially open-ended nature of research enquiry by tying themselves too closely to the short-term interests of government, or to work in a context defined by political assumptions contrary to their own. Consequently, they chose either to ignore the policy dimension completely or to take a hostile stance from the outside. As Payne *et al.* (1981) have said, 'the dominant mood has been anti-establishment and anti-empirical, and this in a period which saw a clear call for more social research by administrators'. To the extent that sociologists, in particular, have been involved in research for policy they have done so 'reluctantly, tentatively, apologetically, as a side-line, moonlighting from their real work, less than fully constructively, much less than fully effectively' (Marsland, 1983).

This stance has been reflected in the theoretical preoccupations of the discipline: especially what Abrams (1981) calls the 'Marxist intrusion', and the backlash against positivism marked by the rise of phenomenology and ethnomethodology. Ironically as their ranks grew in the 1960s, fewer and fewer sociologists were willing to belittle themselves with a-theoretical issues of public policy. Instead they 'resorted to the armchair and spent a decade from the mid 1960s to the mid 1970s contemplating whether society, and hence sociology, actually could exist' (Payne *et al.*, 1981). The opportunities provided by expansion to engage with the problems of the real world were shunned in favour of navel-gazing and the privileged detachment of the ivory tower. As Abrams (1981) warned, 'If British sociology is seriously eroded institutionally it will be, I suggest, because British sociologists have colluded in eroding the market demand for their work'.

On the other side of the equation the failings of social science were matched by the fears of policy-makers. Government, as Kogan and Henkel (1983) have pointed out, may have a limited capacity to tolerate scientific enquiry that intensifies uncertainty, challenges its own working, threatens entrenched views or runs counter to the political wisdom of the day. Chapter 3 of this book has offered many examples to support this view. Even inside government, within the Department of Health and Social Security (DHSS) for instance, professional advisers and statisticians are only rarely accommodated in the same building or close to any of the policy branches they support (DHSS, 1980a). Outside researchers are kept at an even greater distance and regarded even more warily. Certainly, policy-makers are distrustful of their liberal inclinations and underdog sympathies, as well as being suspicious, in the British tradition, of their scientific pretensions. Although there is little hard evidence on the matter, the signs point to many government departments being dissatisfied with the technical competence of sociologists applying for jobs or research grants (Smith, 1975). Serious misgivings, too, have been voiced by policy-makers about the utility and worth of a lot of policy-driven research. Speaking of educational research, for example, Sir William Pile, Permanent Secretary at the Department of Education and Science, said in 1976:

> Part of it is rubbish, and another part leads nowhere and is really rather indifferent; it is, I am afraid, exceptional to find a piece of research that really hits the nail on the head and tells you pretty clearly what is wrong or what is happening or what should be done. (Quoted in Broadfoot and Nisbet, 1980)

The story of the DHSS–SSRC programme of research into transmitted deprivation may help to breathe some life into this all too brisk account of the ups and downs of government social science relations in the UK.

The story begins in 1972 with a speech by Sir Keith Joseph, then Secretary of State for Social Services, to the Pre-School Playgroups Association. 'Why is it', he asked, 'that, in spite of long periods of full employment and relative prosperity and the improvement in community services since the Second World War, deprivation and problems of maladjustment so conspicuously persist?' He suggested that a possible explanation for this puzzle might be found in the existence of what he called 'a cycle of deprivation' linked to patterns of parenting. Poverty and other forms of deprivation might be transmitted from generation to generation through attitudes and processes within the family. People who were themselves deprived in one or more ways in childhood become, in turn, the parents of another generation of deprived children.

Acting on these ideas, Sir Keith Joseph set up a Joint Working Party (JWP) between the DHSS and the SSRC to consider the feasibility of research into the concept of transmitted deprivation. If intergenerational continuities are a feature of the persistence of deprivation, and if the mechanisms underlying them can be understood, then ways might be found of breaking the cycle. The JWP's first step was to commission a review of the literature to establish what was known already and to define the scope for further research (see Rutter and Madge, 1976). With this in front of them the JWP members agreed there was enough evidence to support the hypothesis that deprivation crossed generations but no convincing explanation of how it occurred and that more research might yield an answer.

Accordingly the JWP submitted a report to the Secretary of State, in October 1973, recommending that the DHSS should fund a wide-ranging programme of research through the SSRC into transmitted deprivation. Shortly afterwards, a seven-year contract was signed between the DHSS and the SSRC. Right from the start the programme had the dual purpose of advancing knowledge and contributing to policy. In part it was 'an experiment in co-operation between social researchers and policy-makers' (Brown and Madge, 1982). Eversley (1983) goes further. He says it could be seen as a last chance to save social science from its critics. The signing of the research contract effectively put social science – sociology in particular – on trial.

How did it rise to the challenge? Eversley offers a bruising assessment. Even before the research had begun, many social scientists denounced the programme for conceiving poverty in terms of personal failure, and proclaimed it to be ideologically untouchable. Already in a hole, they carried on digging. Others with their feet on more level ground squared up to the issues while the controversy rumbled on. As a result of their efforts, the combined research output of the programme was substantial. Between 1972 and 1981 over twenty original, empirical studies were completed, along with fourteen reviews ranging from short discussion papers to comprehensive literature surveys (see Brown and Madge, 1982). More than seventy researchers from a wide range of disciplines were directly involved in the programme. Sizing up this accumulated body of research, Eversley concludes that if he were a benevolent, intelligent, independent policy adviser at the DHSS, then very little of what he had read would influence him one way or another for a number of reasons.

To start with, the projects were overly preoccupied with definitional questions and ended up by adopting very different criteria as measures and indicators of deprivation. As Silburn (quoted in ibid.), too, has commented: 'The projects themselves were so varied, so different from one another in their thinking, their theoretical justifications and their proposed research methodologies, even in their basic definition of the problem, that they defy comparison.' All this variety led to the programme drifting away from its original aims and reaching well beyond its intended scope. The initial focus on the concept of the *cycle of deprivation* – with its emphasis on familial processes – soon gave way to a wider concern with the *cycles of disadvantage* that permeate our whole society. In other words, the researchers ignored the questions posed by their sponsors and answered others of their own choosing.

This shift of focus also altered the explanatory thrust of the research and its implications for policy. Concentration on familial mechanisms of transmission tends to lead towards explanations couched in terms of individual behaviour and group dynamics, and tends to point towards intervention at the personal level. By contrast, switching to look at patterns of disadvantage in society as a whole gives more weight to structural explanations and to policies geared towards structural change. The underlying message to come out of the transmitted deprivation programme was that the problems can only be tackled in the context of the wider society. Yet as Brown and Madge (ibid.) acknowledge, policy-makers 'lack the creative power to achieve grand changes to the whole structure'. In short, having evaded the questions initially put by Sir Keith Joseph, the researchers went on to propose solutions that were either too vague to inform action or too far-reaching to be of any practical use. In

Eversley's view this evasion 'damns the whole exercise'.

Overall, then, the research programme produced a shelf of books but little in the way of usable knowledge. Seen as an experiment in co-operation between researchers and policy-makers, the benefits turned out to be pretty one-sided. As Brown and Madge admit in their final report on the programme when, having drawn together the research, they move on to consider its implications for policy and practice: 'Much of the research has added greatly to our understanding of the meaning and causes of various deprivations but very little has provided clear evidence to answer the question of what to do about them.' Eversley arrives at a similar though slightly more sweeping and trenchant conclusion. 'I do not believe', he says, 'that sociological insights, based on specific social research methods, have, on this evidence, much to contribute to policy-making.' Perhaps Sir Keith Joseph, who started the ball rolling, had reached the same verdict when he used his new position as supremo at the Department of Education and Science (DES) under Mrs Thatcher to round on the SSRC just as the programme was winding to a close.

Let us pause for a moment to take stock of the argument so far. In both the UK and USA at roughly the same time, and prompted by roughly the same motives, there occurred a quickening of official interest in the use of social science for policy-making. Government funds were channelled into the expansion of the social sciences; there was a rapid increase in expenditure on social research; and social scientists were drawn into government. For a while optimism ran high that a new partnership was in the making. Before long, however, strains began to show as the overblown expectations of each side were dashed. Social scientists complained that nobody listened to them and their work was ignored. Policy-makers chuntered about the irrelevance of the research they commissioned. Both retreated into their bunkers. What came to be known as 'the crisis of under-utilization' set in.

Theories of Underutilization

The realization that their work was not having the impact they believed it deserved came hard to social scientists. It stung their vanity and seemed to endanger their newly found status. True to their calling, they turned to investigating the reasons for the 'underutilization' of social science research with unremitting vigour. So much so that in the twenty years up to 1976 the number of citations in this field increased fiftyfold (Karapin, 1986).

Coming to terms with this bulky literature is not easy. Caplan (1975) offers a key. He identifies three broad types of 'utilization theories', each of which provides a different explanation for the nonuse or underuse of social science by policy-makers: the 'two communities' hypothesis, knowledge-specific theories and policy-maker-specific theories. A fourth category might properly be added to these three: simple disenchantment.

The 'Two Communities' Hypothesis
According to Caplan (1975), theories of underutilization with the greatest degree of explanatory power are those pointing to the existence of a gap between social scientists and policy-makers due to differences in values, language, reward systems and social and professional affiliations. They live in what Young (1977) has called different 'assumptive worlds'.

Policy-makers tend to draw their values from the prevailing hierarchy of power. Within the social sciences, however, there is a strong tradition of identification with the underdog, the powerless and the outsider. For many sociologists, policy-oriented research is about 'taking knowledge from the people, giving knowledge to the rulers' (Nicolaus, 1969). It turns the researcher into a kind of spy in the service of the master institutions of society providing information that helps to bind people to the state apparatus, to keep them down and to bolster the control exercised by ruling élites on their own behalf (Gouldner, 1970). In rejecting the status of intellectual Uncle Tom, generations of sociologists have aligned themselves with the unofficial, underside of society (Sharpe, 1978) and stressed their role as critics of the social order. Instead of setting out to inform policy, they have set out to debunk it. Rex (1974) makes clear the moral and political bases for this crusade:

> Sociology is a subject whose insights should be available to the great mass of the people in order that they should be able to use it to liberate themselves from the mystification of social reality which is continuously provided for them by those in our society who exercise power and influence.

This stance has fixed self-imposed limits on the incorporation of sociologists as advisers or technicians into policy-making and administration.

The structure of incentives within the academic community has also driven a wedge between social scientists and policy-makers. These incentives attach greater weight to knowledge-building research as against policy-forming research; to authoritativeness rather than usefulness; to the pursuit of rigour as against relevance; to the values of scientific independence as against the virtues of policy involvement; and to understanding rather than action. They also maintain and reinforce the traditional institutional divisions between the disciplines which carve up knowledge in ways that rarely match the world of experience. The chief mechanism for regulating these incentives is the system of peer review which largely determines what gets published, where the grants go and who gets promoted. Faced with the choice, the pressure on academic researchers is to put their careers and their professional standing first and to please their peers rather than their sponsors. Lynn (1977), for instance, quotes from a 1971 National Research Council report on social science research in the US Defense Department:

> High-level officials, both in the Department of Defense and in the former Bureau of Budget, believe that research should be more useful to them than it is. Non-mission-oriented basic research is considered to have lacked policy pay-offs and to have constituted both a subsidy to producers and a source of difficulty and irritation with the Congress. Research producers are sometimes viewed as being more interested in furthering their academic disciplines than producing operational help to the Department of Defense.

The inclination for scholars to see knowledge as deriving from theory and method is mirrored by an inclination among policy-makers to see knowledge as coming from experience and common sense. As Sharpe (1975) says, the British political tradition 'gives much greater weight to knowledge as accumulated experience – *he who does knows* – and in its extreme form sees practical experience as the only legitimate source of knowledge'. Similarly, Mondale (1968b) has remarked on the tendency for politicians in the USA to regard themselves as successful practitioners of applied social science because they know the people and have had their views endorsed by winning elections.

Unlike their colleagues in engineering, the physical sciences or medicine, social scientists often deal with data and with problems about which policy-makers may feel they have acquired substantial knowledge from years of first-hand involvement. From their point of view, it may not be at all clear who is really the expert. Social scientists generally speak most authoritatively on picayune matters, while policy-makers show a better mastery of the parameters within which they operate (Merton, 1949).

One consequence of the pragmatic view of knowledge common among policy-makers is to encourage a dismissive attitude towards research that points to conclusions which are counter-intuitive (Thomas, 1985). Merton (1959) has neatly caught the dilemma this creates for researchers:

> Should his systematic inquiry only confirm what has been widely assumed – this being the class of plausible truths – he will of course be charged with 'labouring the obvious'. He becomes tagged as a bore, telling only

what everybody knows. Should investigation find that widely held social beliefs are untrue – the class of plausible untruths – he is a heretic, questioning value-laden verities. If he ventures to examine socially implausible ideas that turn out to be untrue, he is a fool, wasting effort on a line of inquiry not worth pursuing in the first place. And finally, if he should turn up some implausible truths, he must be prepared to find himself regarded as a charlatan, claiming as knowledge what is patently false.

Here, in a nutshell, is the difference between the world-view of social science and of common sense: the one questions what the other takes for granted.

Merton's dilemma is compounded by another feature of relations between the two communities. As Abrams (1981) has pointed out, in so far as the insights and findings of social science are judged to be of interest or use they tend to be absorbed into the language of everyday discourse and appropriated as common sense. What is left as social science is precisely those ideas which nobody values. Hence its reputation for irrelevance and ill-grounded theorizing, and the ease with which policy-makers see themselves as their own expert.

Finally, in both the UK and USA there exists an institutional divide between government and the social science community. There is a Chief Scientist in Whitehall to advise the government on science policy but no Chief Social Scientist. There is a Chief Economic Adviser at the Treasury but no Chief Social Adviser. Until recently the DHSS appointed a Chief Scientist but the post was always filled from the world of medical research. Indeed, when the Secretary of State for Social Services set up a Chief Scientist's Advisory Group in 1980 to review departmental research needs, it consisted almost exclusively of people of eminence and authority in the field of clinical, medical and health research. The Economic and Social Research Council (ESRC) is very much a lightweight among its bigger cousins from the 'hard' sciences with a research budget of less than 5 per cent of total expenditure by all five research councils and, of course, a correspondingly weaker voice.

Although social science is much stronger in the USA the same institutional weaknesses are apparent. Since the Second World War the President's Office has appointed a scientific adviser from among the most distinguished scholars in the physical sciences. The President's Scientific Advisory Committee also provides a channel between the executive branch and the physical and biological sciences. The Council of Economic Advisers assists the President in the formulation and direction of national economic policy, and the Joint Economic Committee of Congress serves as a forum for public debate of national economic affairs.

There are no similar institutions providing a bridge between the non-economic social sciences and the machinery of government. Federal support for basic social research is channelled through the multi-disciplinary National Science Foundation which is dominated by the natural sciences. Persistent efforts within Congress to set up a separate National Social Science Foundation in the late 1960s and early 1970s foundered in the face of opposition from vested interests within the scientific establishment. Equally, as Chapter 5 has shown, the attempt to create a Council of Social Advisers also failed. As in the UK, the social sciences (excluding economics) lack a prominent public platform of their own.

In sum, the 'two communities' hypothesis explains the underutiliz-ation of social research by depicting social scientists and policy-makers as living in separate worlds. The differences 'make for wide divergences in expectations, in perceptions of mutual impact as well as difficulties in achieving satisfactory and constructive relationships' (Kogan, Korman and Henkel, 1980).

Policy-maker Specific Theories

This second class of theories shares the assumption that the underutilization of research can best be understood from the standpoint of policy-makers themselves and the constraints under which they operate.

Policy-making is about securing agreement between different people who want different things. It involves finding a compromise between the competing claims and conflicts of purpose which fuel the political process. One way of coping with these contending interests is through vagueness and ambiguity (Rein, 1976). Indeed, we might go so far as to say that ambiguity is essential for the agreement on which policy depends, for two reasons. First, because it leaves policies open to a variety of interpretations compatible with the many and conflicting aims and interests of the different groups involved. Secondly, because it allows a measure of flexibility in dealing with the unforeseen problems and special cases arising from the implementation of policy.

Research, on the other hand, endeavours precisely to remove ambiguity and to bring clarity and precision to our thinking about problems. It aims to make the nature of the choices facing policy-makers as clear and explicit as possible; to estimate the costs and benefits of alternative courses of action; and to identify who stands to gain or lose from them. Accordingly, so far as policy-makers are concerned, a better understanding of problems might make it more difficult to reach agreement on how they should be tackled.

This particular conflict between the requirements of policy and the contribution of research shows itself in two ways. First, policy-makers are usually unwilling to be too open and specific about whom their policies are to serve and with what results for fear of stirring up opposition which may jeopardize the support they seek, and because to do so would provide their critics with a yardstick for assessing their own performance. Yet without knowing what objectives are being pursued, the researcher is ill-placed to evaluate how well a policy or programme is working. Part of the charge of irrelevance levelled against much policy-directed research arises precisely because the researcher often lacks such guide-posts.

Secondly, research which is too explicit in revealing the costs and benefits of policies and where they fall feeds the discontent of both the losers and those who had hoped to gain more, so again making it harder to secure the political agreement on which policy is based. An example of both these traits may be seen in the refusal by Norman Fowler, then Secretary of State for Social Services, to publish DHSS estimates of the financial consequences, for different categories of claimants, of the changes in supplementary benefits and housing benefit proposed by the 1985 Social Security review.

This general point, that research aims for clarity while policy often depends on ambiguity, relates to another: namely, that research tends to complicate issues by showing them to be more ticklish than they first appeared, whereas the art of policy-making lies in simplifying things to the point where action becomes possible. Cohen and Weiss (1977) have made the same point more forcefully:

> For the most part, the improvement of research on social policy . . . usually tends to produce a greater sense of complexity. This result is endemic to the research process. For what researchers understand by improvement in their craft leads not to greater consensus about research problems, methods and interpretation of results, but to more variety in the way problems are seen, more divergence in the way studies are carried out, and more controversy in the ways results are interpreted. It leads also to a more complicated view of problems and solutions, for the progress of research tends to reveal the inadequacy of accepted ideas about solving problems.

Indeed, the common assumption that more information makes for better decisions is probably mistaken. As Thomas (1985) has said, there is 'more research than can be assimilated by even the most open-minded and assiduous department'. 'The problem for policy-makers stems more from having to choose what to ignore' (Wildavsky, 1970). Keynes, who had a lifetime's experience advising governments, was well aware of this fact: 'there is nothing', he wrote, 'a government hates more than to be well-informed; for it makes the process of arriving at decisions much more complicated and difficult' (quoted in Sharpe, 1975).

From where the policy-maker sits, then, it may be more rational to accept ignorance as a condition for action than to strive for certainty or to rely too much on the help which research can give (Marris and Rein, 1967). A number of other factors bear out this view from the frontline.

In making decisions, policy-makers usually have to take account of a wider range of variables than research can normally encompass. They must fit the immediate problem into its wider context and weigh up the repercussions of any action they may take (in terms of its immediate impact, possible 'knock-on' effects and any potential 'sleeper' effects) on a string of constituencies (beneficiaries, legislators, officials, professionals, public opinion, etc.) across a range of dimensions (political, administrative, financial, technical, etc.). The methodology of research, on the other hand, is to abstract from the wider context a few variables and to examine them in a controlled and systematic way. In short, research casts events in a fundamentally different light to policy, and rarely provides the breadth of vision that policy-makers require.

An episode from my own spell as a social services researcher in local government illustrates this point. I had been asked by management to undertake a study of the 'meals on wheels' service. Among other things the investigation showed there were many people in greater need of the service than some who were currently receiving it, and that many existing recipients no longer qualified for the service by the established criteria. This situation had arisen partly because the circumstances of some recipients had changed since they first were allocated 'meals on wheels', and partly because the criteria for allocation were being interpreted differently in different delivery areas. On the basis of these findings, I devised a simple procedure for reviewing cases and redrafted the allocation criteria in an unambiguous way. However, no action was taken on these proposals, and for reasons which had not been allowed for in the research: first, because the decision to withdraw the service was more likely to cause distress, inconvenience and bitterness among those who had come to rely on it than was the failure to give it to people, however pressing their need, who so far had managed without; and secondly, because the introduction of tight and uniform criteria would seriously prejudice the professional discretion of the service administrators. The decision not to act on the research findings therefore was based on considerations extraneous to the study which put a different gloss on them. Departmental management simply took a different view of their significance.

Weiss and Bucuvalas (1980a) probe deeper into this difference of outlook. Scientists, they say, are accustomed to judging the validity of findings on the basis of the research *process*. Policy-makers go further: they also judge validity by the *outcomes* of research. They assess the extent to which research outcomes accord with their first-hand experience and professional judgement.

All this is to say that policy-makers have other sources of knowledge than research alone (Lindblom and Cohen, 1979). They learn by doing, by talking and listening to colleagues, by direct observation and practical reasoning. And they draw their information from a variety of sources apart from research: routine statistics, official records, personal briefings, in-house memoranda, special enquiries and reviews, staff reports, complaints procedures, the media, pressure groups, and so on. Research is just one more resource available to policy-makers. In order to understand the use they make of the data it generates, it is necessary to appreciate how research is assimilated into this wider perspective.

Weiss and Bucuvalas (1980a) found that decision-makers apply two tests in screening research and deciding how seriously to treat its findings: a 'truth test' and a 'utility test'. The 'truth test' is a judgement about the technical merit of a study and how far its findings are believable (usually assessed in terms of their conformity with prior understanding and experience). The 'utility test' is a measure of the extent to which the study provides them with practical advice on which they can act or a helpful new perspective on problems.

Research which passes these two tests is more likely to be taken up and absorbed into the stock of knowledge that policy-makers call on to inform or legitimate their actions. This suggests, echoing a point made previously, that findings which are counter-intuitive are unlikely to travel very far. As Aaron (1978) has said, in what amounts to a neat re-statement of the 'truth test', 'the person who finds research in conflict with deeply-held beliefs may think errors in the research are more likely than in his preconceptions'. It also suggests why top-level actors are not hospitable to new definitions of the situation of the kind which original research may offer. Government departments, as Hope (1978) points out, are very liable to be captured by intellectual cliques. Such cliques are bound together by common political and ideological commitments. Research which does not fit their assumptions is generally weeded out by application of the truth and utility tests. Only when some crisis reveals the inadequacy of prevailing ideas, or when a new political leadership emerges, is the door opened to fresh insights (Bunker, 1978).

Other factors have a bearing on the utility of research. Within an action frame of reference, for instance, it is hard to dissent from the view that policy is about more pressing matters than research. Certainly, they often play to a different rhythm.

Data collection and analysis take time and this often conflicts with the urgency of decisions. While the benefits and returns from research tend to increase with time, its value and usefulness to the policy-maker diminishes.

There is another side to the same problem. Career mobility among senior civil servants, who seldom remain in the same post for longer than three years, about the usual life of a research project, makes it difficult to sustain the kind of relationships conducive to the easy flow of ideas and information between the two communities (Thomas, 1985; Bunker, 1978). All too often a piece of research is received by people other than those who commissioned it in the first place. Thomas (1985) quotes an official from the Department of Education and Science (DES) speaking about the Educational Priority Area programme:

> The nursery research programme was launched in the wake of the 1972 research. By the time [researchers] had been found it was 1974. By then several people had moved on. By the time the research work was completed a third generation of people had moved in. It does weaken enthusiasm. Most of these things owe something to individual interest.

Another consequence of high rates of turnover in senior positions is the creation of what Bunker (1978) has called a deficit in 'institutional memory'. People move on, taking their expertise with them, arriving as a greenhorn in their new post and having to start all over again on the learning curve. All too often the lessons of research are lost in the process.

In summary, policy-maker specific theories of underutilization dwell on the barriers to the use of research inherent in the behaviour and attitudes of policy-makers themselves and in the workings of the policy process. The gist is that research and policy are uneasy bedfellows at the best of times.

Knowledge Specific Theories

This third category of explanations for the underutilization of research holds that the reasons are to be found in the nature of social science knowledge, the characteristics of disciplinary research and the behaviour of social scientists.

Rein (1976) has distinguished three different research strategies for social scientists working in the policy arena:

1   A *consensual approach* in which the policy-maker poses the questions and the social scientist provides the answers.

2   A *contentious* *approach* in which the social scientist assumes the role of moral witness to the failings of society or social critic of the government's performance.
3   A *paradigm-challenging* *approach* where the researcher steps beyond the bounds of received opinion to bring a new vision to the definition of problems and the possibilities for action.

Each of these approaches, however, leads to strains in the underlying relationships between the users and producers of research.

The consensual approach appears to be the one most likely to yield information that is relevant and useful to policy-makers. Yet it is riddled with difficulties in practice. On the one hand, it presupposes something akin to an engineering model of the relationship between research and policy, based on the customer–contractor principle (see below), which simply cannot be applied in the field of social policy. On the other hand, it turns the researcher into little more than a technician in the service of officialdom and few career-minded social scientists are prepared to accept such a narrow view of their role or such limitations on the scope of their discipline.

The contentious approach perhaps squares best with the critical stance of most social scientists, their anti-establishment instincts and the argumentative nature of their discipline. But it doesn't go down so well with policy-makers. They have to shoulder enough criticisms as it is without contracting for more. In any case, from their point of view, research aimed merely at showing up the failings of existing policies only tells half a tale unless it goes on to say what can be done about them. And for all their talk and books, social scientists in this tradition have rarely been willing to promise very much (Gottlieb, 1969; Marsland, 1983). Behind this approach lies a clash between two concepts of relevance which drives the two sides apart. For it brings together social scientists who are largely interested in matters of policy only in so far as they are relevant to social theory and practical people who are only interested in social science so long as it is relevant to policy.

The paradigm-challenging approach is the most intellectually rewarding for researchers but, generally speaking, delivers least for policy-makers. Visionary, new perspectives cannot be had to order. It is not possible to contract for this kind of research. The only way is to allow researchers the freedom to follow their own noses. Usually their efforts will lead nowhere. But even when they do come up with something new the ideas are likely to be so much ahead of their time that no politician will touch them and no official will believe them (Moynihan, 1970b). They will not pass the truth and utility tests used by policy-makers for screening research.

But the problems of utilization go beyond the frustrations engendered by these three research strategies. In many ways they go to the heart of what passes for knowledge about society. It might almost be said that some of them, at least, are epistemological in origin.

The 1960s saw a major critical assault on the dominant tradition in social science research: the positivist tradition. This is not the place to begin an excursion into the philosophy of science. Let us just say that positivism is the belief that empirical methods are the only source of true knowledge. This tradition came under attack from within and without (Bell and Newby, 1977; Payne *et al.*, 1981).

From within the critique focused on the shortcomings of quantitative methods and techniques of measurement. The instruments used by social scientists to gather their data about the social world were not up to the job. They were altogether too blunt and crude to capture the true nature of social reality whose essence could not be squeezed into the boxes of a questionnaire or reduced to mere numbers and percentages. The attempt to create a natural science of society had simply led social scientists into imposing order on the events they observe by fiat. All too often the 'facts' they unearthed were no more than an artefact of their own methods, and a reflection of their own categories of discourse. Alternative methodologies were required, which tried to apprehend the world through the eyes of the people in it and to grasp the meanings they attributed to their own actions and doings. The upshot of this self-questioning was a shift away from old-style empiricism, a new emphasis on qualitative methods of research, especially ethnography, and an acknowledgement of the role of insight, intuition and interpretive reasoning as basic tools of social analysis.

The challenge from without came from two sources: ethnomethodology and Marxism. Both of these movements amounted to a far-reaching reappraisal of the nature of the sociological endeavour. Both constituted a frontal attack on the empirical method: ethnomethodology by denying the possibility of objective, disinterested and impersonal knowledge about society; and Marxism by denying the existence of an independent realm of 'social facts' against which propositions about society may be tested. For ethnomethodologists there is no knowledge other than that which comes from participation in society; for Marxists there are no facts outside of theory.

The confluence of these three strands of criticism did a lot to undermine some of the fundamental tenets of positivism. It precipitated a 'flight from method' on the part of substantial sections of the social science community, a rejection of quantitative techniques and measurement, and the abandonment of the fact–value distinction and the ideal of a value-free social science.

These developments had a profound effect on how policy-makers in government regarded social science as an enterprise and the knowledge it produced. Partly they felt let down and cheated, as the next section will show. After all, it had been their conviction that social science would prove useful which had produced the funds for its expansion. Partly, too, they felt released from the obligation to listen and the compunction to act. If social science knowledge is compounded of insights, intuition, common sense and practical reasoning, rather than empirical truths, then it had little to teach them. They were their own experts and could look to their own experience. This may be why policy-makers are reluctant to accept anything other than quantifiable findings in the social policy field (Payne *et al.*, 1981). Everything else lacks the mystery of expertise and the validity of objective fact. Also if all social science is inescapably value-laden (usually with values hostile to those, like themselves, who exercise power), then again it loses its claim to authoritativeness. Moynihan (1970b) summed up the views of most policy-makers when he said that the role of social science 'lies not in the formulation of social policy, but in the measurement of its results'. Values entered the making of policy through the political process but they were seen as inimical to the objective evaluation of outcomes. The abandonment of the fact–value distinction and the flight from method seriously damaged the expectations that policy-makers held of social science.

Of course, large numbers of bread-and-butter social scientists continued to provide policy-makers with the kind of number-crunching research they wanted heedless of the criticisms of 'abstracted empiricism' levelled by their more theoretically minded colleagues. Indeed, in many ways the 'epistemological crisis' sparked off by the assault on positivism had little direct impact on the style of research contracted by government. Its main effects were by the by: in tarnishing the image of social science generally, undermining its claims to scientific status and disparaging the expertise and credibility of its practitioners. But even those researchers who continued in their empiricist ways encountered obstacles deriving from their methodology.

The statistical complexity of a lot of social research can hinder its use. The spread of computer-based techniques such as regression and multivariate analysis has rendered the logic and even the vocabulary of much research inaccessible to all but the specialist. The layman is very much at the mercy of the professional, and of the professional's interpretation of the evidence. For policy-makers this may demand more trust in the researcher's competence and objectivity than they are willing to give, especially in the social services where countervailing views are rife (Weiss, 1978).

More serious, perhaps, is the tendency for researchers to conceptualize problems in terms of the methodologies in which they are proficient, and to formulate questions in ways their methodology can address. The results may be highly praised in professional circles but irrelevant to the needs of policy-makers. Roberts's study (OECD, 1980) of the role of economists in the debate in the USA about how to deal with water pollution is a case in point. He argues that 'the academics were answering questions which the real world was not asking'. The Congress wanted to do something about dirty water, while the economists saw the problem as one of 'market failure'. Two factors contributed to this clash of perspectives. On the one hand, the economists could only see the problem of pollution through the special lenses of their discipline. On the other hand, their tools of mathematical analysis could not handle the non-quantifiable factors that contributed to the problem and exercised policy-makers. The lesson, Roberts concludes, is that social scientists often 'see in reality only a reflection of the conceptual systems they brought to the encounter'.

In summary, then, knowledge-specific theories explain underutilization in terms of the frequent mismatch between the perspectives on reality which research and policy provide. Sometimes research casts events in a light which cannot be accommodated within a framework of action or which cannot be reconciled with the political constraints within which policy is framed. Equally, as C. Wright Mills (1959) has pointed out, when 'many policies – debated and undebated – are based on inadequate and misleading definitions of reality, then those who are out to define reality more adequately are bound to be upsetting influences'.

Disenchantment and Underutilization
Disenchantment runs through the account of each set of theories described above but as a consequence rather than a cause of the underutilization of research. Here it finds a place in its own right. Broadly the argument is that as social scientists and policy-makers came to know each other better from working together, familiarity bred contempt.

During the 1960s, as Premfors (1979) says, social science came of age and emerged as an important social institution with a solid academic base. A necessary condition for this growth was, in most countries, major support from government. And not surprisingly, government looked for something in return for its investment.

For instance, in 1976 the US federal government spent more than $1.8 million on research relating to the identification and solution of social problems (Lynn, 1977). Yet in the same year a review by the National Research Council concluded that the quality of applied social science research was 'highly variable and that on average it is relatively undistinguished with only modest potential in useful application'. On a wider front policy-makers, too, were expressing their discontent with what they were getting: 'It's sad how often when we ask basic questions there's just no intellectual capital to draw on' (quoted in Alexander, 1972). Lynn (1978b) reports that many officials believed the pressures for policy relevance had flooded the market with shoddy products, and that 'the resulting poor-quality research, nonreplicable demonstrations, ambiguous experiments, useless data and biased evaluations have neither policy value nor scientific merit'. Higgins (1980) reports a similar level of dissatisfaction with the quality of research by policy-makers in the UK.

The disenchantment was reciprocated by social scientists. Initially they had hoped their research for government would make a contribution to social betterment. When their own experience confirmed that, in the main, it was only used to support the partisan ends of the holders of power, they grew chary. Furthermore, when it became clear that the costs of incorporation in the policy process were limits on what was studied, the questions asked, how it was studied and the kind of answers given, they drew back. Green (1971) summed up their doubts and fears:

> The involvement of social scientists with government poses a serious threat to the independence of social science. In order that social science may be useful to government officials, it must meet their criteria of reality and practicality. At the technical level this may mean accepting official categories of discourse; more broadly it will mean that certain problems do not get studied, unless the research can be structured so as to suggest 'constructive' and politically tenable solutions, and unless the social scientist adopts a manipulative attitude towards the subjects of his research.

Underutilization, then, is an expression of the unhappiness of policy-makers with the utility of social research and of the unwillingness of social scientists to march to someone else's tune.

Two Models of Research and Policy
There is something to be said for each of these theories. They all contain a nugget of truth. So far as there is a genuine problem of underutilization they help us to understand how and why it comes

about, and also point to ways of narrowing the gulf between research and policy.

But in some respects, too, they lead us down a blind alley by providing answers to the wrong questions, that is, questions based on a misreading of the real nature of the problem. To see why this should be so, we need to uncover the assumptions behind these theories. These assumptions are embodied in two related models of the relationship between research and policy: a purist model and a problem-solving model.

The *purist model* holds simply that research generates knowledge that impels action. It is firmly grounded in a rational view of the policy-making process. In Britain it is perhaps most closely associated with the Fabian tradition in social administration. A common version of the purist model, drawn from parallels with industrial research and development techniques and the process of technological innovation, posits a linear relationship between research and policy in which basic (or theoretical) research feeds applied research that informs policy development leading eventually to implementation (Rothman, 1980b).

The *problem-solving model*, or engineering model as it is sometimes called, differs from the purist model mainly in that it is policy rather than theory which disciplines the research. The link remains a linear one, but instead of it being research that mobilizes opinion and stimulates action it is, on the contrary, the decision to act which generates the demand for research. Policy-makers first spell out the problem and what more they need to know about it. They commission research to fill in these gaps in their knowlede and to explore possible solutions. Policy is then framed in the light of this evidence. In short, the policy-maker asks the questions and the researcher provides the answers.

Perhaps the best-known expression of the problem-solving model is the customer–contractor principle which Lord Rothschild (1971) proposed should guide the commissioning and funding of applied research and development by government departments: 'The customer says what he wants; the contractor does it (if he can); and the customer pays.' Here the 'customer' is the user or sponsor and the 'contractor' is the researcher.

The customer–contractor principle is rooted in three assumptions about the working relationship between researchers and policy-makers (Booth, 1979a):

— that the job of the researcher is to lay before the policy-maker 'the unbiased facts to which future policy should be adapted' (Benjamin, 1973);

— that the use of research is measured in terms of its immediate return in influencing decisions;
— that researchers must work within, rather than challenge, the scale of values through which policy-makers view their task.

The purist model and the problem-solving model have two key features in common. They both see research as the bedrock on which policy is built and they both conceive of utilization as implying the direct application of research to a pending decision.

A number of criticisms can be levelled against this position, suggesting that these two models present too narrow a view of the functions of research and too simple a view of the workings of the policy process. To begin with, research serves far more purposes than merely fact-finding. For instance, it may be used to *legitimate* policies arrived at by other routes (Berger, 1980). Piven (1974) has argued that social scientists and social science did not play much of a role at all in the USA in the design of the ambitious social programmes of the 'Great Society' era: 'Rather than providing the scientific basis for the formulation of policies, they provided the scientific authority which political leaders borrowed to justify these policies.'

In the same way, research may be used (often selectively) by policy-makers to *vindicate* their actions or to advance their own bureaucratic self-interest (e.g. by supporting their claims for extra resources). Thomas (1985) reports that 'ministers were as likely to find shoddy research useful as they were to take up well conducted research findings; for a minister the quality of the research was of secondary importance so long as the findings supported the point of view he was putting forward.'

Equally research may serve as a mechanism of *control* (Rein and White, 1977a; Weiss, 1986). It is used by those at the centre to keep in touch with what is happening at the periphery, or by those at the top of an organization to monitor the performance of those at the bottom. In this sense, research is tied more closely to the functions of management and audit than to policy-making.

Research, too, may have an important *symbolic value* or decorative appeal. One aspect of this is what Lipsky (1971) has called 'the paprika role', where research has no substantive effect other than to add a bit of colour to decisions. Another is to lace policy-making with the appearance of rationality. Similarly, commissioning research may be a useful way of responding to pressures where some visible commitment short of action is required.

Other purposes for which research may be used in the policy arena include political *positioning* (as a tactical ploy for heading off criticism, for delaying the need for action and for stirring up controversy) or as a source of *ammunition* for fighting political wars. Against this backcloth any account which only conceives of research as supplying empirical data for policy-makers leads to a superficial view of how research is used and how policy is framed.

A second major criticism of the two models is that they attribute too much importance to research and fail to recognize that policy-makers have other sources of information available to them on which they draw. Research usually adds only a little to what they already know. As Weiss and Bucuvalas (1980a) say:

> Those social scientists who expect research to be authoritative enough to *determine* policy choices are giving insufficient weight to the many and varied sources from which people derive their understandings and policy-preferences . . . People in official positions often do not catalogue research separately in their minds. They interpret it as they read it in the light of their other knowledge, and they *merge* it with all the information and generalisations in their stock.

Lindblom and Cohen (1979) identify three other kinds of knowledge apart from social research which policy-makers enlist in their work:

1 *ordinary knowledge* – the common-sense understandings and everyday wisdom they possess as members of society;
2 *social learning* – what they pick up on the job and from watching, listening and talking to colleagues and others;
3 *interactive problem-solving* – the experience they acquire in the process of actually grappling with problems and working through them.

Policy-makers, then, use research as only one among many kinds of evidence and weigh up its significance, not by statistical tests in the manner of the analyst, but in the light of their other knowledge (Aaron, 1978). Rarely is policy decided by a concrete, point-by-point reliance on empirically grounded data. This leads us to a much broader notion of utilization than that embraced by the purist and problem-solving models; one in which the use of social research is quite compatible with it having little effect on the outcome of decisions.

Caplan (1975) makes a distinction between the diffusion, utilization and application of research which helps to clarify what this means. Diffusion is the process whereby research reaches the policy-maker. Utilization occurs where the research is taken up: where it is read, criticized, discussed, assimilated, discounted, trimmed, suppressed, manipulated or whatever – so long as it receives some sort of attention. Application is where the research makes a difference to what happens in the sense of having an impact on decisions.

The two models, outlined above, of how research and policy connect confuse utilization with application. For this reason, finding precious little evidence of the impact of research, social scientists have been led to conclude that either it was not getting through or was not being taken up. Accordingly instead of seeing how policy-makers *merge* research with their other forms of knowledge, they have concentrated on looking for the obstacles and blockages to its use. As Patton (quoted in Smith, 1981) suggests, the crisis of underutilization rests as much on social scientists' overly grand ideas about their own importance, and their misconceptions about the nature of decision-making, as on the intransigence of bureaucrats and the impermeability of the policy process.

This last point blends with a third criticism of the purist and problem-solving models which challenges the picture they present of policy-making as a staged and purposeful sequence of events. This criticism comes in two guises: one emphasizes the elusiveness of decisions, while the other stresses the jumbled and undirected ways by which policy often emerges.

Weiss (1980), for instance, found that most government officials do not believe they make anything so crisp and clear as a decision:

> They recommend, advise, confer, draw up budgets, testify, develop plans, write guidelines, report, supervise, propose legislation, assist, meet, train, consult – but decide? It is not a concept that seems to describe aptly the flux of activities that engage officials even on the top rungs of complex organizations.

In government departments, as in most large organizations, the authority for making decisions rarely rests with one person or in one office. There is no single, authoritative decision-maker (Lynn, 1977). The fragmentation of powers and responsibilities ensures that, on most occasions, many people in many offices are involved. Proposals entering this system are subject to modification, amendment and redrafting as they meet up with criticism and opposition from the different constituencies of interest encountered on the way and in the light of the compromises and accommodations reached as a result.

In this slow and cumbersome process the participants themselves are usually not fully aware of the influence they have. Often they lose sight of the connection between their contribution and what eventually happens. Even top officials may feel they do little more than rubber-stamp what others have decided. By the time proposals arrive on their desk so much spadework on the detail may have been done by the ranks below as to leave them with only limited room for manoeuvre. It is not uncommon for the staff of field agencies to feel so hemmed in by the regulations, requirements, instructions and guidelines issued by headquarters as to believe they exercise no choice or discretion over their work, while at the same time top management bemoan how the actions (or inaction) of field staff frustrate or undo their plans. All these facts bear witness to the pervasive sense among office-holders at virtually every level that the 'real' decisions are made elsewhere.

Weiss suggests that all this goes to show how our image of decision-making *as an event* provides only a highly stylized version of reality. Only rarely do officials get together at one time and one place to contrive anything so final and concrete as a decision. More commonly, myriad apparently disjointed actions initiated by different people at different times slowly coalesce to form what is afterwards put down as a decision. Small things with seemingly small consequences (like writing a memo, answering an enquiry, editing a minute, tabling a report) over a period of time gradually foreclose options and limit the range of possibilities until almost imperceptibly, without conscious deliberation, a decision is framed. We might say, after Weiss, that decisions are not made: they accrete.

Much the same can be said about the policy-making process as a whole. The impression given by the problem-solving model, for example, of policy evolving through a succession of orderly stages from problem definition to policy choice belies the truth:

> Looking at specific real-life policies we cannot find stages in which problems are defined, the alternatives analysed, then benefits and costs weighed, then 'the' decision made. Everything not only *seems* to be going on at once, it is. (Heclo and Rein, 1980)

Heclo and Rein (ibid.) pinpoint seven different dimensions which make up the policy process:

1 *Ferment* – marking a general state of readiness or concern.
2 *Conceptualization* – when issues begin to slot into focus.
3 *Translation* – when their implications for action are considered.
4 *Assessment or bargaining* – where the participants weigh and argue over options and alternatives.
5 *Construction* – or the piecing together of concrete proposals.
6 *Decision* – the emergence of a commitment to a particular course of action.
7 *Feedback* – when the commitment is publicly acknowledged.

The point stressed by Heclo and Rein is that these features of the policy process are not sequential steps or stages. They may all be happening at once, or participants may jump backwards and forwards from one to another. Indeed, the process may even begin with a public commitment to a particular course of action only to be followed afterwards by the work of mobilizing opinion in favour of change, building up a consensus and sorting out the details. (Mrs Thatcher's approach to the abolition of the rating system and the reform of local government finance is a case in point.)

The purist and problem-solving models also present policy-making as essentially a deliberative process, whereas in fact policies often emerge in ways that bear little resemblance to any such textbook schema. Weiss (1986), for instance, points to eight different 'routes to policy' that do not involve the weighing of evidence, the careful appraisal of options or the assessment of pay-offs:

1 *Reliance on customary rules and procedures* – officials simply follow the book by applying routine formulae to new problems.
2 *Improvization* – policy-makers act off the cuff, fashioning impromptu responses under the press of events.
3 *Mutual adjustment* – lacking any driving sense of purpose, officials merely adapt to decisions made around them.
4 *Repetition* – policy-makers simply repeat the recipes they have tried before in similar situations.
5 *Negotiation* – officials try to work out solutions to problems by a process of bargaining, or give and take, aimed at appeasing contending interests within the bureaucracy.
6 *Move and counter-move* – policy is shaped out of the organizational games played by offices, agencies and departments as they compete for resources, status and power.
7 *A window for solutions* – sometimes solutions chase problems and partisans will actively seek out opportunities for trying their patent remedies.
8 *Indirection* – policy emerges as the unintended consequence of actions taken for other purposes.

The absence of a single, authoritative policy-maker, the elusiveness of decisions, and the twists and turns of the policy process have one important repercussion: they leave no obvious point of entry for research. The slow accretion of decisions through many small uncoordinated steps by staff in scattered offices who have little sense of where they are heading provides few openings for the systematic use of research findings. Equally when policy so often just happens, there may be no inlet for research. For these reasons, the purist and problem-solving models of the relationship between research and policy, and the concept of utilization they invoke, must be rejected. This, however, is not the end of the story, for the arguments advanced above lead us to two further models of the role of research in the policy process and a different understanding of how it is used.

Political and Enlightenment Models of Research

The *political model* holds that in an adversarial system of policy-making research itself becomes a political activity. The policy process comprises different groups, with different interests, in pursuit of different ends. None of these groups usually has the power to impose its way on the others. Inevitably research becomes entangled in the political debate between these constituencies. In this context research information is almost unavoidably partisan information serving to promote some interests and values and to undermine others. An example from my own experience illustrates the point.

As a research officer in a social services department, I had been asked to help the area managers devise a formula for linking their establishment of social workers to the demands and needs of their areas. Up to that time all six area teams had been allocated equal numbers of social workers despite significant differences in the size of their populations – which ranged from 60 000 to 100 000 – and in rates of referrals.

Over a period of several months repeated attempts were made, in collaboration with the area managers themselves, to devise a formula which they could agree based on population, indices of social need, caseload size and referrals. Each time, however, proposals were effectively vetoed by those managers who stood to lose or gain least from them on the grounds that the formula was insensitive to the pressures and demands on their areas.

On different occasions it was argued by different people that the population statistics did not accurately measure the distribution, incidence or gravity of local problems; that the index of need omitted to give adequate weight to features peculiar to their area; that caseload size was an inadequate measure of workload; and that referral rates were suspect because of significant variations between areas in the way they were compiled.

Despite a great deal of research effort, it proved impossible to devise a formula which, viewed from the self-interested perspectives of the area managers, could not be shown to discriminate unfairly against some of them. In the end, the attempt to produce a standardized formula was abandoned in favour of leaving the area managers to argue their own case for having any new posts allocated to their establishment.

Caught up in bureaucratic politics, the research failed to find a solution. But it did provide a focus for the debate, clarify the issues at stake, keep the matter on the agenda and pave the way for an acceptance by the area managers of the principle of differential staffing *on their own terms*.

For policy research to exert any influence it must inevitably be embedded in political struggle. As part of this struggle some factions will seek to discredit it, others will use it as ammunition for their own ends. In this process researchers act as partisans for the value of their research, and as advocates for the insights and findings it generates. Only rarely will they have any direct influence on the outcome of decisions. But their contribution may influence the course or content of the debate over policy by stimulating thinking, injecting new ideas, clarifying the options or colouring the arguments. At this point the political model begins to touch on the enlightenment functions of research.

The *enlightenment model* holds that research feeds into policy through 'the gradual sedimentation of insights, theories, concepts and ways of looking at the world' (Weiss, 1977). Seldom is it used in a direct and instrumental way in the making of policy. Instances where research can be said to have provided 'answers' to problems are few and far between. It is hard to find examples of decisions that might have been different but for the contribution of research. Instead research *creeps* into policy in diffuse ways: by helping to shape policy-makers' perceptions of social reality and their understanding of the possibilities for action.

Reflecting on his experience of evaluation research in the US Department of Health, Education and Welfare (HEW), Lynn (1973) endorses this view:

> It seems to me a mistake to measure the results of evaluation by whether or not it directly produces a policy change. Evaluation findings can affect the thinking of numerous officials . . . and over time become accepted doctrine. Thus the agency's reflexes, if not its overt short-term behaviour, may be profoundly conditioned by evaluation results. This has been the case at HEW, where today's conventional wisdom about the strengths and weaknesses of HEW programs is often based on yesterday's evaluations, which have had their effect on official thought more by osmosis than by conscious confrontations with the evidence itself.

There is, then, usually no moment of impact, only a slow process of osmosis (reminiscent, according to Thomas (1985) of the passage of water through limestone) by which research seeps into the thinking of policy-makers.

This explains why policy-makers, when asked, frequently say they make use of research but are unable to cite examples showing when and how (Weiss, 1980). Once absorbed, they cannot then unravel it from knowledge acquired from other sources. In terms of the enlightenment thesis, therefore, research is useful for its ideas as much as for the specific data it provides. The diffusion of these ideas into the world of policy can subtly alter the parameters of debate and the angle of vision from which policy-makers view their task. In this way, research may stimulate fresh thinking and open up new ways of looking at things which give a new emphasis and direction to the conduct of policy.

Summary

For social scientists who have looked to make a direct input into policy, and for officials who have looked to them for policy-relevant research, the last twenty-five years have been soured by frustrations. Hence the rocky state of the relationship between social science and government. It has proved difficult to harness an independent, theoretical and critical social science to the constraints of the policy process. Generally speaking, social science research has percolated into policy only in diffuse ways. The only way, it seems, to ensure that research is both *manageable* and *relevant* to the practical administration of social affairs is for it to be disciplined by the demands of policy. This is where policy research, as opposed to disciplinary research, comes in. Chapter 10 spells out some of the characteristics of research geared specifically to the development of policy rather than the advancement of knowledge.

10 Criteria for policy research

'In so far as sociology has a crisis to face it lies precisely in our failure to work out a relationship between ourselves and the domain of public action which could satisfactorily replace the lost innocence of positivism.' (Philip Abrams, 1981)

'No Testimony is sufficient to establish a Miracle, unless the Testimony be of such a kind, that its Falshood would be more miraculous, than the Fact, which it endeavours to establish.' (David Hume)

A key theme running throughout this book has been the underdevelopment of social planning. Part I set the scene. The failure of governments to pursue a co-ordinated approach to the making and execution of social policies was attributed to the social division of planning. The social division of planning describes the fragmentation of powers and responsibilities within the government machine and in society as a whole. It creates problems of information and collaboration that choke strategic thinking, lead to piecemeal ways of working and generally sustain an incrementalist bias within the policy process. Overcoming these problems, it was argued, in order to develop a more coherent framework for the determination of social priorities, calls for better social information about trends and changes in society, about social needs and problems, about the impact of social policies and about the effectiveness of social programmes. Such improved mechanisms of social monitoring and reporting, in turn, require that research should be integrated more closely into the policy-making process. The inadequacy of the information available to social policy-makers was illustrated by comparison with the sophistication of the national economic accounts and statistics, and its consequences traced in terms of the subordination of social goals to economic objectives.

Broadly speaking, the argument in Part I may be summarized in the words of the Fulton Committee (1968) on the civil service. Research, it declared, is 'the indispensable basis of proper planning'.

Part II of the book then turned to looking at the problems of integrating research and policy. This was done through a series of case studies, mainly focusing on American experience. There are sound reasons for crossing the Atlantic in search of examples. The USA has been the most ambitious and systematic of all Western nations in its efforts to harness the social sciences to the business of government, and to make use of social science knowledge in tackling the problems of society. The five case studies presented in Part II may almost be seen as a history of relations between social science and government in the USA over the past twenty-five years. A characteristic feature of this relationship has been its openness. What initiatives have been taken are well documented, unlike the UK where the blanket of official secrecy hides so much from view.

What lessons do the case studies reveal? Much of their interest is in the detail, and this has already been told. Drawing out the common threads running through them all, however, leads us to a number of general points:

- There is no ready-made market for social science information within the policy process.
- Research is not easily integrated into bureaucratic routines.
- There seems to be a definite limit to the capacity of government departments to make use of research, especially when it is critical of the status quo.
- The politics of research often loom much larger than is allowed for in its design.
- There is a potential for conflict between the standards of scientific excellence and the demands of policy relevance.
- Research for policy must be designed around the user's information needs and not the knowledge-building aims of the academic community.

Taken together, the message conveyed is that disciplinary research in the academic mould does not transplant easily into the policy setting. Put another way they suggest, adopting a distinction made by Kogan and Henkel (1983), that the requirements of 'policy-driven research' (aimed at improving decision-making) are not the same as those of 'internally-driven science' (aimed at advancing knowledge). These different tasks call for a different style of research.

Academic social science cannot provide as a matter of routine the kind of research that policy-makers require, *nor should it try*. It cannot do so, as we have seen in Chapter 9, for a medley of reasons, but chiefly because it is not disciplined by the same constraints as policy and because the pull of incentives within the academic community leads away from an action frame of reference. It should not try because there is a need for an independent, theoretical and critical social science.

Single-minded attention to the requirements of policy relevance would tie social science too closely to the short-term, partisan and often self-serving interests of policy-makers. As Lord Rothschild (1982) stressed in his enquiry into the Social Science Research Council, there is a class of research (including, notably, research subversive of existing policies) for which no suitable customer exists within government, but which ought to be done in the public interest if serious consequences for the nation are to be avoided. Townsend (1981) has argued forcefully that the relative subservience of research interests to bureaucratic interests has restricted the interpretation of the role of social policy to the advantage of administrative élites and the governing classes.

Alternative sources of information and analysis about the condition of society must be maintained in order to guard against the monopolization of knowledge by government and its manipulation in the interests of the state. Chapter 3 of this book has shown how official social statistics are vulnerable to such manipulation. Already there is a worrying concentration of research funds in the hands of government and evidence to suggest that this power is being used to influence what is studied and how, and to link research more directly to government priorities (Willmott, 1980). An independent social science is required to subject the official version of reality to continuous, critical scrutiny and to sustain an informed public opinion outside the circles of official administration.

All this leads, then, to the conclusion that integrating research and policy is not just a matter of building bridges between policy-makers in government and social scientists and researchers outside (mainly working in academic settings). Policy-forming research should be kept separate from knowledge-building research. There is a difference between research *for* policy and research *on* policy; between the role of the policy analyst and the role of the academic social scientist.

Merton (1949) recognized long ago that the intellectual (let us say social researcher) working for policy-makers in a bureaucracy 'is in time compelled to accept new criteria of significance'. The findings from the case studies reported in Part II accord with this judgement. As a way of winding up the discussion and bringing this book to a close, we might usefully spell out some of these criteria by extracting them from the case studies and presenting them in their own right as what might properly be called 'criteria for policy research'.

Criteria for Policy Research

Policy research is 'good enough research': research that provides *enough* information with a *sufficient* level of confidence to illuminate the options and choices facing the policy-maker. Accuracy and precision therefore are defined relative to the questions being asked and the kind of information required rather than by reference to external standards of scientific rigour. In much the same way as decision-makers 'satisfice' rather than 'optimize' (Simon, 1957), so policy-makers look for research that is 'good enough' for the job in hand rather than scientifically authoritative.

Policy researchers are required to see and formulate problems not from a disciplinary perspective, but from the perspective of the policy-maker.

'Relevant' research is research that answers the real questions occupying policy-makers. As Weiss (1978) says, the 'pivotal phase in developing relevant research is framing the questions. The most important choice is to decide: whose questions?' Policy research must demonstrate its responsiveness to the information needs of its end-users.

Policy research calls for the active involvement of end-users in all stages of the project: from the beginning phase when questions are formulated; through the design phase when decisions are made about what sort of information should be collected and how; to the end phase when reporting procedures are decided and recommendations are drawn up.

The greater the involvement of policy researchers with their target audience, the more likely it is their research will be used. Patton (1984) has explained why:

> Involving identified decision makers and information users in measurement and design decisions is based on the assumption that utilization is enhanced if users believe in and have a stake in the data. Belief in the data is increased by understanding it; understanding is enhanced by involvement in the painstaking process of making decisions about what data to collect, how to collect it, and how to analyze it. Decision makers who acquiesce to the expertise of the evaluator may find later that they neither understand nor believe in the evaluation data. By the same token, evaluators can expect low utilization if they rely on the mysticism of their scientific priesthood to establish the credibility of data rather than on the understanding of decision makers directly involved with it.

In short, people who have been involved in the collection, processing and weighing of evidence are more likely to feel they have a stake in the outcome.

Policy research is most likely to influence decisions when it accepts the values, assumptions, objectives and categories of discourse of policy-makers.

There are important political limits to the utility of research that is devised, undertaken, reported and considered other than in a fairly close and continuous relationship with operational necessity and the experience and responsibilities attached to it. Only rarely is there a customer for research that does not impinge directly on organizational concerns.

The plausibility of data to its users is just as important as its scientific robustness.

The quality of policy research is not primarily a methodological issue. Good policy research must aim to be useful, understandable, relevant, timely and practical. Technical adequacy alone does not ensure usefulness; usefulness cannot be taken for granted. It has to be planned for and built into the design of studies as an essential aspect of their methodology. Policy research need not be authoritative to be useful.

Options on rigour should be explored. How much is enough? How much can we afford? How much can be accommodated in the time available? The requirements of methodological rigour are not easily reconciled with those of policy relevance, and frequently some sort of judicious trade-off may be called for in the interests of utility and effectiveness.

Policy researchers should operate within the confines of their techniques while being flexible and imaginative in their choice of methods. They must learn to take their cue from policy-makers. Complex statistical designs and analyses put policy-makers at the mercy of the researcher's interpretation. This may demand more trust than they are prepared to give. Where policy-makers are not versed in the methodology being used, a broker may be needed to ensure effective communication (Rich, 1975).

Policy research must not outstrip the comprehension of policy-makers or their capacity to use it. Research is rarely worth while unless it is understood and wanted by its clients.

Policy research should be looked on more as a *process* than a product. Research comprises four phases, each of which may contribute independently to the making of policy: discussing and articulating the issues and problems and framing the questions; collecting the data; producing the report of the findings; and disseminating the results. Traditional academic research has generally conceived its contribution to policy in terms only of producing a report (the product). Policy research pays attention to the opportunities for learning and discovery presented by the first two phases and the need for carefully planning the dissemination of the results.

In the cut and thrust of bureaucratic politics the rectitude of analysis sometimes has to give way to the reality of expedience.

Policy research is no substitute for political judgement which often involves considerations beyond the scope of analysis. Often it may only reveal rather than resolve the choices that have to be made.

In the hurly-burly of the policy process all research is politically charged and may be transformed into just another tool of advocacy.

Knowledge without the concomitant power to act is potentially threatening to governments. Policy researchers should concentrate on issues and problems that policy-makers can do something about, on conditions that can be altered, on variables that can be manipulated and on solutions that are judged to be politically credible.

Policy research that points to conclusions which are counter-intuitive is unlikely to travel very far. The further removed research conclusions are from mainstream opinion, the less likely are they to influence policy in the short run.

Policy researchers must be prepared to accept political assumptions different from their own and to continue working constructively in a context defined by such assumptions.

Policy is about more urgent matters than research and will not wait on definitive analysis.

Research must not outrun the urgency of decisions. Partial information available at the time of decision is better than no information or late information.

The further in the future the research is focused, the less relevant it is to immediate issues; and the more remote its usefulness, the smaller is the constituency who will pay it any heed.

Policy research usually has to be reported on differently from academic research. Although utilization can never be guaranteed, it is more likely if careful attention is given to the information needs of its potential users. Planning for dissemination should be part of the study design.

Reports should be brief, non-technical and free from jargon.

Wherever possible, they should seek to translate findings into recommendations.

Dissemination should not be regarded merely as the end-phase of a study. It should be part of a continuous process of discussion, feedback and review between researchers and their clients that goes on throughout the project.

The mode of dissemination should be determined by the needs and characteristics of the users. Different types of report (summary, technical, popular, comprehensive, issue-specific, etc.) may be required for different audiences. Oral and audio-visual methods of reporting (lecture presentations, seminar-type discussions, personal briefings) may be more effective than the written word.

Finally, policy researchers who follow these criteria and still find their work has little impact should not lose heart, remembering that while it is right for them to believe in the value of what they do it is arrogance to have too much faith in its importance.

Bibliography

This bibliography includes all citations in the text together with other sources used in the preparation of this book but not directly referenced.

Aaron, H. (1978), 'Testimony before the Senate Committee on Human Resources: hearings on program evaluation, Oct. 6 and 27', *Evaluation and Change* (special issue), 15–17.

Abel-Smith, B. (1966), *Labour's Social Plans*, London: Fabian Tract 369.

Abrams, P. (1981), 'The collapse of British sociology?', in P. Abrams, R. Deem, J. Finch and P. Rock (eds), *Practice and Progress: British Sociology 1950–1980*, London: Allen and Unwin.

Abt, C.C. (1976), *The Evaluation of Social Programs*, Beverly Hills, Calif.: Sage.

Abt, C.C. (1979), 'Government constraints on evaluation quality', in L. Datta and R. Perloff (eds), *Improving Evaluations*, Beverly Hills, Calif.: Sage.

Aldrich, H. (1972), 'An organization–environment perspective on co-operation and conflict between organizations in the manpower training system', in A. Negandhi (ed.), *Conflict and Power in Complex Organizations*, Ohio: Kent State University.

Alexander, T. (1972), 'The social engineers retreat under fire', *Fortune*, October, 132–148.

Ares, C., Rankin, A. and Sturz, H. (1963), 'The Manhattan Bail Project: an interim report on the use of pre-trial parole', *New York University Law Review*, 38, 67–95.

Arkava, M. and Lane, T. (1983), *Beginning Social Work Research*, London: Allyn and Bacon.

Ashworth, J.M. (1982), 'On the giving and receiving of advice (in Whitehall and Salford)', *Manchester Statistical Society*, 1–14.

Association of Learned Societies in the Social Sciences (1986), *ALSISS Reports*, 10, May, 2.

Bains Report (1972), *The New Local Authorities: Management and Structure*, London: HMSO.

Ball, R. (chairman) (1978), *Report of the Committee on Policy*

Optimisation (Cmnd 7148), London: HMSO, March.

Ball, S. and Bogatz, G. (1970), *The First Year of Sesame Street: An Evaluation*, Princeton, NJ: Educational Testing Service.

Banks, G. (1979), 'Programme budgeting in the DHSS', in T. Booth (1979b).

Barrett, S. and Fudge, C. (eds) (1981), *Policy and Action: Essays on the Implementation of Public Policy*, London: Methuen.

Batten, P. (1977), 'National income: the accounting framework', *National Income and Economic Policy*, Unit 2, D284, Milton Keynes: The Open University.

Bauer, R. (1966), *Social Indicators*, American Academy of Arts and Sciences, Cambridge, Mass.: MIT Press.

Bell, C. and Newby, H. (1977), *Doing Sociological Research*, London: Allen and Unwin.

Bell, D. (ed.) (1967), Towards the Year 2000, *Daedalus*, Summer.

Benjamin, B. (1973), 'Research strategies in social services departments of local authorities in Great Britain', *Journal of Social Policy*, 2(1), 13–26.

Benson, J. (1975), 'The interorganisational network as a political economy', *Administrative Science Quarterly*, 20, 229–249.

Berger, S. (1980), 'Introduction', in Organization for Economic Co-operation and Development, *The Utilization of the Social Sciences in Policy Making in the United States*, Paris: OECD.

Bernstein, I. and Freeman, H. (1975), *Academic and Entrepreneurial Research*, New York: Russell Sage.

Berthoud, R. (ed.) (1985), *Challenges to Social Policy*, Aldershot: Gower.

Blau, P. (1964), *Exchange and Power in Social Life*, New York: Wiley.

Blume, S. (1979), 'Policy studies and social policy in Britain', *Journal of Social Policy*, 8(3), July, 311–344.

Blume, S. (1982), *The Commissioning of Social Research by Central Government*, London: SSRC.

Bogatz, G. and Ball, S. (1971), *The Second Year of Sesame Street: A Continuing Evaluation*, Princeton, NJ: Educational Testing Service, Vols 1 and 2.

Booth, A. and Coats, A. (1978), 'The market for economists in Britain, 1946–75: a preliminary survey', *Economic Journal*, 88, September, 436–453.

Booth, T. (1979a), 'Research and policy making in local authority social services', *Public Administration*, 57, Summer, 173–186.

Booth, T. (ed.) (1979b), *Planning for Welfare*, Oxford: Blackwell/Robertson.

Booth, T. (1981a), 'Collaboration between the health and social services: pt 1, a case study of joint care planning', *Policy and Politics*, 9(1), 23–49.

Booth, T. (1981b), 'The big cover-up of social realities', *Community Care*, 373, 16–17.

Booth, T. (1986) 'Social research and policy relevance', *Research, Policy and Planning*, 4(1–2), 15–18.

Boruch, R. (1974), 'Bibliography: illustrated randomised field experiments for program planning and evaluation', *Evaluation*, 2(1), 83–87.

Boruch, R., McSweeny, A. and Soderstrom, E. (1978), 'Randomised field experiments for program development and evaluation: an illustrative bibliography', *Evaluation Quarterly*, 4, 455–695.

Botein, B. (1965), 'The Manhattan Bail Project: its impact on criminology and the criminal law process', *Texas Law Review*, 43, 319–331.

Boulding, K. (1958), *The Skills of the Economist*, London: Hamish Hamilton.

Boulding, K. (1967), 'Dare we take the social sciences seriously?', *American Behavioral Scientist*, June, 12.

Braybrooke, D. and Lindblom, C. (1963), *A Strategy of Decision*, New York: The Free Press.

Brayfield, A.H. (1967), 'Inquiry on federally sponsored social research', *American Psychologist*, 22 November, 877.

Breton, A. (1974), *The Economic Theory of Representative Government*, London: Macmillan.

Brittan, S. (1975), 'The economic contradictions of democracy', *British Journal of Political Science*, April, 5, 129–159.

Broadfoot, P. and Nisbet, J. (1980), *The Impact of Research on Policy and Practice in Education*, Aberdeen: Aberdeen University Press.

Brown, M. and Madge, N. (1982), *Despite the Welfare State*, London: Heinemann.

Bruce, R. (1972), 'What goes wrong with evaluation and how to prevent it', *Human Needs* (US Department of Health, Education and Welfare), 1(1), 10–11.

Brush, L. (1983), *The Short-Term Policy Evaluation: A Responsive Evaluation Strategy in a Political Context*, Washington, DC: US Department of Health and Human Services, Evaluation Documentation Center.

Buchanan, G. and Wholey, J. (1972), 'Federal level evaluation', *Evaluation*, Fall, 17–22.

Bulmer, M. (1978), 'Gulf between research and policy', *Times Higher Education Supplement*, 7 July.

Bulmer, M. (1982), *The Uses of Social Research: Social Investigation in Public Policy-Making*, London: Allen and Unwin.

Bulmer, M. (1985), 'The influence of research on policy: how do they relate?, *Research, Policy and Planning*, 3(2), 13–18.

Bunker, D. (1978), 'Organizing to link social science with public policy-making', *Public Administration Review*, May–June, 223–232.

Burns, S. (1975), *The Household Economy*, Boston, Mass.: Beacon Press.

Campbell, D. (1969), 'Reforms as experiments', *American Psychologist*, 24(4), April, 409–429.

Caplan, N. (1975), 'The use of social science information by federal executives', in G. Lyons (ed.), *Social Research and Public Policies*, Hanover, NH: Public Affairs Center, Dartmouth College.

Carley, M. (1981), *Social Measurement and Social Indicators*, London: Allen and Unwin.

Carlson, J. (1969), 'The status and next steps for planning, programming and budgeting', in Joint Economic Committee, *The Analysis and Evaluation of Public Expenditures: The PPB System*, Subcommittee on Economy in Government, 91st Congress, 1st session, Washington, DC: US Government Printing Office.

Central Policy Review Staff (CPRS) (1973), 'Demonstrating the client group approach: socially disadvantaged children', October.

Central Policy Review Staff (1975), *A Joint Framework for Social Policies*, London: HMSO.

Central Policy Review Staff (1977), *Relations Between Central Government and Local Authorities*, London: HMSO.

Chadwin, M. (1975), 'The nature of legislative program evaluation', *Evaluation*, 2(2), 45–49.

Chapman, R. (1975), 'The role of central or departmental policy and planning units: recent developments in Britain', *Public Administration* (Sydney), 34(2), 144–155.

Chelimsky, E. (1978), 'Testimony before the Senate Committee on Human Resources: hearings on program evaluation, Oct. 6 and 27, 1977', *Evaluation and Change* (special issue), 15–17.

Chelimsky, E. (1983), 'The definition and measurement of evaluation quality as a management tool', in R. St Pierre (ed.), *Management and Organization of Program Evaluation*, San Francisco, Calif.: Jossey-Bass.

Chelimsky, E. (1985), 'Linking program evaluation to user needs', in *The Politics of Program Evaluation*, Sage Yearbook in Politics and Public Policy, San Francisco, Calif.: Jossey-Bass.

Cherns, A. (1976), 'Behavioural science engagements: taxonomy and dynamics', *Human Relations*, 29(10), 905–910.

Cherns, A. (1986), 'Policy research under scrutiny', in F. Heller (ed.), *The Use and Abuse of Social Science*, London: Sage.

Coates, D. (1976), 'Politicians and the sorcerer: the problems of governing with capitalism in crisis', in A. King (ed.), *Why Is Britain Becoming Harder to Govern?*, London: BBC Publications.

Cohen, W. (1968), 'Social indicators: statistics for public policy', *American Statistician*, 22(4), October, 14–16.

Cohen, D. and Weiss, J. (1977), 'Social science and social policy: schools and race', *Educational Forum*, 41, May, 393–413.

Conyers, D. (1982), *An Introduction to Social Planning in the Third World*, Chichester: Wiley.

Cook, T., Appleton, H., Conner, R., Shaffer, A., Tamkin, G. and Weber, S. (1975), *Sesame Street Revisited*, New York: Russell Sage.

Crawford, M. and Jacobs, E. (1981), 'How 364 economists said the patient was sick but couldn't agree on the cure', *Sunday Times*, 5 April.

Cronbach, L., Ambron, S., Dornbusch, S., Hess, R., Hornick, R., Phillips, D., Walker, D. and Weiner, S. (1980), *Toward Reform of Program Evaluation*, San Francisco, Calif.: Jossey-Bass.

Crossman, R. (1967), *Socialism and Planning*, Fabian Tract 375, May.

Crowther-Hunt, Lord (1977), 'Civil service reform', Memorandum submitted to the Expenditure Committee (General Subcommittee), Eleventh Report from the Expenditure Committee, *Civil Service*, Session 1976–77, Vol. III.

Crozier, M. (1975), *The Crisis of Democracy*, New York: New York University Press.

Cunliffe, S. (1980), 'Response to the Presidential Address to the Royal Statistical Society', *Journal of the Royal Statistical Society*, series A, 143(1), 29–31.

Davies, V. (1982), Letters to the Editor, *Guardian*, 6 April.

Davis, J., Jr (ed.) (1969), *Politics, Programs and Budgets*, Englewood Cliffs, NJ: Prentice-Hall.

DHSS (1973), *A Report from the Working Party on Collaboration between the NHS and Local Government on its Activities to the End of 1972*, London: HMSO.

DHSS (1974a), 'Collaboration between health and local authorities', NHS Reorganisation Circular HRC(74)19, March.

DHSS (1974b), *Report of the Working Party on Social Work Support for the Health Service*, London: HMSO, June.

DHSS (1976), *Priorities for Health and Personal Social Services in England: A Consultative Document*. London: HMSO.

DHSS (1980a), *Review of the Government Statistical Services: Report of the DHSS Study Team*, June 1980 (available from DHSS, Information Division, Canons Park, Government Buildings,

Honeypot Lane, Stanmore HA7 1AR).

DHSS (1980b), *The Government's White Papers on Public Expenditure: The Social Services* (Cmnd 8086), Reply by the Government to the Third Report from the Social Services Committee, Session 1979–80, London: HMSO.

DHSS (1981), *Public Expenditure on the Social Services* (Cmnd 8464), Reply by the Government to the Third Report of the Select Committee on Social Services, Session 1980–81, London: HMSO: December.

DHSS (1982), *Public Expenditure on the Social Services* (Cmnd 8775), Reply by the Government to the Second Report from the Select Committee on the Social Services, Session 1981–82, London: HMSO.

DHSS (1983), *Health Service Development: Care in the Community and Joint Finance*, HC(83)6/LAC(83)5.

DHSS (1984), *Public Expenditure on the Social Services* (Cmnd 9414), Reply by the Government to the Fourth Report from the Select Committee on Social Services, Session 1983–84, London: HMSO.

Dean, M. (1979), 'Society tomorrow', *The Guardian*, 28 November, 17.

Donnison, D. (1975a), *An Approach to Social Policy*, National Economic and Social Council, Dublin: The Stationery Office.

Donnison, D. (1975b), 'Ideologies and policies', *Journal of Social Policy*, 1, II.

Donnison, D. (1982), *The Politics of Poverty*, Oxford: Martin Robertson.

Douglas, J. (1976), 'Review article: the overloaded crown', *British Journal of Political Science*, 6, 483–505.

Drew, E.B. (1967), 'PPBS: its scope and limits: (2), HEW grapples with PPBS', *Public Interest*, 8, 9–29.

Drewnowski, J. (1971), 'The practical significance of social information', *The Annals*, 393, January.

Edwards, W. and Guttentag, M. (1975), 'Experiments and evaluations: a re-examination', in C. Bennett and A. Lumsdaine (eds), *Evaluation and Experiment*, New York: Academic Press.

Eisner, R. (1970), 'Measurement and analysis of national income (nonincome income)' in National Bureau of Economic Research, *50th Annual Report*, September.

Else, P. and Marshall, G. (1981), 'The unplanning of public expenditure: recent problems in expenditure planning and the consequences of cash limits', *Public Administration*, 59, Autumn, 253–278.

Engquist, C.L. (1970), 'PPBS: an operating agency view', in E. Schwartz (ed.), *Planning, Programming and Budgeting Systems and Social Welfare*, Chicago: School of Social Service Administration, University of Chicago.

Etzioni, A. (1977), 'Social science in the White House', *Evaluation*, 4, 13.

Evaluation Research Society (1980), *Standards for Program Evaluation*, Exposure Draft, May.

Eversley, D. (1983), 'Social science on trial', in C. Jones and J. Stevenson (eds), *The Yearbook of Social Policy 1982*, London: Routledge and Kegan Paul.

Fay, B. (1975), *Social Theory and Political Practice*, London: Allen and Unwin.

Ferge, Z. (1979), *A Society in the Making: Hungarian Social and Societal Policy 1945–75*, Harmondsworth: Penguin.

Ferriss, A. (1979), 'The US federal effort in developing social indicators', *Social Indicators Research*, 6, April, 129–152.

Field, F. (1981), *Inequality in Britain: Freedom, Welfare and the State*, London: Fontana.

Freeman, H.E. (1975), 'Evaluation research and public policies', in G. Lyons (ed.), *Social Research and Public Policies*, Hanover, NH: Public Affairs Center, Dartmouth College.

Fulton Committee (1968), *The Civil Service* (Cmnd 3638), Report of the Committee 1966–68, London: HMSO, Vol. 1.

Galbraith, J. (1978), 'The trouble with economists', *New Republic*, 14 January, 15–21.

Gans, H. (1972), *People and Plans*, Harmondsworth: Penguin.

Garrett, J. (1972), *The Management of Government*, Harmondsworth: Penguin Books.

Garrett, J. (1980), *Managing the Civil Service*, London: Heinemann.

General Accounting Office (1973), *Program Evaluation: Legislative Language and a Users' Guide to Selected Sources*, Washington, DC: GAO.

General Accounting Office (1977), *Finding Out How Programs Are Working: Suggestions for Congressional Oversight*, Report to the Congress by the Comptroller-General of the United States, PAD-78-3, Washington, DC: GAO, 22 November.

General Accounting Office (1978), *Assessing Social Program Impact Evaluation: A Checklist Approach*, Exposure Draft, PAD-79-2, Washington, DC: GAO, October.

General Accounting Office (1984), *Designing Evaluations*, Methodology Transfer Paper 4, Program Evaluation and Methodology Division, Washington, DC: GAO, July.

Gilbert, J., Light, R. and Mosteller, F. (1975), 'Assessing social innovations: an empirical base for policy', in C. Bennett and

A. Lumsdaine (eds), *Evaluation and Experiment*, New York: Academic Press.

Glennerster, H. (1975), *Social Service Budgets and Social Policy*, London: Allen and Unwin.

Glennerster, H. (1976), *Labour's Social Priorities*, London: Fabian Research Series 327.

Glennerster, H. (1980), 'Prime cuts: public expenditure and social services planning in a hostile environment', *Policy and Politics*, 8(4), 367–382.

Godber, G. (1983), 'Is this the right prescription?' Interview with Melanie Phillips, *Guardian*, 12 October.

Goldstein, M., Marcus, A. and Perkins Rausch, N. (1978), 'The nonutilization of evaluation research', *Pacific Sociological Review*, 21(1), 21–44.

Gorham, W. (1967), 'PPBS: its scope and limits – notes of a practitioner', *Public Interest*, 8, 9–29.

Gottlieb, D. (1969), 'Social science and social policy: an introduction to a symposium', *Social Science Quarterly*, 50(3), December.

Gough, I. (1979), *The Political Economy of the Welfare State*, London: Macmillan.

Gouldner, A. (1970), *The Coming Crisis of Western Sociology*, London: Heinemann.

Gray, A. and Jenkins, B. (1983a), *Policy Analysis and Evaluation in British Government*, London: Royal Institute of Public Administration.

Gray, A. and Jenkins, B. (1983b), 'The state of policy analysis and evaluation in government', in A. Gray and B. Jenkins, *Policy Analysis and Evaluation in British Government*, London: Royal Institute of Public Administration.

Gray, A. and Jenkins, B. (1983c), 'Retreat or tactical redeployment? The fate of policy analysis and evaluation in government', in A. Gray and B. Jenkins, *Policy Analysis and Evaluation in British Government*, London: Royal Institute of Public Administration.

Green, P. (1971), 'The obligations of American social scientists', *The Annals*, 394, March, 13–27.

Gross, B. (ed.) (1965), 'The social state of the union', *Trans-Action*, November–December, 14–17.

Gross, B. (ed.) (1967a), 'Social goals and indicators for American society', *Annals of the American Academy of Political and Social Science*, 1, 371, May.

Gross, B. (ed.) (1967b), 'Social goals and indicators for American society', *Annals of the American Academy of Political and Social Science*, 2, 373, September.

Gross, B. and Springer, M. (1967), 'A new orientation in American government', in B. Gross (ed.), *Annals of the American Academy of Political and Social Science*, 1, 371, May.

Gross, B. and Straussman, J. (1974), 'The social indicators movement', *Social Policy*, September–October, 43–54.

Grosse, R. (1970), 'The planning programming budgeting system in the federal government: a planner's view', in E. Schwartz (ed.), *Planning, Programming and Budgeting Systems and Social Welfare*, Chicago: School of Social Service Administration, University of Chicago.

Guttentag, M. (1978), 'Testimony before the Senate Committee on Human Resources: hearings on program evaluation, Oct. 6 and 27', *Evaluation and Change* (special issue), 15–17.

Guttentag, M. and Soar, S. (1977), *Evaluation Studies Review Annual*, London: Sage, Vol. 2.

Haldane Committee (1918), *Report of the Machinery of Government Committee of the Ministry of Reconstruction* (Cmnd 9230), London: HMSO.

Harper, E., Kramer, F. and Rouse, A. (1969), 'Implementation and use of PPB in sixteen federal agencies', *Public Administration Review*, 29, November–December, 623–632.

Haveman, R. (1970), 'Public expenditures and policy analysis: an overview', in R. Haveman and J. Margolis (eds) (1970).

Haveman, R. and Margolis, J. (eds) (1970), *Public Expenditures and Policy Analysis*, Chicago: Rand McNally.

Heath, E. (1970), 'Personal foreword', *Conservative Election Manifesto*, May.

Heath, E. and Barker, A. (1978), 'Heath on Whitehall reform', *Parliamentary Affairs*, Autumn, 363–390.

Heclo, H. (1977), 'A question of priorities', *Humanist*, 37, March–April, 21–24.

Heclo, H. and Rein, M. (1980), 'Social science and negative income taxation', in Organization for Economic Co-operation and Development, *The Utilization of the Social Sciences in Policy Making in the United States*, Paris: OECD.

Heclo, H. and Wildavsky, A. (1981), *The Private Government of Public Money* (2nd edn), London: Macmillan.

Held, V. (166), 'PPBS comes to Washington', *Public Interest*, 39, 102–115.

Heller, F. (ed.) (1986), *The Use and Abuse of Social Science*, London: Sage.

Hencke, D. (1982), 'Society tomorrow: losing the cold war', *Guardian*, 3 March.

Hennessy, P., Morrison, S. and Townsend, R. (1985), *Routine Punctuated by Orgies: The Central Policy Review Staff, 1970–83*,

Strathclyde Papers on Government and Politics No. 31, Glasgow: University of Strathclyde.

Heseltine, M. (1979), 'Why we must curb the bureaucrats', *Sunday Times*, 16 December.

Heyworth Committee (1965), *Report of the Committee on Social Studies* (Cmnd 2660), London: HMSO.

Higgins, J. (1980), 'The unfulfilled promise of policy research', *Social Policy and Administration*, 14(3), Autumn, 195–208.

Hill, M. (1982), 'Street level bureaucracy in social work and social services departments', in J. Lishman (ed.), *Social Work Departments as Organisations*, Research Highlights No. 4, University of Aberdeen, July.

Hogg, S. (1982), 'Think-tank gains a chief but hankers after good old days', *Sunday Times*, 7 March.

Holland, S. and Omerod, P. (1979), 'Why we must increase public spending', *New Society*, 25 January, 193–194.

Hom, R. (1978), 'Government take-over of the social indicators movement', *Social Indicators Research*, 5, 365–367.

Hope, K. (1978), 'Indicators of the state of society', in M. Bulmer (ed.), *Social Policy Research*, London: Macmillan.

Horowitz, I. and Rainwater, L. (1967), 'Social accounting for the nation', *Trans-Action*, May, 2–3.

House of Commons (1979–80), Fourth Report from the Treasury and Civil Service Committee, *Civil Service Manpower Reductions*, Session 1979–80, HC712-I, Report, HC712-II, Minutes of Evidence and Appendices.

House of Commons (1980–1), Third Report from the Social Services Committee, *Public Expenditure on the Social Services*, Vol. I, Report HC324-I, Vol. II, Minutes of Evidence and Appendices, HC324-II, London: HMSO.

House of Commons (1981–2), Fifth Report from the Treasury and Civil Service, *The Government Expenditure Plans 1982–83 to 1984–85*, Session 1981–82, HC316, London: HMSO.

House of Commons (1980), First Report from the Environment Committee, *Enquiry into Implications of Government's Expenditure Plans 1980–81 to 1983–84 for the Housing Policies of the Department of the Environment*, House of Commons Session 1979–80, HC714 and HC578-i.

Hudson, J. and McRoberts, H. (1984), 'Auditing evaluation activities', in L. Rutman (ed.), *Evaluation Research Methods*, Beverly Hills, Calif.: Sage.

Huitt, R. (1969), 'Rationalizing the policy process', *Social Science Quarterly*, 50(3), December, 480–486.

Isserlis, A. (1984), 'The CPRS and after', *Policy Studies*, 4, 3, 22–35.

Jackson, D. (1980), 'Economics, education and the real world', *Lloyd's Bank Review*, October, 42–54.

Jackson, D. (1981), 'Why do we teach economics so badly?', *Guardian*, 10 March.

Jay, P. (1972), 'CPRS: magic circle or fifth wheel?', *The Times*, 21 January.

Joint Committee on Standards for Educational Evaluation (1981), *Standards for Evaluations of Educational Programs, Projects and Materials*, New York: McGraw-Hill.

Joint Economic Committee (1969), *The Analysis and Evaluation of Public Expenditures: The PPB System*, Subcommittee on Economy in Government, 91st Congress, 1st Session, Washington, DC: US Government Printing Office.

Jones, B. (1979), 'Social forecasting in Lucas', *Social Trends*, 9, 20–29.

Juster, F. (1973), 'A framework for the measurement of economic and social performance', in M. Moss (ed.), *The Measurement of Economic and Social Performance*, Studies in Income and Wealth, Vol. 30, New York: Columbia University Press for National Bureau of Economic Research.

Karapin, R. (1986), 'What's the use of social science? A review of the literature', in F. Heller (ed.), *The Use and Abuse of Social Science*, London: Sage.

Kassebaum, G., Ward, D. and Wilner, D. (1971), *Prison Treatment and Parole Survival*, New York: Wiley.

Keegan, W. and Pennant-Rea, R. (1979), *Who Runs the Economy?*, London: Temple Smith.

Keeling, D. (1972), *Management in Government*, London: Allen and Unwin.

Kershaw, D. (1972), 'A negative income tax experiment', *Scientific American*, 227, 19–25.

Kershaw, D. and Fair, J. (1976), *The New Jersey Income Maintenance Experiment*, New York: Academic Press, Vol. 1.

King, A. (1975), 'Overload: problems of governing in the 1970s', *Political Studies*, 23, 162–175.

Klein, R. (1977), 'Democracy, the welfare state and social policy', *Political Quarterly*, 48(4), 448–458.

Kogan, M. and Henkel, M. (1983), *Government and Research*, London: Heinemann.

Kogan, M., Korman, N. and Henkel, M. (1980), *Government's Commissioning of Research: A Case Study*, Hillingdon: Department of Government, Brunel University.

Kopkind, A. (1967), 'The future planners', *New Republic*, 25 February, 19–23.

Kusserow, R. (1986), *Program Inspections: A New Form of Rapid*

Evaluation, Washington, DC: Office of Inspector-General, US Department of Health and Human Services.

Larsen, J. and Nichols, D. (1972), 'If nobody knows you've done it, have you . . .?', *Evaluation*, Fall, 39–44.

Leach, S. (1980), 'Organisational interests and interorganisational behaviour in town planning', *Town Planning Review*, 51(3), 286–299.

Lebergott, S. (1965), *Men Without Work*, New York: Prentice Hall.

Levine, S. and White, P. (1961), 'Exchange as a conceptual framework for the study of interorganizational relationships', *Administrative Science Quarterly*, 5, 583–601.

Lindblom, C. (1959), 'The science of "muddling through"', *Public Administration Review*, 19, 79–99.

Lindblom, C. (1965), *The Intelligence of Democracy*, New York: The Free Press.

Lindblom, C. and Cohen, D. (1979), *Usable Knowledge: Social Science and Social Problem Solving*, London: Yale University Press.

Lipsky, M. (1971), 'Social scientists and the AOL Commission', *Annals of the American Academy of Political and Social Science*, 394, March, 72–83.

Litwak, E. and Hylton, L. (1961–2), 'Interorganizational analysis: a hypothesis on co-ordinating agencies', *Administrative Science Quarterly*, 6, 395–420.

Lumsdaine, A. and Bennett, C. (1975), 'Assessing alternative conceptions of evaluation', in C. Bennett and A. Lumsdaine (eds), *Evaluation and Experiment*, New York: Academic Press.

Lynn, L. (1972), 'Notes from HEW', *Evaluation*, Fall, 24–28.

Lynn, L. (1973), 'A federal evaluation office?', *Evaluation*, 1(2), 56–59.

Lynn, L. (1977), 'Policy relevant social research: what does it look like?' in M. Guttentag and S. Soar (eds), *Evaluation Studies Review Annual*, London: Sage, Vol. 2.

Lynn, L. (ed.) (1978a), *Knowledge and Policy: The Uncertain Connection*, Study Project on Social Research and Development, Washington, DC: National Academy of Sciences, Vol. 5.

Lynn, L. (1978b), 'The question of relevance', in L. Lynn (ed.), *Knowledge and Policy: The Uncertain Connection*, Study Project on Social Research and Development, Washington, DC: National Academy of Sciences, Vol. 5.

Lyons, G. (ed.) (1975), *Social Research and Public Policies*, Hanover, NH: Public Affairs Center, Dartmouth College.

MacDonald, J. and Fry, G. (1980), 'Policy planning units – ten years on', *Public Administration*, 58, Winter, 421–437.

MacRae, D., Jr (1985), *Policy Indicators: Links Between Social Science and Public Debate*, Chapel Hill, NC: University of North Carolina Press.

Macrae, D. (1961), *Ideology and Society*, London: Heinemann.

Mark, M. and Cook, T. (1984), 'Design of randomised experiments and quasi-experiments', in L. Rutman (ed.), *Evaluation Research Methods*, Beverly Hills, Calif.: Sage.

Marris, P. and Rein, M. (1967), *Dilemmas of Social Reform*, London: Routledge and Kegan Paul.

Marsland, D. (1983), 'Sociologists and social policy', *Social Policy and Administration*, 17(1), Spring, 4–16.

Marvin, K. and Rouse, A. (1969), 'The status of PPB in federal agencies: a comparative perspective', in Joint Economic Committee, *The Analysis and Evaluation of Public Expenditures: The PPB System*, Subcommittee on Economy in Government, 91st Congress, 1st Session, Washington, DC: US Government Printing Office.

Marvin, K. and Hedrick, J. (1974), 'GAO helps Congress evaluate programs', *Public Administration Review*, July–August, 327–333.

Merton, R. (1949), 'On the role of the intellectual in bureaucracy', in *Social Theory and Social Structure*, Glencoe, Ill.: The Free Press.

Merton, R. (1959), 'Notes on problem-finding in sociology', in R. Merton, L. Broom and L. Cottrell (eds), *Sociology Today*, New York: Basic Books.

Miller, S.M. (1974), 'Policy and science', *Social Policy*, 3, January, 73–94.

Miller, S.M. (1975), 'Planning: can it make a difference in capitalist America?', *Social Policy*, 6(2), September–October, 12–22.

Miller, S.M. (1979), 'Social policy on the defensive in Carter's America', *New Society*, 1 November, 244–247.

Miller, S.M. and Rein, M. (1975), 'Can income redistribution work?', *Social Policy*, May–June, 3–18.

Mills, C. Wright (1959), *The Sociological Imagination*, New York: Oxford University Press.

Mishan, E. (1969), *The Costs of Economic Growth*, Harmondsworth: Penguin.

Mondale, W. (1967), 'New tools for social progress', *The Progressive*, 31, 28–31.

Mondale, W. (1968a), 'Reporting on the social state of the Union', *Trans-Action*, June, 12–17.

Mondale, W. (1968b), *Congressional Record*, S.6729.

Mondale, W. (1970), 'Social advisers, social accounting and the Presidency', *Law and Contemporary Problems*, Summer, 496–504.

Mondale, W. (1972), 'Social accounting, evaluation, and the future of the human services', *Evaluation*, Fall, 29–34.

Moser, C. (1980), 'Statistics and public policy', *Journal of the Royal Statistical Society*, series A (General), 143(1), 1–27.

Moss, M. (1969), 'New directions in the federal information system', *American Statistician*, 23(2), April, 25–29.

Moynihan, D. (1967), 'A crisis of confidence?', *Public Interest*, Spring, 9–10.

Moynihan, D. (1970a), *Maximum Feasible Misunderstanding*, New York: Random House.

Moynihan, D. (1970b), 'The role of the social scientist in action research', *SSRC Newsletter*, 10 November.

Mushkin, S. (1973), 'Evaluations: use with caution', *Evaluation*, 1(2), 31–35.

Myrdal, G. (1960), *Beyond the Welfare State: Economic Planning in the Welfare States and its International Implications*, London: Duckworth.

National Academy of Sciences (1968), *The Behavioural Sciences and the Federal Government*, Washington, DC: NAS.

National Academy of Sciences and Social Science Research Council (1969), *The Behavioural and Social Sciences: Outlook and Needs*, Englewood Cliffs, NJ: Prentice-Hall.

National Commission on Technology, Automation and Economic Progress (1966), *Technology and the American Economy*, Washington, DC: US Government Printing office, February, Vol. 1.

National Goals Research Staff (NGRS) (1970), *Toward Balanced Growth: Quantity with Quality*, Report of the National Goals Research Staff, Washington, DC: US Government Printing Office.

National and Local Government Statistical Liaison Committee (1981), *Review of Personal Social Services Statistics*, February.

National Science Foundation (1969), *Knowledge into Action: Improving the Nation's Use of the Social Sciences*, Report of the Special Commission on the Social Sciences of the National Science Board (chairman, Orville G. Brim, Jr), Washington, DC: US Government Printing Office.

Nicolaus, M. (1969), 'Remarks at ASA convention, Boston, 1968', *Catalyst*, Spring, 103–106.

Niskanen, W. (1973), *Bureaucracy: Servant or Master*, London: Institute of Economic Affairs.

Niskanen, W. (1975), Interview, *Evaluation*, 2(2), 44.

Nixon, R. (1969), 'Statement by President Nixon on creating a National Goals Research Staff', *Futures*, 1, 458–459.

Novick, D. (1968), 'The origin and history of program budgeting', *Californian Management Review*, Fall, 7–12.

O'Connor, J. (1973), *The Fiscal Crisis of the State*, New York: St. Martin's Press.

Office of the Assistant Secretary for Planning and Evaluation (OASPE) (1980), *Report on Evaluation Utilization in the Department of Health, Education and Welfare*, Washington, DC: Department of Health, Education and Welfare, April.

Office of the Assistant Secretary for Planning and Evaluation (1981), *Report on Evaluation Utilization in the Department of Health and Human Services*, Washington, DC: Department of Health, Education and Welfare.

Olson, M. (1969a), 'The plan and purpose of a social report', *Public Interest*, 15, Spring.

Olson, M. (1969b), 'The relationship between economics and the other social sciences: the province of a "social report"', in S. Lipset (ed.), *Politics and the Social Sciences*, New York: Oxford University Press.

Olson, M. (1970), 'An analytic framework for social reporting and policy analysis', *The Annals*, 388, March, 112–126.

Organization for Economic Co-operation and Development (OECD) 1980, *The Utilization of the Social Sciences in Policy Making in the United States*, Paris: OECD.

Parker, R. (1983), 'Comparative social policy and the politics of comparison', in J. Gandy, A. Robertson and S. Sinclair (eds), *Improving Social Intervention*, London: Croom Helm.

Paterson Report (1973), *The New Scottish Local Authorities*, Edinburgh: HMSO.

Patton, M. (1984), 'Data collection: options, strategies and cautions', in L. Rutman (ed.), *Evaluation Research Methods*, Beverly Hills, Calif.: Sage.

Payne, G., Dingwall, R., Payne, J. and Carter, M. (1981), *Sociology and Social Research*, London: Routledge and Kegan Paul.

Peacock, A. (1977), 'Giving economic advice in difficult times', *Three Banks Review*, 113, March, 3–23.

Peston, M. (1976), 'The philosophy of public spending', *New Statesman*, 12, March, 316–319.

Piven, F. (1974), 'Social scientists and the poor', in P. Roby (ed.), *The Poverty Establishment*, Englewood Cliffs, NJ: Prentice-Hall.

Plowden, W. (1973a), 'The role and limits of a central planning staff in government: a note on the Central Policy Review Staff', Conference on the Study of Public Policy (mimeo.).

Plowden, W. (1973b), 'The Central Policy Review Staff: the first two years', paper presented to the Political Studies Association Conference (unpublished).

Plowden, W. (1977), 'Developing a joint approach to social policy', in K. Jones (ed.), *The Yearbook of Social Policy 1976*, London: Routledge and Kegan Paul.

Plowden, W. (1981), 'The British Central Policy Review Staff', in P. Baehr and B. Wittrock (eds), *Policy Analysis and Policy Innovation*, London: Sage Publications.

Plowden, W. (1987), 'Whatever happened to JASP?', in R. Klein, W. Plowden and A. Webb with L. Challis (eds), *Joint Approaches to Social Policy*, Cambridge: Cambridge University Press.

Pollitt, C. (1974), 'The Central Policy Review Staff 1970–1974', *Public Administration*, Winter, 375–393.

Popper, K. (1957), *The Poverty of Historicism*, London: Routledge and Kegan Paul.

Premfors, R. (1979), 'Social research and public policy making: an overview', *Statsvetenskaplig Tidskrift*, 4, 281–290.

Radin, B. (1977), 'Political relationships in evaluation: the case of the experimental schools program', *Evaluation*, 4, 201–204.

Razzell, E. (1980), 'Planning in Whitehall – is it possible? – will it survive?, *Long Range Planning*, 13, 34–41, February.

Regan, D. and Stewart, J. (1982), 'An essay in the government of health: the case for LA control', *Social Policy and Administration*, 16 (1), 19–43.

Rein, M. (1976), *Social Science and Public Policy*, Harmondsworth: Penguin Books.

Rein, M. (1977), 'Equality and social policy', *Social Services Review* (University of Chicago), 51(4), December, 565–587.

Rein, M. (1983), *From Policy to Practice*, London: Macmillan.

Rein, M. and White, S. (1977a), 'Can policy research help policy?', *Public Interest*, 49, 119–136.

Rein, M. and White, S. (1977b), 'Policy research: belief and doubt', *Policy Analysis*, 3(2), 239–271.

Rex, J. (1974), *Sociology and the Demystification of the Modern World*, London: Routledge and Kegan Paul.

Rich, R. (1975), 'Selective utilization of social science related information by federal policy makers', *Inquiry*, 12, 239–245.

Richardson, J. (1982), 'Programme evaluation in Britain and Sweden', *Parliamentary Affairs*, D35(2), 160–180.

Riecken, H.W. (1967), 'Government–science relations: the physical and social sciences compared', *American Psychologist*, 22, March, 211–218.

Riecken, H. and Boruch, R. (eds) (1974), *Social Experimentation: A Method for Planning and Evaluating Social Intervention*, New York: Academic Press.

Rivlin, A. (1970), 'The Planning, Programming, Budgeting System in the Department of Health, Education and Welfare: some lessons from experience', in R. Haveman and J. Margolis, 1970.

Rivlin, A. (1971), *Systematic Thinking for Social Action*, Washington, DC: Brookings Institution.

Rivlin, A. (1972), 'Why can't we get things done?', *Brookings Bulletin*, 9(2), Spring, 5–9.

Rivlin, A. (1973), 'Social experiments: the promise and the problems', *Evaluation*, 1(2), 77–78.

Robbins Committee (1963), *Higher Education* (Cmnd 2154), London: HMSO.

Rose, R. (1980), *Challenge to Governance: Studies in Overloaded Polities*, London: Sage.

Rose, R. and Peters, G. (1978), *Can Governments Go Bankrupt?*, New York: Basic Books.

Rossi, P. (1969), 'No good idea goes unpunished: Moynihan's misunderstandings and the proper role of social science in policy-making', *Social Science Quarterly*, 50(3), December, 469–479.

Rossi, P. (1975), 'Field experiments in social programs: problems and prospects', in G. Lyons (ed.), *Social Research and Public Policies*, Hanover, NH: Public Affairs Center, Dartmouth College.

Rossi, P. and Wright, S. (1977), 'Evaluation research: an assessment of theory, practice and politics', *Evaluation Quarterly*, 1(1), 5–51.

Rothman, J. (1980a), *Using Research in Organizations*, Beverly Hills, Calif.: Sage.

Rothman, J. (1980b), *Social R and D: Research and Development in the Human Services*, Englewood Cliffs, NJ: Prentice-Hall.

Rothschild, Lord (1971), *A Framework for Government Research and Development* (Cmnd 4814), London: HMSO.

Rothschild, Lord (1982), *An Enquiry into the Social Science Research Council* (Cmnd 8554), London: HMSO.

Royal Institute of Public Administration (RIPA) (1959), *Budgeting in Public Authorities*, London: RIPA:

Royster, V. (1975), 'Britain: a model study', *Wall Street Journal*, 20 August, 14.

Rule, J. (1978), *Insight and Social Betterment*, New York: Oxford University Press.

Rutman, L. (ed.) (1984a), *Evaluation Research Methods*, Beverly Hills, Calif.: Sage.

Rutman, L. (ed.) (1984b), 'Evaluability assessment', in L. Rutman (ed.), *Evaluation Research Methods*, Beverly Hills, Calif.: Sage.

Rutter, M. and Madge, N. (1976), *Cycles of Disadvantage*, London: Heinemann.

Salasin, S. (1973), 'Experimentation revisited: a conversation with Donald T. Campbell', *Evaluation*, 1, November, 7–13.

Salasin, S. (1977), 'From national security to mental health: making analysis count in government – an interview with Laurence E.

Lynn Jr', *Evaluation*, 4, 165–177.

Salasin, S. and Kivens, L. (1975), 'Fostering federal program evaluation: a current OMB initiative', *Evaluation*, 2(2), 37–41.

Sampson, A. (1962), *Anatomy of Britain*, London: Hodder and Stoughton.

Samuelson, R. (1967), 'Council of social advisers: new approach to welfare priorities?', *Science*, 157, 7 July, 49–50.

Sandberg, A. (1977), *The Limits to Democratic Planning*, Stockholm: Liberforlag.

Schick, A. (1971), 'From analysis to evaluation', *Annals of the American Academy of Political and Social Science*, 394, 57–71.

Schick, A. (1973), 'A death in the bureaucracy: the demise of the federal PPB', *Public Administration Review*, 2, March–April, 146–156.

Schlesinger, J. (1968), *Planning – Programming – Budgeting: Uses and Abuses of Analysis*, Memorandum prepared at the request of the Subcommittee on National Security and International Operations of the Committee on Government Operations, US Senate, 90th Congress, 2nd Session, Washington, DC: US Government Printing Office.

Schneider, J. (1974), 'Making government work: political versus technical obstacles to social accounting', *American Behavioural Scientist*, 17(4), March–April, 585–608.

Schonfield, A. (1972), 'Research and public policy: lessons from economics', in A. Cherns, R. Sinclair and W. Jenkins (eds), *Social Science and Government*, London: Tavistock.

Schultze, C. (1968), *The Politics and Economics of Public Spending*, Washington, DC: Brookings Institution.

Schultze, C. with Hamilton, E. and Schick, A. (1970), *Setting National Priorities: The 1971 Budget*, Washington, DC: Brookings Institution.

Seers, D. (1969), 'The meaning of development', *International Development Review*, December, 3–6.

Self, P. (1980), 'Resource and policy coordination under pressure', in R. Rose (ed.), *Challenge of Governance*, London: Sage.

Shankland, G. with Turner, R. (1984), *A Guide to the Informal Economy*, Work and Society Report No. 14, Institute of Manpower Studies, University of Sussex.

Sharpe, L. (1975), 'The social scientist and policy-making: some cautionary thoughts and transatlantic reflections', *Policy and Politics*, 4(4), 7–34.

Sharpe, L. (1978), 'Government as clients for social science research', in M. Bulmer (ed.), *Social Policy Research*, London: Macmillan.

Shostak, A. (1978), 'Updating Mondale's Social Accounting Act',

Policy Studies Journal, 7(2), Winter, 290–300.

Simon, H. (1957), *Administrative Behaviour*, New York: Macmillan.

Smith, C. (1975), 'The employment of sociologists in research occupations in Britain in 1973', *Sociology*, 9(2), 309–316.

Smith, G. (1983), 'Social work, policy, government and research: a mildly optimistic view', in J. Gandy, A. Robertson and S. Sinclair (eds), *Improving Social Intervention*, London: Croom Helm.

Smith, G. and May, D. (1980), 'The artificial debate between rationalist and incrementalist models of decision-making', *Policy and Politics*, 8(2), 147–161.

Smith, R. (1981), 'Implementing the results of evaluation studies', in S. Barrett and C. Fudge (eds), *Policy and Action: Essays on the Implementation of Public Policy*, London: Methuen.

Smithies, A. (1968), 'Government budgeting', *International Encyclopedia of the Social Sciences*, New York: Collier-Macmillan, Vol. 2.

Social Services Committee (1980), Third Report from the Social Services Committee, *Public Expenditure: The Social Services*, Vol. I, Report HC702-I, Vol. II, Minutes of Evidence, HC702-II, House of Commons Papers.

Social Services Committee (1981), *Public Expenditure on the Social Services*, Volume I, Report HC324-I, London: HMSO.

Social Services Committee (1982), Second Report from the Social Services Committee, *Public Expenditure on the Social Services*, Vol. I, Report HC306-I, Vol. II, Minutes of Evidence and Appendices, HC306-II, London: HMSO.

Society of Civil Servants (1977), *Joint memorandum submitted to the House of Commons Expenditure Committee (General Sub-Committee)*, Session 1976–77, HC535-II.

Spengler, J. (1969), 'Is social science ready?', *Social Science Quarterly*, 50(3), 48–64.

Springer, M. (1970), 'Social indicators, reports and accounts: toward the management of society', *The Annals*, 388, March.

Staats, E. (1973), 'The challenge of evaluating federal social programs', *Evaluation*, 1(3), 50–54.

Stacey, M. (1971), 'Sociology and the civil service', *SSRC Newsletter*, 13, November, 8–10.

Stevenson, O. (1983), 'Research and policy in the personal social services', in J. Gandy, A. Robertson and S. Sinclair, *Improving Social Intervention*, London: Croom Helm.

Struening, E. and Guttentag, M. (1975), *Handbook of Evaluation Research*, London: Sage.

Stufflebeam, D. (1980), 'An interview with Daniel L. Stufflebeam', *Educational Evaluation and Policy Analysis*, 2(4), 85–90.

Taylor, R. (1986), 'Tories' way with figures', *Observer*, 3 August,.

Testimony before a Subcommittee of the Committee of Appropriations

(1967), House of Representatives, 90th Congress, 1st Session, Pt 6, Washington, DC: US Government Printing Office.

Thomas, H. (1980), 'Creating a boutique society with firepower a plenty', *Guardian*, 17 September.

Thomas, H. (1982), 'Alternatives', *Financial Guardian*, 13 February.

Thomas, H. (1985a), 'Uninformed in pursuit of unrethinkable', *Guardian*, 3 September.

Thomas, H. (1985b), 'It's time to twin ecology to economics', *Guardian*, 7 November.

Thomas, P. (1985), *The Aims and Outcomes of Social Policy Research*, London: Croom Helm.

Thompson, E. (1978), 'Social trends: the development of an annual report for the United Kingdom', *International Social Science Journal*, 30(3), 653–659.

Thompson, J. (1967), *Organizations in Action*, New York: McGraw-Hill.

Thompson, V. (1969), *Bureaucracy and Innovation*, Montgomery, Ala.: University of Alabama Press.

Titmuss, R. (1968), *Commitment to Welfare*, London: Allen and Unwin.

Townsend, P. (1967), 'The need for a social plan', *New Society*, 14 December.

Townsend, P. (1970), 'The reorganization of social policy', *New Society*, 22 October.

Townsend, P. (1974), 'The social underdevelopment of Britain', *New Statesman*, 1 March.

Townsend, P. (1976), *Sociology and Social Policy*, Harmondsworth: Penguin Books.

Townsend, P. (1979), 'Social policy in conditions of scarcity', *New Society*, 10 May.

Townsend, P. (1980a), 'Guerrillas, subordinates and passers-by', *Critical Social Policy*, 1(2), 22–34.

Townsend, P. (1980b), 'Social planning and the treasury', in P. Townsend and N. Bosanquet (eds), *Labour and Equality*, London: Heinemann.

Townsend, P. (1981), 'Society tomorrow', *Guardian*, 15 July.

Trow, M. (1984), 'Researchers, policy analysts and policy intellectuals', in T. Husen and M. Kogan, *Educational Research and Policy: How Do They Relate?*, Oxford: Pergamon.

US Department of Health, Education and Welfare (HEW) (1969), *Towards a Social Report*, Washington, DC: HEW.

US Department of Health, Education and Welfare (1980), *FY 1981 Guidance for Evaluation, Research and Statistical Activities*, Washington, DC: HEW.

Veitch, A. (1986), 'Survey on chips and biscuits diet to be released', *Guardian*, 4 April.

Walker, A. (1981), 'Social policy, social administration and the social construction of welfare', *Sociology*, 15, 224–250.

Walker, A., Ormerod, P. and Whitty, L. (1979), *Abandoning Social Priorities*, Poverty Pamphlet 44, London: Child Poverty Action Group.

Wallis, K. (ed.) (1984), *Models of the UK Economy*, Oxford: Oxford University Press.

Ward, T. (1983), 'PESC in crisis', *Policy and Politics*, 11(2), April, 167–177.

Wass, D. (1978), 'The changing problems of economic management', *Economic Trends*, 293, March, 97–104.

Wass, D. (1983), 'Cabinet: Directorate or Directory', Reith Lecture No. 2, BBC Radio 4, 16 November.

Watts, H. and Rees, W. (1977), *New Jersey Income Maintenance Experiment*, New York: Academic Press, Vols 2 and 3.

Weiler, D. (1976), 'A public school voucher demonstration: the first year of Alum Rock, summary and conclusions', in G. Glass (ed.), *Evaluation Studies Review Annual*, 1, 278–304.

Weiss, C. (1973a), 'Where politics and evaluation research meet', *Evaluation*, 1(3), 37–45.

Weiss, C. (1973b), 'Between the cup and the lip', *Evaluation*, 1(2), 49–55.

Weiss, C. (1975), 'Evaluation research in the political context', in E. Struening and M. Guttentag (eds), *Handbook of Evaluation Research*, London: Sage.

Weiss, C. (1977), 'Research for policy's sake: the enlightenment function of social research', *Policy Analysis*, 3(4), Fall, 521–545.

Weiss, C. (1978), 'Improving the linkage between social research and public policy' in L. Lynn (ed.), *Knowledge and Policy: The Uncertain Connection*, Study Project on Social Research and Development, Washington, DC: National Academy of Sciences, Vol. 5.

Weiss, C. (1980), 'Knowledge creep and decision accretion', *Knowledge: Creation, Diffusion, Utilization*, 1(3), March, 381–404.

Weiss, C. (1984), 'Increasing the likelihood of influencing decisions', in L. Rutman (ed.), *Evaluation Research Methods*, Beverly Hills, Calif.: Sage.

Weiss, C. (1986), 'Research and policy-making: a limited partnership', in F. Heller (ed.), *The Use and Abuse of Social Science*, London: Sage.

Weiss, C. and Bucuvalas, M. (1980a), 'Truth tests and utility tests:

decision-makers' frames of reference for social science research', *American Sociological Review*, 45, April, 302–313.

Weiss, C. and Bucuvalas, M. (1980b), *Social Science Research and Decision-Making*, New York: Columbia University Press.

Weiss, R. and Rein, M. (1970), 'The evaluation of broad-aim programs: experimental design, its difficulties and an alternative', *Administrative Science Quarterly*, 15(1), March, 97–109.

Wholey, J., Scanlon, J., Duffy, H., Fukumoto, J. and Vogt, L. (1970), *Federal Evaluation Policy*, Washington, DC: The Urban Institute.

Wilcox, L.D., Brooks, R.M., Beal, G. and Mand Klonglan, G.E. (1972), *Social Indicators and Societal Monitoring*, Amsterdam: Elsevier.

Wildavsky, A. (1966), 'The political economy of efficiency', *Public Administration Review*, 26, 292–310.

Wildavsky, A. (1968), 'Budgeting as a political process', *International Encyclopedia of Social Science*, New York: Collier-Macmillan, Vol. 2.

Wildavsky, A. (1970), 'Rescuing policy analysis from PPBS', in R. Haveman and J. Margolis, 1970.

Wildavsky, A. (1980), *The Art and Craft of Policy Analysis*, London: Macmillan.

Will, G. (1976), 'Mondale's idea of "sensible statecraft"', *Washington Post*, 9 September.

Williams, S. (1969), *SSRC Newsletter*, 5, March.

Williams, W. (1971), *Social Policy Research and Analysis: The Experience in the Federal Social Agencies*, Amsterdam: Elsevier.

Williams, W. (1980), *Domestic Program Policy Analysis: Some Observations on its Practice at the Top of the Government in the US and the UK*, Discussion Paper No. 4, Institute of Governmental Research, University of Washington.

Williams, W. (1983), 'British policy analysis: some preliminary observations from the US', in A. Gray and B. Jenkins (eds), *Policy Analysis and Evaluation in British Government*, London: Royal Institute of Public Administration.

Williams, W. and Evans, J. (1969), 'The politics of evaluation: the case of Head Start', *The Annals of the American Academy of Political and Social Science*, September, 118–132.

Willmott, P. (1973), 'The tasks for planning', in P. Cowan (ed.), *The Future of Planning*, London: Heinemann.

Willmott, P. (1980), 'A view from an independent research institute', in M. Cross (ed.), *Social Research and Public Policy: Three Perspectives*, London: Social Research Association.

Wistow, G. and Hardy, B. (1986), 'Transferring care: can financial incentives work', in A. Harnson and J. Gretton (eds), *Health Care UK: An Economic, Social and Policy Audit*, Berkshire: Hermitage.

Wootton, B. (1962), 'Socrates, science and social problems', *New Society*, 4 October.

Wortman, P., Reichardt, C. and St Pierre, R. (1978), 'The first year of the educational voucher demonstration: a secondary analysis of student achievement test scores', *Evaluation Quarterly*, 2(2), 193–221.

Wright, M. (1979), 'Planning and controlling public expenditure', in T. Booth (ed.), *Planning for Welfare*, Oxford: Blackwell/Robertson.

Wright, M. (ed.) (1980), *Public Spending Decisions*, London: Allen and Unwin.

Young, H. and Sloman, A. (1984), *But, Chancellor*, London: BBC.

Young, K. (1977), 'Values in the policy process', *Policy and Politics*, 5(3), 1–22.

Zapf, W. (1976), *Social Indicators Newsletter*, Social Science Research Council, No. 10, November.

Names index

Aaron, H., 107, 133, 154, 231, 240
Abel-Smith, B., 34, 53
Abrams, P., 219, 220, 227, 247
Abt, C., 150, 164, 183, 187
Agricultural Research Council, 208
Aldrich, H., 40
Alexander, T., 218, 236
Alum Rock Union Elementary School District, 176
Ares, C., 171
Ashworth, J., 104, 193, 195, 208, 211, 212
Association of County Councils, 22
Association of Learned Societies in the Social Sciences, 220
Association of Metropolitan Authorities, 80

Ball, R., 35, 36, 69, 70
Ball, S., 175
Bancroft, Lord, 189
Banks, G., 101
Barker, A., 11, 100
Bauer, R., 113
Bell, C., 234
Bell, D., 116, 119, 133
Benjamin, B., 238
Benson, J., 40, 41
Berger, S., 217, 239
Bernstein, I., 183
Berrill, K., 201, 205, 212
Blau, P., 39
Blume, S., 208, 211
Bogatz, G., 175
Booth, A., 56

Booth, T., 46, 55, 74, 152, 156, 238
Boruch, R., 168, 170, 181, 182, 185, 186, 187
Botein, B., 171
Boulding, K., 35, 56, 69, 115, 131
Brayfield, A., 128
Breton, A., 42
British Sociological Association, 219
Brittan, S., 15
Broadfoot, P., 221
Brookings Institution, 98
Brown, M., 222, 223
Bruce, R., 146, 147
Brush, L., 162
Buchanan, G., 142, 147
Bucuvalas, M., 230, 231, 239
Bulmer, M., 137, 189, 219
Bunker, D., 112, 231, 232
Bureau of the Budget, 91, 94, 95, 226
Burns, S., 61
Business Statistics Office, 71

Cairncross, A., 56
Califano, J., 110, 111
Californian Adult Authority, 173
Callaghan, J., 203, 210
Campbell, D., 165, 169
Caplan, N., 218, 224, 240
Carlson, J., 86, 89, 90, 91, 94
Castle, B., 47
Central Policy Review Staff, 3, 11, 12, 14, 26, 28, 37, 102, 104, 189, 191, 194, 195, 196, 197, 198, 199, 200, 201, 202,

Subject index